# A Literal Chinese Translation Illustrated Encyclopedia
## And my China Adventure Story

**Copyright**

Title: A Literal Chinese Translation Illustrated Encyclopedia
Author: Kevin Bruce
Cover: Cody Fennell

ISBN: 978-1-7776607-5-8

Dedicated to Brandon,
a friend gone too soon.

# Contents

# Forward
Where's the cloth wrapper?


The word we use today in modern Chinese when we refer to "humour", i.e. 幽默 (pronounced in standard Mandarin Chinese as yōu mò) is comprised of two characters: 幽 which could mean any of these things: "deep, remote, secluded, dim, hidden, secret, tranquil, and/or serene", and 默 which denotes something "quiet, silent, and/or dark". At first glance we wouldn't be too keen to think of 'gloomy remote hidden silences' as a desirable semantic cornerstone for the word 'humour', and surely many students of the Chinese language have scratched their heads when confronted with this particular word. Kevin Bruce, the author of this marvellous encyclopedia, however, would greet with a chuckle this strangeness of thought and carry on with his day, since for him the irony of humour being the exact opposite of what we expect it to be is far greater than the frustration of it being counter-intuitive.

Now, the reason for our word 幽默 to be this oddly chosen meta-linguistic-wink lays, as usual, within the history of China. In this case, we don't need to dive hundreds of years into the past, since the word was coined by the famous writer Lin Yu Tang during May of 1933. The main reason to use these characters should (or at least it ought to be) evident to any English speaker, since it is a transliteration of the English word 'humour'. Lin Yu Tang argued that despite the many comical forms of preexisting Chinese literature, the Chinese people had not yet developed a proper sense of humour, not at least one conceived as a "humanistic virtue". And so, on May 1933, Chinese people discovered humour...

...or well, not quite. If Chinese people had indeed not a funny bone in them, how else could've one of China's most prominent writers have come up with such a satirical way of expressing the source of all laughter? Humour is not a matter defined by how funny or unfunny things are, rather it is a yardstick that measures how well you communicate. You know, it's not the joke that is funny but the way you tell it. There is one way you can say punchline in Chinese, 包袱, which translates to "cloth wrapper" so even the punchline, the phrase that

8

cannot go wrong or else the whole joke crumbles, is more about the packaging than the actual content.

This book is packed with the best kind of laughter: the kind that comes from innocence, from stripping things of their solemnity and just laughing at how strangely we have decided to name the world that surrounds us. Laughing can be therapeutic, but laughing at what one cares more deeply might well be a life-saver these days. The way Chinese write laughter speaks for itself: 笑 is exactly what it looks like, and at the same time exactly what it represents: a drawing of a person laughing and a young 夭 bamboo 竹; an ode to flexibility.

I met Kevin back in 2016 when we were both majoring in Ancient Chinese Language and Literature at Guizhou University, and one of the things that struck me the most about this Canadian, based for years in the middle of rural China, was how easily he seemed to communicate with the locals. Not because his grammar was concise and precise, or because his tones where impeccable (as it is sometimes the case with many students of Chinese in China and abroad), but rather because he did not fear to make a fool of himself. "I *am* dumb" he would brush a random native speaker's sneer off with, while pointing his index finger to his nose, demonstrating to everyone he was not only *not* dumb but rather perfectly capable of getting a grasp of Chinese culture, since few things are as Chinese as that gesture.

Kevin's tones —which I claim where not faulty but merely 'southernized', and they only sounded wrong to anybody who expected him to speak in flawless Standard Northern Mandarin Chinese—, were no match to his empathy towards Chinese. But personally I believe that his connection to China comes through his hands rather than his ears. Whilst he might not be reciting Tang poetry on TV any time soon, his intuition with a brush when writing calligraphy one day might lead him there. The illustrations on this encyclopedia speak for themselves, as also does the fact of Kevin learning dialectal varieties of Chinese Sign Language on top of learning spoken and written Chinese. The book you have in your hands has been written by hands that have helped at orphanages, taught at schools and rode motorbikes. Read with the attention and care you would do any of those things.

—Antonio Rodríguez Durán.

# Introduction
(You can't afford not to read this.)

Firstly, at a glance it may seem as though I am, in a way, making fun of the Chinese language. But the fact is I am not, and my intentions are not to demean an entire people group or language. While we can laugh at things they say like 'Adam's apple' (throat knot), I actually do find their language infinitely fascinating and am continually drawn to it.

The point of this book isn't to mock the makeup of their language, but to merely find a fun way to appreciate it. I like to think of it this way: There's two kinds of 'funny'; one is funny-interesting and the other funny-stupid. Something like 'an Adam Sandler movie' would be funny-stupid, but something like 'a shrimps heart is in it's head' (true story) would be funny-interesting. I think the differentiation is important in this regard, simply to reinforce the fact that I know some people will just see an apparent mockery of one of the oldest languages to exist. So again, this book doesn't exist solely to 'take the piss', as they say.

Besides all that, I hope that looking at this book it may peak your interest in the Chinese language. I would recommend you study it a little. Chinese is definitely not as hard as people tend to think it is, and for every two words you learn, you can combine them to make a new one! Refer to 'computer' in the next paragraph.

Secondly, these translations are absolutely done to the best of my ability and knowledge, but that's not to say they are all 100% correct. I did close as I could with my 6.5 years of language studies and the few apps that helped me translate. If you're curious, Pleco is objectively the best app, and I've tried almost every one. I'd also like to point out that Chinese people don't actually think in regard to individual characters like this book makes out. That is to say, if we take a word like computer (电脑 = electric brain), they don't think 'computer = electric brain'. They just think 'computer = computer'. It's not like they're breaking down every word into literal meanings. We don't do that in English either... and I bet if you try it you'll find many words that are quite funny in English that you didn't think about before, like 'pineapple'...

Keep in mind as well that many characters have multiple meanings (some had more than fifteen!), so again, I did my best to figure out which made the most sense. And if you're curious, I was in China about seven years and studied the language most of that time. At the time of my departure from China in early 2018, I was studying for HSK 5 and knew about half. HSK is the 'Hanyu Shuiping Kaoshi' - literally 'Chinese Level Exam', and there are 6 levels in total, each vocabulary load doubling as it progresses. At my prime I could speak about 4000+ words, read about 2500-ish and write about 750, give or take. To put it in perspective though, I had trouble reading children's books, and couldn't even begin to understand the news paper.

One more thing. I put the index of all the words (and their phonetics) at the back. I didn't manage to draw every single word I collected over the years, so I **put them in bold** so that they're easier to locate. Words like 'Celibacy' or 'Cognitive Dissonance' I didn't have the patience to draw, nor did I know *what* to draw. Also, after 500+ hours of drawing, I just didn't care enough, sorry. With that being said however, this may be the only book that you should/need to read the index in. Seriously, check it for 'the ultimate book experience'.

# About Mandarin Chinese
(You shouldn't skip this, but you can. This will be the most compact Chinese lesson perhaps ever written, so get ready.)

Chinese is made of characters. Each character represents an idea/meaning. For example 我爱你 (wǒ ài nǐ) means: I love you. Each character represents those english words. 我 = I - 爱 = love - 你 = you. So basic Chinese grammar isn't actually super difficult, really. Much of it is the same as English.

The longest word (character) in Chinese is six letters long, and every character is only one syllable. So once more, not as complicated as people think.

The Chinese language, unlike English, is unable to create new words due to being a non-phonetic language. Thus while we are free to invent words (like Spork) Chinese must use already existing characters in order to make new words; hence this book.

There is also a character '者' (zhě), which means 'the one who'. You may see it from time to time. It's usually attached to the end of a verb to change the meaning. For example 'creator' would be '创造者' (chuàng zào zhě); to create - 'the one who' = the one who creates. 'Reporter' would be '记者' (jì zhě); to record - 'the one who' = the one who records. And on and on…

Chinese has four 'tones', making some words which phonetically sound the same have entirely different meanings. (See the 'shi' poem on page 213.) I added them (the phonetics with all the tones) to the index as I felt if they were part of the art it would have been to much information.

Mandarin is spoken in most of China. Cantonese is mostly spoken in Hong Kong and near the very south of China. Mandarin uses 'simplified' characters, and Cantonese uses 'traditional' characters. Some differences being (love) '爱' and '愛', or (book) '书' and '書'. They also speak differently. This book covers Mandarin Chinese.

# Random Stuff

Many words are transliterated from English like coffee, 'kā fēi' (咖啡). I threw a few in at the end, but they aren't that funny, really.

If you're wondering why there's not more words, that's because those words probably already have their own character, for example dog = 狗 (gǒu). Also, for some words that had three or more characters, sometimes the literal translation *really* made no sense, so I combined the characters (as it actually is in Chinese) to make more sense. So you may see three characters but only two english words. Deal with it eh!

Lots of these you'll have to sort of read backwards. You'll get the gist once you see a few of them. Or if there's more than one meaning for a character, choose what you think suits the translation best.

Some of these words may not be 'commonly used' by Chinese people (or are slang), but I added them anyway because many were so funny. See 'testicles'.

If you're familiar with the etymology of English, this book not may be as funny, as many words in English will translate the same if you examine them close enough. Like hippo being 'river horse' etc... Ignorance is bliss, in this case at least.

# Fair Warning

Since it's 2022 I thought I'd take a moment to let you know that this book has been deemed 'not politically correct' by me, however please note that nothing written in here was done with any intent to purposely offend anyone. Everything in here has been made with utmost sincerity and love, and my only hope is that you are entertained and smile while reading.

E-mail: stairwaytokevin@mail.com
Instagram: yorik_bruhl
Tiktok: yorikbruhl
Website: www.kevinsbook.ca

(The 'Rated R stuff' is available upon request.)

# 房子与技术

House & Technology

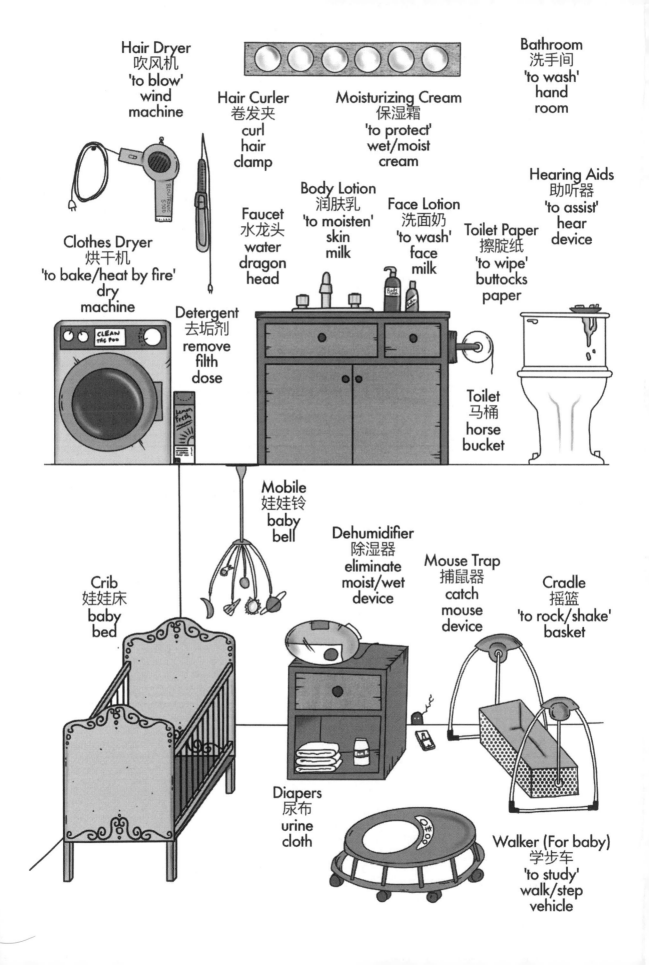

Hair Dryer
吹风机
'to blow'
wind
machine

Hair Curler
卷发夹
curl
hair
clamp

Moisturizing Cream
保湿霜
'to protect'
wet/moist
cream

Bathroom
洗手间
'to wash'
hand
room

Hearing Aids
助听器
'to assist'
hear
device

Body Lotion
润肤乳
'to moisten'
skin
milk

Face Lotion
洗面奶
'to wash'
face
milk

Toilet Paper
擦腚纸
'to wipe'
buttocks
paper

Faucet
水龙头
water
dragon
head

Clothes Dryer
烘干机
'to bake/heat by fire'
dry
machine

Detergent
去垢剂
remove
filth
dose

Toilet
马桶
horse
bucket

Mobile
娃娃铃
baby
bell

Dehumidifier
除湿器
eliminate
moist/wet
device

Mouse Trap
捕鼠器
catch
mouse
device

Cradle
摇篮
'to rock/shake'
basket

Crib
娃娃床
baby
bed

Diapers
尿布
urine
cloth

Walker (For baby)
学步车
'to study'
walk/step
vehicle

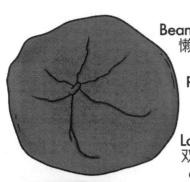

Beanbag Chair
懒人沙发
lazy
person
sofa

Living Room
客厅
guest
hall

Radio
收音机
'to receive'
sound
machine

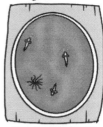

Love Seat
双人沙发
double
person
'sha fa'

Toy
玩具
play
device

Aquarium
养鱼缸
'to raise'
fish
jar/vat

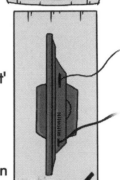

Ottoman
软垫凳
soft
cushion
bench

T.V.
电视
electric
'to look at'

Internet
互联网
mutual
connect/join
network

Video Games
电玩儿
electric
fun/to play/toy

Blinds
百叶窗
hundred
leaf
shutter

Sound Proof Wall
歌声强
separate
noise
wall

Thermometer
温度计
temperature
degree
guage

Abstract Art
抽象艺术
obtain by drawing
shape
art

Humidifier
加湿器
'to add'
moist/wet
device

Boombox
噪音盒
noise
sound
small box

Bunk Beds
上下床
up
down
bed

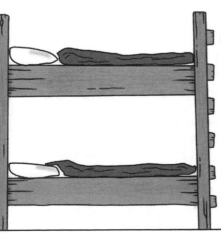

Mattress
床垫
bed
cushion

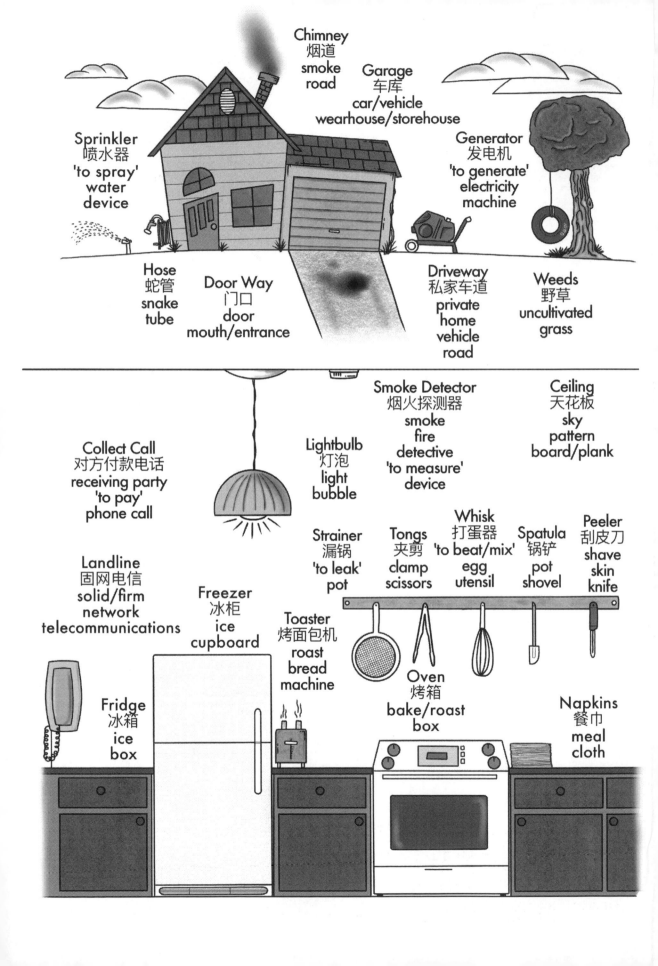

Chimney
烟道
smoke
road

Garage
车库
car/vehicle
wearhouse/storehouse

Generator
发电机
'to generate'
electricity
machine

Sprinkler
喷水器
'to spray'
water
device

Hose
蛇管
snake
tube

Door Way
门口
door
mouth/entrance

Driveway
私家车道
private
home
vehicle
road

Weeds
野草
uncultivated
grass

Smoke Detector
烟火探测器
smoke
fire
detective
'to measure'
device

Ceiling
天花板
sky
pattern
board/plank

Collect Call
对方付款电话
receiving party
'to pay'
phone call

Lightbulb
灯泡
light
bubble

Whisk
打蛋器
'to beat/mix'
egg
utensil

Spatula
锅铲
pot
shovel

Peeler
刮皮刀
shave
skin
knife

Strainer
漏锅
'to leak'
pot

Tongs
夹剪
clamp
scissors

Landline
固网电信
solid/firm
network
telecommunications

Freezer
冰柜
ice
cupboard

Toaster
烤面包机
roast
bread
machine

Fridge
冰箱
ice
box

Oven
烤箱
bake/roast
box

Napkins
餐巾
meal
cloth

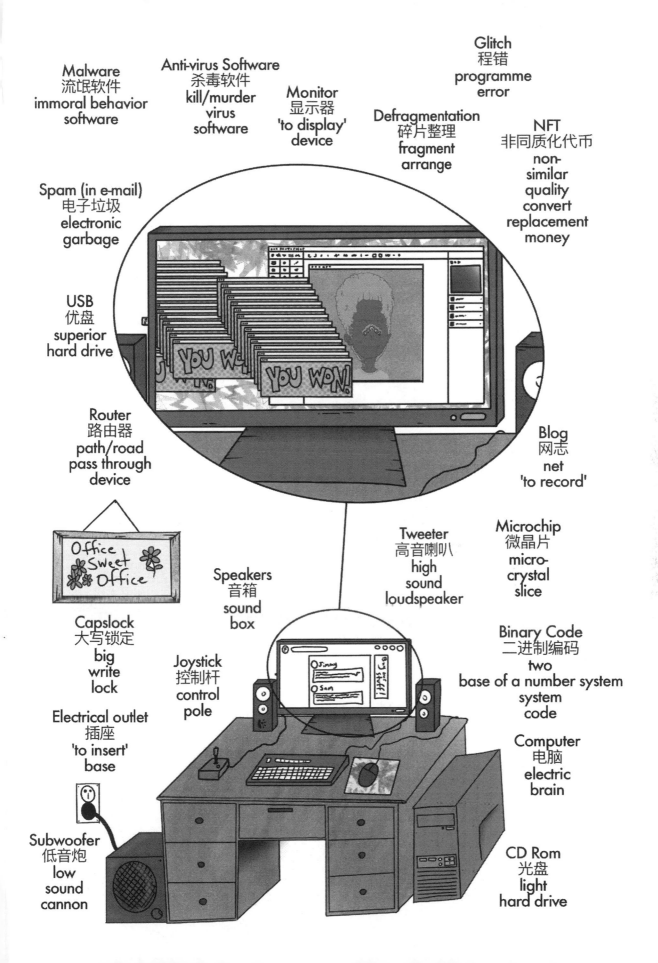

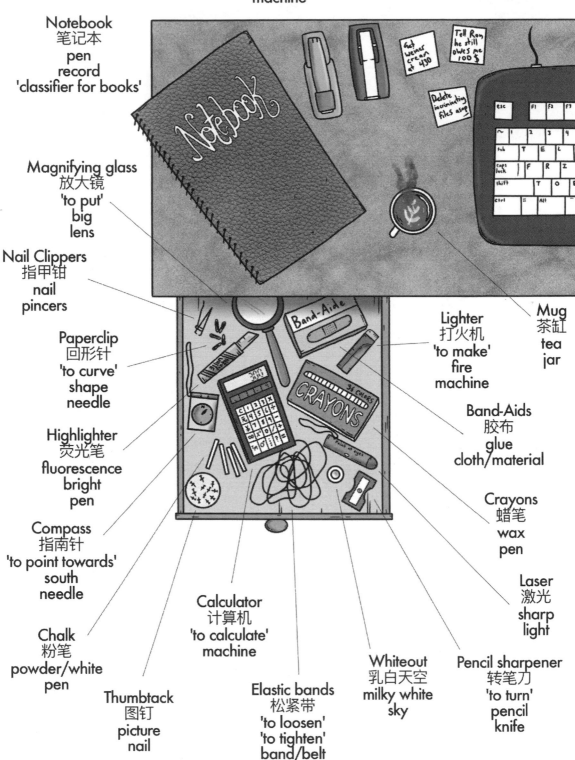

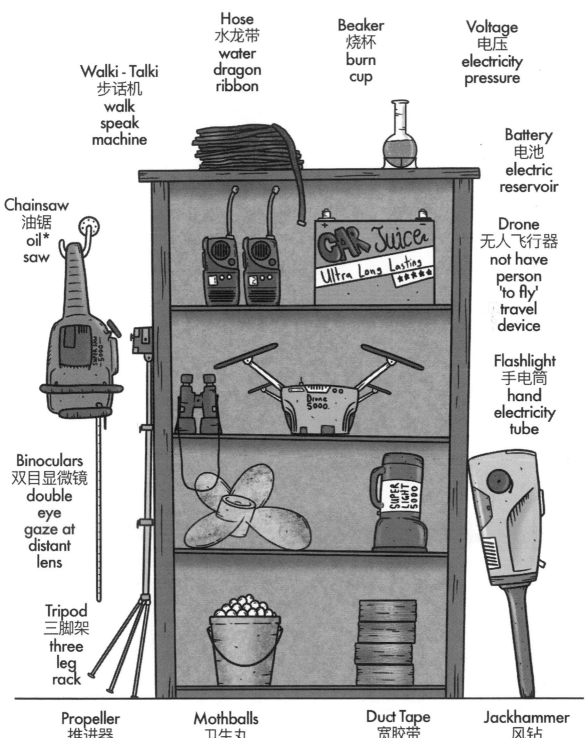

Hose
水龙带
water
dragon
ribbon

Beaker
烧杯
burn
cup

Voltage
电压
electricity
pressure

Walki - Talki
步话机
walk
speak
machine

Battery
电池
electric
reservoir

Chainsaw
油锯
oil*
saw

Drone
无人飞行器
not have
person
'to fly'
travel
device

Flashlight
手电筒
hand
electricity
tube

Binoculars
双目显微镜
double
eye
gaze at
distant
lens

Tripod
三脚架
three
leg
rack

Propeller
推进器
'to push'
'to go forward'
device

Mothballs
卫生丸
hygiene/sanitation
ball

Duct Tape
宽胶带
wide
glue
belt

Jackhammer
风钻
wind
'to drill/bore'

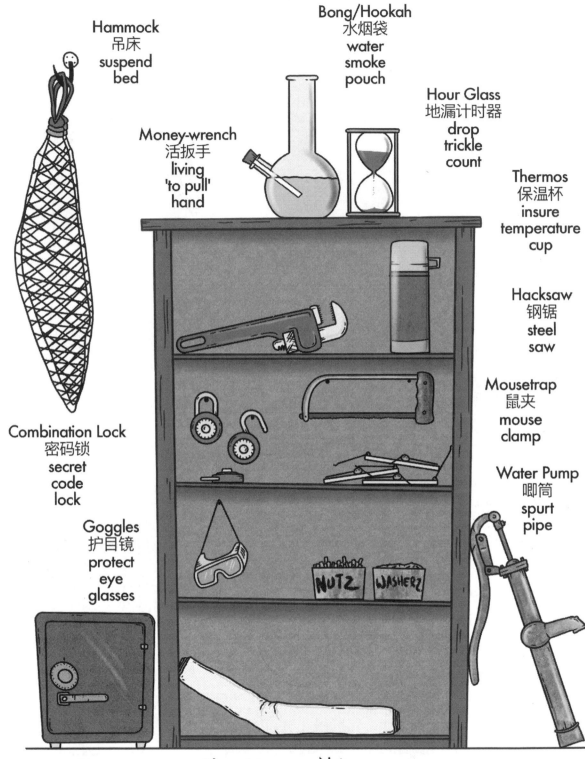

Hammock
吊床
suspend
bed

Bong/Hookah
水烟袋
water
smoke
pouch

Hour Glass
地漏计时器
drop
trickle
count

Money-wrench
活扳手
living
'to pull'
hand

Thermos
保温杯
insure
temperature
cup

Hacksaw
钢锯
steel
saw

Mousetrap
鼠夹
mouse
clamp

Combination Lock
密码锁
secret
code
lock

Water Pump
唧筒
spurt
pipe

Goggles
护目镜
protect
eye
glasses

Safe
金柜
money
cabinet

Blueprint
图纸
chart
paper

Nuts
螺丝帽
screw
hat

Washer
螺丝垫
screw
cushion

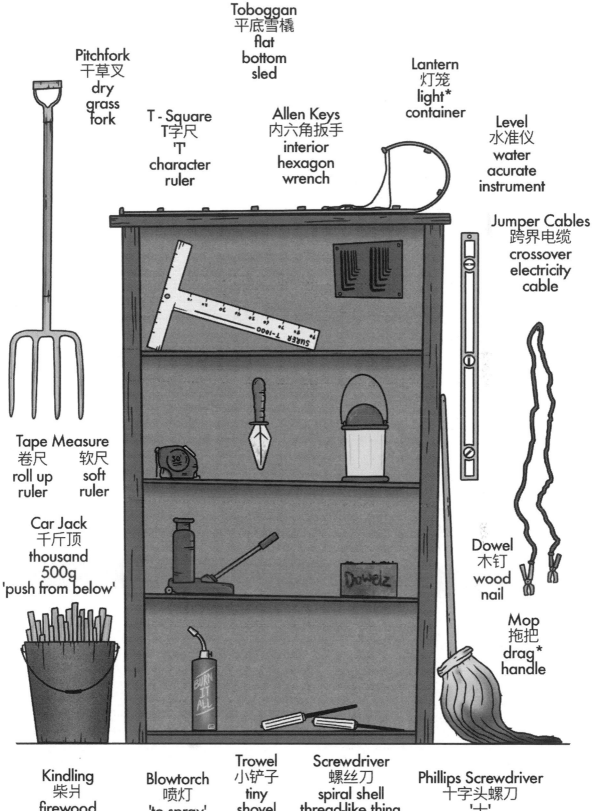

(*拖 also means 'to mop the floor' & 灯 also means 'lantern'.)

Toboggan
平底雪橇
flat
bottom
sled

Pitchfork
干草叉
dry
grass
fork

T - Square
T字尺
'T'
character
ruler

Allen Keys
内六角扳手
interior
hexagon
wrench

Lantern
灯笼
light*
container

Level
水准仪
water
acurate
instrument

Jumper Cables
跨界电缆
crossover
electricity
cable

Tape Measure
卷尺          软尺
roll up      soft
ruler        ruler

Car Jack
千斤顶
thousand
500g
'push from below'

Dowel
木钉
wood
nail

Mop
拖把
drag*
handle

Kindling
柴爿
firewood
split wood

Blowtorch
喷灯
'to spray'
burner

Trowel
小铲子
tiny
shovel

Screwdriver
螺丝刀
spiral shell
thread-like thing
tool

Phillips Screwdriver
十字头螺刀
'十'
character
head
screwdriver

Rock Garden
假山
artificial
mountain

Sled
冰排子
ice
raft

Water Dispenser
饮水机
drink
water
machine

Flint
火石
fire
rock

Bar Code
商品条码
merchandise
stripe
code

674921337855

Goblet
高脚杯
tall
base
cup

Canvas
画布
painting
cloth

Fountain Pen
自来水笔
naturally
arrive
liquid
pen

Easel
画架
painting
rack

Fax
电传
electric
'to transmit'

Cling Wrap
保鲜膜
protect
fresh
film

SUPER CLINGY WRAP

Air Blower
喷粉器
'to spray'
powder
device

Fax your face

Spork
叉勺
fork
spoon

Quill
羽毛笔
feather
writing brush

Telescope
望远镜
gaze into the distance
far away
looking glass

Clothes Pin
晾衣架
'dry in the air'
clothes
clamp

Electric Kettle
快煮壶
rapid
boil
kettle

Electric Clock
音叉钟
sound
fork
clock

Doll
玩偶
toy
image

Wok
炒菜锅
sauté
vegetables
pan

人类

People

**Monk (Mocking)**
秃驴
bald
donkey

**Sleepwalker**
梦游者
dream
travel
'the one who'
(the one who travels
while dreaming)

**Executioner**
刀斧手    刽子手
knife    'to amputate'
hatchet    tradesman
tradesman

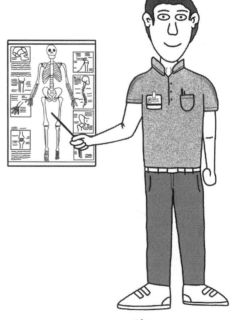

**Scrooge (Miser)**
守财奴
'to guard'
wealth
slave

**Nun**
出家人
'to leave'
home
person

**Chiropractor**
脊椎指压治疗师
vertebra
accupressure
medical treatment
expert

Pirate
海盗
ocean
bandit

KKK
三K党
three
'K'
club/party

'Smartphone Addict'
低头族
'to lower'
head
ethnicity/race

Assassin
刺客
stab
guest

Transvestite
异装癖
unusual
clothing
hobby

Scarecrow
稻草人
rice plant
grass
person

Chef
厨师
kitchen
expert

**Alchemist**
炼金术士
'to refine'
gold
method
scholar

**Cart Driver**
掌鞭的
'to wield'
whip/flog

**Nazi**
纳粹
'to accept'
unmixed

**Ventriloquist**
口技表演者
mouth
skill
preformance
'the one who'
(the one who is skilled at mouth
preformances)

**Bartender**
调酒师
'to blend'
liquor
expert

**Elvis**
猫王
cat
king

**Priest**
祭司
'to offer sacrifice'
department (of a ministry)

**Geek**
理工男
science and engineering
man

**Stenographer**
速记员
rapid/speedy
record
personnel

**Milkman**
送奶人
'to deliver'
milk
person

**Fraternal Twins**
异卵双胞胎
different
egg
twins

**Identical Twins**
同卵双胞胎
similar
egg
twins

**Lawyer**
律师
law
expert

Hermit
幽人
secluded
person

Inmate
收容人
put away
contain
person

Shepard
牧羊人
'to herd'
sheep
person

Barbarian
野蛮人
wilderness
savage*
person

Conductor
指挥家
'point to'
'to conduct'
specialist (in a certain field)

Wealthy
有钱人
'to have/possess'
money
person

**Poet**
诗人
peom
person

**Referee**
裁判员
judge/decide
pass a verdict
employee

**Stripper**
脱衣舞女郎
'to cast off'
clothes
dance
girl

**Skeleton**
骨人
bone*
person

**Loan Shark**
大耳窿
big
ear
hole

**Plumber**
水管工
water pipe
worker

**Cobbler**
修鞋匠
repair
shoes
craftsman

**Peeping Tom**
偷窥狂
secretly
peep/spy on
crazy

**Detective**
侦察员
investigate
examine
personnel

**Freak**
畸胎
abnormal
birth

**Cat Burglar**
飞贼
'go quickly'
thief

**Carpenter**
木匠
wood
craftsman

**Arsonist**
防火犯
light
fire
criminal

**Busker**
街头艺人
street corner
art
person

Robot
机器人
machine
person

Midget
袖珍人
pocket - size
person

Butcher
卖肉者
to sell
meat
'the one who'
(the one who sells meat)

Ninja
忍者
to endure
'the one who'
(the one who endures)

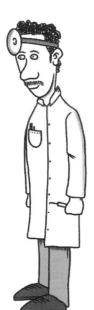

Dentist
牙医
tooth
doctor

Postman
邮递员
mail
'to hand over'
employee

Old Person
老头
old
head

Farmer
农民
agriculture
nationality

(*狗 means 'dog' too, so translate how you like.)

Lifeguard
救生员
rescue
life
employee

Magician
魔术师
slight of hand/magic
specialist

Paparazzi
狗仔
damned*
young man

Bodyguard
保镖
safeguard
throwing weapon

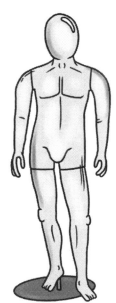

Undertaker
殡仪员
funeral
ceremony
personnel

Mannequin
人体模型
human body
model

Hitch-hiker
便车旅行者
convenient
vehicle
travel
'the one who'
(the one who travels with a
convenient vehicle)

Alien
外星人
outside
planet
person

Santa Clause
圣诞老人
Christmas
old
person

Bidder
出价人
'to go beyond'
price
person

Peking Man
中国猿人
China
ape
man

Martian
火星人
fire
planet
person

White Trash
泥腿子
mud
leg

Albino
白化病人
white
-ization
illness
person

Pacifist
和平主义者
peaceful
ideology
'the one who'
(the one with the
peaceful ideology)

Mayor
镇长
small town
chief

Bimbo
胸大无脑
breasts
large
be without
brain

Veterinarian
兽医
animal
doctor

Fool
傻瓜
stupid
melon

Electrician
电工
electricity
worker

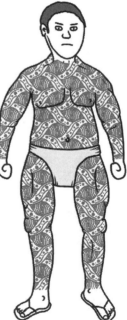

Yakuza
日本黑道
Japan
underworld

Animals

Rodent
啮齿动物
nibble
teeth
animal

Aardvark
土猪
earth/soil
pig

Alpaca
羊驼
sheep
camel

Squirrel
松鼠
pine tree
rat

Owl
猫头鹰
cat
head
eagle

Turkey
火鸡
fire
chicken

Centipede
百脚
one hundred
foot

Puma
美洲狮
american
lion

Cobra
眼镜蛇
eye glasses
snake

Panda
熊猫
bear
cat

Giraffe
长颈鹿
long
neck
deer

Kangaroo
袋鼠
bag
rat

Hippopotamus
河马
river
horse

Raven
大乌鸦
big black crow

Skunk
臭鼬
smelly weasel

Venom
毒液
poison liquid

Koala
树袋熊　无尾熊
tree pouch bear　without tail bear

Viper
毒蛇
poison snake

Zebra
斑马
stripe horse

Mammoth
长毛象
long hair elephant

Tusk
长牙
long tooth

Reindeer
驯鹿
tame deer

Woodpecker
啄木鸟
peck tree bird

Lemur
狐猴
fox monkey

Tarantula
捕鸟蛛
to seize bird spider

Pilot Whale
圆头鲸
sphere
head
whale

Marlin
枪鱼
spear
fish

(The pilot and the bottlenose look smilar so i didnt draw both, so there.)

Bottlenose Whale
巨齿鲸
huge
teeth
whale

Sponge
海绵
ocean
spineless

Humpback Whale
座头鲸
seat
head
whale

Killer Whale
杀人鲸
kill
people
whale

Blowfish
河豚
river
pig

Tiger Shark
鼬鲨
weasel
shark

Lobster
龙虾
dragon
shrimp

Octopus
八爪鱼
eight
claw
fish

Dolphin
海豚
ocean
pig

Sperm Whale
抹香鲸
'to smear'
sweet smelling
whale

Porpoise
鼠海豚
rat
dolphin

Narwhal
独角鲸
single
horn
whale

Jellyfish
海蜇
ocean
'to sting'

(*The character 小 means 'small', but also 'child', so this would also be 'child horse'.)

Porcupine
箭猪
arrow
pig

Gecko
壁虎　蝎虎
wall　scorpion
tiger　tiger

Toad
癞蛤蟆
skin disease
frog
toad

Seal
海豹
ocean
panther

Moose
驼鹿
camel
deer

Walrus
海象
ocean
elephant

Anteater
食蚁兽
eat
ant
beast

Bald Eagle
白头鹰
white
head
eagle

Coyote
郊狼
suberbs
wolf

Blue Jay
冠蓝鸦
champion
blue
crow

Racoon
浣熊
'to wash'
bear

Pony
小马
small*
horse

Caterpillar
毛毛虫
hair
hair
worm

Peacock
孔雀
hole
sparrow

Lemming
旅鼠
'to travel'
rat

Gnu
角马
horn
horse

Hornbill
犀鸟
rhinoceros
bird

Polar Bear
北极熊
north
pole
bear

Chipmunk
栗鼠
chestnut
rat

Dalmation
斑点狗
spotted
dog

Penguin
企鹅
'to stand on tip toes'
goose

Rattlesnake
响尾蛇
sound
tail
snake

Wombat
袋熊
bag
bear

Gerbal
沙鼠
sand
rat

Jaguar
美洲虎
America
tiger

(*Trout also has a different name 鳟鱼, which would translate to 'trout fish', so I used the other one.)
(虫 can be 'insect' or 'worm'. I used my discretion.)

Beetle
甲虫
shell/armor
insect

Ladybug
瓢虫
ladle
insect

Trout
尊鱼
honour*
fish

Slug
鼻涕虫
snot
worm

Stink Bug
放屁虫
fart
insect

Piranah
水虎鱼
water
tiger
fish

Flounder
左口鱼
left
mouth
fish

Grizzly Bear
灰熊
ash
bear

Poodle
卷毛狗
curl
hair
dog

Greyhound
灰猎犬
ash
hunting
dog

Chimpanzee
黑猩猩
sinister
ape
ape

Pomeranian
博美犬
rich
beautiful
dog

Gopher
沙龟
gravel
turtle

Canary
金丝雀
gold
silk
sparrow

Beaver
河狸
river
fox-like animal

Sloth
树懒
tree
lazy

树獭
tree
otter

懒熊
lazy
bear

Chameleon
变色龙
'to change'
colour
dragon

Kingfisher
鱼狗
fishing
dog

Gorilla
大猩猩
large
ape
ape

Dung Beetle
屎壳郎
dung/feces
shell
gentleman

Iguana
鬣蜥
fin
lizard

Wolverine
狼獾
wolf
badger

Falcon
猎鹰
hunting
hawk

Meekrat

狐獴
fox
mongoose

招狸
pond
racoon dog

细尾獴
tiny
tail
mongoose

Tazmanian Devil
袋獾
pouch
badger

Golden Retriever
金毛狗
golden
hair
dog

Guinea Pig

天竺鼠
India
rat

荷兰猪
Holland
pig

豚鼠
pig
rat

(*The Brontosaurus and Brachiosaurus look similar so, whatever.)

Pterodactyl
翼手龙
wing
hand
dinosaur

Dinosaur
恐龙
fearful
dragon

Triceratops
三角恐龙
three
horn
dinosaur

Platypus
鸭嘴兽　鸭獭
duck　　 duck
mouth　 otter
beast

Hadrosaurus
巨龙
chief/huge
dinosaur

Brontosaurus
迷惑龙
confused
dinosaur

Brachiosaurus*
腕龙
wrist
dinosaur

Herbivore
草食动物
grass
'to eat'
animal

Carnivore
肉食动物
meat
'to eat'
animal

Stegosaurus
剑龙
sword
dinosaur

Archaeoraptor
古盗鸟
ancient
thief
bird

T-Rex
霸王龙
tyrant
king
dinosaur

Ostrich
驼鸡
camel
chicken

Giant Salamander
娃娃鱼
baby
fish

Pika
鼠兔
rat
rabbit

Swan
天鹅
sky/heaven
goose

Husky
雪橇犬
snow
sled
dog

Chihuahua*
吉娃娃
lucky
baby

Flamingo
火烈鸟
fire
upright
bird

Earthworm
地龙
earth
dragon

Marmot*
旱獭
dry land
otter

Groundhog
土拨鼠
ground/soil
distribute
rat

Stray Dog
流浪狗
wander
stroll
dog

Sea Otter
海龙
ocean
dragon

Hamster
仓鼠
barn
mouse

Jackal
胡狼
whiskers
wolf

To Migrate (of animals)
回游
'to return'
'to travel'

Water Flea
金鱼虫
goldfish
insect

Loon
潜鸟
'to dive/submerge'
bird

Toucan
大嘴鸟
large
beak
bird

Kiwi
无翼鸟
without
wing
bird

Llama
美洲驼
North America
camel

Addax
旋角羚
spin
horn
gazelle

Partridge
班翅山鹑
spotted
wing
mountain
quail

Longhorn beetle
天牛
sky/heaven
cow

Ferret
雪貂
snow
mink

Lay Eggs
甩子
'to leave behind'
offspring

Pangolin
穿山甲
'to bore through'
mountain
shell

Cuttlefish
墨鱼
ink
fish

Pug
八哥狗
eight
elder brother
dog

Hummingbird
蜂鸟
bee
bird

Flea
跳蚤
jump
louse

Velociraptor
伶盗龙
clever
thief
dinosaur

Leech
吸血者
suck in
blood
'the one who'
(the one who sucks blood)

Bumblebee
大黄蜂
large
yellow
bee

Mammal
哺乳动物
'to feed'
milk
animal

Reptile
爬行动物
'to crawl/climb'
walk
animal

Amphibian
两栖动物
two
'to dwell/live'
animal

Sawfish
尖齿锯鳐
sharp
teeth
saw
ray (fish)

Caterpillar
小毛虫
small
hair
worm

Dingo
澳洲野狗
Austrailia
homeless dog

Larva
幼虫
infant
insect

Anglerfish
琵琶鱼
'pi pa'
fish

Clothes

Onesie
连身衣
'to join'
body
clothes

Wallet
钱包
money
bag

Mask
面具
face
equipment

Scarf
围巾
'to encircle'
kirchief

Loafers
懒人鞋
lazy
man
shoes

Lingerie
亵服
obscene
clothes

Wig
假发
false
hair

Headband
头箍
head
hoop

Lipbalm
唇膏
lip
ointment

Cape
披风
'to drape over
ones shoulds'
style

Sunglasses
墨镜
ink
glasses

Split-pants
开裆裤
open
crotch
pants

Slippers
拖鞋
drag
shoes

.BRUH.

Bowtie
蝴蝶领带
butterfly
shape
neck
ribbon

Bullet Proof Vest
护甲
'to protect'
armor plating

Camouflage
迷彩服
confused
colour
clothes

Contacts
隐形眼镜
invisible
eye
glasses

S.W.A.T.

Sweater
卫衣
'to protect'
clothes

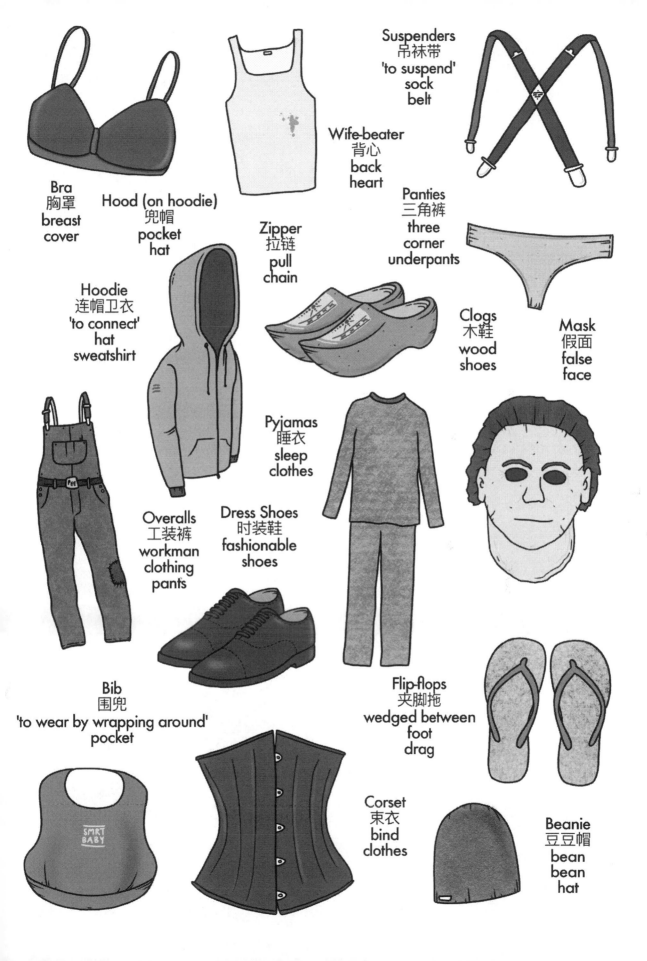

Bra
胸罩
breast
cover

Hood (on hoodie)
兜帽
pocket
hat

Wife-beater
背心
back
heart

Suspenders
吊袜带
'to suspend'
sock
belt

Zipper
拉链
pull
chain

Panties
三角裤
three
corner
underpants

Hoodie
连帽卫衣
'to connect'
hat
sweatshirt

Clogs
木鞋
wood
shoes

Mask
假面
false
face

Pyjamas
睡衣
sleep
clothes

Overalls
工装裤
workman
clothing
pants

Dress Shoes
时装鞋
fashionable
shoes

Bib
围兜
'to wear by wrapping around'
pocket

Flip-flops
夹脚拖
wedged between
foot
drag

Corset
束衣
bind
clothes

Beanie
豆豆帽
bean
bean
hat

Beret
四角帽
four corner hat

Apron
油裙
oil skirt*

UGG Boots
雪地靴
snowfield boots

Mittins
连指手套
join/connect finger gloves

Miniskirt
超短裙
super short skirt

Moccasins
鹿皮靴
deer hide boots

Flared Skirt
喇叭裙
trumpet skirt

Sailor Hat
水手帽
river 'person skilled at certain types of work' hat

Top Hat
大礼帽
large etiquette hat

Bonnet
苏格兰猫
Scotland hat

Sweat Pants
绒裤
cotton pants

Nightgown
睡裙
sleep skirt

Open-toe Shoes
鱼嘴鞋
fish mouth shoes

Earmuffs
耳帽
ear hat

(*裙 also can mean apron, but 'oil skirt' is definitely better.)

# Body Parts

(*身 can also mean 'pregnant'.)

Brains
脑汁
brain
juice/fluid

Pony Tale
马尾
horse
tail

Part (in one's hair)
分头路
separate
hair
path

Crow's Feet
鱼尾纹
fish
tail
wrinkle

Ear Wax
耳屎
ear
feces

Bangs
齐眉穗儿
level with
eyebrow
fringe

Sleepies
眼屎
eye
feces

Braces
牙套
teeth
harness

Tonsils
扁桃腺
flat
peach
gland

Braces
牙齿矫正器
teeth
'to straighten'
device

Spine
背骨
back of the body
bone

Armpit
肋窝
rib/chest
'hollow of the
human body'

Face Cream
香脂
fragrant
fat

Twins
双胞胎
set of two
womb
fetus

Pregnant
双身子
double
body*
seed/child

Ovary
卵巢窝
ovum
nest
nest

Uterus
子宫
child
temple

Fertile Egg
受精卵
receive
sperm
ovum/egg

Veins
血管
blood
tube

Ankle
腿腕
leg
wrist

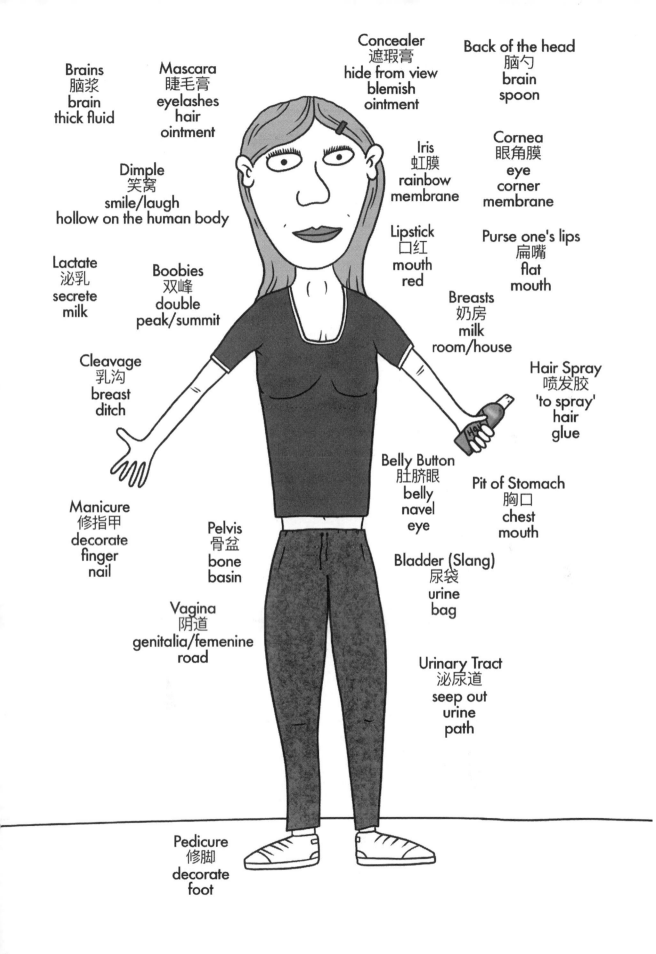

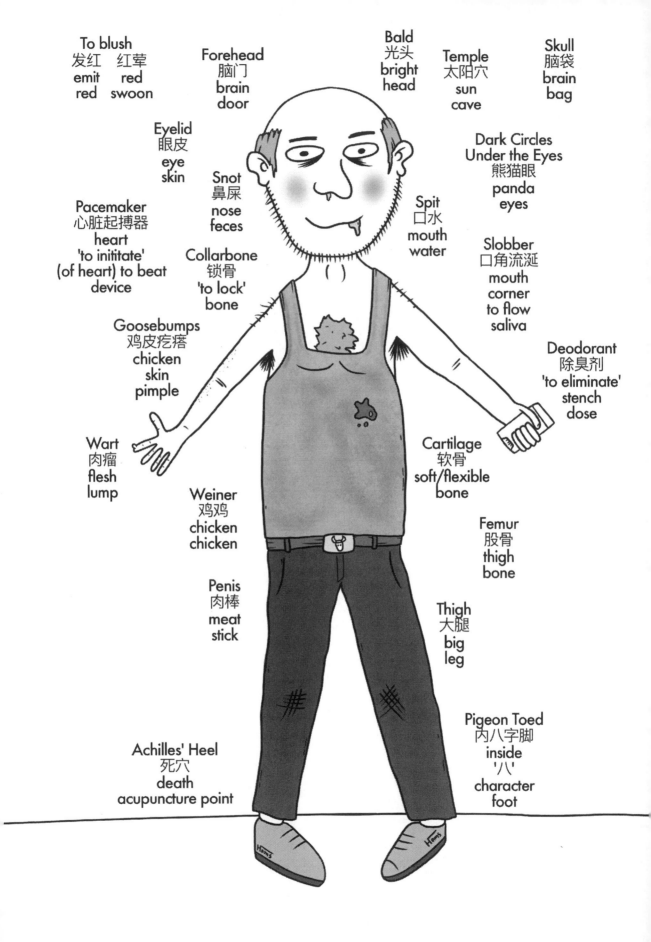

To blush
发红　红晕
emit　red
red　swoon

Forehead
脑门
brain
door

Bald
光头
bright
head

Temple
太阳穴
sun
cave

Skull
脑袋
brain
bag

Eyelid
眼皮
eye
skin

Dark Circles
Under the Eyes
熊猫眼
panda
eyes

Snot
鼻屎
nose
feces

Pacemaker
心脏起搏器
heart
'to inititate'
(of heart) to beat
device

Spit
口水
mouth
water

Slobber
口角流涎
mouth
corner
to flow
saliva

Collarbone
锁骨
'to lock'
bone

Goosebumps
鸡皮疙瘩
chicken
skin
pimple

Deodorant
除臭剂
'to eliminate'
stench
dose

Wart
肉瘤
flesh
lump

Cartilage
软骨
soft/flexible
bone

Weiner
鸡鸡
chicken
chicken

Femur
股骨
thigh
bone

Penis
肉棒
meat
stick

Thigh
大腿
big
leg

Pigeon Toed
内八字脚
inside
'八'
character
foot

Achilles' Heel
死穴
death
acupuncture point

(*屁 can also mean 'fart'...)

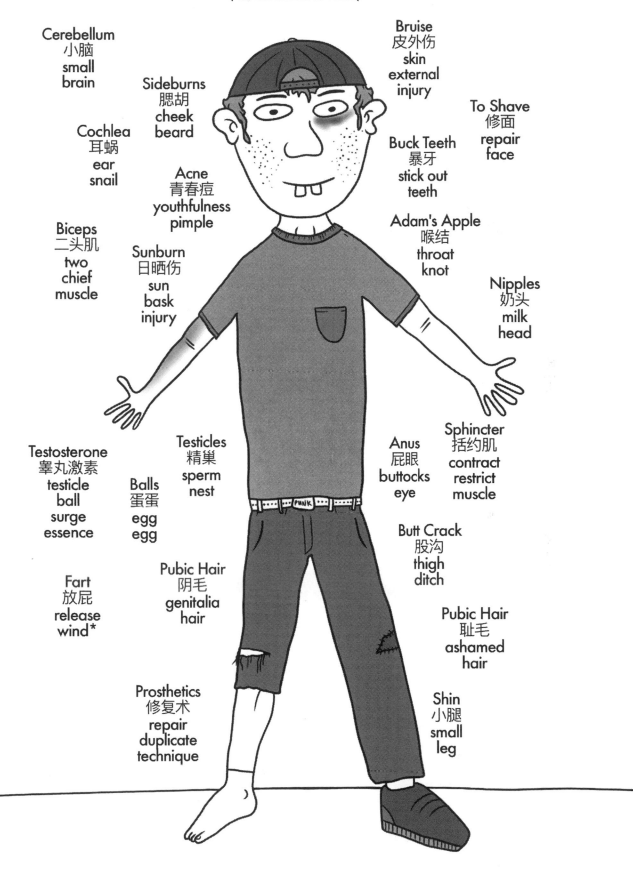

Cerebellum
小脑
small
brain

Sideburns
腮胡
cheek
beard

Bruise
皮外伤
skin
external
injury

To Shave
修面
repair
face

Cochlea
耳蜗
ear
snail

Acne
青春痘
youthfulness
pimple

Buck Teeth
暴牙
stick out
teeth

Biceps
二头肌
two
chief
muscle

Sunburn
日晒伤
sun
bask
injury

Adam's Apple
喉结
throat
knot

Nipples
奶头
milk
head

Testosterone
睾丸激素
testicle
ball
surge
essence

Balls
蛋蛋
egg
egg

Testicles
精巢
sperm
nest

Anus
屁眼
buttocks
eye

Sphincter
括约肌
contract
restrict
muscle

Butt Crack
股沟
thigh
ditch

Fart
放屁
release
wind*

Pubic Hair
阴毛
genitalia
hair

Pubic Hair
耻毛
ashamed
hair

Prosthetics
修复术
repair
duplicate
technique

Shin
小腿
small
leg

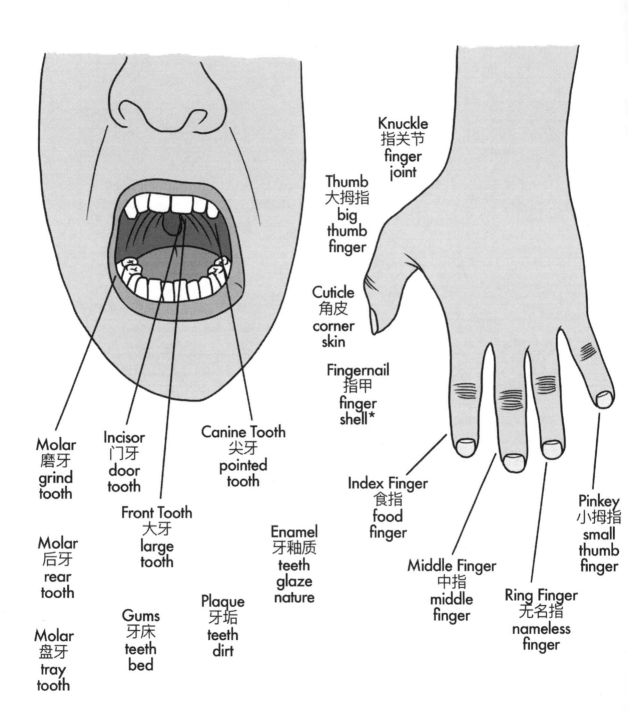

Knuckle
指关节
finger
joint

Thumb
大拇指
big
thumb
finger

Cuticle
角皮
corner
skin

Fingernail
指甲
finger
shell*

Molar
磨牙
grind
tooth

Incisor
门牙
door
tooth

Canine Tooth
尖牙
pointed
tooth

Index Finger
食指
food
finger

Pinkey
小拇指
small
thumb
finger

Molar
后牙
rear
tooth

Front Tooth
大牙
large
tooth

Enamel
牙釉质
teeth
glaze
nature

Middle Finger
中指
middle
finger

Ring Finger
无名指
nameless
finger

Molar
盘牙
tray
tooth

Gums
牙床
teeth
bed

Plaque
牙垢
teeth
dirt

Instruments

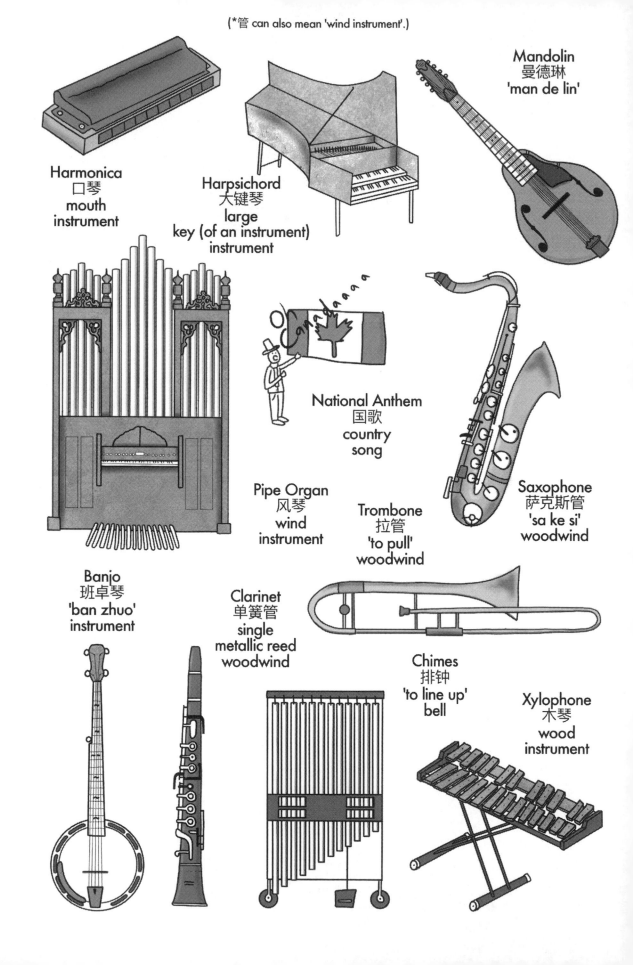

(\*管 can also mean 'wind instrument'.)

Harmonica
口琴
mouth
instrument

Harpsichord
大键琴
large
key (of an instrument)
instrument

Mandolin
曼德琳
'man de lin'

National Anthem
国歌
country
song

Pipe Organ
风琴
wind
instrument

Saxophone
萨克斯管
'sa ke si'
woodwind

Trombone
拉管
'to pull'
woodwind

Banjo
班卓琴
'ban zhuo'
instrument

Clarinet
单簧管
single
metallic reed
woodwind

Chimes
排钟
'to line up'
bell

Xylophone
木琴
wood
instrument

Tambourine
铃鼓
(small) bell
drum

Accordian
手风琴
hand
wind
instrument

Piccolo
短笛
short
flute

Piano
钢琴
steel
instrument

Bagpipes
风笛
wind
flute

Trumpet
小号
small
horn

Tuba
大号
large
horn

Harp
竖琴
upright
instrument

Oboe
双簧管
double
reed
woodwind

Violin
小提琴
small
lift/raise
instrument

Viola
中提琴
middle
lift/raise
instrument

Cello
大提琴
large
lift/raise
instrument

Double Bass
低音提琴
low
sound
lift/raise
instrument

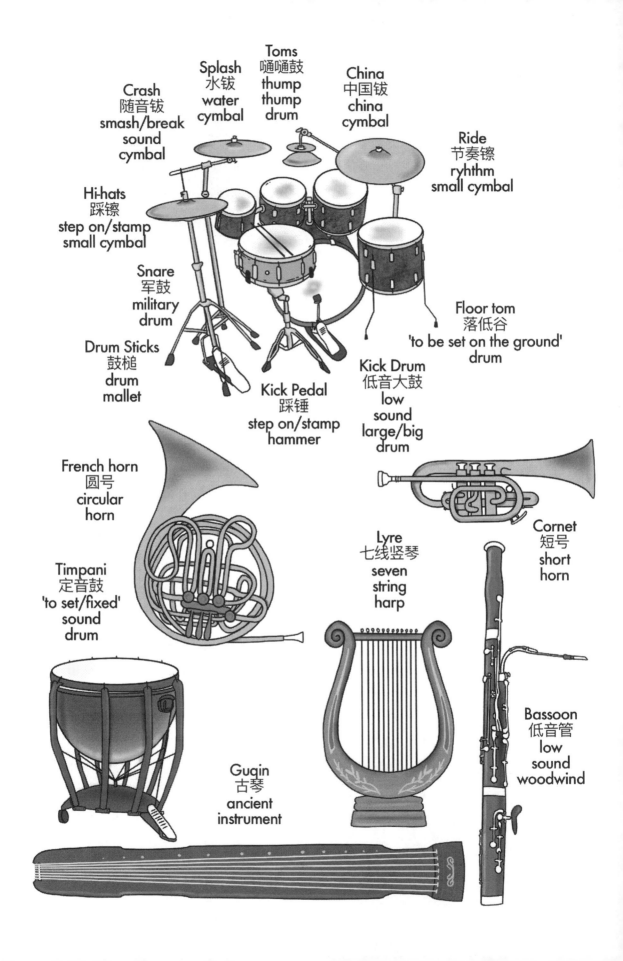

Crash
随音钹
smash/break
sound
cymbal

Splash
水钹
water
cymbal

Toms
嗵嗵鼓
thump
thump
drum

China
中国钹
china
cymbal

Ride
节奏镲
ryhthm
small cymbal

Hi-hats
踩镲
step on/stamp
small cymbal

Snare
军鼓
military
drum

Drum Sticks
鼓槌
drum
mallet

Kick Pedal
踩锤
step on/stamp
hammer

Kick Drum
低音大鼓
low
sound
large/big
drum

Floor tom
落低谷
'to be set on the ground'
drum

French horn
圆号
circular
horn

Cornet
短号
short
horn

Lyre
七线竖琴
seven
string
harp

Timpani
定音鼓
'to set/fixed'
sound
drum

Bassoon
低音管
low
sound
woodwind

Guqin
古琴
ancient
instrument

(*See the last page in 'Randoms' for 'onomatopoeia'.)

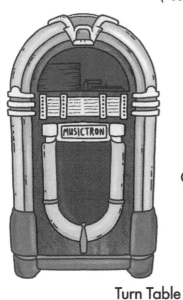

Jukebox
自动点唱机
automatic
'to choose'
gramophone

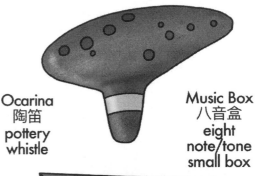

Ocarina
陶笛
pottery
whistle

Music Box
八音盒
eight
note/tone
small box

Gramophone
唱机
song
machine

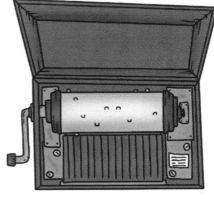

Recorder
竖笛
upright
flute

木笛
wood
flute

Turn Table
唱盘
song
plate/tray

Tuning Fork
声叉
sound/tone
fork

A Capella
无伴奏合唱
without
'to accompany with musical instruments'
chorus

Microphone
传声器
'to transmit'
sound
device

Tempo
速度拍子
speed
degree
beat

Choir
唱诗班
'to sing'
(the) verse
group

Scat Singing
拟声唱法
onomatopoeia*
singing style

Skibiddy bop doo
ba dee, dee doodle
a goo da bop

Boots 'n cats 'n
Boots 'n cats 'n
Boots 'n cats 'n
Boots 'n cats 'n
Boots 'n cats 'n

Soprano
女高音
female
'of a high level'
note

Tenor
男高音
male
'of a high level'
note

Falsetto
假声
false
voice

Pitch
音高
sound
height

Beat Boxing
节奏口技
beat/rhythm
mouth
skill
(Translates also to
'Rhythm Ventriloquism')

# Vehicles

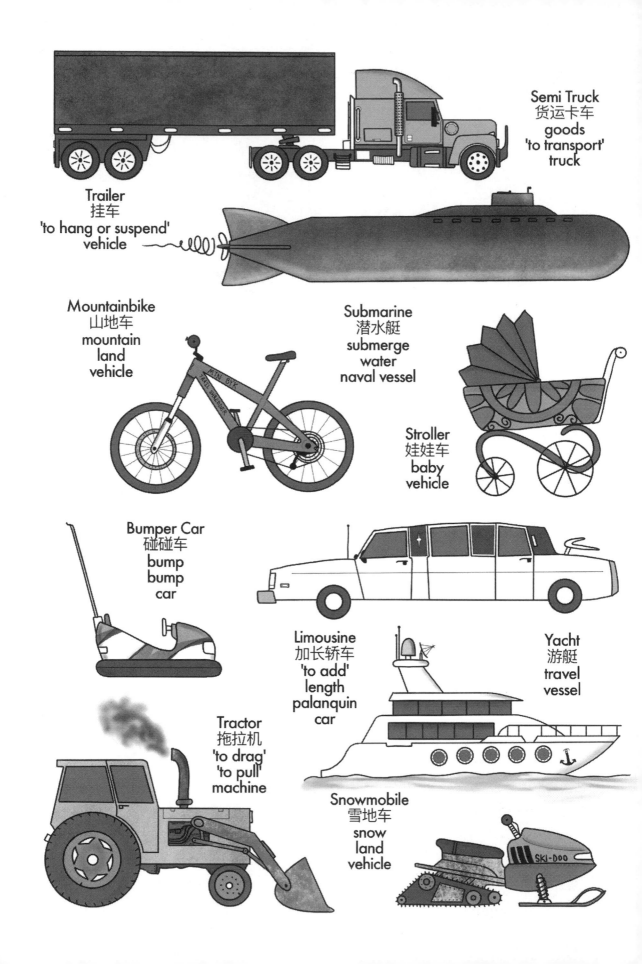

Semi Truck
货运卡车
goods
'to transport'
truck

Trailer
挂车
'to hang or suspend'
vehicle

Mountainbike
山地车
mountain
land
vehicle

Submarine
潜水艇
submerge
water
naval vessel

Stroller
娃娃车
baby
vehicle

Bumper Car
碰碰车
bump
bump
car

Limousine
加长轿车
'to add'
length
palanquin
car

Yacht
游艇
travel
vessel

Tractor
拖拉机
'to drag'
'to pull'
machine

Snowmobile
雪地车
snow
land
vehicle

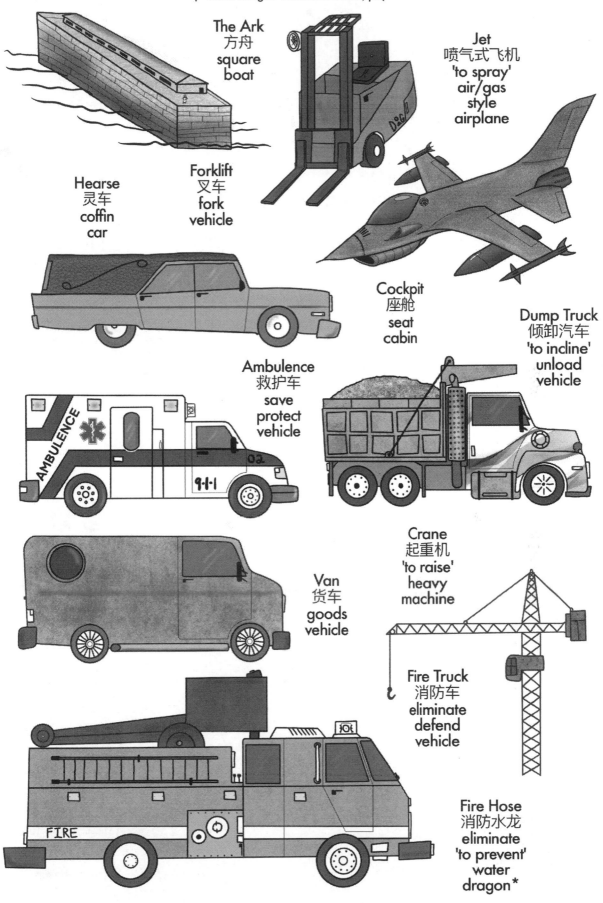

(*'Water Dragon' translates to hose, ps.)

The Ark
方舟
square
boat

Jet
喷气式飞机
'to spray'
air/gas
style
airplane

Forklift
叉车
fork
vehicle

Hearse
灵车
coffin
car

Cockpit
座舱
seat
cabin

Dump Truck
倾卸汽车
'to incline'
unload
vehicle

Ambulence
救护车
save
protect
vehicle

Crane
起重机
'to raise'
heavy
machine

Van
货车
goods
vehicle

Fire Truck
消防车
eliminate
defend
vehicle

Fire Hose
消防水龙
eliminate
'to prevent'
water
dragon*

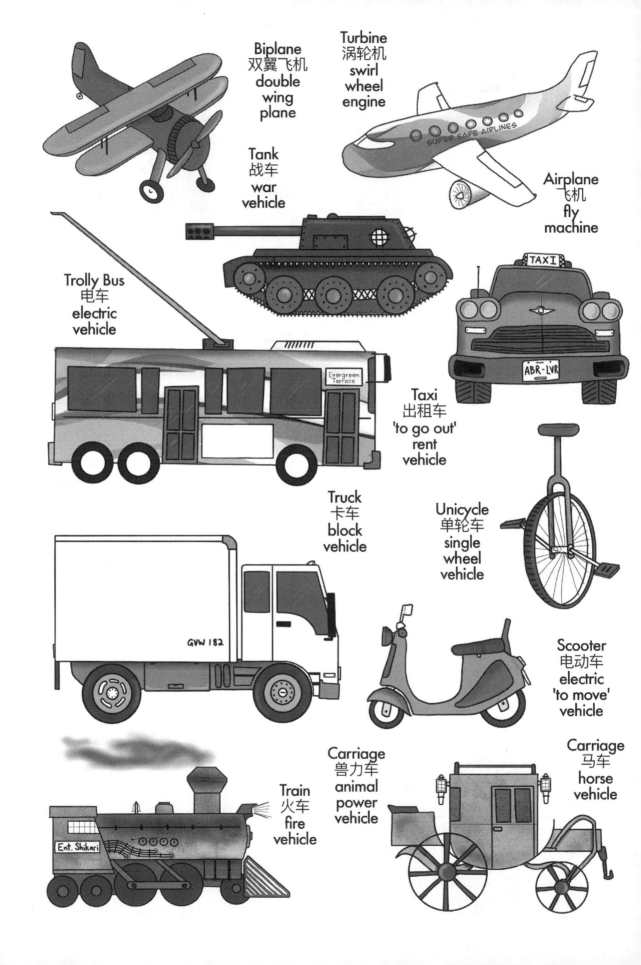

Biplane
双翼飞机
double wing plane

Turbine
涡轮机
swirl wheel engine

Tank
战车
war vehicle

Airplane
飞机
fly machine

Trolly Bus
电车
electric vehicle

Taxi
出租车
'to go out' rent vehicle

Truck
卡车
block vehicle

Unicycle
单轮车
single wheel vehicle

Scooter
电动车
electric 'to move' vehicle

Train
火车
fire vehicle

Carriage
兽力车
animal power vehicle

Carriage
马车
horse vehicle

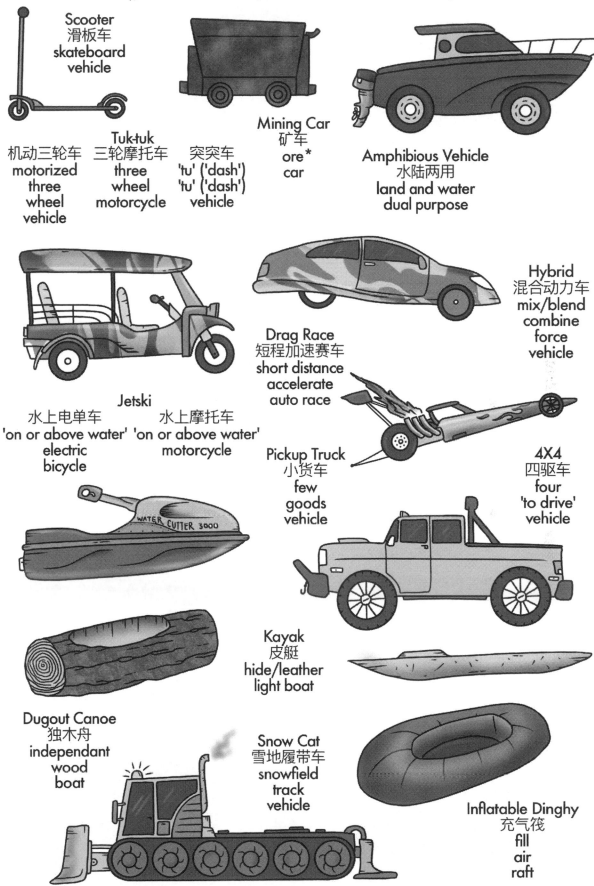

(矿 can also mean 'to mine', but I like 'ore car' better than 'mine car'.)

Scooter
滑板车
skateboard
vehicle

机动三轮车
motorized
three
wheel
vehicle

Tuk-tuk
三轮摩托车
three
wheel
motorcycle

突突车
'tu' ('dash')
'tu' ('dash')
vehicle

Mining Car
矿车
ore*
car

Amphibious Vehicle
水陆两用
land and water
dual purpose

Hybrid
混合动力车
mix/blend
combine
force
vehicle

Drag Race
短程加速赛车
short distance
accelerate
auto race

Jetski

水上电单车
'on or above water'
electric
bicycle

水上摩托车
'on or above water'
motorcycle

Pickup Truck
小货车
few
goods
vehicle

4X4
四驱车
four
'to drive'
vehicle

Kayak
皮艇
hide/leather
light boat

Dugout Canoe
独木舟
independant
wood
boat

Snow Cat
雪地履带车
snowfield
track
vehicle

Inflatable Dinghy
充气筏
fill
air
raft

Aircraft Carrier
航母
ship
mother

Helicopter
直升机
vertical
ascend
aircraft

Hovercraft
气垫船
air
cushion
boat

Rickshaw
东洋车
eastern
foreign
'carry in a cart'

SUV
休旅车
'to rest'
travel
car

Glider
滑翔机
slide
glide
aircraft

Moped
激动自行车
motorized
bicycle

Seaplane
水上飞机
'above the water'
airplane

Bulldozer
推土机
'to push forward'
soil/land
machine

**RV**
房车
house
car

**Oil Rig**
钻井船
'to drill'
a well
vessel

**Rollercoaster**
过山车
'to cross'
mountain
vehicle

**Blimp**
软式小型飞船
soft
small scale
fly
boat

**Spoiler**
导流板
'to direct'
'to circulate'
board

**Sunroof**
天窗
sky
window

**Antenna**
天线
sky
wire

**Windshield Wiper**
雨刷
rain
'to brush'

**Windshield**
风挡
wind
cover

**Hood**
引擎盖
'to extend'
'to raise' (ones hand)
cover

**Trunk**
行李箱
luggage
box

**High Beams**
远光灯
distant
bright
light

**Muffler**
减声器
'to reduce'
sound
device

**Rim**
车圈
vehicle
circle

**Fibreglass**
玻璃钢
glass
steel

**VW Bug**
金龟车
tortoise
car

**Turn Signal**
泵灯
pump
light

**Bumper**
保险杠
'to protect'
danger
bar

Tachometer
转速表
classifier for revolutions
velocity
meter

Rearview Mirror
后视镜
rear
'to reveal'
mirror

Ignition
点火开关
'to ignite'
fire
'to switch on'
'to switch off'

Defroster
除霜器
'to get rid of'
frost
device

Clutch
离合器
seperation
reunion
device

Brake Pedal
制动踏板
'to regulate'
movement
step on
plate

Gas Pedal
油门
petroleum
door

Emergency Brake
紧急闸
urgent
hurried
brake

Stick Shift
变速杆
change
speed
shaft

Oil Filter
机油滤清器
engine
oil
'to filter'
'to clean'
device

Spark Plug
火花塞
fire
flower
cork
(spark cork)

Piston
活塞
living
cork

Alternator
交流发电气
'to exchange'
'to develop'
electricity
machine

Dipstick
油尺
oil
ruler

V-Tech

Honder

Carburetor
化油器
transform
oil
machine

Radiator
散热器
'to disperse'
heat
device

Grille
护删
'to protect'
fence

ABS
防抱死系统
'to guard against'
'to embrace'
death
system

食物

Food

Anchovy
凤尾鱼
phoenix
tail
fish

Corncob
玉米芯
corn
core

Raspberry
山莓
mountain
berry

Almonds
扁桃
flat
walnut

Macadamia Nut
火山豆
volcano
bean

Brussels Sprouts
球芽甘蓝
sphere
sprout
cabbage

Asparagus
龙须菜
'shaped like a dragon'
tassel
vegetable

Nectarine
油桃
greasy
peach

Rutabaga
芥菜疙瘩
tiny
vegetable
pimple

Snow Pea
荷兰豆
Holland
bean

Thaw Food
退冰
remove
ice

Kimchi
韩式泡菜
South Korea
style
pickled vegetables

Pecan
山核桃
mountain
walnut

Artichoke
洋蓟
foreign
thistle

Porkchop
排骨
row
bone

Lentils
小扁豆
small
flat
bean

Beet
甜菜
sweet
vegetable

Macaroni
空心面
hollow
centre
noodles

Strawberry
草莓
countryside*
berry

Cranberry
酸梅
sour
berry

Lime
酸橙
sour
orange

Protein
蛋白
egg
white

Cottage Cheese
乡村奶酪
countryside
cheese

Diet
节食
conserve
food

Pasteurized Milk
无菌牛奶
without
bacteria
milk

Marmalade
柑橘酱
mandarin orange
tangerine
jam

Mayonnaise
蛋黄酱
egg
yellow
sauce

Instant Noodles
方便面
convenient
noodles

Cotton Candy
棉花糖
cotton
anything resembling a flower
candy

Sushimi
生鱼片
raw
fish
slice

Frappuccino
星冰乐
small amount
ice
pleasure

Dairy Product
乳品
milk
product

Margarine
人造奶油
artificial
butter

Cabbage
洋白菜
foreign
white
vegetable

Menu
菜单
cuisine
list

Pasta
意大利面
Italy
noodles

Salami
意大利香肠
Italy
sausage

Broccoli
西兰花
west
orchid
flower

Bubble Gum
泡泡糖
bubble
bubble
candy

Potato
土豆
earth/soil
bean

Oatmeal
麦片
wheat
slice

Fondue
奶酪火锅
cheese
hot pot

Skim Milk
脱脂牛奶
'to shed'
fat
cow
milk

Walnut
胡桃
beard
peach

Popsicle
冰棒
ice
stick

Avocado
牛油果
cow
fat
fruit

Syrup
糖水
sugar
liquid

Syrup
糖汁
sugar
juice

Pancakes
热香饼
hot
savoury or
appetizing
round flat cake

Smoothie
冰沙
ice
sand

Buffet
自助餐
self
'to help'
meal

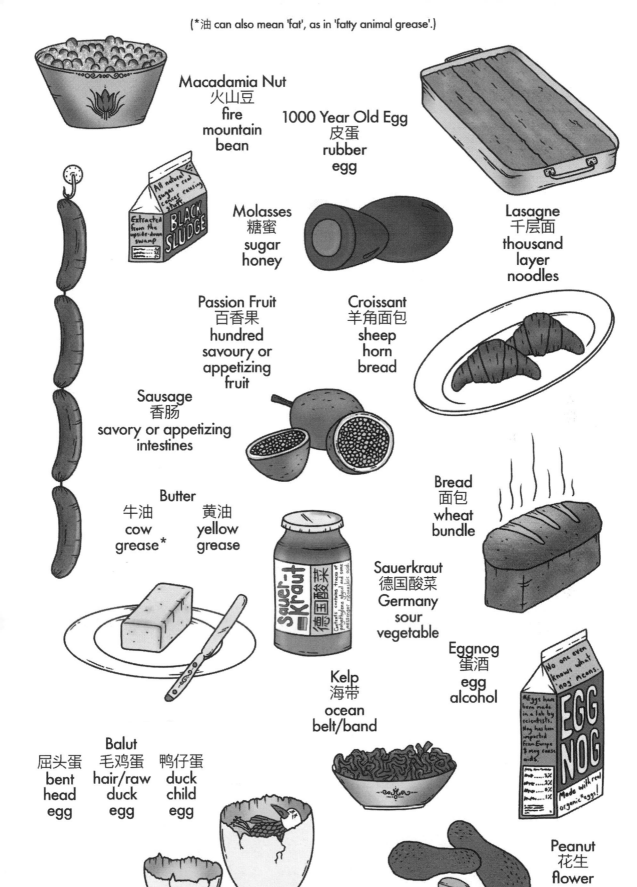

(*油 can also mean 'fat', as in 'fatty animal grease'.)

Macadamia Nut
火山豆
fire mountain bean

1000 Year Old Egg
皮蛋
rubber egg

Molasses
糖蜜
sugar honey

Lasagne
千层面
thousand layer noodles

Passion Fruit
百香果
hundred savoury or appetizing fruit

Croissant
羊角面包
sheep horn bread

Sausage
香肠
savory or appetizing intestines

Butter
牛油
cow grease*

黄油
yellow grease

Sauerkraut
德国酸菜
Germany sour vegetable

Bread
面包
wheat bundle

Eggnog
蛋酒
egg alcohol

Kelp
海带
ocean belt/band

Balut
屈头蛋
bent head egg

毛鸡蛋
hair/raw duck egg

鸭仔蛋
duck child egg

Peanut
花生
flower raw

Pretzel
椒盐卷饼
hot pepper
salt
curl
pastry

String Bean
豆角
bean
horn-shaped

Icecream Cone
甜筒
sugary
tube

Pumpkin
南瓜
south
mellon

Lollipop
棒棒糖
stick
stick
candy

Hay
马草
horse
grass

Patato Chips
炸薯片
'to fry in oil'
potato
slice

Doughnut
油炸圈饼
deep-fry
ring
cake

Whipcream
奶油
milk
fat

Watermellon
西瓜
west
mellon

MSG
味精
taste
extract

Soda
汽水
air
water

Yogurt
酸奶
sour
milk

Pizza
意大利肉饼
Italy
meat
round flat cake

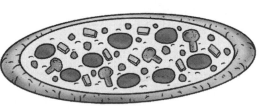

Dumpling
团子
lump

Wild Peach
毛桃
hair
peach

Zucchini
意大利青瓜
Italy
cucumber

Cracker
饼干
biscuit
dry

Taco
墨西哥卷饼
Mexico
'to roll up'
round flat cake

Marshmallow
果汁软糖
fruit juice
soft
candy

Carrot
胡萝卜
whiskers
radish

Loaf Cake
枕头蛋糕
pillow
cake

Ginger Ale
姜汁
ginger
juice

Popcorn
玉米花
corn
flower

Root Beer
跟汁汽水
root (of a plant)
juice
soda

Mead
蜂蜜酒
honey
alcohol

Jalapeño
墨西哥辣椒
Mexico
hot pepper

Horseradish
辣根
spicy
root

Fortune Cookie
签语饼
inscribed bamboo stick (used in divination)
words
cookie

奇幻

Fantasy

Faun
洋男
sheep
man

Werewolf
狼人
wolf
person

Goblin
灵怪
spirit
monster

Cyclops
独眼巨人
single
eye
huge
person

Sphinx
狮身人面
lion
body
person
face

Valkyrie
女武神
female
military
deity

Dryad
树妖
tree
evil spirit

Mermaid
美人鱼
beautiful
person
fish

Siren
妖精
witch/devil
spirit

Basilisk
蛇怪
snake
monster

Pegasus
飞马
flying
horse

Satyr
色魔
sex
demon

Elf (Leprechaun)
仙童
immortal
child

Centaur
半人马
half
person
horse

Frankenstein
科学怪人
science
monster
person

Vampire
吸血鬼
(to) suck
blood
devil

Orc
半兽人
half
beast
person

Griffin
鹰头狮
eagle
head
lion

Minotaur
人身牛头怪物
person
body
cow
head
monster

Golem
魔像
demon
appearance

Gargoyle
石像鬼　　滴水嘴兽
stone　　drip
image　　water
devil　　mouth
　　　　beast

Phoenix
凤凰
male phoenix
female phoenix

Unicorn
独角兽
single
horn
beast

Kraken
北海巨妖
north
sea
gigantic
monster

Grim Reaper
死神
death
god

Saskquatch
大足野人
big
foot
wild
person

Zombie
僵尸
rigid/stiff
corpse

Troll
山精
mountain
mythical goblin spirit

Gnome
土神
earth
deity

Ogre
食人魔
'to eat'
person
demon

Boogyman
夜半鬼开门
midnight
demon
open
door

(*Genie also means 'fairy or elf' as well. It's a hard one to translate.)

Banshee
丧门神
mourn
gate
deity

Yeti
雪人
snow
person

Incubus
梦魔
dream
demon

Jackalope
鹿角兔
deer
horn
rabbit

Spectre
魔影
evil spirit
shadow

Genie*
精灵
energy
spirit

Succubus
魔女
demon
woman

Harpie
鸟身女妖
bird
body
woman
devil

Cerberus
地狱三头犬
underworld/hell
three
head
dog

# 运动与游戏

## Sports & Games

Rugby
橄榄球
olive
olive
ball

HED KIKRZ
GEORGE

Cricket
板球
board/plank
ball

Hockey
冰球
ice
ball

PUCK SLAPPERS
EASTON
EASTON

Baseball
棒球
stick/club
ball

Tennis
网球
net
ball

中

FAT BATZ

Basketball
篮球
basket
ball
(go figure eh)

DUNK MASTERS

Squash
壁球
wall
ball

Vollyball
排球
'to line up'
ball

44
+

Badminton
羽毛球
feather
ball

Football
美国足球
America(n)
foot
ball

BALL DESTROYERZ

Soccer
足球
foot
ball

Pool/Billiards
桌球
table
ball

Cue Ball
主球
master
ball

Pool/Billiards
撞球
bump against
ball

Ice Skates
冰鞋    冰刀
ice     ice
shoe    knife

Bowling
滚球
'to roll'
ball

Curling
冰壶
ice
pot/kettle

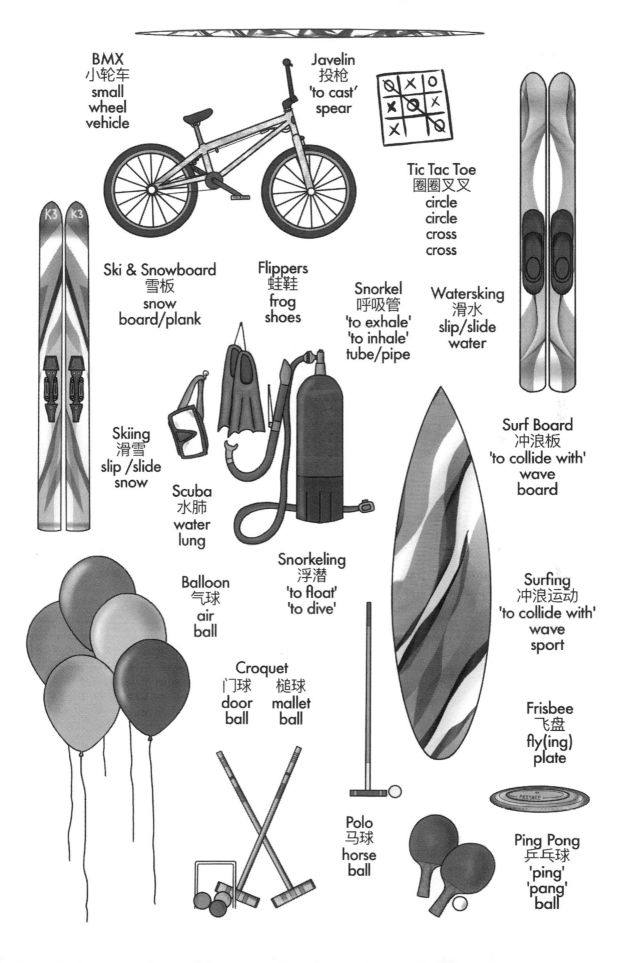

BMX
小轮车
small
wheel
vehicle

Javelin
投枪
'to cast'
spear

Tic Tac Toe
圈圈叉叉
circle
circle
cross
cross

Ski & Snowboard
雪板
snow
board/plank

Flippers
蛙鞋
frog
shoes

Snorkel
呼吸管
'to exhale'
'to inhale'
tube/pipe

Watersking
滑水
slip/slide
water

Surf Board
冲浪板
'to collide with'
wave
board

Skiing
滑雪
slip /slide
snow

Scuba
水肺
water
lung

Snorkeling
浮潜
'to float'
'to dive'

Surfing
冲浪运动
'to collide with'
wave
sport

Balloon
气球
air
ball

Croquet
门球    槌球
door    mallet
ball     ball

Frisbee
飞盘
fly(ing)
plate

Polo
马球
horse
ball

Ping Pong
乒乓球
'ping'
'pang'
ball

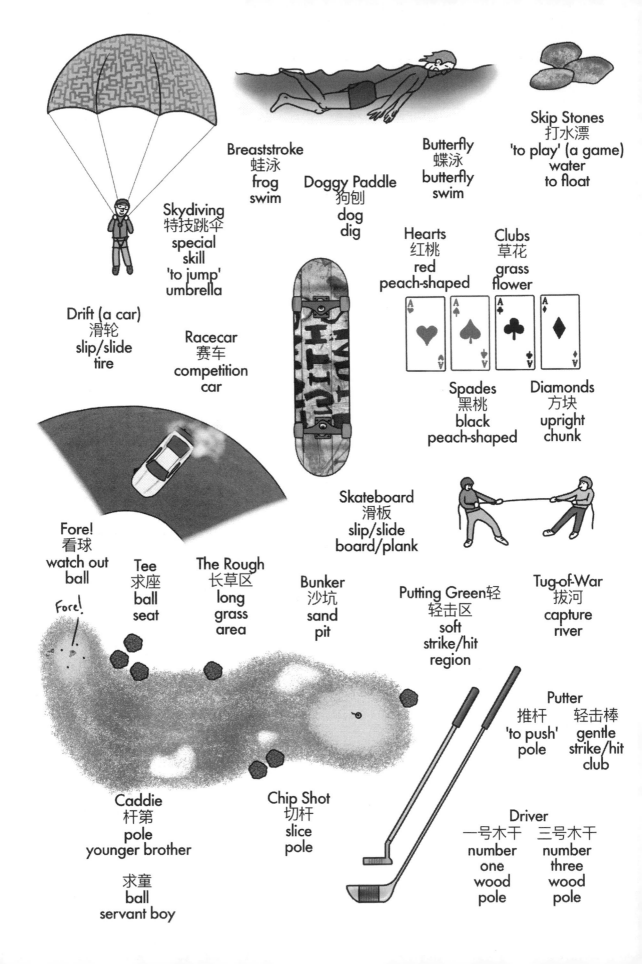

Skydiving
特技跳伞
special
skill
'to jump'
umbrella

Breaststroke
蛙泳
frog
swim

Doggy Paddle
狗刨
dog
dig

Butterfly
蝶泳
butterfly
swim

Skip Stones
打水漂
'to play' (a game)
water
to float

Drift (a car)
滑轮
slip/slide
tire

Racecar
赛车
competition
car

Hearts
红桃
red
peach-shaped

Clubs
草花
grass
flower

Spades
黑桃
black
peach-shaped

Diamonds
方块
upright
chunk

Skateboard
滑板
slip/slide
board/plank

Fore!
看球
watch out
ball

Fore!

Tee
求座
ball
seat

The Rough
长草区
long
grass
area

Bunker
沙坑
sand
pit

Putting Green轻
轻击区
soft
strike/hit
region

Tug-of-War
拔河
capture
river

Putter
推杆           轻击棒
'to push'       gentle
pole         strike/hit
club

Caddie
杆第
pole
younger brother

Chip Shot
切杆
slice
pole

Driver
一号木干      三号木干
number      number
one        three
wood       wood
pole        pole

求童
ball
servant boy

轮滑
wheel
slip/slide

**Roller Skates**
四轮鞋滑冰
four
wheel
shoes
skate (on ice)

旱冰鞋
dry land
ice skates

Hooray for me!

First looser

#1

There are no such thing as loosers

Three

**Ice Skates**
冰鞋
ice
shoes

**Grand Prix***
大奖赛
large
prize
race

**Figure Skating**
花样滑冰
fancy pattern
manner
slip/slide
ice

**Parallel Bars**
双杠
double
thick stick

**Pole-vaulting**
撑杆跳高
'to push'
pole
jump
high

**Push-up**
俯卧撑
face down
'to crouch'
prop up

**Seesaw**
跷跷板
'to lift/raise'
'to lift/raise'
board

SUPER DINGER 7000

Why do people even try this?

..oO

MAD SKILLZ

**Do the Splits**
劈叉
'to split open'
crotch

**Swimming Goggles**
泳镜
swimming
glasses

**Slam Dunk**
扣篮　　暴扣
dunk　　fierce
basket　dunk

**Hula Dance**
草裙舞
grass
skirt
dance

**Merry-go-round**
旋转木马
'to move in orbit'
revolve
wood
horse

(*I just realized 'prix' means 'prize' in French. Oh well eh!)

**Marbles**
玻璃球
glass
ball

**Carnival**
狂欢节
wild
joyous
festival

**Sudoku**
九宫格数独
nine
imperial palace
square
count
independant

**Puzzle**
拼图玩具
'to join together'
picture
toy

**Horse Spur**
题马刺
kick
horse
thorn

Hut!

I'm super not lame.

**Tap Dance**
踢跶舞　踢踏舞
kick　　kick
slip　　stamp
dance　dance

**Quarterback**
四分卫
four
distribute
defend

**'Twerk'**
电臀舞
lightning
buttocks
dance

**Pull-up**
引体向上
pull
body
towards
up

**Break Dance**
霹雳舞
(slang) awesome
dance

**Callisthenics**
柔软体操
flexable
gymnastics

**Board Game**
桌游
table
game

**Rubik's Cube**
魔方
magic
square

**Peek-a-boo**
躲猫猫
hide (oneself)
hide
hide
(猫 also means cat...)

**Dominos**
多米诺骨牌
'duo mi nuo'
bone
mahjong tile

**Yo-yo**
悠悠球
'to swing'
'to swing'
ball

**Balance Beam**
平衡木
level/flat
weight
wood

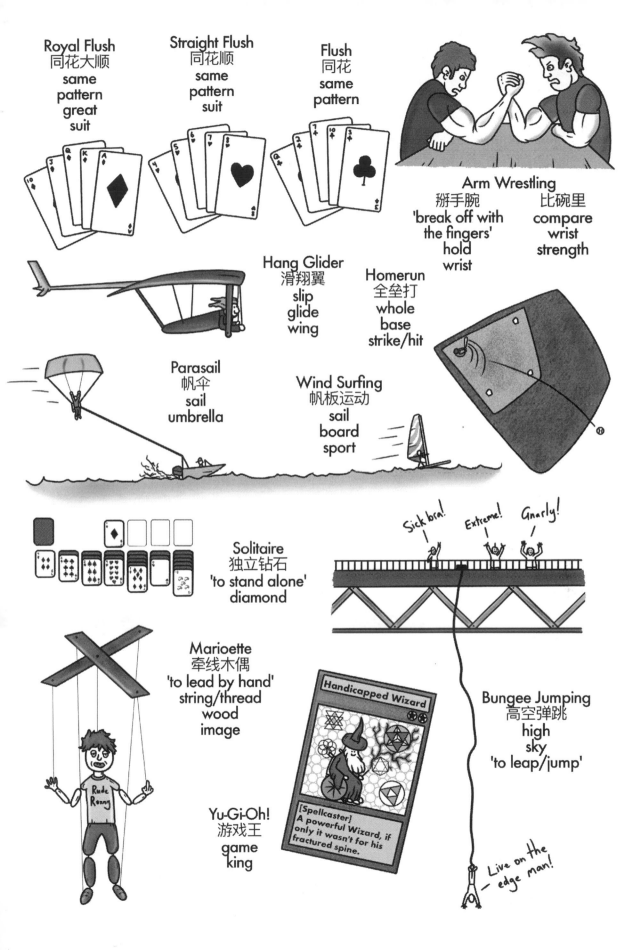

Risk (Board Game)
大战役
large-scale war
campaign

Blackjack
二十一点
twenty one
count

Fencing
击剑
attack/assault
sword

Arcade Game
街机游戏
street
machine
game

Twister
扭扭乐
twist
twist
enjoyment

Uppercut
上钩拳
send up
hook
fist

Hadouken
波动拳
wave motion
fist

Water Polo
水球
water
ball

Token
代币
'to take the place of'
money

Rock-Paper-Scissors
剪刀石头布        包剪锤
scissors        bundle
rock            scissors
cloth           hammer

手足球台    Foosball    足球游戏桌
hand       桌上足球    soccer
soccer     table       game
table      top         table
           soccer

Juggle
边抛边接
side
throw
side
connect/join

Wipeout (Gameshow)
勇敢向前冲
courageous
forge ahead
thoroughfare

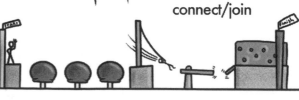

# Weapons

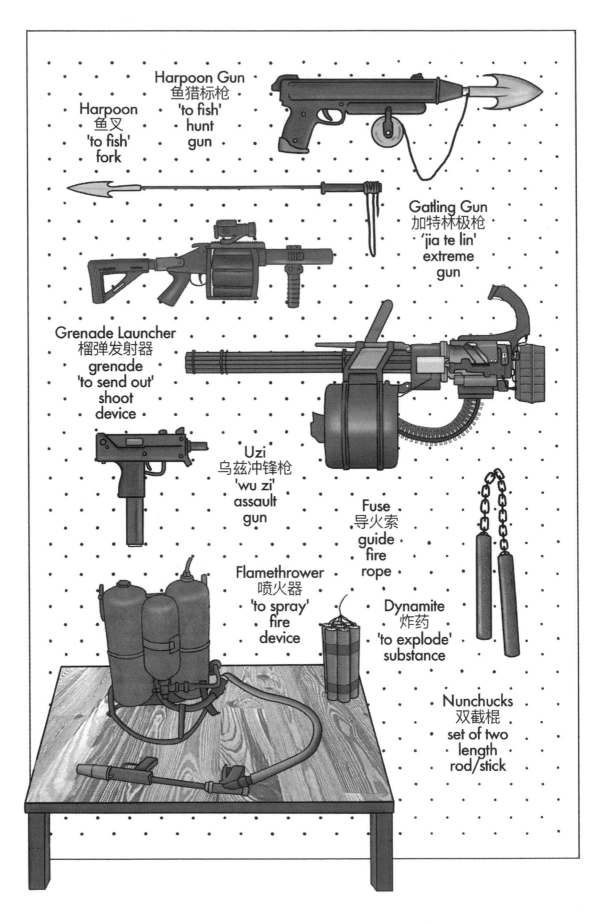

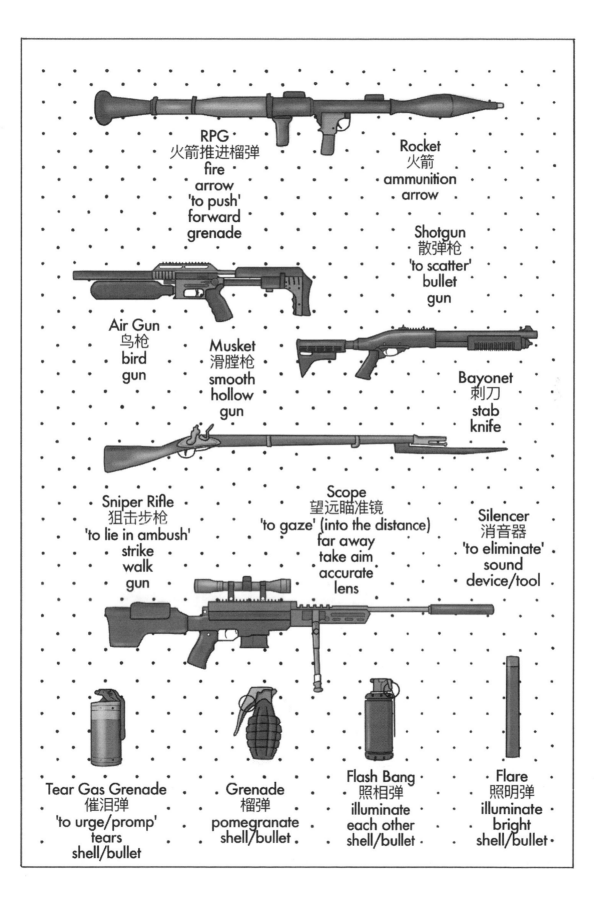

RPG
火箭推进榴弹
fire
arrow
'to push'
forward
grenade

Rocket
火箭
ammunition
arrow

Shotgun
散弹枪
'to scatter'
bullet
gun

Air Gun
鸟枪
bird
gun

Musket
滑膛枪
smooth
hollow
gun

Bayonet
刺刀
stab
knife

Sniper Rifle
狙击步枪
'to lie in ambush'
strike
walk
gun

Scope
望远瞄准镜
'to gaze' (into the distance)
far away
take aim
accurate
lens

Silencer
消音器
'to eliminate'
sound
device/tool

Tear Gas Grenade
催泪弹
'to urge/promp'
tears
shell/bullet

Grenade
榴弹
pomegranate
shell/bullet

Flash Bang
照相弹
illuminate
each other
shell/bullet

Flare
照明弹
illuminate
bright
shell/bullet

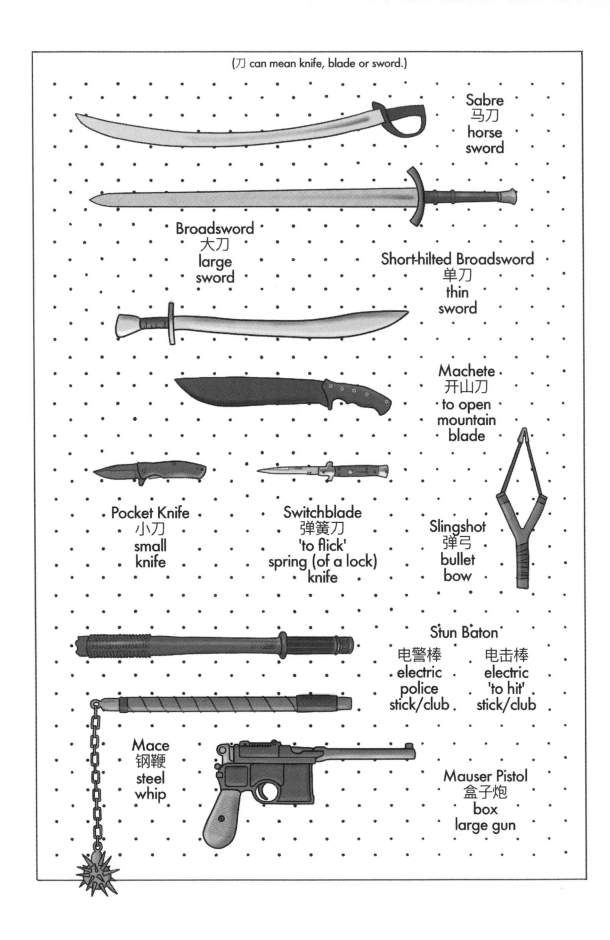

(刀 can mean knife, blade or sword.)

Sabre
马刀
horse
sword

Broadsword
大刀
large
sword

Short-hilted Broadsword
单刀
thin
sword

Machete
开山刀
to open
mountain
blade

Pocket Knife
小刀
small
knife

Switchblade
弹簧刀
'to flick'
spring (of a lock)
knife

Slingshot
弹弓
bullet
bow

Stun Baton

电警棒
electric
police
stick/club

电击棒
electric
'to hit'
stick/club

Mace
钢鞭
steel
whip

Mauser Pistol
盒子炮
box
large gun

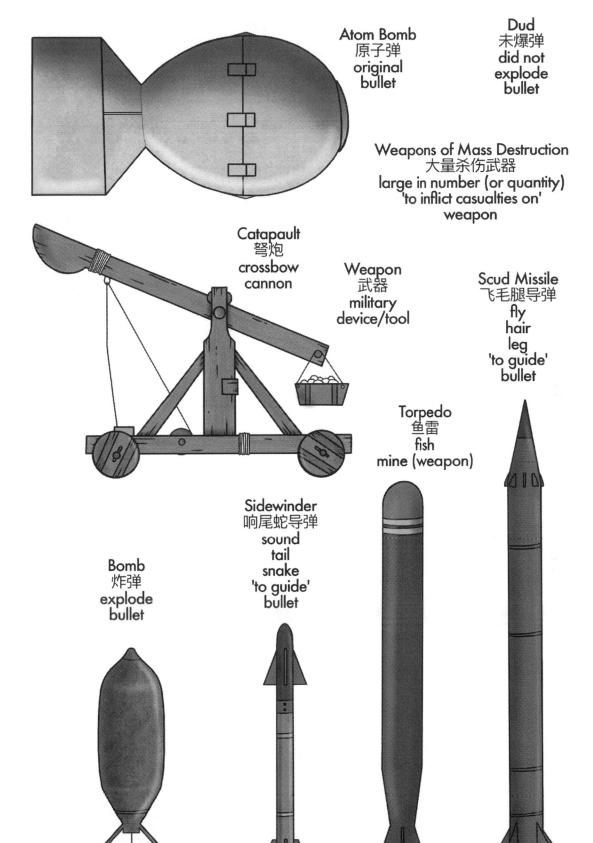

Atom Bomb
原子弹
original
bullet

Dud
未爆弹
did not
explode
bullet

Weapons of Mass Destruction
大量杀伤武器
large in number (or quantity)
'to inflict casualties on'
weapon

Catapault
弩炮
crossbow
cannon

Weapon
武器
military
device/tool

Scud Missile
飞毛腿导弹
fly
hair
leg
'to guide'
bullet

Torpedo
鱼雷
fish
mine (weapon)

Sidewinder
响尾蛇导弹
sound
tail
snake
'to guide'
bullet

Bomb
炸弹
explode
bullet

# 病与感情
## Diseases & Emotions

(*烧 also means 'fever', but I like 'emit heat' better.)

Lockjaw
牙关紧闭正
teeth
'to close'
tight
shut
illness

Tapeworm
绦虫
ribbon
worm

Battlecry
喊杀声
'to yell/howl'
"kill"
voice

Dyslexia
诵读困难症
read aloud
difficulty
illness

失读症
mistake
pronounce
illness

'Butthurt'
玻璃心
glass
heart

Scoliosis
脊柱侧弯
vertabra
'to lean'
bend

eht yob

Snivel
假哭
artificial
'to cry'

Fever
发烧
emit*
heat

Allergies
花粉病
pollin (flower powder)
disease

PTSD
创伤后压力紊乱
trauma
afterwards
burden
disorderly

Bloodthirsty
嗜杀成性
addicted to
murder
'by nature'

Cerebral Palsy
脑瘫
brain
'be physically
paralyzed'

Revenge!

Manic Depression
躁狂抑郁症
restless
extremely
gloomy
illness

Bored
无聊
without
'to chat'

# Religion

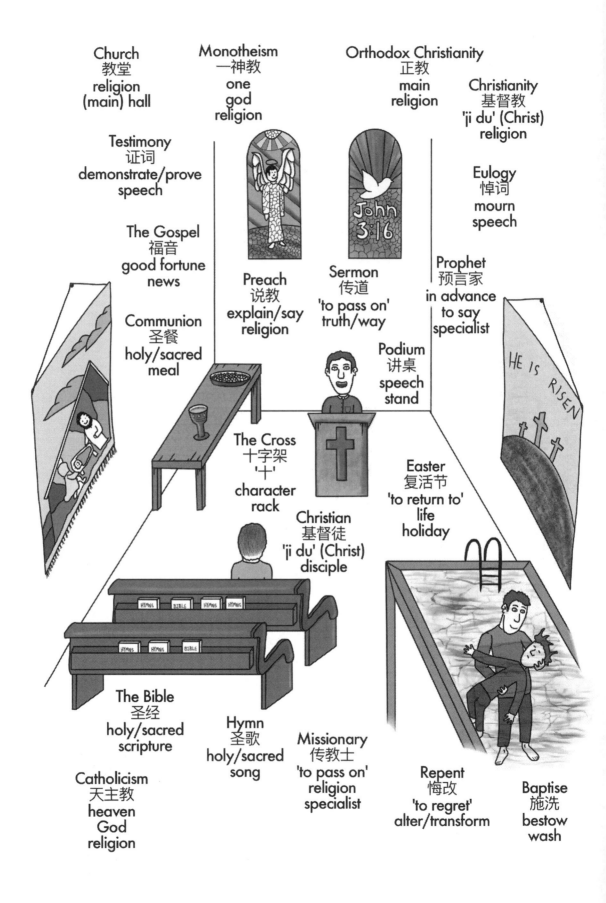

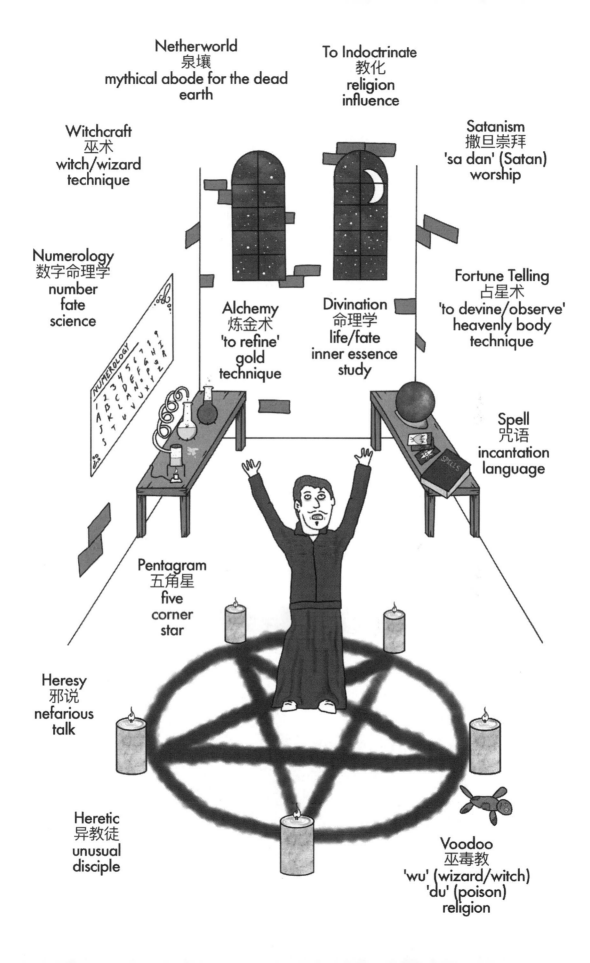

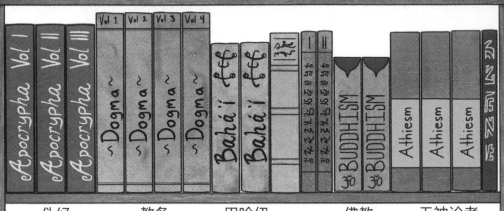

伪经
false/forged
scripture

教条
religion
law/order

巴哈伊
'ba ha yi'
*transliterated*

佛教
Buddah
religion

无神论者
none
deity
critic

神道教
deity
truth/path
religion

转世
'to transfer'
life

不可知论着
not
can
'to know'
critic

拜火教
'to worship'
the sun
religion

道教
'the way'
religion

印度教
India
religion

孔教
confucius
religion

圣诗
holy
poem

宗教
school/sect
religion

泛神论
non-specific
deity
doctrine

天堂
sky
room

炼狱
'to smelt'
prison

地狱
earth
prison

诠释学
'to explain'
interpret
study

多神教
many
deity
teaching

虚无主义
emptiness
'to lack'
ideology

启蒙主义
'to awake'
blind/ignorant
ideology

因果
cause
result

犹太教
just as
highest
religion

全知全能
entire
'to know'
entire
ability

Christmas
圣诞节
holy
birth
holiday

**Monastery**
修道院
repair
doctrine/principle
school

**Convent**
女修道
female
repair
doctrine/principle

**Orthodox School**
正宗
correct one's thinking
sect/school

**Exorcism**
驱邪
expel
evil

**Coffin**
寿木
funerary
coffin

**Effigy**

假人像
false
person
likeness/state

模拟人像
imitate
person
likeness/statue

**The Arc of the Covenant**
约柜
covenant
cupboard

**Hanukkah**
光明节
radiance
holiday

Orange man bad

**Sleep Paralysis**
鬼压身
spirit/demon
weigh down
body

**Passover**
逾越节
'to jump over'
pass through
holiday

Study

# Harvard Class Schedual 2022

| Monday | Tuesday | Wednesday | Thursday |
|---|---|---|---|
| Math<br>4:00am - 6:00am<br>数学<br>number<br>study | Chemistry<br>4:00am - 6:00am<br>化学<br>'to change into'<br>study | Sociology<br>4:00am - 6:00am<br>社会学<br>society<br>study | Radiology<br>4:00am - 6:00am<br>放射学<br>'to release'<br>radio (chemestry)<br>study |
| Algerbra<br>6:00am - 9:00am<br>代数学<br>'to replace'<br>number<br>study | Physics<br>6:00am - 9:00am<br>物理学<br>thing/object<br>logic/reason<br>study | Theology<br>6:00am - 9:00am<br>神学<br>God/deity<br>study | Psychiatry<br>6:00am - 9:00am<br>精神病学<br>mental disorder<br>study |
| Geometry<br>9:00am - 12:00pm<br>几何学<br>how many<br>why<br>study | Philosophy<br>9:00am - 12:00pm<br>哲学<br>wise man/sage<br>study | Mythology<br>9:00am - 12:00pm<br>神话学<br>fairytale/myth<br>study | Geology<br>9:00am - 12:00pm<br>地质学<br>earth<br>quality/nature<br>study |
| Trigonometry<br>1:00pm - 3:00pm<br>三角学<br>triangle<br>study | Biology<br>1:00pm - 3:00pm<br>生物学<br>organism<br>study | Linguistics<br>1:00pm - 3:00pm<br>语言学<br>language<br>study | Astronomy<br>1:00pm - 3:00pm<br>天文学<br>sky<br>culture<br>study |
| Calculus<br>3:00pm - 7:00pm<br>分析学<br>'to allocate'<br>'to analyze'<br>study | Botany<br>3:00pm - 7:00pm<br>植物学<br>plant<br>study | Neurology<br>3:00pm - 7:00pm<br>神经学<br>nerve/mental state<br>study | Architecture<br>3:00pm - 7:00pm<br>建筑学<br>building<br>study |
| Statistics<br>7:00pm - 10:30pm<br>统计学<br>'to unify'<br>calculate<br>study | Zoology<br>7:00pm - 10:30pm<br>动物学<br>animal<br>study | Anaesthesiology<br>7:00pm - 10:30pm<br>麻醉学<br>'to feel numb'<br>intoxicated<br>study | Pharmacology<br>7:00pm - 10:30pm<br>药物学<br>pharmaceuticals<br>study |

# Harvard Class Schedual 2022

| Friday | Saturday | Sunday | Mersday |
|---|---|---|---|
| Toxicology<br>4:00am - 6:00am<br>毒理学<br>poison/narcotics<br>'to manage'<br>study | Forestry<br>4:00am - 6:00am<br>森林学<br>forrest<br>study | Archaeology<br>4:00am - 6:00am<br>考古学<br>test/inspect<br>ancient<br>study | Glaciology<br>4:00am - 6:00am<br>冰川雪<br>glacier<br>study |
| Business<br>6:00am - 9:00am<br>商业<br>commerce<br>'to engage in' | Aesthetics<br>6:00am - 9:00am<br>美学<br>'to beautify'<br>study | Criminology<br>6:00am - 10:30pm<br>犯罪学<br>'to violate/assault'<br>crime<br>study | Traumatology<br>6:00am - 10:30pm<br>外伤学<br>external<br>injury<br>study |
| Literature<br>9:00am - 12:00pm<br>文学<br>culture/language<br>study | Optics<br>9:00am - 12:00pm<br>光学<br>light/ray<br>study | Horticulture<br>9:00am - 12:00pm<br>园艺学<br>gardening<br>study | Cryptography<br>9:00am - 12:00pm<br>密码学<br>secret<br>code<br>study |
| Anatomy<br>1:00pm - 3:00pm<br>解剖学<br>cut open/dissection<br>'to analyze'<br>study | Demography<br>1:00pm - 3:00pm<br>人口学<br>population<br>study | Paleoanthropology<br>1:00pm - 3:00pm<br>古人类学<br>ancient<br>human being<br>type/kind<br>study | Palaeontology<br>1:00pm - 3:00pm<br>古生物学<br>ancient<br>living things<br>study |
| Anthropology<br>3:00pm - 7:00pm<br>人类学<br>people<br>type/class<br>study | Science<br>3:00pm - 7:00pm<br>科学<br>branch of study<br>study | Toxicology<br>3:00pm - 7:00pm<br>毒理学<br>poison/toxin<br>study | Virology<br>3:00pm - 7:00pm<br>病毒学<br>virus<br>study |
| Engineering<br>7:00pm - 10:30pm<br>工程学<br>profession/trade<br>regulations<br>study | Mechanics<br>7:00pm - 10:30pm<br>力学<br>force/power<br>study | Ornithology<br>7:00pm - 10:30pm<br>鸟类学<br>bird<br>type/kind<br>study | Robotics<br>7:00pm - 10:30pm<br>机器人学<br>robot<br>study |

电脑游戏

Video Games

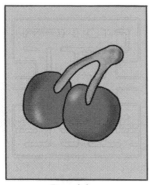

**Pac-Mac**
吃豆人
'to eat'
bean
person

**Twisted Metal**
烈火战车
raging inferno
tank

**Metroid**
银河战士
milky way
soldier

**Castlevania**
恶魔城
evil
devil
city

**Carmageddon**
死亡赛车
death
race car

**Quest for Glory**
荣耀任务
honourable
task/mission

**Trials**
特技摩托
stunt
motorbike

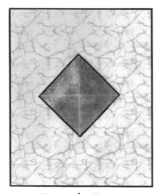

**Temple Run**
神庙逃亡
religious shrine
runaway

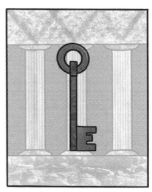

**Tomb Raider**
古墓丽影
ancient
tomb/grave
beautiful
photograph

**Street Fighter**
街头霸王
street
leading overlord

**Mortal Kombat**
格斗之王
fist fight
king

**Left 4 Dead**
求生之路
'to seek'
life's
road

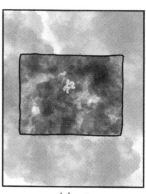

**Myst**
神秘岛
mysterious
island

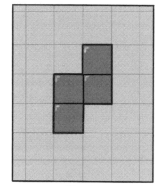

**Tetris**
俄罗斯方块
russia
square
piece

**World of Warcraft**
魔兽世界
magic
beast
world

**Starcraft**
星际争霸
star
edge
'contend for power'

**Portal**
传送门
deliver
door

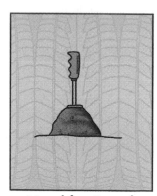

**Need for Speed**
极品飞车
highest grade
go quickly
car

GTA
侠盗猎车手
heroic
poach
car
skill

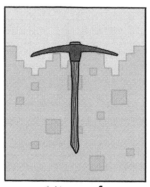

Minecraft
我的世界
my
world

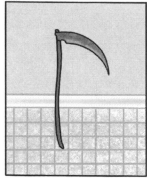

Grim Fandango
冥界狂想曲
ghost world
rhapsody

The Sims
模拟人生
simulate
life

Wolfenstein
德军司令部
germany
army
headquarters

Quake
雷神之锤
thunder
god
'of'
hammer

Diablo
暗黑破坏神
dark
'to destroy'
deity

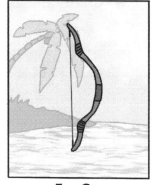

Far Cry
孤岛惊魂
isolated island
'the state of being frightened'

Doom
毁灭战士
exterminate
soldier

Movies

**Click**
人生遥控器
life
remote control

**Spy Kids**
非常小特务
extremely
small
spy

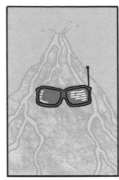

**Tron**
电子世界争霸战
electron
world
'to contend for power'
battle

**Spongebob**
海绵宝宝
sponge
baby

**Ferris Bueller's Day Off**
春天不是读书天
springtime
'is not'
study
day

**Karate Kid**
功夫梦
kung-fu
dream

**Wall-E**
机器人总动员
robot
general mobilization

**Mallrats**
耍酷一族
'to act'
cool
social group

**Benjamin Button**
返老还童
return (to)
old
'go back'
child

**A-Team**
天龙特攻队
sky
dragon
attack
team

**Tarzan**
泰山归来: 险战丛林
Mt. Tai
return (to)
dangerous
war
jungle

**The Muppet Show**
大青蛙布偶秀
big
frog
'cloth image' (muppet)
show

**Kick-Ass**
海扁王
'to beat somebody up'
king

**High School Musical**
歌舞青春
sing
dance
youthfulness

**Music & Lyrics**
共谱恋曲
mutual
compose
love song

**The Big Labowski**
谋杀绿脚趾
murder
green
toe

**Final Destination**
死神来了
death
god
comes

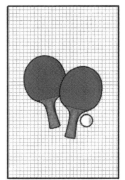

**Balls of Fury**
愤怒乒乓球
anger/rage
ping pong

**Eight Below**
南极大冒险
south pole
big
adventure

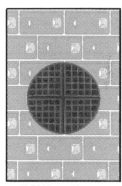

**50 First Dates**
初恋五十次
first love
fifty
times

**Meet the Fockers**
拜见岳父大人
pay a visit to
wife's father
adult

**Anchorman**
王牌播音员
trump card
announcer

**The Matrix**
黑客帝国
hacker
kingdom

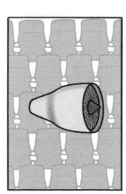

**Donnie Darko**
死亡幻觉
death
hallucination

**Resident Evil**
生化危机
biochemistry
crisis

**Guardians of
the Galaxy**
银河护卫队
milky way
protect
team

**The Jungle Book**
奇幻森林
strange
forrest

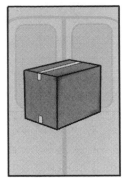

**The Smurfs**
蓝色小精灵
blue
small
spirit

**Where the Wild
Things Are**
野兽家园
wild
beast
homeland

**Knocked Up**
一夜大肚
one
night
big
belly

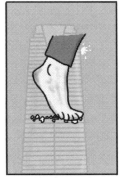

**Die Hard**
虎胆龙威
brave
gallbladder
dragon
strength

**Sex and the City**
欲望都市
lust
metropolis

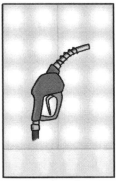

**Zoolander**
超级名模
super
top model

**Ghost Rider**
灵魂战车
soul
war chariot

**Evan Almighty**
冒牌天神
imposter
deity

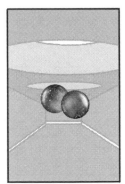

**Men in Black**
黑衣人
black
clothes
people

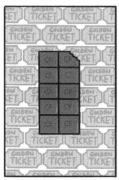

**Charlie and the Chocolate Factory**
欢乐糖果层
happy
candy
house

**Tangled**
长发公主
long
hair
princess

**Toy Story**
玩具总动员
toy
general mobilization

**Big Hero 6**
超能陆战队
super
land battle
team

**Ponyo**
悬崖上的金鱼公主
on the cliff
gold fish
princess

**Wreck-it Ralph**
无敌破坏王
unmatched
destruction
king

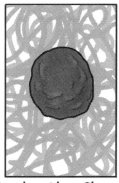

**Cloudy with a Chance
of Metalballs**
天降美食
sky
drop
delicious food

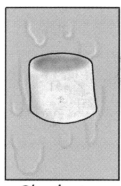

**Ghostbusters**
捉鬼敢死队
'to catch'
ghost
suicide team

**Shrek**
怪物史瑞克
monster
'shi rui ke'

**Bambi**
小鹿斑比
small
deer
'ban bi'

**Pinocchio**
木偶奇遇记
'wood image'
strange meeting
record

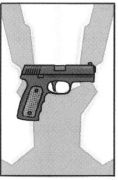

**Ghost in the Shell**
攻壳机动队
attack
shell/casing
power driven
team

**Totoro**
龙猫
dragon
cat

**Sisterhood of the Traveling Pants**
牛仔裤的夏天
jeans'
summer

**Up**
飞屋坏游记
fly
house
bad
travel
memory

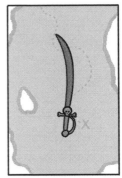

**The Goonies**
七宝奇谋
seven
treasure
ingenious
plan

**Star Trek**
星际旅行
interstellar
journey

**Homeward Bound**
看狗在说话
look
dog
at
speaking
(lit. look at the speaking dog)

**Pokémon**
口袋妖怪
pocket
monster

**Finding Nemo**
海底总动员
seabed
general mobilization

**Frozen**
冰雪奇缘
ice
snow
witch

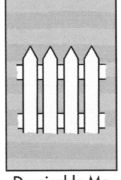

**Despicable Me**
神偷奶爸
lively
thief
milk dad
(milk dad = stay at home dad)

**Zootopia**
疯狂动物城
crazy
animal
city

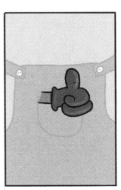

**Minions**
小黄人
small
yellow
people

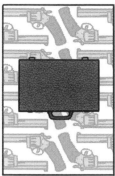

**Pulp Fiction**
低俗小说
vulgar
fiction

**The Nightmare Before Christmas**
圣诞夜惊魂
christmas
night terror
spirit

**Good Will Hunting**
心灵捕手
clever
catcher

**Lord of the Rings**
指环王
(finger) ring
king

**Pleasantville**
欢乐谷
pleasure
valley

**Scream**
惊声尖叫
frightened
voice
scream

**Joe Dirt**
摇滚电台
rock and roll
radio station

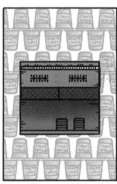

**Punch Drunk Love**
思恋失调
private
love
imbalance

**Childs Play**
鬼娃回魂
terrible
'to toy with'
go back/'to return'
spirit

**Gremlins**
小魔鬼
small
fiends

**Psycho (1960)**
惊魂记
frightened
notes/record

**Evil Dead**
鬼玩人
spirit
'to trifle with'
person

(*Refer to page 374 for some more info on this one.)

**Shawn of the Dead**
僵尸肖恩
zombie
'xiao en' (Shawn)

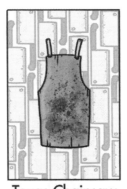

**Texas Chainsaw Massacre**
德州电锯杀人狂
Texas
electric chainsaw
homicidal maniac

**Coco**
寻梦环游记
seek
dream
tour around
record

**Dr. Jeckle & Mr. Hyde**
化身博士
incarnation
doctor

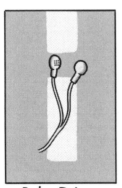

**Baby Driver**
极盗车神
extreme
thief
car
deity

**Dumbo**
小飞象
small
flying
elephant

**Ratatouille**
美食总动员
gourmet food
general mobilization

**Dumb & Dumber***
阿呆与阿瓜
simple/stupid
and
melon

**The Truman Show**
楚门的世界
'chu men' (Truman's)
world

**No Country for Old Men**
老无所依
old (of people)
'to lack'
location
depend on

**Blade Runner**
仿生人会梦见电子羊
'to imitate living things'
person
to be able to
'to dream about'
electronic
sheep

**Pitch Black**
星际传奇
interplanetary
fantasy sega

**The Mask**
变相怪杰
convert
monster
hero

**Jumanji**
勇敢者的游戏
brave
'the one who's'
game
(The game for the brave.)

**John Carter**
异星战场
unusual
planet
battlefield

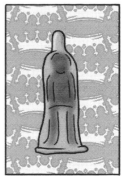

**Naked Gun**
白头神探
white
hair
clever
detective

**The Flintstones**
摩登原始人
modern
primitive
people

**Ace Ventura**
神探飞机头
clever
detective
airplane
hair style

**Home Alone**
小鬼当家
mischievous child
'to manage the household'

**A Night at the Roxbury**
舞翻天
dance
behave wildly

**Clueless**
独领风骚
independant
guide
flirtatious behavior

**Teletubbies**
天线宝宝
antenna
baby

**There's Something About Mary**
我为玛丽狂
I
for
'ma li' (Mary)
crazy
(I'm crazy for Mary.)

**The Grinch**
圣诞怪杰
christmas
monster
hero

**Robocop**
机械战警
machine
war
police

**John Wick**
疾速追杀
great speed
pursue
murder

**The Devil Wears Prada**
穿普拉达的女王
'to wear'
prada
queen

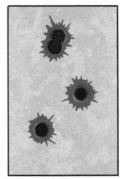

**Judge Dredd**
特警判官
special police
judge
government official

**Snow Piercer**
雪国列车
snow
country
train

**IT**
小丑回魂
clown
'to return'
spirit

**Point Break**
极盗者
extreme
thief
'the one who'
(The (one who is an) extreme thief.)

**Virtuosity**
时空悍将
space and time
heroic
general

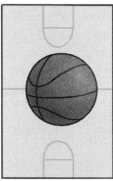

**Space Jam**
空中大灌篮
'in the sky'
big
slam-dunk

**6 Underground**
鬼影特攻：以暴制暴
ghost
special
attack:
'to use violence to
curb violence'

**Big Trouble in Little China**
妖魔大鬧唐人街
evil spirit
'to cause havoc'
chinatown

**Half Baked**
半仙半死
half
immortal
half
dead

**Snakes on a Plane**
航班蛇患
scheduled flight
snake
trouble

**Momento**
记忆碎片
memory
fragment

**Event Horizon**
黑洞表面
black hole
surface

**Rons Gone Wrong**
天赐灵机
bestowed by heaven
clever
machine

**Blind Side**
弱点
weak point

**Trainspotting**
猜火车
guess
train

**Billy Madison**
超龄插班生
overage
'a student who
joins the class in
midstream'

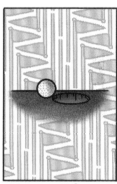

**Happy Gilmore**
高尔夫球也疯狂
golf
crazy

**Wedding Crashers**
婚礼傲客
wedding
overbearing
guest

**Taken**
飓风营救
hurricane
rescue

**Stranger Than Fiction**
奇幻人生
fantastic
life

**Rad**
单车小子
bicycle
boy

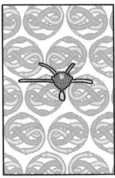

**The Never Ending Story**
大魔域
huge
monster
region

**The Burbs**
邻居
neighbour

**Willow**
风云际会
stormy or unstable situation
opportunity

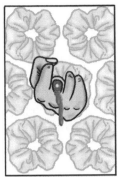

**Heathers**
希德姐妹帮
uncommon
morals
sisters
gang

**Short Circuit**
霹雳五号
thunderbolt
number five
(actually is 'five number')

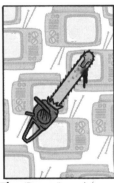

**The Running Man**
过关斩将
'go through a
strategic pass by
killing the garrison
commander in battle'

**Game of Thrones**
权力的游戏
power
game

**Death Becomes Her**
飞越长生
unexpected
surpass
'to live forever'

**Dazed and Confused**
年少轻狂
young
extremely frivolous

**Fast Times at
Ridgemont High**
开放的美国学府
'unconstrained in
one's sexuality'
America
'educational
establishment'

**Strange Brew**
神奇酒酿
magical
'fermented glutinous
rice wine'

**Pee-Wee's Big Adventure**
荒唐小混蛋奇遇记
preposturous
young bastard
adventure
'to record'

# 大自然与基础设施

## Nature & Infrastructure

Traffic Light
红绿灯
red
green
light

Emergency Exit
太平门
peace & security
door

EMERGENCY EXIT

Tunnel
地道
earth/ground
road

Address
地址
place
location

Subway
地下铁道
underground
iron
road

Concrete
石屎
rock
excrement

Windmill
风车
wind
vehicle

Cement
水泥
water
mud

Manhole
检查口
inspect
opening

Sewer
下水道
down
water
road

Storm
风暴
wind
violent/cruel

Tornado
龙卷风
dragon
roll
wind

Population
人口
people
mouth

Cactus
霸王树
rule by force
king
tree

**Lighthouse**
灯塔
lamp
tower

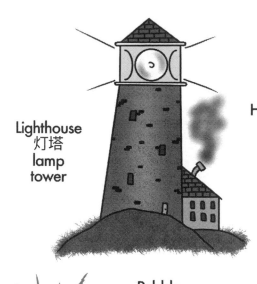

**Puddle**
水坑
water
pit

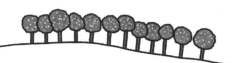

**Horticulture**
园艺
garden
art

**Orchard**
果木园
fruit
tree
garden

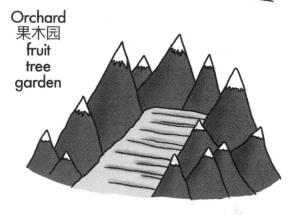

**Pebble**
河卵石
river
seed
stone

**Glacier**
冰河
ice
river

**Aloe Vera**
芦荟胶
reed
flourishing
gel

**Log**
圆形木材
round
shape
tree
timber

**Iceland**
冰岛
ice
island

**Pollination**
传粉
spread
powder

**Bird's Eye View**
俯瞰图
'to look down'
look down from a height
diagram

**Peninsula**
半岛
'in the middle'
island

**Pollin**
花粉
flower
powder

**Sweatshop**
血汗工厂
blood and sweat
factory

I shop to fill the hole in my heart.

**Pyramid**
金字塔
'金'
character
tower

**Yurt**
圆顶帐篷
dome
tent

**Escalator**
电扶梯
electric
staircase

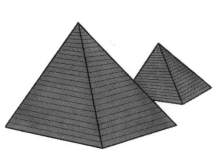

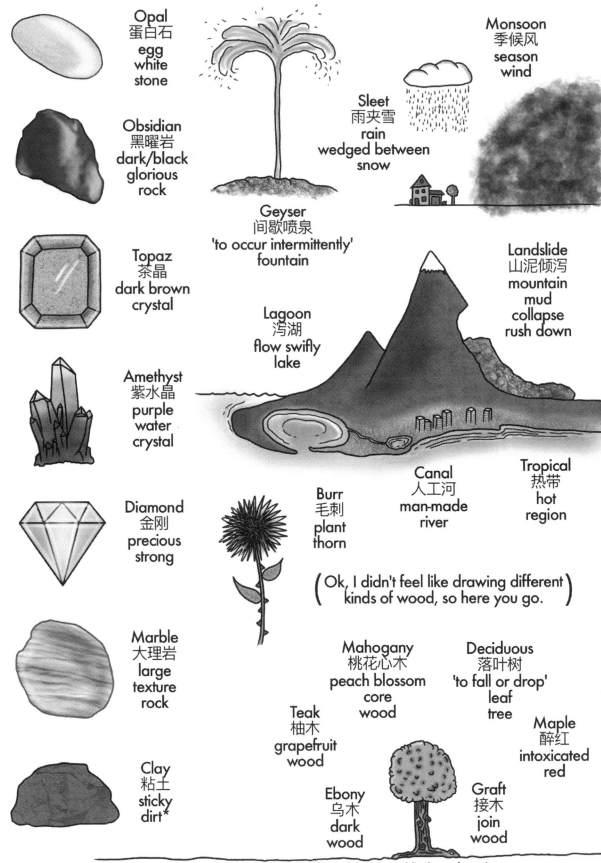

Opal
蛋白石
egg
white
stone

Obsidian
黑曜岩
dark/black
glorious
rock

Topaz
茶晶
dark brown
crystal

Amethyst
紫水晶
purple
water
crystal

Diamond
金刚
precious
strong

Marble
大理岩
large
texture
rock

Clay
粘土
sticky
dirt*

Geyser
间歇喷泉
'to occur intermittently'
fountain

Lagoon
泻湖
flow swifly
lake

Sleet
雨夹雪
rain
wedged between
snow

Monsoon
季候风
season
wind

Landslide
山泥倾泻
mountain
mud
collapse
rush down

Burr
毛刺
plant
thorn

Canal
人工河
man-made
river

Tropical
热带
hot
region

(Ok, I didn't feel like drawing different
kinds of wood, so here you go.)

Mahogany
桃花心木
peach blossom
core
wood

Deciduous
落叶树
'to fall or drop'
leaf
tree

Teak
柚木
grapefruit
wood

Maple
醉红
intoxicated
red

Ebony
乌木
dark
wood

Graft
接木
join
wood

(*The character 土 also means 'clay', but if I used that, it wouldn't be as funny.)

Petroleum
石油
rock
oil*

(*油 also means petroleum.)

Sunflower
向阳花
'to face'
(the) sun
flower

Volcano
火山
fire
mountain

Switchback Road
之字路
'之'
character
road

Magma/Lava

岩石
mountain
rock

岩浆
mountain
thick liquid

熔将
smelt
thick liquid

DEAD END

Dead End Road
死路
impassable/dead
road

Snowflake
雪花
snow
flower

Icicle
冰柱
ice
pillar

Fossil
化石
'to change into/transform'
rock

Sunset
日落
sun
'to drop/lower'

Rare Unicorn Vampire Fish

Stalagmite
石笋
rock
bamboo shoot

Sunrise
日出
sun
'to come out/rise'

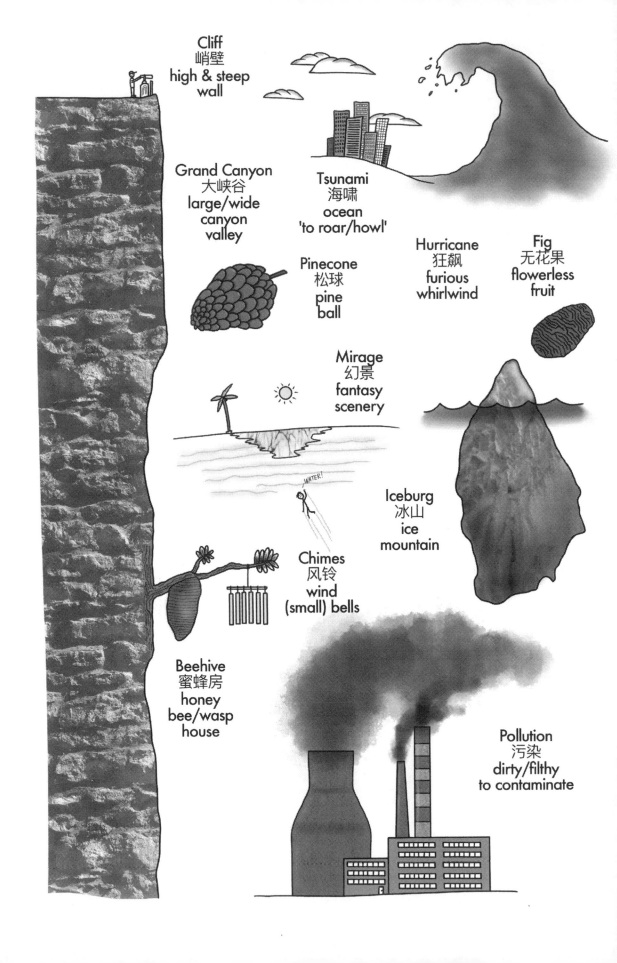

Cliff
峭壁
high & steep
wall

Grand Canyon
大峡谷
large/wide
canyon
valley

Tsunami
海啸
ocean
'to roar/howl'

Hurricane
狂飙
furious
whirlwind

Fig
无花果
flowerless
fruit

Pinecone
松球
pine
ball

Mirage
幻景
fantasy
scenery

WATER!

Iceburg
冰山
ice
mountain

Chimes
风铃
wind
(small) bells

Beehive
蜜蜂房
honey
bee/wasp
house

Pollution
污染
dirty/filthy
to contaminate

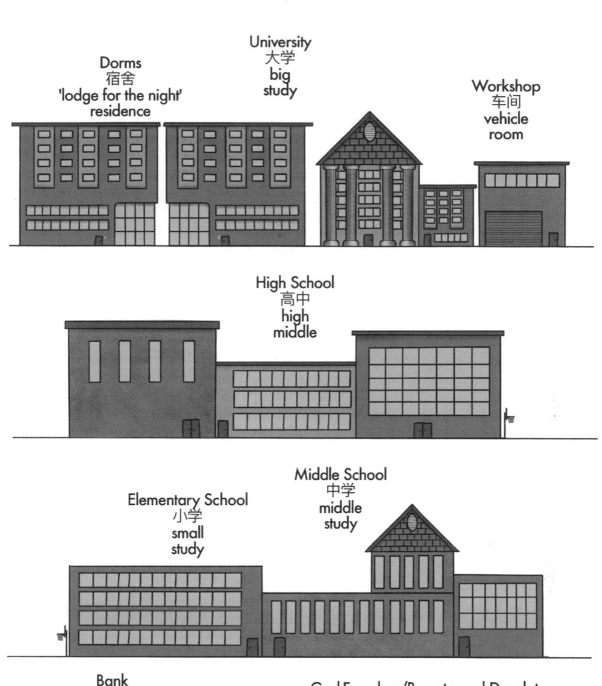

**Dorms**
宿舍
'lodge for the night'
residence

**University**
大学
big
study

**Workshop**
车间
vehicle
room

**High School**
高中
high
middle

**Elementary School**
小学
small
study

**Middle School**
中学
middle
study

**Bank**
银行
silver
profession

**Ghetto**
贫民区
poor
citizen
district

**God-Forsaken/Remote and Desolate**
鸟不拉屎鸡不生蛋
'birds don't shit'
'chickens don't lay eggs'

Idioms

(*See page 186 for reference.)

Shotgun Wedding
因孕而婚
because
pregnant
and so
wedding

No, seriously, it
was THIS big!

Brag*
吹牛
'to blow'
cow

To talk big
满嘴跑火车
'to fill'
mouth
'to run away'
train

'To toot your
own horn'
自炒
self
fry/sauté

Extravagant
大手大脚
big
hand
big
foot

To endure all sorts of
hardships
一把尿一把屎
one handful (of)
pee
one handful (of)
poo
(to raise ones children while
they pee and poo.)

**Lottery winner dies
by his own cash**

After getting
diagnosed with AIDS,
Cancer, Covid 21,
Alzheimers and
A.D.D., Sigfried
Munchler who
recently won 100
million dollars in the
lottery died while he
lay in bed. Reports
say, he stacked all the
money up beside his
bed, and when it all
fell on him he
suffocated and died.
He was schedualed to
be married this
weekend as well.

He is outlived
by his dog,
Rover, who
also has AIDS.

To hoodwink people
偷天换日
'to steal'
sky
'to exchange'
sun

One disaster on
top of another
雪上加霜
snow
go up
increase
frost

Unexpected
Misfortune
山高水低
mountain
high
water
low

For
Sale RealMonalisa 20k

Fame has it's price
人怕出名猪拍肥
people
'to fear'
fame
pig
'to fear'
fat

Hi, I'd like to
speak with the
manger.

I just want
people to
think I'm hot.

To cheat
挂羊头卖狗肉
hang
sheep
head
sell
dog
meat

To make life difficult
for someone
穿小鞋
'to wear'
small
shoes

To be the object
of flattery
戴高帽子
'to wear'
tall
hat

Sup gurl. YRU so hawt?
Yer shirt is so fire. I
wanna BU! #jelly

Complete confusion
翻天覆地
turn over
sky
tip over
the earth

Sponge of others
吃白饭
'to eat'
white
rice

My dad can do 200 push-ups. He was in the Russian Mafia.

Well, my dad can do 250 push-ups. He was in the Navy Seals.

Looking for a needle in a haystack
大海捞针
big
ocean
fish for
needle

Outdoing one another
争先恐后
contend
first
fear
last

Eyes brimming with tears of excitement
热烈盈眶
hot
tears
'to be full of'
eye socket

Light Fingered
手脚不干净
hand
foot
not
clean

A brief period of enthusiasm
三分钟热度
three
minutes
hot
temperature

To wolf down ones food
狼吞虎咽
wolf
swallow
tiger
swallow

To have a brainstorm
心血来潮
heart
blood
'to arrive'
tide

To suddenly see the light
恍然大悟
all of a sudden
correct
great
awaken/become aware

I work out every day for 12 hours (and take mad amounts of steroids).

To do one's utmost
尽心竭力
'to the greatest extent'
intention
exhaust
strength

To pledge one's undying love
海誓山盟
ocean
vow
mountain
oath

You get out what you put in
一分耕耘一分收获
one part
cultivate
one part
results

I'll be there, maybe, probably, more like 49% yes, I think...

Fickle/Erratic
反复无常
repeatedly
changable

I've worked eight days this week.

Burning the candle at both ends
劳累过度
work/labour
fatigued
excessively
degree of intensity

To punish an individual as an example to others
杀鸡儆猴
kill
chicken
warning
monkey

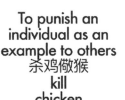

My dog just died.

Yeah, but I mean, now you don't have to clean up his poo every day right? So there's that...

Every cloud has a silver lining
雨过天晴
rain
'to cross/pass over'
weather
clear

I can't believe Jessica cheated on Breven, er, wait, was I supposed to say that to anyone?

I love rice, eating dogs and am good at math!

Stereotype
刻板印象
inflexable
impression

To let the cat out of the bag
漏泄天机
divulge
let out
season
secret

# 关系与行为

## Relationships & Behaviour

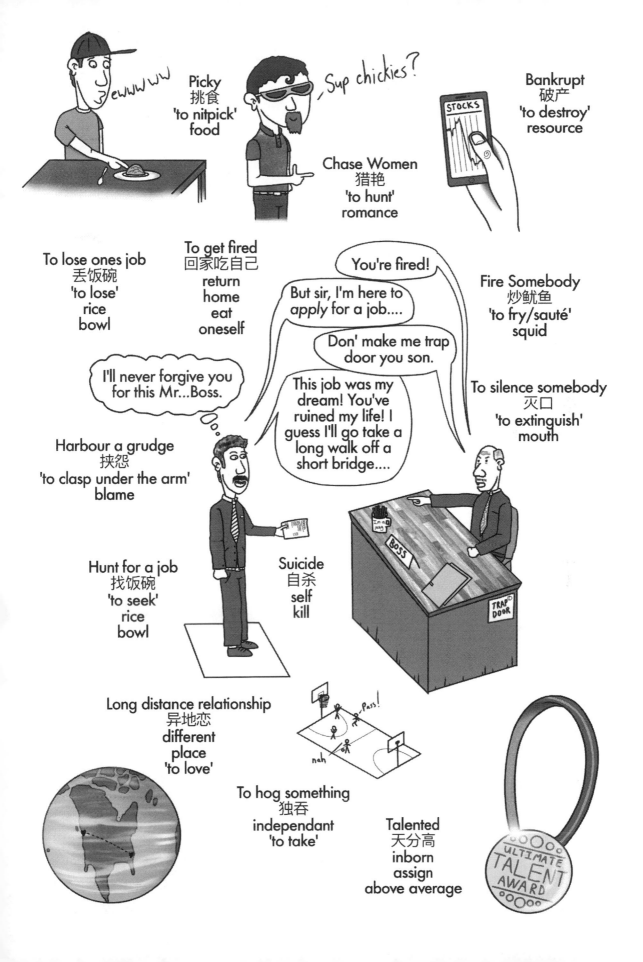

(休 also can mean 'retire' but I don't even care.)

I can do whatever you need

'Jack of all trades'
杂家
miscellaneous
'specialist in a certain field'

Attempted Murder
杀人未遂
'to kill'
person
did not
succeed

Retire
退休
quit
rest*

I could retire on this much mad cash...

Ill-gotten gains
邪财
nefarious
fortune

Did yuh hear 'boot Meloneesha? I can't believe she cheated on Gereth with Roy.

Gossip
绯闻
slander
story

WANTED
- Attempted murder by strangling
- Drug trafficking & being a dick
~ REWARD ~
$100,000,000,000

Drug Traficking
毒品交易
narcotics
business deal

Strangle
扼杀
choke
kill

Characterization
人物塑造
personage
portray

Having a hangover
宿酒卫星
stay overnight
liquor
have not
sober up

Eavesdrop
偷听
stealthily
to listen

听墙根
'to listen'
wall
source

J-Walk
乱穿马路
random
cross
road

Juicy details!

And then a dragon burst forth from the depth of the darkness and swallowed all the Trumpers!

Imagination
想象
'to believe/wish'
image

# 药与东西

## Medicine & Stuff

LSD
迷幻药
confused
fantasy
drug

Drugs
毒品
poison
product

Facelift
拉皮
'to pull'
skin

Plastic Surgery
整容
repair
appearance

Amputate
截肢
'to cut off'
limb

Cesarean section
剖宫产
'to cut open'
temple
reproduce

Stoma
气孔
air/gas
opening

Ketamine
K粉
K - powder

Nicotine
烟碱
tobacco plant
base/alkali

Scalpel
解剖刀
a dissection
'to analyze'
knife

Ecstasy
摇头丸
'to shake'
head
pill

Magic Mushrooms
迷幻蘑菇
confused
fantasy
mushroom

NIAGRA

Methamphetamine
冰
ice

Surgery
手术
hand
art

Viagra
伟哥
large
elder brother
(elder brother = slang for penis.)

Latex Glove
胶乳手套
rubber
milk
hand
cover/sheath

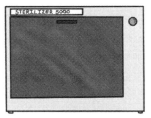

Hieroglyph
象形文字
shape
'to appear'
written language

Sterilize
消毒
'to eliminate'
poison

Radioactive
放射
'to release'
radio- (chemistry)

Herbicide
杀草剂
kill
grass
dose (medicine)

Insecticide
杀虫剂
kill
insect
dose (medicine)

Antidote
解毒药
'to remove'
poison

Tonic
补品
nourish
product

Digest (food)
消化
'to eliminate'
change into/-ization

XXX
Tonic

Snake bite
Antidote蛇

In

Out

CT Scan
电脑断层扫描
computer
judge
layer
scan

Rhythm of the
heartbeat
心律
heart
law

Ayahuasca
死藤水
death
vine
beverage

Cremate
火葬
fire
bury (the dead)

Urn
骨炭
bone
jug

Stethoscope
听诊器
'to listen'
examine (a patient)
device/tool

Cremate
火化
fire
transform/-ization

Virus
病毒
illness
poison

Catheter
导尿管
'to guide'
urine
tube

Deep distress
落汤鸡
'to fall or drop'
soup
chicken

# Time Related

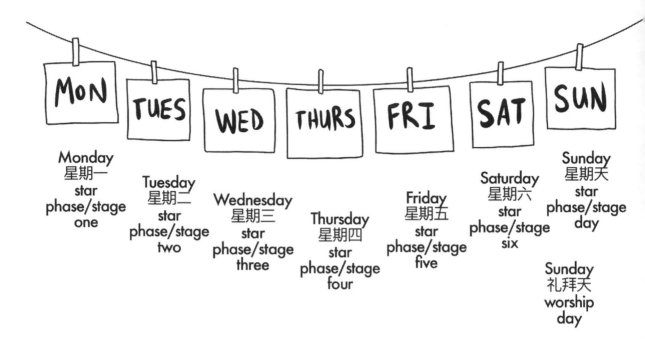

Monday
星期一
star
phase/stage
one

Tuesday
星期二
star
phase/stage
two

Wednesday
星期三
star
phase/stage
three

Thursday
星期四
star
phase/stage
four

Friday
星期五
star
phase/stage
five

Saturday
星期六
star
phase/stage
six

Sunday
星期天
star
phase/stage
day

Sunday
礼拜天
worship
day

8　八 = **eight**

9　九 = **nine**

10　十 = **ten**

11　十一 = **ten - one**

12　十二 = **ten - two**

20　二十 = **two - ten**

21　二十一 = **two - ten - one**

100　(一) 百 = **(one) hundred**

101　一百零一 = **one - hundred - zero - one**

102　一百零二 = **one - hundred - zero - two**

110　一百一十 = **one - hundred - one - ten**

111　一百一十一 = **one - hundred - one - ten - one**

112　一百一十二 = **one - hundred - one - ten - two**

999　九百九十九 = **nine - hundred - nine - ten - nine**

1000　(一) 千 = **(one) thousand**

10,000　(一) 万 = **(one) ten thousand**

100,000　十万 = **ten - ten thousand**

1,000,000　一百万 = **one - hundred - ten thousand or 亿**

January: 一月 one month

February: 二月 two month

March: 三月 three month

April: 四月 four month

May: 五月 five month

June: 六月 six month

July: 七月 seven month

August: 八月 eight month

September: 九月 nine month

October: 十月 ten month

November: 十一月 ten one month

December: 十二月 ten two month

Early morning
早上
5am - 8am

Morning
上午
9am - 11am

Noon
中午
12pm

Afternoon
下午
1pm - 6pm

Evening
晚上
7pm - 12am

Night
凌晨
1am - 4am

# 偶然的

Random

(*Refer to page 186 for explanation.)

(*Refer to page 183 for explanation.)

Ghostwriter
捉刀人
grab/clutch
knife
person

Novel
小说
small
speak/to say

Moral (of a story)
寓意
to contain
meaning

DVD
Anaconda15
Rise of the Snake

Irony
反话
reverse
talk

Phrase
短语
short
speech

B Movie
二级影片
second
grade
movie

Index
检字表
gather
word
list

Plot
情节
situation
section/part

十四四十十四四，四十十四四四十。
四十十四四十四，不知是十还是四

$$\left( \begin{array}{l} 十 = shí \\ 四 = sì \end{array} \right)$$

Tongue Twister
绕口令
confuse
mouth
'to cause'

Foreshadow
预兆
beforehand
'to foretell'

Parade
游行
'to walk'
travel

Emoji
表情符号
facial expression
symbol

COPY
COPY

Fireworks
烟花
smoke
flower

Copy
复印
to duplicate
image

Weeeee

Streaking
裸奔
naked
run quickly

Hide & Seek
(Is also Peek-a-boo)
藏猫猫
'to conceal/hide away'
cat
cat

CENSORED

Circus
马戏团
horse
show
group

WELCOME

Waltz
慢三步
slow
three
step

Poker Face
板脸
stiff/hard
face

**Stonehenge**
巨石柱群
gigantic
stone
pillar
group

**Pop rocks**
跳跳糖
jump
jump
candy

**X-Rated movie**
儿童不宜片
children
unsuitable/inadvisable
film

**Vulgar/Indecent**
不雅
not
elegant

**Birth defect**
畸态
abnormal
appearance

**Funny**
搞笑
'to produce'
laugh

**Mosaic**
镶嵌画
rim/edge
inlay/set
picture

**Scale**
体重器
body
weight
device/tool

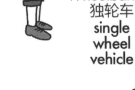

**Syringe**
注射器
'to inject'
discharge in a jet
device/tool

**Yodel**
岳得尔歌
mountain peak
like
song

**UFO**
不明飞行物
not
reveal/sight
'to fly/move swiftly'
behaviour
object

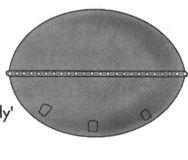

**Diamond**
金刚石
precious
unyielding
stone

**Wheelbarrow**
独轮车
single
wheel
vehicle

**Jewelry**
首饰
head
decorations/ornaments

**Breakfast**
早饭
early
meal

**Lunch**
午饭
midday
meal

**Dinner**
晚饭
evening
meal

**Flea market**
小市
small
market

**10:00-ish**

Approximately
左右
left
right

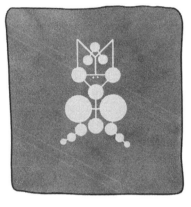

**Crop circle**
麦田怪圈
wheat
field
bewildering
circle/ring

**Yinyang**
阴阳
moon
sun

*Come on Jhonny, I don't give up on me!*

**CPR**
心肺复苏术
heart
lung
'to resume'
'to revive'
technique

**Nocturnal**
夜行
by night
behaviour

**Uneven/Bumpy**
凹凸
concave
convex

*One of my favourite sets of characters.*

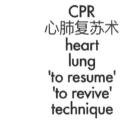

**Burn the Midnight Oil**
吃夜草
'to eat'
night
grass

**Seppuku**
切腹自杀
cut
abdomen
suicide
(suicide = self - kill)

**1 + 1 = ?**
(Hint: it's not 3)

**Hint**
暗示
secret
'to reveal'

Guidebook
指南
indicate/point to
south

Magnum Opus
巨著
tremendous
book/work

Telepathy
心电感应
feeling
'to get an electric shock'
response

Cog
轮牙
wheel
tooth

'@' Symbol
小老鼠       A圈儿
small       'A'
mouse       circle

Glitter
金葱粉
gold
green onion
powder

Vowel
元音
fundimental
sound

AEIOU
And sometimes 'Y'?

Movie trailer
预告片
in advance
announce
film

Harness
挽具
'to pull'
tool

Pink
粉红色
peach
red
colour

Meter
公尺
metric
ruler

Partition
瓜分
melon
divide

Booth (in a restaurant)
火车坐
train
seat

Styrofoam
保丽龙
safeguard
elegant
dragon

Password
密码
secret
code

Plasticine
蜡泥
wax
mud

(*This also means 'micro'.)

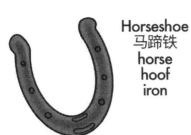

Horseshoe
马蹄铁
horse
hoof
iron

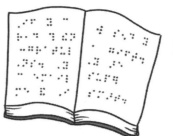

Braille
点字
dot
word

Dub (in movies)
配音
'to replace something'
sound

Paperback Book
简装书
simple
'to wrap'
book

Suffix
字尾
word
end

Black Friday
黑五
black
five

All your base are
belong to us.

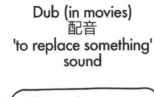

Infinite
无限
without
limit

Decapitate
斩首
'to cut'
head

An extra in a movie
临时演员
temporary
actor

UNIVERSE STUDIOS
SCENE 51  TAKE 7  ROLL 3
Nov 30/2022
John Holmes

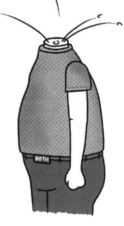

John
Killed by his
time-traveling
grandson John
the third.
1883 - 1979.

Paradox
悖论
contrary
theory

Microscope
显微镜
display/show
miniature*
looking glass

Lawnmower
剪草机
'to cut'
grass
machine

Cryptocurrency
电子钱
electronic
money

Good-night!
晚安
evening
peaceful

MIKE DEER

Sports Jersey
球衣
(sports) match
clothes

毛织运动衫
woollen
sports
garment

Sleep In
睡懒觉
sleep
lazy
sleep

Velcro
魔术贴
magic
stick/glue

粘扣带
sticky
'to fasten'
strap

Monochrome (Art)
单色话
single
colour
drawing/painting/picture

Outhouse
茅厕
grass
toilet

Hand Sanitizer
消毒洗手液
'to disinfect'
liquid soap

Sold! To number 420 for $420.⁹⁹

Weeds
杂草
miscellaneous
grass

荒草
wilderness
grass

**Hand Sanitizer**

How to use:
Step 1: Open hand
Step 2: Pour some liquid on hand
Step 3: Rub hands till dry
Totally proven to not give you cancer

Auction
拍卖
'to slap/swat'
sell

Barbed Wire
刺钢丝    刺铁丝
'to stab'  'to stab'
steel      iron
wire       wire

The Nutcracker Ballet
胡桃夹子
walnut
clamp

Dunce Hat
高帽
tall
hat

Oh me? Yes, I only eat vegetables. It's much more ethical.

Vegetarian
素食者
vegetable
'to eat'
'the one who'
(the one who eats vegetables)

Crowbar
撬杠
'to pry open'
bar/rod

IDIOT

D Size Battery 一号电池 = one - size - battery
C Size Battery 二号电池 = two - size - battery
AA Size Battery - 三号电池 = three - size - battery
AAA Size Battery - 四号电池 = four - size - battery
AA Size Battery - 五号电池 = five - size - battery
AAA Size Battery - 七号电池 = seven - size - battery
(Also dont ask why there's no 'six size battery'. I couldn't find that they existed.)

SUPER BATTER-EEE 7000 Size AAA⁴

Sofabed
两用沙发
two
use
sofa

Humble Abode
蜗庐
snail
hut/cottage

(Upholstered) Armchair
单人沙发
single
person
sofa

Lay-z-boy™
睡椅
sleep
chair

Laxative
泻药                  轻泻剂
flow swifty          relaxing
medicine             flow swiftly
                     dose (medicine)

Laxative
For when you feel
like there's a full
apple sitting in
your rectum.

Straw
吸管
'to suck liquids'
tube

Compass*
指北针
'to point towards'
north
needle

(*Don't ask why they also call this 'point south needle'. I legit dunno.)

Shampoo
洗头膏
'to wash'
hair
paste

ShamPoo

Sled
冰床
ice
'something shaped
like a bed'

Crayon
炭棒
charcoal
stick

Cray-On

N
W        E
S

Mr. Sled 3000

Cleans the
pores &
makes you
look at least
five times
more attractive

Clean Yer Face!

Eye of the needle
针鼻
needle
nose

Cleansing Lotion
洁面乳        洗面奶
clean         'to wash'
face          face
milk          milk

And then I climbed this mounatin with two broken legs and managed to make a huge body-kite and fly back home only to find my house being robbed so I fought the theif and killed him.

Talk bullshit
满嘴喷粪
full
mouth
'to blow out'
excrement

Stop-motion Animation
逐帧动画
one by one
frame
cartoon

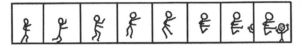

Onomatopoeia
拟声
imitate
sound

Silhouette
侧影
side/lateral
shadow/image

Dictation
听写
listen
write

Sketch
写生画
draw
life
picture

Graffiti
涂鸦          涂鸭
scribble     scribble
crow         duck

Semicolon
分号
seperate
mark/sign

An Epic & Poetic Saga
史诗
history
poem/ode

Fragile
易碎
easy
break

Contraband
禁运品
banned
'to transport'
goods

Jack-o-Lantern
鬼火
devil
flame/fire

Why?
为什么
'for the purpose of'
what

Transliterated

Pizza Hut
必胜客
'bi sheng ke'

# Transliterate

Transliterate
音译
sound
translate

KFC
肯德基
"ken de ji"

Walmart
沃尔玛
'wo er ma'

**Walmert**

Putting Mom&Pops outta business for 52 years.

Microphone
麦克风
'mai ke feng'

Cocaine
可卡因
'ke ka yin'

Heroin
海洛因
'hai luo yin'

Mescaline
麦司卡林
'mai si ka lin'

FACE

+ Bad = $

Coffee
咖啡
'ka fei'

Typhoon
台风
'tai feng'

Facebook
非死不可
'fei si bu ke'

Mocca
摩卡
'mo ka'

Generic
Corporate
Coffee
· Unfair trade coffee ·

SODA

Coke
可口可乐
'ke kou ke le'

Vit-D
Who needs
the Sun?

Vitamin
维他命
'wei ta ming'

Latte
拿铁
'na tie'

Poker
扑克
'pu ke'

Tiramisu
提拉米苏
'ti la mi su'

Cool
酷
'ku'

SUPER TANK 8000

Tank
坦克
'tan ke'

Cartoon
卡通
'ka tong'

Radar
雷达
'lei da'

"I think, therefore I shred."
-Dragonforce

Logic
逻辑
'luo ji'

Golf
高尔夫球
'gao er fu'
ball

Hamburger
汉堡
'han bao'

# AIDS
Auto Immune Disease Something

AIDS
艾滋
'ai zi'

Guitar
吉他
'ji ta'

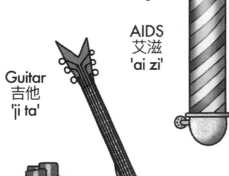

Salon
沙龙
'sha long'

FREE THE WEED

Hippy
嬉皮
'xi pi'

Salad
沙拉
'sha la'

Hello!
哈罗
'ha luo'

Pudding
普定
'pu ding'

Bacon
培根
'pei gen'

Curry
咖喱
'ka li'

Yoga
瑜伽
'yu jia'

# 外太空
## Space

Space
太空
greatest
void

Spaceship
宇宙飞船
universe
fly
ship

Satellite
卫星
'to guard'
star

Milky Way
银河
silver
river

The Sun
太阳
greatest
light

Nebula
星云
star/planet
cloud

Solar System
太阳系
sun
system

Astroid
小行星
small
travel
star

Meteor
流星
'to drift or move'
star

Neptune
海王星
ocean
king
planet

Pluto
冥王星
obscure
king
planet

Venus
金星
gold
planet

Mars
火星
fire
planet

Atmosphere
大气层
big
air
layer

Earth
地球
land
sphere/globe

Mercury
水星
water
planet

Planet
行星
travel
star/planet

Uranus
天王星
heavenly
king
planet

Saturn
土星
earth/soil
planet

Big Bang
大爆炸
large/big
explosion

Jupiter
木星
wood
planet

# 解释偏胖

# Explaining Radicals

# An Introduction to Chinese Radicals
(Explained to the best of my ability.)

Chinese characters are comprised of 'radicals', this is to say, they are made of structural parts or character components, which are basically just a combination of characters; radicals are characters combined - characters within characters; *a radical is a character,* essentially. Generally speaking, most characters have with one or two radicals (although many have much more). Obviously single characters don't have a radical thus they aren't defined as a radical. I mean, this is how I understand it at least...

Take the first example: 人 (rén) means person or people and is a character unto itself. But combine it with itself, and you get 从 (cóng), which is two people or persons; meaning 'to follow'. Add in another person character (aka radical) and you get 众 (zhòng) - three 'people' which means 'crowd'. Thus when learning Chinese characters, there is often a way to figure out the general relationship of the character and it's meaning based on the radicals. With 从 or 众 you could wager a guess that it has something to do with 'people', and while not knowing the exact meaning, you'd be closer than randomly guessing. Although I'm pretty sure this isn't true for all radicals; why would Chinese make it too easy?

On top of all that as well, many radicals' shape will change depending on where it is. 人 when put with 休 changes slightly - can you see it there on the side (亻)? Hand (手) changes into 扌, eye (眼) contains the radical for 'eye/look' which is 目, mother (妈) contains the character for woman (女), 合 contains the radical/character for mouth (口) and so on.

Once you know a fair amount of characters, it's much easier to see how the more complex ones are made. 胃 is made of 田 and 月, 江 is made of 氵 and 工, 刘 is made of 文 and 刂 etc... For reference, I mostly used the app 'Pleco" and the book '汉子痛' (hàn zi tòng) as a reference. So while I do consider both as quite reliable, I'm not gonna say all these are 100% unquestionably correct. Take lots of this with a grain of salt. I'm no expert. On a side note too, often the radicals are merely there for phonetic purposes only, so this "breaking down of characters" only goes so far...

# 众
## (zhòng)

人 means 'person or people'. Two together 从 means 'to follow' - two people walking together, and put three of them together and you get 'crowd' - 众.

# 串
## (chuàn)

Looks like meat on a stick? It is. Means 'to skewer' or 'string together' (like a rope stringing up two items). Made of 丨 and two 口; in fact these don't actually break down into anything interesting, sorry.

# 品
## (pǐn)

The character for 'mouth' is 口, and three of them together means 'to taste'. It also means 'commodity/product/goods' and 19 meanings altogether, according to Pleco.

# 伞
## (sǎn)

Looks like an umbrella? It is. Actually this is an example of a character looking like it's meaning. Another one you can't break down the radicals, but characters that look like their meaning are called '象形字' which means 'pictograph'. This is the same for 串.

# 聪
## (cōng)

This one means 'clever, wise, sharp-witted, or intelligent'. It's comprised of an ear 耳 and 总 'to collect or gather'. Ears that collect information.

# 学

(xué)

To learn (or study). The old script depicted two hands arranging chips; representing counting. Now, the character is mostly comprised of a child 子 and a cover ⼧, which seems to imply a child learning at a school (school being 'the covered place').

# 指

(zhǐ)

Finger or 'to point'. The radical for hand 手 = 扌 is on the left combined with 旨 'tasty or delicious' on the right; a hand reaching for yummy food. Yum!

# 瓶

(píng)

Bottle. Made of the left radical/character 幷 which means 'to join' or 'to merge/amalgamate', and 瓦 - earthenware pottery (aka a bottle or jar) for drawing water back in 'the day'. When water and the jar join they become one; a bottle.

# 哭

(kū)

Does this look like someone crying? Well, that's what the character means; to cry. Originally meant 'the wailing of a dog' as it has two mouths 口 over a dog 犬. It eventually came to mean 'a person crying'.

# 噩

(è)

Bad, ill-omened, unlucky, shocking, or upsetting, or more accurately 'terrifying'. Long ago the character had a different radical instead of 王 which means King or Monarch. It had only two mouths 口 and a 屰 , a man upside down - an ill omen.

王 can indicate the victim of a crime as well here, and the 口s can mean 'public uproar'.

# 笔
## (bǐ)

Means writing brush or pen/pencil. Bamboo on top 竹 which turns into 𥫗 and 'hair' on the bottom 毛 which resembles a tuft of hair. Writing brush handles (or whatever they're called) were made of bamboo and the 'hair' was obviously hair of some sort.

# 茶
## (chá)

Tea. On top is grass 艹 or in this case tea leaves, and also includes 'people' 人 and 'wood' 木 on the bottom. Suggests people drinking tea.

# 炒
## (chǎo)

To stir-fry, sauté, roast, boil or cook. Comprised of fire 火 and 少 meaning 'little, few or inadequate' or 'a short amount of time'. A short period over a good flame.

# 酒
## (jiǔ)

Booze! The water (水) radical 氵 means liquid and 酉 is a wine vessel. Need I say more?

# 果
## (guǒ)

'Cultivated or field' is 田 and tree is 木. So trees in a field are 'fruit'.

# 听
(tīng)

To hear. Comprised of mouth 口 and axe 斤, ie hearing the sound of an axe, or sounds of speech; diverse sounds. The Seal Script included the characters for ear, virtue and 'straighten up', ie listen respectfully to virtuous words.

# 窗
(chuāng)

A window. On top is cave 穴 and on bottom in window/chimney 囱. A opening or 'cavern' in the cave wall to let in light and air.

# 忍
(rěn)

Endure. Made of knife 刃 and heart 心. "One has to endure, even with a knife pointed at their heart". This is also the character Naruto uses to mean 'ninja'.

# 中
(zhōng)

(Not 'Red Dragon Skateboards'.) This one means centre, or middle; a line through a square. That's as much info as I can gather for this one...

# 话
(huà)

The radical on the left (讠) is talk and the right is tongue 舌.

# 帽
(mào)

The radical on the left (巾) means 'general purpose cloth', and on the right is 冒 which means 'hat'. That one is made of head (冃) and eye (目). In the old days hats were made of cloth, like turbans, and worn on the head above the eye.

# 唱
## (chàng)

Made of mouth (口), obviously, and on the right side, 昌; 'light of the sun' made up of the sun (日) and 'to speak' (曰) representing 'ready to say something', speaking openly. Means 'to sing'.

# 尿
## (niào)

So this one is made of a corpse (尸) and water (水); corpse water. It's pee! In fact 尸 can mean 'person' as well, but corpse water is much more funny.

# 屎
## (shǐ)

Can you guess this one? corpse/person (尸) and rice (米). As in, your body digests food. It means poo!

# 好
## (hǎo)

From what I hear, this character 'good' is made of a girl and a boy (女 and 子), as in, it is good to have a boy and a girl (as children). 子 can also mean 'child'. My 汉子痛 book says a woman with a child is 'good'.

# 饭
## (fàn)

This one means 'cooked rice' or 'food'. It's made of eat (饣) and 反 which means 'repeat' (or reverse), as in put the food in your moth over and over. One thing also said it can be 'reverse', as in your hand flips (reverses) as you turn it to put food in your mouth.

# 休

(xiū)

To rest. Made of a person (人) and a tree (木). A person sitting next to a tree implies 'resting in the shade of the tree on a hot day'.

# 坐

(zuò)

Sit. Has two people (人) sitting together on the earth/soil (土).

# 安

(ān)

Means 'safe/calm' (and 16 other things according to Pleco). Made of two radicals. A roof (宀) and a woman (女), meaning ' a women in a house is safe'.

# 明

(míng)

'Clear or bright', this one is made of sun (日) and moon (月); as bright as the sun and moon.

# 婚

(hūn)

This one means 'marriage or wedding'. It's made of a woman (女), and dusk/ twilight (昏). Apparently in ancient times marriages were held at the time of dusk.

# 草

(cǎo)

Grass, made of grass (艹), and 'early morning' (早); seeds sprouting under the morning sun.

# 妈

(mā)

So don't ask me, but this one means mother, and is made of woman and horse (女 and 马). Apparently the 马 in this character is merely phonetic, so...

# 宝

(bǎo)

Precious or treasure, this one is made of a roof (宀) and jade/gem (玉). The traditional character is 寶, made of (can you even see it?) roof (宀), precious (珎) and money (貝). Same thing, basically.

# 漏

(lòu)

'To leak'. Made of water (水), and person (尸) and rain (雨). Yup.

# 嬲

(niǎo)

'To pester'. It has two men (男), with a girl (女) between. like the dance floor, two guys bothering a girl. You've never seen Night at the Roxbury?

# 鞋

(xié)

This character means 'shoes'. Shoes are made of hide (革) and they walk on the ground (圭) (that character is two 'earth/soil's (土). Yay!

# 好玩的事实
## Fun Facts

-A polite way of saying 'die' is 'passed away', 去世 (qù shì): the 去 means 'to go to' and the 世 means 'the world'.

-好久不见 (hǎo jiǔ bù jiàn) literally means 'long time no see' in Chinese. That's where we get the saying.

-In Chinese there's not really a word for 'no'. Instead, they say 'not yes'. (Similar to 'isn't' in English.) They do however have '不' (bù) which means 'no/not/negative prefix', but generally speaking they almost never say '不' by itself to answer a question.

-There's three ways to say 'can' in Chinese, which is quite brilliant I think.
能 (néng) = Ability: I'm not busy, so I <u>can</u> come over. I broke my arm, so I <u>can't</u> throw the ball.
会 (huì) = Be able to/acquired the skill: I <u>can</u> speak Chinese. I <u>can't</u> use chopsticks.
可以 (kěyǐ) = Permission/possible: <u>Can</u> I use your pen? I <u>can't</u> smoke in here.

-If you ever use a tooth pick in China you must cover your mouth with your other hand, otherwise it's rude.

-Chinese movies and TV all have Chinese subtitles. I assume because so many words would similar. Like the 'shi' poem you probably read.

-Swearing isn't 'cool' in China. In fact, for the most, it makes you lose face.

-I never saw one RV in China during my entire time there. Retirement doesn't exist. (Actually I was recently told there are RV's in China.)

-520 (wǔ èr líng) sounds like 'wǒ ài nǐ' in Chinese, which means 'I love you'. So 520 is often written to mean I love you.

-It was rare to get a cold drink in China. They were either room temperature (I don't recommend drinking warm beer) or boiling hot water/tea. I did grow accustomed to the hot water, and still drink it to this day.

-People in University can (and sometimes do) pay people to write their thesis. So, it makes it harder to trust people you need to trust (like doctors) when they say "I've graduated University" but you know there's a chance they only passed due to money power and not brain power.

-Chinese people take two hours for lunch. It was great when I worked, because I could nap. But not great when you went to the hospital and the doctors were away for two hours.

-The simplified character for love is 爱 (ài). The traditional is 愛. The character for heart is 心 (xīn) . When they simplified 'love' they took out the character for heart from the middle of the traditional character.

-When you take a business card from someone in China, you must use both hands and take it from both sides.

-In China the number 250 means idiot. I did some research and found a few differing stories as to why this is. For plagiarism reasons, I'll summarize my findings.

Story 1: One day 'someone' (unclear who) was killed. The King wanted revenge on the murderer named Su Qin, so he put out a request for his head. It was to be hung on the city gate. One day, there was Su's head, hanging on the gate. Next to it said 'Su was a traitor and whoever killed him is entitled to one thousand of taels (an ancient weight measurement in China) of Gold. Well, four guys stood up and all said they were the murderer. After the King said "do not lie!" they all insisted it was them. So he asked them "if I divide 1000 between you, how much does each of you get?" They all answered 250. The King was furious and said "take these 250 away to be beheaded!" Now it is used to refer to stupid people after being passed down through the years.

Story 2: A long time ago a string of a thousand copper coins was called a 'diao', and half a string (five hundred coins) was called a 'diao zi'. The term 'diao zi' at this time was used to describe someone with mediocre skills or mental abilities. It's said that due to this, many scholars, out of humility or modesty would often refer to themselves as a 'diao zi', or half of a 'diao'. Out of this grew the term '250', as half of a half of a diao was used as an insult.

-Chinese people don't like super sweet things as much as the West, thus they use 'red beans' as a flavour in things like the pie's at McD's, and milk. It's not bad, but takes some getting used to. Although the red bean milk was horrific.

-Speaking of McD's pies, I only found apple once. Otherwise, they usually had red bean, pineapple and taro. They (and KFC) also served little half corn on the cobs.

-My students would eat Halls cough candy as actual 'candies'.

-Since there are tones inherent in the language, Chinese actually must use a word/character at the end of a sentence to ask questions. With English, while we intonate the end of our sentence upwards, Chinese can't do that (lest it change the meaning of the words). The character is 吗 (ma). An example would be 你喜欢我吗？ Literally "You like me *question mark*"

-The word for contradiction is 矛盾 (máo dùn), which translated to 'spear - shield'. A basic example would be two opposing things. For example, one country wants to go to war and attack, but the other wants to defend. Or as one guy put it; you want money, but you don't want to go to work.

-In Chinese, if you want to say something (usually for foreigners it's your language skills) is 'mediocre' you would say 马马虎虎 (mǎ mǎ hǔ hǔ), which means 'horse horse tiger tiger'. There's a few differing stories, but the main one I found goes like this:

In ancient times, there was a painter surnamed Jia in the capital and he was very famous. Many people came to ask him for his paintings. The man gradually became proud and thought that he would draw a few strokes as a masterpiece. Therefore, when he painted, he began to do whatever he wanted and wasn't very serious.

One day, he was drawing a picture of a fierce tiger going down the mountain. As soon as he drew the tiger's head, someone rich came to his door to buy the picture and asked for a picture of a horse. Painter Jia was too lazy to start again, so he painted the body of a horse under the tiger's head. The visitor looked at it and asked him, "master, are you painting a horse or a tiger?" painter Jia said, "Ma... Hu, just so-so. You see? Both the tiger's power and the horse's vigour are rare masterpieces!" Of course, the man wasn't satisfied so he smiled and left.

Painter Jia liked his masterpiece very much, so he hung it at home. At this time painter Jia had two sons who were a little short of intelligence and had no brains. When his eldest son saw the painting, he asked him what it was. The painter knew that his son was stupid and that he could not fool his son with carelessness, so he said it was a tiger. Unexpectedly, the next day when his eldest son went out hunting, he saw someone else's horse and thought it was a tiger so he shot it. As a result Jia had to pay a lot of money.

After a few days, the second son saw the 'sloppy' picture and went to ask him what it was. The painter has gained experience and learned a lesson. This time, he dare not say it's a tiger, so he said it's a horse. The second son kept it in mind. The next day, he went to the countryside to play. On the way, he met a tiger which he thought was a horse, so he happily welcomed it. He grabbed the hair on the tiger's neck and was about to ride on it. How could the tiger be polite to him? He turned his head and bit him to death.

Painter Jia was very sad, but it was too late to regret. He went home to tear down the careless picture and burned it to ashes. Later, he wrote a poem to blame himself. "Careless picture, careless picture, like a horse and like a tiger, the eldest son shot the horse, the second son fed the tiger. If the thatched cottage is burned, please don't learn from me. Since then, the word 'ma hu' has been handed down. Meaning careless or mediocre or so-so[1].

-One funny term Chinese use to mean 'flirt' is 吃豆腐 (chī dòu fu), which means 'to eat tofu'. There's a story behind it but I didn't feel like writing it...

-To cheer in Chinese is 加油 (jiā yóu) which translates to 'add oil'. I found many versions of why this came about. One was this: In the past, in the oil press workshop, the production of oil from raw materials had to go through a variety of complicated procedures, and some procedures required the cooperation of several people to complete, especially the final procedure, which required several people to work hard at the same time. For this purpose, several people chanted chants, and as soon as the bell struck, the oil squeezed out was added to the oil container. This is the origin of the word 加油[2].

-How you say 'brag' in Chinese is 吹牛 (chuī niú) which means 'to blow the cow'. The one story I found went like this.

> The allusion of this word is actually related to slaughter. In the past, the "puffing method" was used to kill pigs and sheep. After slaughtering pigs and sheep their blood is released. The butcher would then make a small opening on the leg of the pig or sheep near the hoof, insert something into it and poke it. He'd then blow into it which would make the whole body of the pig or sheep swell up. This would make the skin split by itself as long as it was pulled gently with a knife. This is called 'blowing a pig' or 'blowing a sheep'.

> However, this method cannot be applied to cattle, because the cow is not only huge, but the skin is also tough. If you want to inflate the entire cow, you must have an amazingly huge lung capacity, which is basically impossible for ordinary people to do. So bragging is equivalent to an impossible thing. If a person often says something that he can't accomplish at all, he will be said to be bragging[3].

-The word for 'stuff' is 东西 (dōng xī), which means 'east - west'. There's two legends. One was basically that there were two cities far apart, East and West of each other, naturally. So to buy things you had to either go East or West, depending on where you were, to get there. The other pertains to the four elements; East = wood, West = gold, South = fire, and North = water. Since you can't put water and fire in a basket, the natural thing was wood and gold.

-November 11th is called 双十一 (shuāng shí yī) which means 'double eleven'; singles day. That day in China there is a crazy sale on Taobao (their Amazon), and you can save *insane* amounts of money.

-If you're using the internet and would like to tell someone "go die" (or 'piss off/ get lost etc...'), they use the word 狗带 (gǒu dài), which literally means 'dog belt'. But since it sounds like the English "go die" that's what they use. Chinese internet slang!

-I've heard that in order to join the communist party in China you need to confirm that you are an atheist. Not sure this is 100% true, but I do believe it is; I'm 95% sure its 100% true.

-The number four is unlucky in Chinese because it sounds similar to death. 'Four' - 四 (sì) and 'death' - 死 (sǐ).

-The character 小 (xiǎo) means 'small or little' but it also means 'young or child'. It's put before the names of most animals to indicate their 'young'. Puppy - young dog, fawn - young deer, kitten - young cat, calf - young cow, piglet - young pig etc..

-I asked a few Chinese people about this, and for some reason they don't differentiate between a 'blindfold' and an 'eye-patch'. The same word is used (眼罩 (yǎn zhào) = eye/look/glance - cover/shade/hood. Anyway, I thought that was interesting.

-Ok, the story behind 'son of a bitch' (or bastard) in Chinese is pretty interesting. First of all, son of a bitch in English isn't super super bad (I think), but in Chinese, this is one of the more sever things you can say, I believe. Second, the story goes like this, so I've been told. After mild amounts of research I can see this isn't the most widely accepted one, but it's interesting none the less.

So 'son of a bitch' in Chinese is 王八蛋 (wáng bā dàn), which translates literally to 'king - eight - egg'. Apparently it's a 'false legend' going way back to The Eight Virtues of Buddhism. Sounding much like 'wáng bā dàn' is 忘八端, wàng bā duān, which means 'forget - eight - end', 'to forget The Eight Virtues'. So you verbally have similar sounding words 'wáng bā dàn' vs 'wàng bā duān'. And I guess over time, it's said, the characters changed, but the pronunciation stayed the same (except for duān which changed to dàn).

One website I found says this (translated from google): In the long-term oral transmission process, the misrepresentation of "forgetting the eight virtues" as "the bastard" is related to the pronunciation of the three-character combination, because "forgetting the eight virtues" in spoken language is called out, not read out, the called word is important in Chinese[4].

-If someone compliments you in China, unlike Canada where you say something like 'thanks man', in China, you must deny the compliment with '哪里哪里' (nǎlǐ nǎlǐ), which means 'where? where?'. It's a form of being humble.

-If you want to split the bill in China, you can say 'AA'. Not sure why, but I will say, I've seen drunk Chinese dudes almost literally fight to pay the bill. Something about 'face' (see page 229).

-One thing I don't think I mention is at every (literally every) somewhat 'middle-to-high end' restaurant has greeters. Even some fast food. And every time you enter they say "welcome" (欢迎光临 - huān yíng guāng lín) and sometimes do a little bow. And when you leave they say, literally, "go slow" (慢走 - màn zǒu), which really means 'go safely', or something like that...

My China Adventure Story

# Preface

Well, since you're reading this I thought I should preface it with a little note, as, after spending *almost* seven (I'm calling it seven for simplicity sake) years in China, there were many experiences I had, many of which were good, and many of which were bad. Thus, I hope this book (if it can be called that) doesn't wholly reflect the fact I left China hating almost everything about it. Maybe I was there too long, maybe it was just life's circumstances, or maybe it was just my attitude. There are an infinite number of things that change one's experience, so I don't want those to make China seem worse than it is. With that being said, what you will read is merely my personal experience and view of China, relative to me. It's not my intention to verbally malign an entire race of people even though at times it comes across that way. Overall, I still do have a deep love of the Chinese culture (for the most) and it's people.

Also, it might be noted that not everything I write is 100% truth. I heard a lot of stuff in China about China from random people, and there were times I asked a Chinese person if 'it was true' and they said 'I've never heard of that before'. So maybe somethings are true, and maybe I was told a lie. I'll write about it anyway because I think it's interesting, and I'll at least let you know when information may be unreliable.

Lastly I have to apologize for what you will discover is maybe one of the most sporadic and unorganized stories ever told. My excuse is that my memory sucks, I have A.D.D. and I simply don't care enough right now to fix it all. One day I will, but for now, it's a raw account of my insane life in China. That's not to say I didn't edit it, but more like 'I'm too exhausted to spend any more time on this book right now' sorta thing. For now, enjoy the read eh.

# Chapter 0: The Beginning

I think now, I need to back up to 'before the beginning'. You can skip this part if you don't care about the reasons for me wanting to go to China. But, if you do care, here it is. Without getting into it too much, back in around 2008 Jesus changed my life and my heart. I lived in Vancouver then, and at that point I realized I'd been basically just living for myself, and I wanted to change that. So I decided that doing something to help people was the best thing. Coincidentally, there was something called 'Missions Fest' around that time, so I went. What this Fest was, was basically tons of Christian outreach programs from all over the world getting together to find volunteers. It sounded just like what I needed; that is, until I went.

I walked around looking at all the options. Every country seemed to be there, but as I talked with some, it was like they didn't really care about their organization. They just gave a little speal and a pamphlet. Then, when I was talking to this one guy I told him "ok, I'm willing to go anywhere, do anything, for any amount of time". His literal quote was this: Do you have any education? (I answered no). Well, then you'd have to go to school first and come back and talk. People like you are a dime a dozen, and we need people who have some skills.

Imagine my heartbreak and anger.

So I left, just completely disgusted with the whole scene. What a bunch of jokers. Fortunately, about a few weeks later this guy came and spoke at my Church about an orphanage* in China. It sounded awesome, and so I talked with him. He asked me if I liked kids, to which I replied 'yes'. He said "Sounds good! If you wanna go to China that would be great!" So we talked a little, and after figuring out some things I joined a team. That was the experience I was expecting at Missions Fest, but hey, it worked out in the end I think.

*[ *I use the term orphanage loosely, mostly because when people think of an orphanage, they may think of something like Oliver Twist, or simply a dingy place with lots of street kids with no parents. In China, from the four 'orphanages' I visited, I feel like saying 100% of the kids I met were disabled to some degree. On*

*top of that, many had parents, but they were abandoned due to various reasons, which I'll get into soon.*

*It should also be noted that we used the term Welfare Center to describe an 'orphanage', as, I believe, that's what it was in Chinese. In Chinese it's 孤儿院, which translated to 'orphan' (lonely person) 'institution'. No matter the choice of words, they were basically a building that housed the 'rejects of society'/disabled people. ]*

**Important side note**: I was told that it was very difficult to get into the Chinese orphanages due to the fact (maybe you heard about this) that the BBC went there many years ago and filmed a bunch of things. They then proceeded to return home to England and make a documentary about how "bad China was" and how they treated their abandoned children so poorly. After that China basically said 'No' to any foreigner wanting to go to the orphanage. So, the guy who I met from Church, in 2009 had been working with China almost 20 years by then. He'd built a very good relationship with the local government. Thus, we were allowed to go. At that time he was working alongside the government in three different cities.

# Chapter 1: Sanmenxia, China - 2 Weeks

In 2008, after having my entire heart do a 180, I worked hard, and paid off my debt. Then in 2009 I saved and had money to do this short term trip. It was to be two weeks. The team was made of about 20 people, some from America, most from the UK, a few from other places like Singapore or Ireland, and me from Canada! (Yay me!). We met in Hong Kong and man, what a tall city. If you've never been there, I can't explain it. It just seemed like every building was about 200 stories high. It was insane. So that was cool. One thing I liked there, as well as China, is that cars don't stop for pedestrians. It's so much easier to cross the road. In China especially, you can just 'frogger' your way across the highway, stop in the middle of the lane and cars will pass you. It's ideal.

The other funny-ish thing about Hong Kong is there are hundreds of East Indian men who target foreigners, asking if they 'want to buy a suit'. It's legit. But, who wants a suit? (Funnily enough I *would* need a suit mere years later.) But it wore thin pretty quick while I was walking around that amazing city. Every few blocks I would encounter a different East Indian guy trying to sell me a suit or a watch. Not sure the watches were legit...

Hong Kong was also insanely clean. There were always workers wiping hand rails or whatever. Anyway, I met the team and we finally flew to Sanmenxia.

I don't remember much of the first while, but I do remember, so vividly being in the bus for our first day to the Welfare Center (orphanage). It was on the outskirts of town, down a small unpaved road. Dirt everywhere. It felt like the countryside in a way. Bumpy and super ghetto. Finally we drove in through a metal gate and parked in a small lot. The entire facility was in the shape of a somewhat oblong circle, with high brick walls. Inside were various two story buildings and some other metal fences. I would find out later that the mentally disabled were separated from the physically disabled. There was also a second story which none of us were allowed to go to. This was where the 'worst cases' and babies were.

Now, I didn't mention that there were also older 'orphans'/abandoned people there. After all, as I said before, disabled people are often shunned and put aside in China. All ages, including some super cute mentally challenged grandpas and grandmas. So the people in charge kinda just divided us up, and we all went to our respective areas to begin to play. I volunteered to be with the mentally disabled kids/seniors as I was about 28 years old, and ready to do mad amounts of physical output. One thing we all realized very quickly is all toys that we had brought can be used as weapons. And, of course there were many fights. But more fun than fights to be honest. The fun was unparalleled for those kids. One guy at the Welfare Center was a kleptomaniac, so we often found him walking around with a large misshapen belly. It turned out most of the toys were hidden down his shirt and pants. I mean like, at one point probably 80% of the toys were hidden in his clothing.

During this time we found out that there basically weren't enough workers there, thus most of these kids/seniors were ignored. So the fact that, for the first time ever the kids and seniors had someone to play with was overwhelming. They never had so much fun. It was great. We were giving piggy back rides, throwing and rolling basketballs, using the little peg boards we brought, trying to paint, play badminton, and so much more. We just tried our best to love them as hard as we could with the time we had. There was one thing however which wasn't ideal. That is, some of the kids decided that some of the seniors could also give piggy back rides, and would jump on their backs without warning. It was especially not ideal when the chubby kid (who was about 13 or 14) would hop on the granny's back. Needless to say, some of them bailed pretty hard, so we gave that up pretty quick. At one point too we had them brush their teeth, which I guess they'd never done. There was so much blood! But it was ok.

So the days went by, and we were tired but happy. Side note, there was one Chinese girl who volunteered there and me and her fell in love during that time. She spoke some English. Anyway, nothing came of it of course. I heard she got married (as every Chinese girl does by the time she's 28*) and had a kid.

[ *Interesting fact: there's a term used in China for girls who aren't married by the time they're 28. It's "leftover women". It is what you think it is. Chinese culture thinks girls over 28 years old and not married are basically useless. There's a 30 min Documentary from Vice on youtube if you're curious. Look up 'left over women vice'. ]

The days in the Welfare Center went quick. We had tons of fun and were burnt out by the end of two weeks. During those two weeks, I really made some great friends, mostly from England. (No one likes Americans eh! Just kiddingggggggg.) Two guys from England in particular I bonded with as they played in a band together, and were a little crazy, if I do say so myself. But in the good way. They were around 40 years old. At one point we were listening to the 'new' Metallica album in their hotel room, and John was jumping on the bed playing air guitar.

Other funny things that happened during those two weeks were as follows: we had a Chinese translator and most nights we would go to various restaurants to eat. Most of us liked this one place where they served "Chinese hamburgers", which was just a fried bun with meat. Needless to say, the Chinese food we ate there was zero percent like any in Canada unless you're in Richmond or some places in Vancouver. Even then, you gotta know where to go.

Anyway, the other thing that was hilarious for those two weeks, but I would later find out to be annoying for the next 6.5 years was people staring at us for being foreigners. Especially the city where we were in. There was maybe literally only a few foreigners there, in a city of 400k (in 2010). We went shopping, and had people just following us, looking and listening to us. Some people asked to take pictures with us (keep in mind this was 2009 so there wasn't many smart phones).

One night in the 'town square'* my two buddies brought out their acoustic guitars and started playing. They had about 100 people watching.

[ *Every city in China has a town square. It consists of a large flat cement square. Most of the time, during summer, you can see families hanging out, kids on bikes, old men whipping their tops and flying kites, and in the evening (usually) there will be about 100 to 1000 or more people, often seniors, dancing to the most random techno. Or traditional Chinese music with techno over it. ]

Martin, my new buddy who was in the band with John got a SIM card for his phone, and he got a free bag of rice! Nice!! haha. One night we found a Karaoke (KTV in China) but as it turned out, the people there cared more about us than the person singing, so we left. We also ran into a white guy named Tony, and he said he hadn't seen foreigners in two months! There really wasn't many I guess.

Another monumental thing that happened was I had La Mian (literally: pulled noodles) for the first time, and it changed my life. Fresh hand-made noodles. In my entire life, I will tell you that these are the best noodles on Earth, and it's worth going to China just for these. The cool thing is almost every shop that sells them is Muslim people from the province of Xin Jiang, in the Northwest. So they speak an entire different dialect of Chinese and look quite different. I love them and their noodles so much. Seriously.

One super rad thing that happened was that our translator, or was it the bus driver, knew about these insane underground houses. (You can find it on Youtube.) So we drove for about 45 minutes to this place which looked like a large field with whiteish coloured hard dirt on the ground. When we drew closer, we realized this is where the houses were. They were basically square holes cut out of the earth, with stairs going down. They were joined by hallways, and between some houses was a large courtyard area, which you could totally fall into easily if you were walking without paying attention. Just a large hole in the ground. Oh, and their beds were so so hard. I mean literally they were just plywood and a blanket. Not cool. Well, at least we didn't sleep there.

But we did eat there, and there was a ton of food. Usually in China, they share food. That is to say, there would be rice and many different shared dishes you can take from. Most tables have a lazy-susan. Another interesting 'rule' that I heard is that they try to have one food item for every person. So since there were ten of us at the table, there were ten different things to eat. The food was awesome!

One thing that was funny in hindsight, but annoying at the time was my first 'hot-pot' experience. Hot pot is basically a huge pot in the middle of the table with boiling soup broth. The servers bring you uncooked food, and you have to put it into the broth. Only to do this you need to reach near a boiling liquid and almost burn your hand with steam. Meanwhile when you drop things or pick them out the water splashes all over your hand and arm. Then you had to wait for the food to cook. Then you would get about one bite, and do it all over again. It was slow, steamy, hot, and frustrating. I just want one big thing to myself so I can turbo eat it. That's how I roll.

Another evening we all went out for dinner with the Welfare Center boss, which means you HAVE to drink. In China there's two super important things that their entire society is built upon. One is 关系 (guanxi) and the other is 面子 (mianzi). Relationships and 'face'/reputation. I'll expand a lot more on them later, but for now, all you need to know is we HAD to drink. They had wine, which I'd never had until then. As you could probably guess, it tasted like straight vinegar. I'm honestly not sure how people "acquire a taste" for wine. I'm still convinced they're just lying to themselves, as I can't imagine anyone genuinely liking drinking that stuff. Anyway, the women didn't have to drink, but we did. I had a little, but not even close to enough to get drunk. Just enough to be respectable.

On a day off we ventured to a cool temple on a hill. The view was fantastic, and people everywhere were flying kites. Then we discovered that there was a slide made of smooth rock the whole way down the mountain! Of course some of us had to try. So we had to put on gloves (to hold the railings for speed control) and a sack over our legs and bums to slide on. It was fun, but ramming into solid rock corners wasn't ideal for my hips. But one of the girls managed to lose a glove half way down, and bail just at the last part. She was bruised and cut up a little but survived. It was then that my camera died. Lame! Remember cameras?

We also got to go to Chinese Church, which was long to say the least. Many songs and *two* sermons! It was like, "Ok finally this never ending sermon is done", and then there was *another*! Of course we couldn't understand either, which was rough. Afterwards, a bunch of people took pictures with us. Classic China. I think it was about 2.5 hours in all.

On the next morning, I went to get a camera but 'we're open' means that all the employees sing and dance outside the shop for a while before they start their shift. It worked out though, and I got a new camera. (On a side note, I just found that camera a few days ago, but it was a pretty haggard and I threw it in the garbage.)

On the second last day at the Welfare Center, I was losing my mind. I was basically watching over six kids by myself and trying to keep them occupied. There were punches and hits and it was mayhem as it is with disabled kids. Now eventually they let us care for a few babies, so while I'm dying the other members of our team had a single cute little baby all to themselves while I ran around like a madman. Keep in mind I'd dealt with this for almost two weeks, so I was exhausted. Overall however, it was an amazing experience.

After the two weeks we left to Xian to see the Terracotta Warriors! I was so stoked to see real ninjas! I envisioned Shaolin monks doing sweet fights. But alas, my ignorance was my downfall. All they were was rock statues in the ground. So me and some of the girls left immediately, because it was mad boring and went to KFC for ice cream cones. After, we went to the hotel and then toured around the city. It was super cool, but that area we were in was a little touristy. Let me quote my journal here: "So me and Martin walked around, found some people and got some noodles (which I just pooped out) and came back to the hotel." That night, we went to the market which was awesome, but every fifty feet or so you just found the same items over and over. It was still amazing and beautiful and strange. The smells and the sights. It's one of those 'you had to be there' things. I'd explain it, but I don't want to.

So finally we all went back to Hong Kong and all parted ways. And in case you're wondering, McDonalds taste the same everywhere I went in China (and Hong Kong). Yum! I left those two weeks really lost, not knowing what to do with my life, but happy for my experiences. Little did I know I'd be going back 7 months later for half a year! Only to a different city and different orphanage, but with the same organization. (International China Concern if you're wondering.)

# Chapter 2: Changsha, China - 6 Months

January 2010, the middle of winter and here I am, leaving Vancouver (my home of eight years) heading to the centre of China, alone, to a place I've never been meeting people I've never met and staying in an apartment I knew zero about. The adventure was really about to begin!

I flew into Hong Kong with my buddy who worked for Air Canada. He flew me there free on his account, I paid him cheaper than a regular ticket, and he made money. Win win. And we hung out a few days in Hong Kong together. When we arrived I was like, "Yeah I know where there's good hotels that are cheap". I'd been to that area before and I'd looked on the internet for 'cheaper' hotels than the one I used before, which was the YMCA. Little did I know that area was dodgy as it gets. It was like in the movies, when people enter some sketchy place, and slowly as they get deeper in it gets darker, and people seem to notice them and begin to follow them. Kinda like that. We finally bailed and went to the YMCA a few blocks away, so it worked out ok. In fact the price wasn't a ton more anyway.

This time in Hong Kong I got to adventure a little more than last time and it ruled. There was the world's longest (or 2nd longest?) escalator, which is actually split into parts, but it still went for about a kilometre up the hill. So fun. We found some cool shops too. One old bookstore was so so amazing, and I wanted to buy a bunch of stuff but didn't have room in my luggage, nor did I need it. We looked for the tram up the big mountain, but after not finding it we decided to walk up, regretting it about half way. Whoops. Still fun though. The peak had a lookout where you could see all of Hong Kong. It was epic!

In the evening, we went to 'The Symphony of Lasers' by the Victoria pier, which is just a few of the skyscrapers in the downtown area shooting patterns all over themselves. But, due to the legitly bad 80s music, it turned out to be pretty weak. Nice to be near the ocean anyway. We hit up the night market after that and got some food. Went back and slept, and then I was off to Chinaland!

Changsha, a.k.a. one of the hottest cities in China. China has something they call the 'three furnaces of China', which are apparently Chongqing, Wuhan and Nanjing. But sometimes there is a fourth added, and that is Changsha. Of course it wasn't hot in Jan, but by June....well, we'll get to that. Population in 2010 was just over 7 million. So, a super large city for me. I arrived, the only foreigner on the airplane to be met by a large 6'5" (or more) Australian guy about 40 years old named Justin. We were immediately best buddies. Friendliest and funniest guy

I ever met. He drove me to my apartment, which was in the same apartment complex as him, and set me up. The complex consisted of many buildings, most of which were about 20 stories high. I think in my entire six months living there I never even walked around the whole thing to be honest.

Anyway, my apartment was a bachelor, or whatever it's called when there isn't a bedroom. It was a little ghetto, but actually better than I expected. It had a shower, toilet, air conditioner, and a bed. That's all. No internet too. But it sufficed. I was home. And it was only 150$ Canadian a month, so that helped. Also, due to the fact I had no internet I'd often go to the nearby 'internet bar'. It was 24 hours, of course. I'd just email people and leave. Eventually I just used Justin's wifi when I was at his place.

The next day Justin brought me to the police station as you need to register with the local authorities that you are in town. He told me it was so that in case there was ever an emergency they would have a record of all the foreigners in town, if something needed to be done for some reason and needed to evacuate them all. We had to park in an underground parking lot, which was exactly this: An unlit tunnel into the ground with no exit and room for about twenty cars. I'd never seen that before. Just a legit road into the earth and that's it. And, by dark I mean pitch black, with no lights. So we had to Austin Powers™ turn and park.

After that I met up with Justins family. They had been there, I think it was about seven years when I arrived. His wife was awesome, and she read fantasy books like me, so that was great. They had three kids, which at the time were around nine, seven and four years old, give or take. Their apartment was much bigger than I expected. A large three-bedroom. It was classic China, with marble floors and a small kitchen with low countertops. I've never thought the stereotype that 'Chinese people are short' was true, but it must have been, because all the places I lived in had low counters in the kitchen. It was especially brutal for Justin as he was a giant of a man.

The next day me and Justin hung out, and he took me around the city. We went to the DVD shop, which ruled. Only I didn't have a DVD player and they wouldn't play in my computer. $2.00 CDN for a DVD. Justin had hundreds as he'd lived there so long. It was fun. After, we went to Walmart and I bought the necessities: speakers for music, fake hardwood puzzle mats, sheets and a pillow.

Those nice blue sheets I bought I never washed, and yeah they turned me into a Smurf™ the first night I slept on them. Whoops.

During these days there was, as you may expect from a group of Christians; Church. Only, we held it in Justin's apartment as it was illegal for us to attend an underground (legit) Church and the Government approved Church wasn't totally 100% reliable theologically. Plus of course, lots of us didn't speak Chinese... So I met a nice Canadian family during that time. They had been there... I forget. Maybe four or five years? They had five kids, two of which were adopted (I'm pretty sure, my memory is bad.) They were aged about 8-15. We hung out and I sometimes played Nintendo wii with them. It was nice to be in China and have some friends. The first week went by quick, but I hadn't got to visit the Welfare Center/orphanage yet. It was nice to settle in though. And I did finally get a DVD player, so I was set up!

I will write this, as I look at my journal remembering all these things. I couldn't have asked for a better dude to hang out with than Justin. He was so so chill, super friendly and super funny, as I said. Especially since he was completely fluent in Chinese, and spoke exactly like a Chinese person, which not many foreigners can do. He was actually quite famous in that city, and was known all over China. He'd been on TV a few times too. Like I said, just one of the best guys I ever met. And looking back I can't even begin to tell you how much he helped me enjoy life during my stay in China. He took me all over and let me experience things I never would have had I just gone as a tourist or whatever. Justin knew everyone, and everyone knew him. In China, there's a few things you need to know. Here's cultural lesson #1.

## Chinese Culture: Relationships

Relationships are one of the most important things in China. There's a word for it, 'guanxi' (关系), and their entire society revolves around it. If you have good guanxi you can get away with almost anything. I mean, literally almost anything. Life is easier and better with guanxi and everyone is always trying to get more. (This is also what I would consider a negative aspect of their culture as it makes you question the motives of almost everyone you meet. Because they may want to know you just to get something from you, which I found to be quite true.)

And so, due to Justin's mad amounts of guanxi, and plain old proficiency in Chinese and their culture, he knew just about everything and everyone. He invited me out on a few occasions too. One thing in China, as I said before is drinking to build guanxi. It's a form of bonding. One story Justin told me was he was at a dinner with some business men. They all had baijiu (white alcohol which taste like drinking flower juice extract and vodka), which you drink a little of at a time, slowly. Anyway, he said he accidentally ate some huajiao, which you may call Sichuan pepper. Well, they explode in your mouth with a gnarly amount of relentless spice and numb your tongue. It sucks and happened to me more than a few times. So he grabs his cup of water and just chugs it down. Meanwhile, it was actually the baijiu, and all the business men were quite impressed with his manliness. So he acquired more guanxi.

Another time (when I was actually with him) we drank baijiu and had snails. If I could just give a little advice, don't ever eat spicy snails. They weren't even big. I mean, you had to use a toothpick to get it out, and then it was basically just a large booger with spices on it. 100% no different. Anyway, we had fun. If you can put aside all the guanxi and mianzi (face/reputation) stuff, it was almost always a good time going out with rich Chinese dudes. They get pretty rowdy. Especially when the bill comes. Here's another funny cultural thing. In China, for some reason, you need to fight to pay the bill. Not actually, but sometimes, actually. I saw a few fights get a little serious, but nothing too bad. It's funny to watch. Especially since more often than not they are half cut.

Another interesting thing is Chinese people always will try to pay, and if you end up letting them, they keep track of it. Like a little mental note in the back of their head. So next time, you have to treat them. It's very back and forth that way, but to be honest that one didn't bother me too much. And the last funny thing about relationships is, I heard if you wear a green hat in China it means you're spouse is having an affair, or something like that.

~

Moving on, one day Justin took me for a massage, as one does in China. Nothing dodgy, although I do have a story I'll tell you that *IS* dodgy, but that's for later. It was a regular massage. And the best part about China is, it's cheap! 90 minutes for $10.00 CDN. Head to feet (minus private parts duh). That became a routine in my entire stay in China. Always a massage. It was great.

Then I started my official 'Chinese Language Lessons'. It was just two hours a week, once a week on Friday. Over the next six months I learned the basics. The first and second lessons were consecutive, and solely focused on tones only. Chinese, as you may know has different tones, which change the meanings of certain words; four tones in all (and a fifth if you count the 'no tone' characters). For example the word 'shi'. Let me give you all the words it can mean if you ignore the tones, and yes I know all of these: 'to be', time, matter/thing, ten, to 'use', true, era, city, teacher, style, lose, begin, soldier, room, stone, history, to look at, meal, to know, feces, lion etc... And there's a ton more I don't know....

Here's a poem, famous in Chinese that uses 100% the word 'shi'. *That's right, every character here is 'shi'.* If you want to find it, search the internet for 'Lion-Eating Poet in the Stone Den'. Try reading it! If you want to hear it, search youtube.

《施氏食狮史》

石室诗士施氏，嗜狮，誓食十狮。氏时时适市视狮。十时，适十狮适市。是时，适施氏适市。氏视是十狮，恃矢势，使是十狮逝世。氏拾是十狮尸，适石室。石室湿，氏使侍拭石室。石室拭，氏始试食是十狮尸。食时，始识是十狮，实十石狮尸。试释是事。

《Shī Shì shí shī shǐ》

Shíshì shīshì Shī Shì, shì shī, shì shí shí shī. Shì shíshí shì shì shì shī. Shí shí, shì shí shī shì shì. Shì shí, shì Shī Shì shì shì. Shì shì shì shí shī, shì shǐ shì, shǐ shì shí shī shìshì. Shì shí shì shí shī shī, shì shíshì. Shíshì shī, Shì shǐ shì shì shíshì. Shíshì shì, Shì shǐ shì shí shì shí shī. Shí shí, shǐ shí shì shí shī shī, shì shí shí shī shī. Shì shì shì shì.

After those couple lessons back to back, we started on the basics the next Friday. Keep in mind, it's still January, and it's decent cold and raining half the time. At this point I've been in Changsha about ten days only. I'm adjusting and having fun. Had a few Chinese lessons and met most of the team of volunteers there. Besides Justin and his family, there were a few people I became close with. Of course the Canadian family, and there was also two other Australian girls

213

there, in their 30's, who had been there about six years. They were pretty fluent in Chinese.

Anyway, around this time a dude a few years younger than the then 27 year old Kevin came to visit. His name was Tom, and he was legit. We were instant friends. He was teaching Chinese in Changchun, way way up North in China, where they build the super famous world's largest ice festival. Google it. So epic, although I never got to go. Anyway, he was just visiting for two weeks, so that was great. Me and him hung out lots, and he took me around the city. His Chinese was decent and he could speak and write enough to communicate. So we purposefully got lost, had an adventure, then just got a taxi back home. I still keep in touch with him too, here and there. Miss you dude! He ended up going back to Aussie and marrying a Chinese girl.

The one really funny story I remember with him was going to the absolute ghettoist hole-in-the-wall restaurant ever. I mean, in my entire time in China, that could have been the sketchiest. Anyway, Changsha is notorious in China for super spicy food (they even call their sexy girls 'spicy girls'), and Tom ordered me spicy noodles. Well, I couldn't even finish them. It was beyond anything I'd ever eaten. I guess the good news was, I only wasted about forty cents CDN.

### Chinese Culture: Abandoned Children

Ok, let's get serious for a second. I mentioned before about the kids being 'abandoned', and that it's not really fitting to call them orphans as many of them do in fact have parents. So here's what I often tell people, because when you hear the word 'abandon' you think things like 'heartless' and the likes. When really that's not always the case. Sometimes it is, but not always. So here's a few reasons parents will abandon their child in China.

Reason one is superstition. This is the worst reason there is, I think. From what I was told (and later experienced) was that Chinese people are very superstitious about many things. They believe that having a disabled child is bad luck, thus, since they don't want bad luck running in their family they will discard the child. That's rough, and I'll touch more on that later when I get to a different city and different orphanage.

The second reason, which I feel like is more common, or maybe I just want to believe it is, is this. There's no choice. You see, in Chinese culture you take care of your parents when they're old. There is no retirement money from the government, no help, no old folks home for them to go to. They live with you until they die. So put yourself in these shoes, and imagine that the child you just had is physically or mentally disabled. How is he/she going to grow up, get a job, and provide for you and take care of you when you're old and need help? They can't. Now add on top of this the fact you probably don't have much money anyway. You're trapped. Thus, many parents figure things like "If I give my child to the Welfare Center maybe they'll have a better chance at a life". Which to a degree is true, but it also isn't. To be honest, there's no easy answer.

Another reason is simply money. Say you have a newborn and it needs a surgery, but it will cost you 300,000元 ($60,000 CDN), could you afford it? Most people can't, although I heard some people sell their house. So again, they think "Maybe if I give my child up, they will be able to get the surgery paid for by the government and have a better life". Which could be true, but also not. Again, no easy answer.

I did hear one story in Changsha, of a boy who was abandoned. He lived in the Welfare Center for over a year, or two or three, I forget. Anyway, he did end up getting a surgery to save his life. Normal boy, no disabilities except the required surgery. In the end, they somehow tracked down his father and asked if he wanted his child back. The father said yes, of course!!! So, situations like these are quite complicated but happen.

So when you think about these abandoned kids, most of which are disabled to some degree, just know it's never as simple as it seems. And one more thing. At the age of fourteen the kids are 'aged out' which means after that age they can no longer be adopted and stay in the the system forever.

~

Ok, back to the story. So I got 'the tour' of the few places I would be working over the next six months. One was a government building, maybe fifteen stories high, but only one floor was the designated 'orphanage'. These kids I didn't personally work with much, but we (me and the two Aussie girls) would take 3-5 of them out at a time for fun. Same kids every week. It was great. These kids were about 13 years old.

Then there was 'The Lighthouse', which was out of town a little ways. Like a good hour on a bus. A singular three story building in the middle of an apartment complex. This is where the younger kids lived. The third was the apartments that some of the young adults rented. I'll get back to these places soon. As it was, it was exciting to meet the kids I'd been hanging out with, and by kids I mean some were like 40 years old, but all were disabled. The last place we visited was the VTC - Vocational Training Centre, and the "kids" (young adults and adults) who actually lived in apartments would go there five days a week and make jewelry; like a job of sorts. The organization I was with (International China Concern) would sell the jewelry and then the money would go back to the kids to live, pay rent, eat etc... It was genius. It gave them purpose.

After the day of touring around, in the evening me, Tom and Justin hung out more. The best part at that time was that there were lots of street vendors. And we would buy meat on a stick. It was amazing! And cheap! Tom, for some reason I forget, put a 10元 bill in his mouth. Ha. What a guy. Surprised he didn't die from some weird disease... So gross.

Here's another insane thing. We saw a dog being trained for underground illegal fighting. It looked just like that mean dog Hector (I googled it) from the Looney Tunes. It had a huge torso, pure muscle. Like a body builder. It wore small dog socks tied around its ankles/feet, a huge muzzle, and was in a harness pulling a huge semi-truck tire behind it. Three men were walking beside it while it took up an entire lane of the two lane road. Zero effs given.

The next day I finally got to officially hang out with the young kids from The Lighthouse. We took them (more like they all took me) to the park. Chinese parks however have things like little trains, and mini rides for kids. We walked around. They even had a haunted house, which we went in, although I don't remember doing this. Thanks journal!

After that day, on the way home I found a shop and bought legit, actual ninja shoes. Well, maybe not ninja, but Kung Fu shoes. Still got em, somewhere in my room...

During my time in Changsha, one guy who I met was Allen. He was British, maybe about 60 years old, and I forget how long he'd been in China. He and his wife lived there, and had one of the floors in that government building I was talking about before. They had their own organization called 'China Kids' or something like that, I forget, but they basically took care of dying babies. That was their deal. One day I went to his house, and I got to meet one of these little junior nuggety babies. He said the baby was abandoned and would die soon. That's heavy man.

Another day, Justin brought me and Tom to The Lighthouse. There I went for a walk with Tan Pu. This little guy, maybe 12, wears a vest with all his information printed on it. Why you ask? Because he bolts any chance he can get. You watch him like a hawk, and that I did. He was a handful, but a good kid. Mischievous, but great. One time (or probably many times) they got a phone call saying he had got on some random bus alone... Anyway, near the point in the walk when we have to return and go back he dropped to the ground and refused to move. I then had to basically carry him back. A decent sized 12 year old. He had fun though, by the time it was over.... haha

After almost a month, I was in the groove, and had my schedule. Tuesday to Thursday I was going to The Lighthouse with the little kids in the AM, and the afternoon was the VTC with the older kids/adults. It was good. And Fridays I usually had Chinese lessons near downtown which wasn't super far away. Lots of what I did was hanging out. Just being with the kids and loving them. As it was, ICC (International China Concern) paid for Chinese workers, but of course, there's always a lot to do. So that's where I came in. My job was to make the kids feel loved as the workers were so busy. And I loved them already, so it was easy enough. Also, before Tom left back to Changchun me and him walked near downtown and got on this insanely huge ferris wheel together. It was pretty epic. Overlooked the entire city. Another side story, Changsha is where Mao Zi Dong grew up (or something) and they have this little island in the middle of the river with 'the worlds largest Mao head statue'. Yay?

At the VTC (where the older adults made the jewelry), Liu Mi was a character, and talked a lot of gibberish. She was/is downs, and the funniest girl I ever met there. She was always laughing and acting like a dog or whatever. And I joined in. Still to this day I almost never had as much fun as I did there with them. Another girl, Tang Xiaoni loved me and she was the best. She couldn't really talk, but thought I was hilarious. I would often help her make the jewelry as her hands didn't work super good, but the workers would always insist I let her do it. She was too cute not to help! The nice thing there was that the the workers there liked me more, and appreciated me more. The VTC was my favourite.

I should add too, that during the first month (and the next five) most of my time was spent with Justin and his family. His wife had a friend there named Samantha and she was over at their apartment often too. We all played Carcassonne a ton and watched movies a ton. And the best part, I didn't even mention yet! Xbox's are chipped in China, which means you can play pirated games, which means that for $1.00 CDN you can buy an $80.00 CDN game. And Justin, well he had them all. And we played a ton. One of my best memories was staying up until 3AM playing Rainbow Six. His wife was not impressed. Man, those were the days. Also, his eldest kid Tyson would stand and play xbox, only he'd be running all over the living room while in front of the TV. It was quite entertaining to watch.

Now, enter the infamous Chinese New Year, which at the time I knew zero about. Chinese New Year is usually around early Feb, and it was insane! Let me tell you. Justin brought me and the kids out to buy fireworks. Changsha, he told me, is a massive producer of fireworks for a lot of China. So we got a ton, for cheap. And I don't mean little ones like roman candles. I mean a box of like thirty large cylinders full of explosives. One super insane thing was just watching little kids, like seven years old, play with huge firecrackers. Justin told me lots of kids blew their hands off or got maimed from them, but since it was China and they lack any sort of foresight/safety it was common to see. We also saw kids all the time standing with their torso out the sunroof of the car while driving down the roads. Not the smartest. Especially since they drive so crazy in China.

Anyway, we bought a ton of fireworks. Then, when midnight came, we all went to the roof of the building. Since we lived in a large apartment complex, as most people do in China, we went up to the roof-top. So our view was of the entire city, 360 degree. Then it happened. Midnight came and it was like a war zone. If you've never experienced it, I don't even know where to begin. Imagine a city of seven million people all letting off fireworks on almost every rooftop for a straight hour. That's about it. It was insane. It never ended. Colours of all sorts exploding in every direction, everywhere! Pure and utter mayhem.

That week I met with Liz and Claire. Those are the two Aussie girls I talked about already who'd been there about six years. I had met them before for their Big Brother Big Sister programme, but I was having a hard time connecting with those kids. Of course my Chinese wasn't really useful after a month, so that didn't help. But it was still fun. We took them to Häagan-Dazs ice cream, and yes it was expensive as you can imagine. I forget the exact prices, but it was more than Canada I think. Anyway, you can't put a price on fun! And it was great. After, we played some games at their apartment.

So life in Changsha was going pretty good. It had its struggles, but overall, it was amazing. Having good friends helped a ton. One main struggle I was having was adapting to the new culture. Some things I loved, some I didn't, and some I began to hate. One funny thing that I really vividly remember was the first time Justin took me to the restaurant just across from the apartment complex. It was the first time I really saw/hear someone hork up an enormous loogie and just spit it onto the restaurant floor. It was gnarly. The other thing that was one of the main things to begin to bother me was the staring. My most dreaded moments were waiting for the bus. Because every time a bus would stop which wasn't the one I wanted, every single person on the bus would look out the window at me. I mean, like every single person. So, let me expand.

### Chinese Culture: Staring & Pointing

There's some cultural difference that I can let go as just 'cultural differences'. I don't expect it to be all the same. But there's a few things I think are rude no matter when or where you are. That is pointing and staring. I think this one is objectively rude mostly because if you're pointing and staring at someone, that someone most likely has a reason to be pointed and stared at. For example, if I had two heads. But the fact remains it's still rude to point out my two heads. Do you think I'm insecure about being so different? Of course. Anyway, I don't have two heads, but I am white, and it's basically the same thing in China, depending where you are. But also, with all of that being said, yes I understand that in their culture pointing and staring wasn't considered rude. Maybe it really isn't. Who am I to say?

As I mentioned, getting stared at annoyed me to death, and would end up being one of the main reasons for me leaving China. Now, maybe you're thinking "Get over it dude", but it wore super thin when you heard "foreigner!" dozens of

219

times *every single day* for seven years. Every day, always. *Always*. What made it worse was eventually knowing Chinese, and knowing all the things people were saying about you 'behind your back', as they assumed you didn't understand. Trust me, it really got me. It just never let up. I would even have parents tap their kids on the shoulder and point me out just so their kids could see me. I can't put to words how frustrating and relentless it was.

The best advice I ever got, which really helped me get through my time in China without killing people was from one of the Aussie girls. She said "No matter the situation, *you* choose how you will react". She knew how hard it was being White in China, so she told me that. And it really did help. Not always, but often. In the words of that Frozen chick, "let it goooooo!"

~

Anyway, after my first month I was feeling pretty alone, as you can imagine. It was great having Justin and his family, but I wasn't there 100% of the time. And being in a random city in the middle of China, across the entire planet from 'normality' was a hard adjustment. Especially, I remember hanging out with some of the kids. Maybe you think it was all sunshine and fun, but I would say most of the time I spent at The Lighthouse with the younger kids was hard as hell, and I often left discouraged and frustrated. If you've worked with disabled kids, you know how frustrating it can be to get punched and spit on all the time. Have fights break out. Have kids steal food from each other and break things. It kinda just never ends. So, it was hard. But I still loved it for the most.

So, the Lighthouse was hard. By the end of six months I often would skip going simply because it stressed me out too much and I was just losing my mind. It became so daunting even thinking about going and what may happen while I was there. Kids just have never ending energy, but I had very limited. Moreover, the workers usually ignored me as, I could tell, they saw me as more of a burden than anything. They had a well-oiled machine, and when I came it changed it up just enough to get them out of synch. I understood though. That's not to say it was all bad. I did have some mellow kids who I loved to chill out with.

Side story, as I remember it: I came into work there at The Lighthouse one day and all the kids were pointing out the window. Next door, just in the doorway of a convenient store was a dead body just lying there. It had a blanket over most of it, but still. As I hung out for the morning, I saw that it took a few hours for someone to come get it. I guess it was super bad luck for that store to have someone die in their entrance...

Anyway, the VTC was always amazing. And I never had a bad time there. It was great. Well, there was sorta one bad time. They had this one guy who was huge. I mean, not fat, but tall (like 6' 5") and pure muscle and he had some mental disability. Anyway, one day he just started freaking out big time, and all the workers were super scared (as they were all women). So I used my absolute zero knowledge to defuse the situation as best I knew how; yell and grab him. Probably/definitely not the best method, but it eventually worked, and we calmed him down. Honestly, if he tried he could have chucked me out the window. Although in China all, and I mean ALL the windows on every building in every city have bars (due to thieves climbing in they said) so he couldn't have. So that was a fun time.

By the end of February it was already beginning to get hot! I dreaded the coming months of heat. I spent lots of time studying Chinese on my own, and continued my weekly lessons. The basics of Chinese are actually not super hard to pick up. You get a few words and then a few more. The hardest thing was being able to listen and understand. That took a good year or more to get to the point where my brain could translate in real time. I heard Chinese, and my brain just knew the words. Same as hearing English. That's when I felt like I was really getting decent with Chinese.

The Big Brother Big Sister programme often went bowling. So that was fun. One thing I never did ever in Canada was bowl. My journal says I got a 125, but I can't imagine. I do remember getting a turkey or two though. Just, the worst part was watching the kids do bad, then be bummed. Here, I wrote a poem in my journal:

> Poo on your shoe
> Pee on your key
> Fart on your cart
> Barf on your poo

Profound eh? Anywho, one day Justin took me on a trip a few hours South, to the other city where ICC was working. What a difference! We went from legit city to countryside town. It was a nice change. Pretty ghetto though, and very dirty. I got to tour the orphanage there, which was fun. It was also way on the outskirts of town. After that, for dinner we went for pizza. And look! Banana pizza! No lie. Well, more yummy pizza came anyway, so I was happy. The only downfall of said "yummy pizza" was that I got mad sick and almost pooed my pants during the drive home. Puked a ton once I got back. China food eh. That also happened to me another time. I got fake KFC (on purpose, out of convenience sake) and I had insane diarrhoea for about ten hours straight. To this day it was the worst I ever had. And you're welcome for that story.

Moving on. China has this thing called 'English Corner', where the University students or whoever come to a designated place; a restaurant in this case, to practice speaking English. It was fun, but sometimes got a bit awkward. Mostly because some Chinese people want to immediately be best friends and share contact info. But for the most I had fun. On another English corner, I was trying to explain to some girls (who were asking me) that if I had a girlfriend, I'd like her to be a female version of myself. I feel like most people want that. Anyway, since their English wasn't very good what they heard was 'female virgin', not 'version', so I had to yell at Justin for help, because it was getting *super* awkward. It was about this time, visiting the Universities that I noticed something funny. It would be sunny out, but girls would have umbrellas. That's because in China, dark skin represents being poor, as only poor people (farmers) worked in the fields. White skin meant "rich", because you didn't have to be a 'lowly farmer'.

Vacation time. Here we go. So, Justin had his annual vacation, and decided to bring me (and the xbox) along. Best week of my life. But let's be begin at the beginning. We got on the train. Trains in China are so convenient and great, depending on what ticket you buy. Now Justin, being experienced bought the best tickets, which was a room with a door and two sets of bunks; four beds. We were even alone! The other options, which I did every other time in China was the open bunks, three to each (so six bunks). And finally, if you're poor or stingy, you can buy a seat.

I had one friend who took a 24 hour train ride in a seat to save a little money. What a nut job. Anyway, back to our amazing room. It was amazing, until at about 1:30AM some women came in, plopped down and fell asleep snoring like Zeus clapping the winds and summoning a storm to destroy worlds. I didn't sleep the rest of the night. Yay!

Back to the trains. The six bunk option was always hit or miss, but mostly miss and the odds of getting someone who snores/yells are greater. And that almost always happened to me. The nice part though, about trains, was that whenever I was on one, it was always to go somewhere for an adventure. So no matter what, it was always fun, even when it wasn't.

Well, we arrived in Guilin, and got a cab for an hour. One thing nice about China is the taxis are mad cheap. I forget what we paid, but it wasn't a ton. Maybe twenty bucks. Then we got to the famous and beautiful Yangshuo. What a place! So famous, you've probably seen pictures of it. A little village tucked away in the strange mountains that jutted up from the earth all around. Many small mountains everywhere.

Yangshuo is pretty touristy during the busy season, but while we were there it wasn't bad. We spent the week going around to a bunch of different nice little restaurants eating "normal" food (there were many 'western style restaurants' there) and playing a bit of xbox. One of the best things we did was rent scooters. It was pretty easy and again, pretty cheap. We went all over! Even got to see this place they call 'Moon Mountain', so that was cool.

We drove all around the country side too, and saw water buffalo in fields! The one funniest thing I ever saw in my life (literally my entire life) also happened while we were scootering around. I'm driving behind Justin, maxed out speed, cruising along the road when I see him lean down pretty hard, and at maximum speed run over a giant water buffalo turd. It exploded so so hard in every direction. I was absolutely dying laughing. Dying. I actually almost crashed my bike I was laughing so hard.

After a while it began to rain, so we quit, but that night got a massage. Always a massage. They're the best! The next day we decided to drive way up into the middle of the mountains. Just random roads here and there getting super lost on purpose. It was great. Here's another funny story. So in China there's often a set of cement stairs, but on the edge of the staircase there's about two feet of flat. I guess it's for driving motorbikes up. Which we did. Only, since I was an idiot, I lost balance, pulled the throttle and just turned and drove off of an eight foot cliff. Ha. Lucky I was wearing a helmet! Just kidding. It's China. We didn't have helmets. But I was ok. The bike; minor damage. Whoops.

Anyway, I got it sorted. We were laughing pretty hard. The bike was making a bit of a noise after that, but it worked, and got me back...

We also went to the 'Worlds Largest Outdoor Light Show'. It was epic, of course! We were seated on a small hill (in seats, not the grass), looking over the river, which was super large. And on the river, all the mountains were lit up, and boats came out with actors dancing, and there was music and it was insane! I think it has like 600 actors in all. Well, no matter, you had to be there. It was magical.

Here's some side notes. We found a rad Kung Fu school while on our scooters in the middle of nowhere. So that was cool. Didn't get to go in though. I think it was super legit and strict. I got some fake Prada sunglasses for ten bucks CDN, and almost hit a water buffalo while scootering down the road. Good times. Not much else to say about that trip. We mostly chilled out, played xbox, ate food and got rubs. Overall, it was an amazing week.

Back in Changsha it was life as normal. Did some work at The Lighthouse and VTC. Had some fun. One thing we did though is go to a movie theatre! My first time in China. Now, maybe your'e thinking 'who cares dude', but this was a VIP one! Here's how it went down. You pay for a ticket, which includes snacks and drinks. You go in, and the theatre room is smaller, and has just about twenty super large recliner chairs. HUGE! So cozy. And, we were the only ones in there. And the people working brought our snacks and drinks right to our chairs. And it was so weird to be in a huge Lazy-Boy in a movie theatre. In fact in my years after I never had that experience again.

It was April by now, and my new adventure would bring me back to Sanmenxia (where I went the first time to China)! I was going on another short term trip! Back to the train I went, only this time it seemed to have some problem. Every time it would slow down to stop, the cars would all slam into each other, which meant my entire body would slam into the wall. I didn't mention before, but the beds on the trains were thin, even for me. And I'm not a big guy. So for many hours (I want to say ten hours?) I just kept rolling and slamming into the wall every hour or so, when they'd stop at a station to get more people. Yay!

It turned out this team was only about seven people. So that was ok. Not many stories really. Just played with the kids. Was good to see them again, and I tell you, knowing a few words in Chinese went a *long* way. I also noticed the kids (and grandpas and grandmas) were behaved a little better. The good news was the government was building a new Welfare Center, so we got to tour it one day, and it was awesome. Really impressed with the government for really stepping up their game in regard to the 'orphans'.

Saw some camels on the street there too, so that was funny and super random. So here's the dodgy story I was talking about before. There was this dude, let's call him "Jim" for the sake of the story, who I got along with really well. One night I was like 'hey man let's go find a massage place, they rule in China', so we went walking. There's so many in every city, I figured we'd find one, and we did. So, now that I had some language skills I asked "how much?", and the counter girl said 100元 for both of us, which was super normal. So we went in.

The first thing I noticed was that the girls weren't dressed in the usual 'professional' and modest uniform you often see, but *much* sexier. The room we went into was empty, except for two beds and a poster on the wall of a guy and girl... you know, smooching naked. Weird. So we laid on our stomachs and started our massage. It wasn't good. Not really. So after a few minutes we hear a 'click' and look up to one of the other girls taking pictures while she giggled. This always happens, so it wasn't a big deal. Looking back, maybe it was, but whatever.

Anyway, not sure why, but the girls left the room for a minute. So I turn to Jim and am like "dude, I think this place isn't what we were looking for", and he agreed. Quickly we got up and begin to leave. I grab 100元 from my pocket and plop it on the counter while we non-stop walk out the door. Easy! But then, just as I am exiting the building there is some guy leaning on the wall just outside the entrance smoking and smiling, exactly like you'd imagine in the movies. He's wearing a sort-of suit, and is 'a good looking older gentleman'. He says something I don't understand and wants to shake my hand. So I kinda turn around, and reach out to shake it. Then he pulls me in for a kiss.

I tell you, when an old strange creepy Chinese man tries to kiss you, you gain level 100 ninja-like reflexes. My left arm came up faster than you could blink and I pushed him off. He was laughing. To be honest I was too. Then I told him "I like girls" while I laughed, and we scurried off into the darkness. I guess he thought since we didn't want sex we were gay. Haha. Fair enough. Anyway, we never told anyone about that. Maybe I shouldn't have even written it, but there it is. A super China adventure! #noragrets

So yeah, I spent two weeks there hanging out with all the abandoned people. This time however, since we were back for a second time, some of us got to go up to the second floor that we weren't allowed to before. ICC had built enough relationship with them that it was now ok. So I went up, and life changed.

I can almost guarantee you that you've never seen a baby so deprived of love that it gave up crying. Well, I did. That was by far the hardest thing I've ever had to witness in my life, bar none. A bunch of little fresh few month olds snuggled into a crib together staring at the ceiling, doing nothing. Never loved, never held. Well, we got to hold a few of them, and it was great. One baby had that disease where their bones break super easy. From the time he was born many of his bones had broken, but then, because no one really cared for him properly they had healed at all the wrong angels so his limbs were all bent. I think I held him. I also held 'peanut', the smallest baby to ever exist.

Anyway, I don't remember much else about that trip. It went fast, and was hard to leave the kids again. On the way back (and on the way there) I was traveling with two other people. One was a lady, about 45 years old, on our team in Changsha from Singapore. I didn't like her much to be honest. The other was a nice guy about 50 years old from Australia. Well, we decided to stop in at this other city on the way home called Luoyang. It's super famous in China for having an amazingly huge and beautiful garden with crazy flowers. Only it was April, and almost none of the flowers were in bloom. So that was kinda a bummer.

Then while we were walking around we met these random middle aged Chinese dudes. I guess because me and the guy I was with were foreigners they invited us out to dinner. This often happens in China, and it's not really weird to be honest. China was cool that way. The entire time I was there I met tons of random strangers and just hung out with them. Despite all my 'slander' against the Chinese, most of them are really friendly people. I had countless people invite me into their home for tea or meals or whatever. Here's an example. Fast forward about five years. I'm moving to another area, and standing in the road with a 48" TV flagging down taxi after taxi, but there wasn't many where I was. Then this guy pulls up in a super nice car and offers me a lift. I throw the TV in his back seat and he drives me forty minutes for free to where I wanted to go. Stuff like that was so legit. And it always happened. Ok, back to the story.

So me, the Singapore lady, the Aussie guy, me and the three guys have dinner at some outdoor place nearby. We ate, then we ate some more. The food kept coming. And then when I thought it was over, we moved tables, and more food came.... haha. It was insane times two. I'm also not sure we ate dog, or lamb. Whatever it was, it was amazing, so probably not dog. But there were dogs in cages over on the side. All in all it was about three hours. For real. After that we headed back to the train to Changsha.

Back it Changsha it was the usual. Worked a bit, went to English Corner just about once a week, played xbox and watched movies. By the end of April I was still stressed about going to The Lighthouse with the little kids. It was really hard on me. Looking back now, ten years later, it's obvious I had super high anxiety. I even had that in Vancouver before, but I couldn't put a name to it. And I still have it now.

I was still at Justins apartment almost every day hanging out with them and their kids, playing board games and xbox. They really got me though my time there. If it wasn't for them I would of had no friends and gone totally insane. I wouldn't have got out much, adventured anywhere or seen all the cool things. We sometimes went downtown too, which was pretty big time. In a city of 7 million, it's big. Oh one epic thing about China is the arcade. You know in Canada it's like $1.00 to play games now. in China it's so cheap, and since our money is (was back then) $1.00 to 6.5元 I was rich! So the arcade was always fun to go to and drop 20 元 and play forever. Then you win tickets, and buy toys!

As I read though my journal figuring out what you'd like to read, it's funny how many times I wrote about napping. If you know me, you know I love naps. But mostly because my body can't get through a day without one. It's crazy to think that I've been tired for more than ten years now. And incase you're wondering, yes I've been to the doctor here in Canada and in China many times to try to figure it out. I even went to a traditional Chinese doctor in Gui Yang, but I'll tell you about that later.

Here's one I remember even without my journal. There was this one girl I was hanging out with a little, for a little while. Nothing nefarious, don't worry. We were just friends. Honestly, Chinese dudes my age were kinda strange and awkward. Anyway, one evening we parted ways and I went to meet up with Justin and his family at a restaurant. Then about ten minutes later she calls me and asks how to get home. (She wasn't the smartest girl I ever met.) And so I was like "dude, I can't read Chinese, I don't know. *Why* would I know?" It was *so* weird. Like at that point I could speak some words of Chinese, but my reading ability was absolute zero. Anyway, I thought that was funny though I shook my head quite hard for some time afterwards.

By May the weather had turned, according to my journal; "mental hot". Yeah, I remember. You walk outside and you might as well have just dived into a pool. Sweat immediately would spew from every pour on your entire body like a fountain. I literally showered after every time I went outside. Go get noodles, fifteen minutes outside, shower. No matter what, shower.

Around this time Justin (who I also forgot to say was one of the main people with the organization here in Changsha) told me that I may not be able to get another Visa. You see, you need a reason to be in China, or at least a "skill". (That asshole at Missions Fest *WAS* right!) Well, it turned out that there was no way to extend my Visa or get another one. We tried some loop-holes, but it never worked out. So, at that point I was really bummed. It was kinda like, ok, now I don't know what I'm going to do with my life. I thought I'd go away forever and just stay, but now I have to go home with no clue about the future. Looking back, I really wish I could have stayed there longer, but life goes on.

While I was in Changsha I spent some time working on my second fantasy novel, which I have parts of still, but it wasn't really a finished idea. I think it was mostly an amalgamation of many ideas and I never actually started writing the actual book. But, during that time I did have a super strange dream, and that dream turned into a short story I wrote, which I still have, and it's amazing. I will add it at the end, if you'd like to read it. It's called 'The Alchemist and the Turtle'. It's an instant classic.

By the end of June I was sick of Chinese food. Go figure. Only 6.5 more years of the same thing! Anywho, May and June were more of the same. Nothing special to report except many naps and I think I was sick for a while. Let me quote my journal again. "I'm tired. Always tired. My brain feels soggy & heavy. My eyes are fuzzy balls, and my limbs wet noodles." Outside my apartment, in the 'common ground' or whatever it's called, were speakers. And every day they'd play some operatic Chinese music. It was super annoying. My journal says "It's shit!" Haha. And I do now remember it, and it *was* pretty bad. One day I got woken up by a marching band and fireworks.

Here's a note I have. "Yesterday a father and son pushed crippled people out of their way to get on the elevator before them." One thing that bothered me in China was the 'me first' mentality. So let's back it up.

**Chinese Culture: Mentality**

So from 1979 to 2015 there was, in China, what is called the 'One-Child Policy'. However, many rural families/minorities still were able to have two children, thus the name isn't exactly accurate. Read the Wiki if you want more info. I'll tell the basics, according to *my view*.

This One-Child Policy lead to what I like to call 'The Spoiled Brat Syndrome'. Since you were only allowed one child, that child got treated like a King or Queen in the family. From my time in China I saw many things, like parents holding the phone for their child while he ate and watched cartoons, or simply letting the child (ten years old mind you) hold the phone while the parents fed them. I saw a complete lack of proper discipline, and an excessive use of verbal and physical abuse. Even in the schools.

Also, more often than not the Grandparents would raise the child. Usually because to live both parents had to work. So you now had a new generation of kids with an old generation mindset raising them. It must have been very confusing for the children. Anyway, in all my years in China, I would say way over half of the kids I saw getting picked up from school or whatnot were by Grandparents.

So, with all that being said, I believe this led to children feeling entitled. They were basically being told 'you're special and more important than anyone else'. This is evident by the following:

-**Bus lines**. They don't exist in China*. People just push each other to get on. Nothing matters except 'self'. I saw seniors, disabled people and kids (often kids) get pushed and shoved out of the way almost daily. I was always last to get on the bus, not only due to this, but also because I never cared enough to push people out of my way. It was always an amusing adventure just merely watching people get on the bus to be honest.

[ *Or I should say 'most of China' as I did see a few times in bigger cities like Wuhan people lining up, but it was almost non-existent everywhere else I went. I'm talking, I saw lines like a handful of time only in seven years. ]

-**Fast food**. Ordering fast food in China is a nightmare. No one lines up. They just shove and yell their order at the cashier while waving money in their face. The cashier basically takes care of whoever is the most aggressive. I had many many times people just cut in front of me and order. This didn't always happen, but more often than not. The good thing was, I adapted, and did the same after a while. It worked out. (Story: I'm in Wuhan, at the train station KFC, with only a few people in front of me, so I wait. I get cut once or twice by people, but then it's my turn to order. Just as I'm about to, this dude just pushes in and starts talking to the cashier ordering food. So I snap. I hit the counter top super hard with my palm and yelled at him to 'line up' and that I've already been waiting to order. You can only get cut so many times before you snap. I didn't even feel bad.)

-**Trains**. Trains in China have designated seats, assigned to you when you buy the ticket. So there's never a reason to push to get on the train. But, of course, it happens. I had one time trying to exit the train. As soon as the doors opened to let us off people just started trying to come aboard. I could barely get off as I had about thirty people trying to push me aside to get in. I was very proficient in Chinese at this time, and yelled super hard at them to wait. I was genuinely mad. And they all laughed because 'a foreigner got mad'. You're not allowed to get mad in Chinese culture or you 'lose face'. I'll get back to that soon as it's like 50% of their culture.

Now, as I said, the correlation between the One-Child Policy and the 'me-first mentality' is definitely my own conclusion, although it makes sense. It was weird though, because as I said before, Chinese are very kind and friendly, so it was a very odd dichotomy. One that I never really figured out, although I do have hints. Here's one I got. When I was flying to China from Vancouver I was next to a nice Chinese lady. We got talking a little (although not much) and I told her I was living in Guiyang. This is like another five years in the future of the story but it's my story so there. Anyway, she says she's from Beijing, and that she didn't like the 'southern Chinese' as they are so uncultured and uneducated and rude and ignorant. Things like that. So I think a lot of the inability to line up springs from a mere lack of culture, or you could say a 'small town mentality'. I'm not sure the right word to use. China's economy and everything changed so much so fast that a lot of China had a hard time keeping up. Hence why you'd see poor people pulling fruit carts next to eighty thousand dollar Land Rovers, and why you'd also see said Land Rovers driving like idiots. Which leads to another kinda fun-fact.

-**Chinese drivers**. You've probably all heard the oft repeated stereotype "Chinese are bad drivers", and it's simultaneously true and not. Let me break it down. Here's what Justin told me, and I found it to be very true. If you're driving in China, there's two rules. One is, you yield to larger vehicles, and two is you yield to whoever is in front of you. So what happens is, there's no need to 'check your blind spots'. You just swerve where you want to go, and if there's a person behind/beside you, they swerve as well without looking. If there's a person near them, they swerve, and every one flows, turning this way and that dodging whoever in on front of them. (That's why when Chinese come to Canada, they are in fact "bad drivers" as they simply drive like they are in China.) So in China, when everyone drives the same it works, and I can honestly say they are actually really *good* drivers which is ironic. I mean, consider this. I was there seven years and very rarely saw a crash. So to fix the stereotype, it should be 'Chinese are great drivers, unless they drive in Canada like they do in China, then they are bad drivers'. Another fun fact I heard (but the Chinese people I asked said wasn't true) was that if you put your seatbelt on in a taxi the drivers get offended as it means you don't trust their driving.

**-Chinese pedestrians**. There's not much to say except Chinese people walk like they drive. Aimless, random, and without any consideration. But to be fair, most people were like this in Vancouver though too so...

Ok, so back to the One-Child Policy, this was interesting. I met a lady who got pregnant with her second child. She "divorced" her husband and "married" another guy she knew. Of course all this was merely on paper, and legal. She actually continued to live with her real husband and kept the second child. This was to avoid the fine of having two kids. I think she said it was about 250,000元 ($25,000CDN) I think. Something like that. Maybe more or less. It was a lot though.

I knew another girl who basically just never told the government she had the kid. I heard there were many 'unregistered' kids in China. And with being unregistered, you basically can't survive in a normal society. You need ID to do *everything* in China. Not sure what ever happened with her. Anyway, the One-Child Policy is super interesting, and there's a ton of info on the internet about it. I don't wanna bore you and just copy stuff, so I'll leave it there. Do more research if you're curious.

~

Moving on, I had a few days left before I went back to Canada. Leaving there was so hard. The VTC had a little party for me, and I cried a ton. Looking back, that was by far the hardest time of my life as far as emotions go. It was so so hard. The drive to the train station was mostly silent with Justin. We said our good-bye and I thanked him for everything. Then I got the fast train (which goes over 300k/h) to Shen Zhen and crossed the boarder via bus into Hong Kong. There was a guy I met in Changsha who lived in Hong Kong, so I got a taxi to his place and stayed with his family. As we were driving I saw the meter going up and up. Finally it passed how much money I had. Luckily my buddy covered me once I arrived and it worked out. Anyway, the next day, went back to the airport and flew home. Six months gone. Life changed forever.

The last story for this chapter is this: While coming back home through the Vancouver airport I was searched. They even took my laptop from me and plugged it into some other computer. The guy explained that they'd had people go to China to "teach" or "do volunteer work", but in actuality they were making child porn. Needless to say, my computer came up clean and I was free to go! I stayed in Vancouver for a while and met some friends. Blah blah blah.

# Chapter 3: Canada - 11-ish Months

Well, here's the short story of Canada. I went home to live with my parents in BC. I spent months floating aimlessly through life, and during that time I was trying to figure out a way to get back to China. Through a series of events, I had an old friend contact me and say he found me a job teaching English at a middle school. It was only six hours from Changsha which meant I could visit my old stomping grounds! So that sounded cool. All I needed was to do the TESOL (Teaching English to Speakers of Other Languages). So I was able to do that. Two weeks for $2000. I think I was home almost a year, summer 2010 to summer 2011, when I flew back to China to teach English!

# Chapter 4: Huangshi, China - 1 Year + 1 Year

Alright, well, I'm out of journal entries so the next few years worth are straight up from my memory. Let's see how much I know... Again, this will be a sporadic timeline.

I flew to Detroit airport, and I tell you, I've never seen so many black people. It was so strange for me; I'm from Canada eh. (Maybe I should have remembered that moment when all the Chinese people stared at me, but I didn't.) Anyway, I met some people there and we got a bus to Spring Arbor, near Jackson in Michigan. There I met up with about twenty other people who would be also traveling to China to teach. The backstory is this: basically a nice lovely American couple had set up this organization where they found teachers for Chinese schools and the Chinese schools would pay them. Like a finders fee. The one reason it worked was because this American couple had been in China and built up some good Guanxi (relationships). Moreover, they had integrity, and everyone loves people with integrity. So this couple would find other like-minded and hardworking people to work in China. It was great.

We hung out for a day or two and had a meeting, getting filled in on what our job would entail etc... I met my future room mate who turned out to be super super awesome. Couldn't have asked for a better dude. He was my age almost exactly, super mellow, made hiphop and was a male model. Anyway, we got along super good and would end up hanging out the entire time we were in Huangshi teaching together. Finally we all went back to Detroit and flew to China.

Flying across the entire planet wears you out. By the time we were on our last plane we were basically drunk on lack of sleep. I've never been that tired in my whole life. We were on the last plane to Wuhan just haggard, slurring words, laughing like idiots and just off our rockers. Once in Wuhan me and my buddy Aaron got picked up in a van towards our new life. Huangshi was about an hour south. The population then was about 700,000. (Wuhan was about 7.5 million.) We met our waiban - foreign boss, aka Chinese teacher who would take care of us while we were there. She was great, and did so much for us during our stay. Got a bank account, phone number, did all the paperwork blah blah blah and got settled into our new apartment, which the school paid for. They also paid for our plane tickets, and we made 5000元 a month, working a total of eight hours a week. Score.

So the schedule was we both had 12 classes a week, 40 minutes each class. I decided to take grade seven and Aaron took grade eight. It worked out. Our apartment was furnished, and pretty huge. We did however have to clean it. I wiped everything three times it was so filthy. It was seven stories up, with no elevator. I heard that there was a law that in China if the building was eight stories or more it could have an elevator, but if seven or less no elevator. Something like that. Could have been nine floors, I forget. But we went up that staircase a hundred million times over then next two years. It was also right on a busy street, and the honking in China is constant. *Constant* I tell you! Thus, after a few months, we requested that new windows be installed to block out the noise level. One day when we got home, there were new windows! Only, they'd just basically put the new ones in front of the old ones. So we had double windows. Well, it worked, so we were happy.

A few things that were cool was that the girls who taught at the school previously left me some old lesson plans, so that helped me get started. To be honest, I had zero clue what I was doing. So we got the book we were supposed to teach and the fun began. But before I get into the insane experience of teaching a sardine can classroom of 50-60 kids I'll tell you this fun fact. There are many many jobs that hire you simply for being white. I had a few, which I will tell you more about later. Our job at *this* school was for Mianzi mostly.

### Chinese Culture: Mianzi (Face)

Remember I said Guanxi (relationships) were one of the most important things in Chinese culture? Well, Mianzi (面子) is second. And we were at this school to make the Headmaster look good. Speaking of the Headmaster, everyone hated him. I guess he thought he was the greatest person in the city. Ego the size of a football field. All the teachers I worked with hated him, and he'd make them all sit through meetings for hours and talk about how amazing he was. Our waiban (foreign boss) lady Sophia told me this story. As a Chinese teacher, she didn't make much money. She worked more than full time for less money than us, who worked eight hours a week. Well, she needed a new laptop and bought one. I guess the headmaster came into her office one day and saw it and basically told her it was garbage. Just crazy.

Anyway, we were the white guys he got to show off like three times a year. It proved to others that *his* school (and in turn him I suppose) had money, which was very important. Otherwise, the school didn't really *actually* care about what we taught. Let me explain.

The kids (middle school kids) had class Monday to Friday, 8AM-5PM. But they had to be at school around 7AM. They had tons of homework, and never had any time for fun. High school was worse. I think it was about 7AM-10:30PM, and a half day Saturday morning and a half day Sun afternoon. They had to work hard for good grades, as the school would post each students grades publicly after every semester. So to have bad grades is to have bad mianzi, which was the worst thing that could happen to you in China.

Speaking of Mianzi, I'm just going to throw two stories in here as they take place years later and at two separate times, but pertain to this. One was, one day me and Aaron were out with our waiban boss lady and some business people she knew. Of course it was drinking time, only Aaron had a life rule (which I entirely respect) to never drink ever. Well, that didn't go over too well as all the men there were pressuring him to drink and he would *not* compromise. The main

235

thing about this whole 'you must drink culture' for me was they way they'd pressure you. We heard so so many times "you're not a man if you don't drink". Me and Aaron would say 'we don't care dude'. That meal he almost walked out. The other time was when I was at University with some people my age and again, pressure to drink. This time, I walked out. I was over it. Ok, on to high school. (One last Mianzi story: Chinese people would never admit they didn't know something. It meant they'd lose face. It was also sad to see the kids afraid to try to speak English. They were scared if they said something wrong people would laugh.)

## Chinese Culture: High School

High school in China is *extremely* important. Like I just said, they go to class seven days a week, and have a ton of homework on top of that. I heard about kids doing homework until 1 or 2AM many nights. Many even lived at the school. They study so hard that their last year, grade 12, is *entirely review*. At the end of grade 12 they take a test that is so important most of China shuts down. There are even noise restriction laws, and this test will determine almost the rest of the students life and career. If you want a good University (which you do) you need to get good grades. You must get a good job to make good money to get good Mianzi. Money is god in China.

And the competition is fierce. Some of students end up killing themselves from stress. If they can't get good enough grades, their parents may beat them or whatever. The stress is so great my buddy had students in grade eight with grey hairs. The pressure to succeed was maximum.

~

So with all that being said, *my* class was the one chance the kids had during the week to slack off. I didn't give an exam, or tests, or homework. I just went in, taught some stuff and left. It was fun. Of course, due to this the kids let loose pretty hard. The first year was super rough, learning how to discipline and teach properly. You had to choose your battles, which took me a while to learn.

Ok, let's back up. I forgot to mention I flew to Wuhan with five other Americans. Two were super rad chicks from Louisiana who were about five years younger than me. They were teaching at a high school. There was another girl who was teaching at a middle school, and a nice couple teaching at another high school. The rest of the team was in Wuhan at various Universities and high schools. The people I was with were cool, and we often all met up and do fun stuff; walk around the city, eat food or whatever. The one fun (if it could be called that) thing to do in China when you don't know Chinese is order food. You see, without knowing how to read Chinese, you can't really know what you're ordering. So when me and Aaron went out we'd do what most foreigners do, just point at items on the menu and hope they are good. Most of the time they weren't.

Oh, one funny (to me) story was the one girl I traveled to Huangshi with got her luggage lost, and she didn't get it back for about three weeks I think. She had one set of clothes. So she had to find some clothes in China to wear, which wasn't easy being a foreigner. Foreign girls are slightly 'larger' than Chinese. But she wasn't even big. A normal size girl. But the Chinese clothes were still small and awkward for her to buy.

Anyway, teaching was tons of fun, for the most. Like I said, the first year was quite hard though. Just learning the best ways to go about things. For example, if you're learning a new language, I bet one of the first things you will want to know is the bad words. It's the same for twelve year olds. So the first few times the students said 'fuck you!' while laughing I snapped. Of course none of them had a clue how bad it was. I got really mad a few times. One time I made a kid stand at the back of the classroom looking at the wall as a punishment. The worst part was his homeroom teacher came in and basically beat him in front of the class. I felt so bad. So, I learned to let it go. By the second year I learnt how to *teach* the 'offensiveness level' of bad words. I'd write some on the board, and ask "how bad do you think this is out of 10?". More often than not the students didn't know how bad some words were. Some students even asked "teacher, what's the worst word in English?", but I never told them. That's all I needed eh. The kids telling their parents 'today we learned the worst words in English'.

Another thing I let go the second year was phones. I had a few times trying to 'take away' kids phones that turned into a disaster. So I just told them I don't want to see them. I had a set of rules. That was one. Anyway, I'm getting ahead of myself. My first year teaching was fun, but hard. I had twelve classes, and there a few who were legit strife. With one I had to make a deal. I said "you listen for ten minutes, and then for thirty minutes we can watch whatever on the computer". This worked. It was that or forty minutes of pure death. All the classrooms had projectors, so that was rad. It helped.

The classrooms were filled, front to back with little wooden desks, and there was usually three rows of three, to the back wall. My biggest class was about 65 kids I think. Smallest maybe 25. But most were about 40-50 kids. One other story from second year was, I often would kinda bug kids if they weren't listening in class. It was never malicious, but sometimes was perhaps over the line. One girl was doing her homework while I was teaching, which I usually didn't care about. So I decided to scare her a little. I crept up to her desk like Ace Ventura and slammed my fist down on her desk.

Unfortunately for me, my fist was too close to her glasses case and snagged the edge, opening up my hand. Blood just poured out, although I didn't notice. Then one of the girls told me "teacher, your hand has blood". I just wrapped up in some tissue and kept teaching. To be honest they were one of my favourite classes. I also had many many students ask "teacher, who is your favourite singer?" I always found that funny as in Canada it's usually 'who is your favourite *band*?" And if you're wondering my answer, I usually told them Dallas Green.

What else can I say? I might as well blend in the two years...as my brain can't separate them. The second year, the one couple I was working with left, but another came, and they had a baby girl! The two girls from Louisiana also came back, as did my room mate Aaron. Aaron was rad, and since I had a bit of Chinese language by then he relied on me a little for some things. We often went out to get KFC, which was like five minutes walk away. He also went to the gym almost every day. It was, I think about 500元 for the ten months, which was about $100 CDN. I got a membership, but literally only went about five times. The funniest thing was Aaron had to literally *teach* them to spray and wipe down the exercise machines. He said they'd legitly just workout, sweat all over and walk away. Also, some people smoked while they worked out.

Random memories include: there was a show at the gym, where all Aarons muscle buddies wore little undies, put oil on themselves and flexed while techno music played. There was about one hundred people there. At one point, the greased up muscle men came over to the girls from Louisiana and asked them if they wanted to touch their muscles. It was *so* awkward; and they didn't. Here's the

238

one thing that sucks about hanging out with a good looking dude, especially when you're not particularly good looking. All the girls liked him. One girl even told us straight up "if I was going to date one of you I'd choose Aaron". I guess that leads to this...

### Chinese Culture: Straight talk, and non-straight talk - Part 1
### -Honesty on steroids-

One thing that bothered me a lot was the way Chinese were super blunt about some things, and never straight forward about other things. For example, that chick above. There were countless (countless I tell you) times where people told me all my physical shortcomings. The most common one was "your head is too small". I had strangers on the street tell me this. Or 'your nose is big' or 'you have a pimple'. It's like "yeah I know these things, thanks". So that was always hard for me. And then of course, when you want them to be blunt, they aren't. If it's ever anything like planning or whatever, they will say a hundred words without saying their actual answer. The most round about way. Like my buddy said, "they have ten ways of saying yes in order to say no".

~

Where was I? I don't even know. Teaching was good. My schedule was split as well, so some days I had one class, some I had two to four. It just depended. The second year, a new couple came (from America) and they had a small kid, I want to say 1.5 years old, named Leila. Anyway, if I thought that I got stared at lots before, it was nothing compared to the Chinese people seeing a cute little white baby with curly blonde hair. And I must say, the parents were better about it than I would have been. So often grandmas would literally just reach into the stroller without warning and try to pick the baby up. Of course she was strapped in, so it never worked. It was crazy to just see strangers grab at her. But Brad and Dana usually obliged and would let the grandmas hold her for a while. They were basically famous.

I also celebrated my 30th birthday there with them as well. We went this this sushi restaurant, which was mediocre at best, but for the town we were in, it was amazing. The irony is, the best sushi I had in Vancouver was made by Chinese people. Anyway, it is a memory I still have to this day.

Also, I guess I should go back to first year, sorry. The girls who left me lesson plans also left me a note that said: Call our friend Dawn, she's cool. So I called this random Chinese girl. She ended up becoming a long time friend, and we all did lots with her. She even opened her own bakery shop, which we helped renovate. She named it after our friends baby, Leila: Leila's Bakery. And it was, like many shops in China, just set up in a shopping mall illegally. Just pay the rent and here's your hole in the wall. It was great though. We hung out there lots and had yummy food. I still talk with her to this day, though not often as I would like. I should also kinda reiterate, Brad and Dana (with their baby), the Chinese girl Dawn, the two girls from Louisiana, me and Aaron hung out all the time. We were super close during that second year. And having all them there, I mean *actually* cool people that I genuinely loved to be around was a life saver. There was also a super super amazing family from America Dawn introduced us to. They we an 'older'-ish couple, who had adopted three girls. One was American, and the other two Chinese. They were all about 9-12 years old then. So that was really nice too, knowing them. We had a good crew that second year.

During that time (the second year) we would randomly go to Wuhan. The first year we took the bus, which wasn't ideal. And on the way back, we just would go stand on the highway and wave it down, then hop on. The second year Brad (the guy with the baby) had access to a van, and got his licence, so he drove us. This one time I was craving McDonalds. Our city didn't have one, I heard because the mayor offended the boss of McDonalds or something, so he said "you don't get a McDonalds". There's the Guanxi acting up eh. So we traveled an hour plus to get McDonalds, and when we arrived they said "we're out of burgers". Can you believe it? I mean, I can. It's China...

That also happened at Pizza Hut once. We went and they said "we're out of pizzas". I told them their name was literally 'Pizza Hut'. Actually, when Pizza Hut opened, the second year I was there, we (me, Aaron, Brad & Dana and Dawn I think) decided we'd join the hype and wait in line. It was winter-ish, and cold. It took about an hour and a half. Needless to say, it's Pizza Hut, so it was definitely not super amazing. Anyway, back to Wuhan. We would sporadically go and meet up with all the other foreigners, sometimes have little parties, or go to the local Church for foreigners. There was usually about 80-100 people attending. The problem with Wuhan is, if you wanna get somewhere, it's an hour *minimum* on the bus, if not more. So we usually got taxis if there was less than five people. One time on the bus in Wuhan one evening I was sitting near the back, and some drunk dude legit just puked on the floor and passed out. We all moved forward and opened the windows, but the whole bus still smelled like barf. Yum!

The other girl I mentioned who had her luggage lost finally got it returned to her. Thankfully. Although, the one problem she had was Chinese girls don't use tampons and she was a little distraught. I guess they only use pads in China, referred to as "bread" as they resemble slice of bread I guess. Anyway, enough about that. Actually, side note, randomly, girls would tell me they are having their period. I guess it wasn't weird to say that in China. Needless to say, I thought it was mad awkward. So the middle school she was at had an old guy for a waiban (foreign boss) who worked there. The best old Chinese man ever, named William. We became good friends and I hung out with him a lot over the years. He was great, and his Guanxi was unequaled. He literally knew everyone. So since he had some pull, I asked him about the local orphanage/Welfare Centre. He knew a lady from the news, and she knew the boss. So me and Aaron met up at the entrance one day and got to go in. It was awesome. We hung out for a few hours, brought them a ton of toys and then left. I tried to get back in, but I guess the boss thought it was more of a one time thing. Whenever I talked with her asking to come back there was always a million words just to say no. But it was cool. And the kids there were super fun. I wish I could have gone back.

William also made his own Hongjiu, which I guess would translate to 'red alcohol'. Imagine vodka but like, much much stronger. Like 80% alcohol strong. He said the Chinese use it medicinally, which I think was true. But they also used it to get hammered, which happened a few times. He was also one of the Chinese people who enjoyed teaching me (and my buddies) about Chinese culture, so it was always great to hang out with him. One time I did a 'cheers' (Ganbei which translated to 'dry cup' in Chinese) and then put my cup down. He said you can never do that. If you Ganbei you *have* to drink after.

The other funny thing he taught me is that I can never say 'maybe' when it comes to planning things. I must say 'yes' or 'no'. But it's best to say yes, even if it's a maybe. Then if I can't make it just bail last minute. I thought that was weird, but that's how it was. So I always just told him 'yes', and then often would just bail. Not on purpose. Just life happened. And he didn't mind.

During those two years in Huangshi I took to using Instagram. Back then it wasn't blocked. I also became infatuated with hunting down abandoned buildings in disrepair, and, since there's zero safety precautions in China I could just walk anywhere I wanted. I began to make it my mission and I took *tons* of pictures. It became my hobby and obsession. And without a word of a lie, I think I walked 90% of every road in that entire city. I went to every alley and every street. Every nook and cranny looking for good pictures. I went out almost for the entire second year I was there, searching for cool stuff. And I found a ton. I also managed to get featured on Instagram, and in 48 hours received 20,000 followers! (That went down over the years to about 13,000, but I think even then, most of them were bots.)

When my mom visited I also took her around to some of the cooler places I found. One was an abandoned hospital and a hotel. She was stoked. The only thing was finding human turds in some of these places. Oh well, I took pictures of some of it! Mom visited twice actually. But that's a story for later.

I also found a few places to get good massages in Huangshi. Although I will say one thing. It was hit and miss. The girls they hired I highly doubt were trained professionally. So you sometimes got one who was good or one who was bad. One time we and Aaron went in, and the girl doing me was just talking with us the whole time. That happens, and it doesn't bother me too much, but the fact is I do go there to relax.

Anyway, her massage was similar to something a three year old would give you. She was rubbing my arms and shoulder with 0.0001 pounds of pressure. So I told her, do it harder. She did for about thirty seconds, then just stayed on my arm. She didn't move around. She was just talking and wasn't focused. I finally snapped and told her to go away. When we left I paid for half a massage and told the boss that was the worst I ever had. Arg. The secret was going to the blind people. They gave the best rubs. I didn't find that out until a few years later though, sadly.

I'll tell you one thing I only recently learned about myself. Well, more like, I can now put a name to what I have. It's call high anxiety and panic attacks. I had this since I lived in Vancouver. I would randomly get panic attacks and literally just bail in the middle of hanging out with friends. They all thought I was an asshole. But I couldn't help it. Now I know what it was. Well, that's been part of my life until now, and still very much is. So at times, teaching for me was a *real* nightmare. I can't even tell you how nervous I got before each class. And I had many other jobs too, most of which were worse than my middle school. It was extremely hard to deal with.

During my time two years in Huangshi, I still managed to get down to Changsha back to the orphanage. The bus ride, I tell ya, was often an absolute nightmare. For one, it had no toilet, and I pee a *ton*. One time I had to pee so bad I whipped out my weiner while sitting in the seat and tried to go in a water bottle. I was near the back, and no one could see. But I didn't want to pull my pants down too far. After a few minutes, due to the angle of said weiner and precarious location in the bus, I ended up not going. Dang it! Well, they did stop once after 3 hours...

One day the school me and Aaron worked at was having some sort of ceremony. We were up front, on a stage, with all the other teachers. The kids were all seated on the ground. The school was shaped like an oval, with the school being the outside walls, and the inside being the courtyard/basketball courts. Anyway, the P.A. cut out, and the Headmaster basically was just shouting. Of course no one could hear him and no one was listening.

Now, about the city. Huangshi was an awesome city. It had a lake where you could rent little pedal boats. It was super beautiful, and the walkways were all lit up in the evenings. Classic China style. One night while walking I passed by a grandma for her evening walk. She was holding a walkman, old school, with a built in speaker. The music she was listening to, basically Dragonforce. I swear to you. I laughed so so hard.

Down the road from our apartment was a market, where I often went to buy cheap crap. Always was looking for more ninja shoes... There was also a nice little meat market near us. During winter solstice (fall) they would sell dog meat, aka dead dogs, skinned and hung up by their jaws with their chests cut open. Gnarly. We had a veggie market near our apartment too, where I became pretty good friends with the people selling veggies. Because I spoke Chinese we were always chatting a ton. I ended up buying from a different person each time. I told them I'd have to make it fair haha. I felt bad just buying from the same person. Especially since I bought a ton of veggies all the time.

Another usual sight in Huangshi we saw was ladies with little kids, often babies begging for money. They were dirty and looked poor, but many Chinese people who I knew said they were cheaters. They would rent the baby and use it to gain sympathy in order to get more money begging. Not an ideal situation. (You may have heard about the story where a little girl got hit my a car, and was laying in the road dying while people just walked on by and were thinking 'who wouldn't help someone like that?', and I'll tell you who. The people who didn't help are the same people afraid of what could happen if they do. You see, due to the substantial amount of scammers in China, people are afraid to help. I never witnessed it, but have seen many videos on the internet of people punching a car hood, then throwing themselves on the ground pretending to be injured. People will fake an injury, then when you go to help them they accuse you and you may have to pay tens of thousands of dollars. So, it's not that Chinese people don't *want* to help, it's that they're *scared* to because if they do, and they get involved with a scammer, they could lose everything. Look up 'the broken vase scam' if you want to know more. )

Under our apartment, under the cement stairs on the first floor, in a small maybe 7" x 15" area lived an older couple who sold stuff like drinks or snacks or whatever. I'm not even sure what they did but they were always busy doing something. And in the alley where our main entrance was were many small tables with many Chinese men smoking and playing card games. It was a form of gambling, and I heard lots of them did that for a job. So crazy. And they were there almost every day of the year except the two weeks for Chinese New Years. or when it rained a ton. There was also a sort of "arcade" with games you could win money. I also heard people just played them as a job too. A form of gambling, but not a casino.

Another nice thing was the street vendors, although as time went by China clamped down on that whole thing, and there were basically none after a few years. But anyway, back in 2011 there was. And these guys, a father and his two sons sold 'bing', which was basically flat bread. We called it 'trash can bread' because most of them sold it from an actual barrel. One has sugar in it, and the other salt and chives. They were great and mad cheap. We also had a little super ghetto Lamian (pulled noodle) shop next to the school entrance. When I say ghetto, I mean exceptionally ghetto. It wasn't what I'd call an 'official' Lamian shop, so their noodles weren't the best. Plus they didn't have many options. Basically just noodle soup. I literal hole in the wall, and so so dirty. Beyond gross walls. But it was great despite all that.

One other funny story was, one day in Wuhan, I guess there was some sort of explosion (or something), and a power plant (or something) was leaking bad air. But we didn't hear about this, and one night when it was "foggy" I wanted to go adventuring for some good picture opportunities. I guess the "fog" had floated down to us. Anyway, we went out, and noticed that no one was around, and the few that were had face masks on. It was curious. Then we began to smell the air, and realized it wasn't fog, but some chemical smell. We bailed on the photo session and just went to KFC for a bit. Then we went home.

Anyway, on the way to school just outside our alley I would often see deaf people hanging out. So I befriended them and began to learn Chinese sign language. The one problem I faced was that, just like spoken Chinese, the deaf also have dialects. Let me tell you what I know. I lived in Huangshi. Forty minutes south there was a different dialect and one hour north there was a different dialect. Basically, almost every city and town I visited had their own unique dialect, and I visited about fifteen cities in China. For example in normal Chinese "what are you doing?" would be 'gan shen me?'. In another dialect it would be 'gao mo si?', or another 'gao na yang?'. So you can see how Chinese gets pretty hard after a while. You have people speaking an entire different language while you're trying to learn Mandarin (translated as the "common language" in Chinese). Sign language was the same!

But hanging out with them was fun. I didn't do it super often, but when I did the one guy who I befriended always was asking me if I wanted to marry girls that walked by. Haha. If they were pretty I usually said yes. It was fun. This was all due to my very limited vocabulary (about twenty words) so our conversation was mostly limited to 'yes or no' questions. I lost contact with them over the years though, which still bums me out to this day. I was also forced to leave behind my Chinese sign language books when I moved home in 2018 mostly because I didn't have room in my two huge suitcases, backpack and box. Oh well.

Well, the first year went by pretty fast. I learned a lot, had some rough times in class, but most of it was amazing. As I said before, the school paid for our flights home. Sooooooo, I thought 'I might as well go to England' this summer instead of Canada. The ticket price was the same, and my boss (the teacher who was cool, not the Headmaster) didn't care so she booked me. That summer I spent a month in England. The best part was I stayed for free everywhere because I knew a bunch of people from my 2009 trip to Sanmenxia and my six months in Changsha. I went to London, Croydon (south of London), Exeter, Bath, Derby (and visited Nottingham), Newcastle (which was amazing!), visited Edinburgh and stayed a night in Glasgow. It was a month of pure fun. My friends even took me to see a bunch of castles, two of which were where they filmed Harry Potter. It was legit as it gets.

After England I flew back to Huangshi for a second year. I know I already mentioned some second year things, but whatever. Here I go. I was back. This time, the one girl who had her luggage lost stayed in America. The two girls from Louisiana were back again, as well as that rad couple Brad & Dana with the baby (who were from North Carolina). That year was much much better than the second, For one, I had a year under my belt teaching, which meant it would be easier and better. I knew what worked and what didn't. The games I played in class were better, I was more confident, and relaxed. Like I said, I let lots go the second year, and it was much better.

Aaron also stayed another year too! So that was great. I think given the fact we had two new cool people life was better. We all got along really really well. And like I said, Brad had the van, so we had some good trips to Wuhan. For Chinese New year (in around Jan/Feb) I went back to Changsha to see all the kids! It was great, although I'm not gonna lie. I literally don't remember any of it except walking into the VTC and everyone yelling my Chinese name because they were so stoked to see me.

Now, I mentioned before that you could be hired in China just for being white. One job I got was for this bank, who was having some sort of party/ceremony. It was mostly people in a big room, sitting in chairs with a stage. I'm not really sure even what it was, but I got paid to sit around for three hours. It was easy. During that time too, we met someone who knew someone, I forget it all by now, and they opened up their own coffee shop made of shipping containers. We went a few times. The cool thing was they had a little audio booth setup, like a small recording studio. I never got to use it though.

So, the second year flew by and I had tons of fun. The goal of the second year was to save money. After the first year of teaching, one lady from Texas who taught in Wuhan, Melodie, decided to move to Guiyang to take over this foster care for an elderly Dutch couple who'd been there about ten years already. So I decided that after the second year I would move down there to help. The story went like this.

Me and Aaron had some time off and wanted to visit Guiyangto help Mel out for a few days. So we booked the tickets, but the annoying part being a foreigner and buying train tickets is that in order to acquire them it's much more trouble. All Chinese have an ID, and it gets them everywhere. For us, we had to line up with humans, as opposed to the quick-and-easy machine, and wait. Then when we got to the window, they rarely knew what to do. We gave passports and waited. That's ideally, but this time Aaron didn't bring his passport. What a guy.

Luckily I had a picture on my phone of his passport. We went to a place to print it, but I had to somehow transfer it to the print shop guy from my phone. After I added the owner on QQ (the 'Facebook' of China) I finally managed to send it to him. After it was printed we had to go back to the line up and wait. Finally we gave the passport and the phone to the clerk, got our tickets, raced through the gate and sat on the train. Literally one minute later the doors closed and we departed. So, we arrived at Mels, had some fun, and I decided shortly after that I wanted to move there. After that, I went back to Canada for the summer.

# Chapter 5: Guiyang Foster Care - 1.5 years

This time going to China, my mom came. We went to Huangshi first for a few days, and stayed in my old apartment. It was empty as they hadn't managed to find any more teachers for that year, so we did have to clean it. A year without cleaning in China is about ten years of *not* cleaning in Canada. For real, the dust was gnarly. Mom, needless to say, *loved* China. I showed her all around Huangshi, and even went to some abandoned buildings together. She met some of my friends there, and we had some nice meals. The one old guy William I knew from before invited us to his house too, which was really nice. She also loved the food and we visited Shanghai, but I forget if that was at the beginning or the end. Anyway, it was fun too.

Anyway, we took the train to Guiyang to start my new life helping Mel. The fast train goes over 300 kph, and is smooth as butter. It was cool. When I arrived, it was one of those 'hit the floor running' situations. It was pure work, from 6AM to 'evening', whenever that came. The nice part was we had the guest apartment, which helped. In said apartment, we met another volunteer, Kandice, who would be my best friend while I was there. She was legit as it gets and we hung out a ton. Mom was there for about two weeks-ish. One funny story with mom was, Mel took us to this famous waterfall. But the drive took a while, and by the time we walked through the giant garden and got to the million stairs down to see the waterfall we didn't have time to look. We just looked at it quickly from a distance, then left and sped home to deal with more stuff.

So the days, at that time, went kinda like this: we would get up at 6AM and go to Mels apartment and get up the ten babies, change them, and feed them. Once they were up the Ayis (阿姨 - ayi = auntie. A common term for women in China) would come, around 7 or 8AM, I forget. Mel had, I think, two Ayis in her apt, and about 2-3 for each other apartment. She paid them 100元 (20$ CDN) a day. At that point she had:

2 Cars
15 Ayis (aunties)
1 Guest apartment
Mels apartment (10 babies and Yamei, a funny girl I'll tell you about soon.)
4 Apartments with kids (separated by disabilities.)

1 "Fun" apartment. (It had a trampoline, and the people below hated us. When I arrived the fun apartment was also the apartment where the two ladies cooked all the meals for the kids. And by all, I mean dinner. Breakfast was oatmeal, and sometimes something else. The babies had bananas and peanut butter. My literal nightmare, if you know me. For lunch, each apartment had a bread maker, and the Ayis would make bread every day for the kids. I think they had PB and J most days, except when there was time to make other things. We did our best to switch up the meals when we could. Dinner was just classic Chinese food: rice and veg/ meat.

I ended up working about six days a week, and eventually more. There was an infinite amount of things to always be done. Go to the bank, pick up groceries, get food at the market, bring kids to school downtown, fix broken things, move things, bring things places, feed and take care of kids, program iPads, download music, organize things and more. Not to mention all the kids were disabled physically or mentally to some degree. Back then, Mel had been there only about a year. When she came, the elderly Dutch couple had fourteen kids. When I came, it was twenty-seven. Back then, Mel was still sorting things out, finding the ways to be most efficient, and over the time I was there we figured out a lot together, changed a lot, and everything was better, or rather good as we could make it.

Of course winter was coming, and having so many kids all living together meant they all got sick when a few got sick. So there was that to deal with too. Vitamin C and Acidophilus was shipped in from America, so we routinely gave the kids that. It helped. We had space heaters in all apartments, and the bill for one month for all of them was over $2000 USD. We didn't have air conditioners because Guiyang never got super cold or super hot. (Air conditioners in China also put out heat.)

At that time, we got two new kids as well. Jerry and Ruby. Both had Apert syndrome, which meant their heads were a little large, and they had webbed hands and feet. Jerry was about 1.5 years old, and Ruby was about 4-ish. Jerry was in Mels apartment, and because his head was so big, he couldn't sit upright without tipping over. But he was the cutest kid ever, and he eventually became my favourite kid we had during my time at Mels. Anyway, we made him a little pillow sort of wall, so he could drink his bottle and not tip over. His little webbed hands were so cute! Ruby was sassy, but a ton of fun. She liked fun, and often that meant hitting me in a friendly way. Little did she know, she was at perfect height to punch me right in the balls. So I learned quickly to be weary of her when I was around. Gotta watch out for my guys!

After them we got another kid. During my whole time at Mels, he was the only one I got to name, and I named him Elvis. I think it was very fitting, but when he got adopted (which is amazing) they changed his name to Garrett. He had/has downs and was so cute. I guess I don't need to say that as all babies are cute! He was about one when we got him. On a side note, we drew on all the kids faces whenever Mel would go out. That was great.

Ok, so let's explain the kids. One apartment had the 'young' kids, one had the 'autistic kids', one had the 'school girls', and another had the rest. Plus Mels with all the babies. The school girls went to school, I believe, five days a week. More often than not I would accompany Mels driver as having five spunky hyper down syndrome girls, all aged about 13, is a bit of a handful. Plus I helped him walk them into the school ground etc... It was actually a shock to me that China had a public school for disabled kids. I though that was amazing, because all my experience in China had led to believe that they shunned those kinds of people (which they still did to a degree, but not always). So that was really cool.

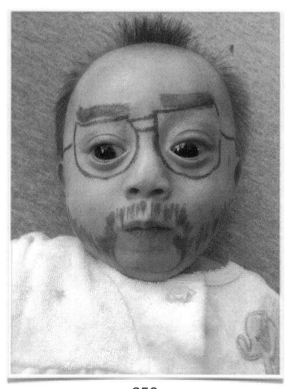

Besides school, the rest of the kids would all take walks and go the 'fun apartment', dance, or whatever. Mel had set up a sort of schedule for them all, which got better as time went by. The apartment complex we lived in was enormous. I mean, I think there was like 10,000 people living there, and at rush hour it was non-stop honking of horns. (Don't forget the driving style. In this case, there was no 'consideration for others' or 'letting people merge'. It was: get as close to the car in front of you as possible and don't let anyone let anyone cut in front of you.)

The walks were always just around the roads within the complex. It was fenced off too, as they are. There was also a nice little pond area, a few small 'playgrounds' and shops to buy stuff. Oh, and the playground was one of those whatever they're called, plastic jungle gyms, with the slide, and pole etc... But it was old, and ghetto, and the slide had a chunk out of it, so you could very easily get physically damaged. Sketchy, to say the least. But it was close, and fun. Something else that boggled my mind for my entire time in China was this. Once it was hot out, I would continue to see people in large winter jackets. They thought you got a cold be being cold. I also saw every single baby bundled up like a marshmallow. Their little hands and legs just jutted straight out, as they couldn't bend them from all the layers. The funniest part was, it would be like plus 25 out, and you'd see babies like this, just sweating to death. Then the Chinese grandmas would have the nerve to scold Melodie because our kids were in t-shirts. It was crazy. And finally, the best thing I always saw was young kids, maybe 3-9 years old with a ton of layers on, and a towel handing out their back like Superman to catch the sweat running down their back. It never occurred to them to take a layer off. Just be hot as hell or nothing.

Mel also got her drivers licence around this time. She told me this story. She went in to do the test. There's two tests; one in Chinese and another in English, but the English one is translated so bad it quite literally made no sense. (I can confirm this as I got the app to study for mine, but realized it was completely useless.) So she goes in and tells the lady working "I need my friend to help me translate the Chinese test". For some reason, this was ok, and when they did the test, the girl just told her all the answers. Ha! Amazing. So Mel got her licence.

Ok, so back to Mels apartment. Ten babies and Yamei. Yamei was about nine at the time, I think. She had some sort of disability, which wasn't super severe, but given that the first nine years of her life she been treated like she was 'useless', she didn't receive the education or love she needed. Mel said, once she adopted her she allowed access to the documents revealing the circumstances on how the orphanage (welfare centre) found her. I guess she was just wandering the streets alone. Imagine. Anyway, incase I spoiled it, it took a while, and money, but Mel adopted her. The funny part was she (Mel) had to go through all the usual 'adoption' drama. They asked her things like "what would you do if your child do something bad, how would you discipline her?" Of course Mel didn't need to imagine what she'd do, because she'd been doing it for a year. So she had to go through all the hoops, but that day when the paperwork went though was quite monumentous, I must say.

Anyway, Mel had a British friend, Alex, who was about my age. He was and is a super awesome dude, and Yamei loved him! He'd been in China for a few years, and his Chinese was basically fluent as it gets. He worked *full time* for a legit business, spoke, read and wrote Chinese all day every day for work. So it was handy having him around sometimes, so sort out problems or translate. He eventually married another friend of Mels who is Chinese.

Another side story is, when I was testing the milks temperature (as one does) I squirted it into my mouth (as one does), but forgot it was from a human. So now, I can say, I've drank human milk. Ha. Whoops. We had got the milk from a nice lady who had lost her new baby.

Ok, so maybe you're wondering, where did Mel get all these kids? Here's the answer! Once upon a time there was a Chinese man who worked for the government. He retired, but had a big heart, and wanted to help the disabled kids on Guiyang and surrounding areas. So he started his own sort of 'foster care' programme. Now I'm not super sure, but I think it was ok for Chinese to care for the kids, but not ok for foreigners. So what we did was technically illegal. But I heard, since Guiyang is quite far from Beijing, and "poor", the government turned a blind eye. That lasted until about later 2018 when they clamped down, and Mel was forced to move back to America. Long story. Anyway, he was a sort of 'middle-man', between people like Mel and the Welfare Centre. The Welfare Centre would talk to him, say 'we have a kids with whatever disability, can you find them a home?' and he would. There was also a few other American/foreign couples in Guiyang who did the same. Two nice older couples, and a family also from the Netherlands.

The other two nice older couples I mentioned were the sweetest people ever, and I became good friends with the one guy Sam. He was about 50 or 55 years old, and a large jolly very funny guy. He would meet up with me sometimes to help me cope, give advice and stuff like that. So that was nice. He and his wife sold everything they had to be in China doing this work. They took care of four babies and one girl about ten years old who was just lovely. The other couple I'm not totally sure about, but they had about the same situation.

Well, that was the first two months summery. Let's move on. December 2013, we got two more kids. Becca, with CP and Sean, with....something. He had a tube in his head that went to his guts, I guess to release fluid in his skull. From what I heard, the 'middle-man' guy (I forget his name by now) said he didn't trust a Chinese family to take care of him, because if he fell on his head he'd die. So we took him. It was even last minute. When they went to get Becca the guy said "can you take one more?" and Mel did. She always did.

By then, Mels apartment had twelve kids. Feeding time in the AM was a conveyer belt of mouths. Feeding two to four kids at a time, and changing a never ending storm of poopy diapers. The fun never stopped. I had about one day off a month at that time, but that was life. One time I was trying to do too much at once and Sammy fell out of his highchair. Luckily he was strapped in, but he *did* hit his face on another chair and bled a little. Meanwhile Benji, who was strapped in to his lowchair would just slowly slip down and down until he was 80% on the floor.

Oh ya, you may be wondering 'how did you get a visa to stay in China?'. Well, we knew of a small loophole in the system. The old Dutch couple and Mel did what I did. We went to the University, explained the situation, and "attended University". They knew about our work, and they allowed it. We got the Visa from them for the price of schooling, which was about $2000 CDN a year, and I did have to have a teacher come to the house about once a week, although we were so crazy busy that that rarely happened. By late December Mel managed to rent three more (unfinished) apartments. Let me break it down.

### Chinese Culture: Apartment buildings

In China, apartment buildings are made 100% of cement. There's no wood, gyprock or whatever. If you wanna put a nail in the wall, you don't. It's cement. When you buy one new, it's literally a hollow, grey cement box. There's nothing.

And I mean, there's no water, water pipes, electricity, or electrical outlets/wires. All of that needs to be installed by means if using a jackhammer to grind away a six inch ditch all over the walls and floors. It's a *ton* of work and louder than anything you've ever heard. Unless you've put your head next to an *actual* construction worker while he jackhammers a sidewalk. And that's what you'd hear for hours upon hours. When I was in Huangshi teaching, the neighbours decided they wanted to modify their apartment. That meant new wiring I guess, which meant an actual earthquake above my head. It was so loud I couldn't hear the tv. Hours of drilling the walls and floors.

~

So we had to hire someone to build them all. They gave a price, and started to work. A few weeks later, when they'd put in the water and electricity, they said 'we need more money'. Of course, renting about nine (?) apartments, paying for food, diapers, Ayis wage, cars, insurance, electricity etc... we had no more money left. So they sat there, half done for about two months. I'll get back to that soon.

There was a time there, in December when Mel had to go away for some reason; I forget now. I was in charge. Well, the school girls had a performance/ activity day one day, so I subbed in as their 'parental figure'. The performance was mostly dancing (which I watched - I didn't dance), and I also had to play games with some of the girls. Dribble a basketball and race. Things like that. It was fun. December was also Xuwei's birthday. She was turning nineteen and had downs. She was hilarious, and wanted to get married *so* bad (in general, not to me). Anyway, she talked about her birthday plans for a month straight. Every detail, over and over, every day. Then the day finally came. We went to Pizza Fun downtown. It was a nightmare to get there, and parking was even worse. Finally, tired and annoyed we all went in. The girls ate so much pizza one or two puked in the car ride home. But they had fun - Pizza fun!!!

Mel's British friend Alex also introduced us to a new bar/pub around this time. It had the *best* Western style food in all of Guiyang, maybe even China. Real, actual, fish and chips *and* legit burgers. Needless to say, we went there as often as we could, which wasn't often. December also brought two of our kids going to the hospital. I'll spare the details, but it was not fun as you can imagine.

They eventually were ok after a few days and came home. Six kids had fevers too during this time.

Then, Christmas.

The Tuesday before Christmas brought about 'The 4th Annual Christmas Gathering' for the entire foster care programme, also known as the epitome of my nightmare. What it was was, every family in the programme (which could have been about 70 to 100, I'm not sure) came together with their kid for this party. Most of the Chinese people just had one disabled child, but it added up to about a few hundred people, plus me and some of our Ayis and some of our kids. So they did things like had a performance, which is basically mandatory in China. Dancing etc... They also had some 'games' for the parents. They played tug of war with about fifteen people on each end of the rope. Then the end was in sight, and I was ready to go. If you know me you'll know I don't like noise, lots of people and "fun" games. By the end my patience was getting low, but it wasn't over. Yamei had a few tickets to get a free prize.

Now, if you've lived in China, and you read the word 'free', you'll know where this is going. If not, I'll tell you. Chinese people LOVE free things. And I don't mean merely sort-of love. I mean they will do almost anything to anyone to get something free. So I'm in line with Yamei. Ha, a line. Well, that didn't last long. Some granny with a kid on her back just starts cramming in and crushing Yamei, who starts freaking out. This lady is sandwiching her so so hard, so I put my full weight into this lady to stop her, and yell at her my hardest to stop pushing. There's now a large commotion, people start to cut and push and grab and yell, and it's utter mayhem. One thing (among many) that I really hated about Chinese people was their lack of consideration for others. Like I said before, with the whole one child policy thing, the top priority is 'self' in China. The strange thing was they were, besides those times, the friendliest people ever.

So people are getting rowdy, and I'm trying my best to guard Yamei while she's freaking out. Of course the lady and everyone else is ignoring me and grabbing at their toys for their kids. Finally we got her toy and left. It was insane. That made my blood boil, I'll tell ya what. I really almost began to fight people. Eventually we got back, and it took me a long while to calm down. Oh Christmas, a time of loving others eh... But overall, the kids had fun, so that was good.

Another thing that happened was the Dutch couple had to fly home for a while. Their son died that Christmas from cancer. Hard times. Otherwise, let's back up a bit. I made it my goal, as soon as I got to Guiyang to find Lamian (pulled noodles made by the Muslims). I finally found a shop downtown after moths of searching, and tried to go every day off I had. It took over an hour on the bus, but 100% worth it. We had Christmas parties in each apartment for the kids, and they dressed like elves. New years (Dec 31st) I was so tired I slept at 10PM.

## Welcome, 2014!

The new year. I went to my first symphony of my life with Mel and some of her friends. It was so amazing. My favourite part was that there were many signs posted everywhere "no pictures", but it's China, and there was flashes going off half the time. Sheesh. But it was wonderful none the less. What else, apartment 15 had an electrical fire, so that was fun. Apartment 21 had their buildings power go out, so I had to run their dinner up 21 flights of stairs. That was fun too. This all happened while Mel was gone for five days, of course.

One day Yaoling fell on the trampoline and cut her lip open and broke her tooth off. Another thing that bugged me China (sorry, there's just so many) was that Chinese people would often say '没关系' which means 'it doesn't matter', for things that *did* matter. So the whole time she's bleeding everywhere the Ayis are telling me "it doesn't matter", but it did. And I was snapping at them saying 'of course it matters!' Anyway, she was ok and back to playing within no time, with one less tooth.

Ok, here's another funny story, but I gotta back up a little. When I got to Mels she introduced me to these two Dutch dudes from a different family who also did the same sorta work. They were a little weird, but decent guys. They'd been in Guiyang a while and knew lots of people. They also had one of those three wheel motorbikes with the box on the back. Anyway, they let me drive it the first week I was there and I almost hit a car. It was a bit crazy. Fast forward a year and I wanna buy a scooter, so I call those two Dutch dudes and they tell me they can help. They took me to this place and I walk in, check out the scooters, and see one I like. I paid 3000元 cash, started it and drove off. No licence, no helmet, nothing. Something good about China! We drove around the long way home (as to avoid some streets with cops) and I made it. Once home I checked the front tire, and the lug nuts (is that their name for motorbikes?) on the front whccl were almost falling off. Not even hand tight. So, that was sketchy. But otherwise, it was all good. I was stoked.

I parked the scooter in the apartment. Yes, I did take it up the elevator; it's China. I even spray painted it flat black. It was legit! And I used it all the time. Just had to be a little careful on what streets I went on, and never went downtown. When Mel came back I had a few days off to rest. Yay! Soon Chinese New Year would come! Not yay.

I didn't mention this before, but during Chinese New Years, almost everyone in China travels. I mean, like *one billion people*. It's their biggest holiday, and most people who work, work every day of the year except these ten days. Our Ayis were this way. One day off a week, and ten days off a year. That's it. So for those ten days, Mel needed volunteers to help. And so they came. Youth With A Mission (YWAM) students from America and some from Mel's church in Texas.

Now, the people from Mels church were awesome. The YWAMers, not so much. Most of them were young 20s, so fair enough they didn't entirely know what to do, but it's not that hard to play with kids. Only they didn't. Some just sat on their phones and ignored the kids, others sat off to the side and just talked to each other. At one point Kandice (the rad chick helping Mel for a year) said "you know it's more fun if you actually *play* with the kids". The girl rolled her eyes and was offended. Can you imagine?

The other super funny story about the YWAM kids was there was one girl who, when she arrived, told Mel she was allergic to a lot of food, and gave a list of things she couldn't eat. So Mel, on top of all her work (and I mean insane amounts of work) obliged this girl and made special meals for her. Then, when the ten days were basically up, and we were tired, annoyed and burnt out, someone told us "oh she's not really allergic to those things, she just doesn't like eating them because it alters her mood". Dude, Mel was so mad. We just shook our heads and were glad they were leaving.

Anyway, some (cool) people brought gifts. Some gifts were autistic toys for Qiaoqiao! He had some chew toys he loved. I think we even got a weighted blanket. And now that I'm talking about Qiaoqiao, I'll tell you more. He was a hilarious boy, with non-verbal autism. He loved to eat. So much so that when he went to bed we had to wrap him in a sort of body blanket with arms. The hands were sewn shut, so he couldn't use his hands, and his bed was made into a cage. Now, if you're thinking 'you horrible people', wait a sec. This kid would eat his own poo, mattress, garbage, and just anything. Literally. So it was for his safety. And the caged bed, same. He would escape and wreak havoc. To be honest he didn't mind. He was always happy no matter what. It was just normal for him.

One not ideal story about him. One day I'm with someone else chatting near the door of the kitchen, and Qiaoqiao came over to us, trying to sneak in to pilfer food no doubt. So we just closed the door and kept talking. Then we noticed he was acting weird. It took a second, because usually he is a little crazy, but this was a bit abnormal for him. Then I look. He had tried to reach into the kitchen as I was closing the door, and it caught his finger. The rest was a blur. I tried the door and it wouldn't open, so I drop kicked it my hardest. Of course, a tin door gave way to my foot easily, as did the sheet of glass which shattered everywhere. But Qiaoqiao was free. Man, whoops. Poor little guy. That was one of my few 'guardian parent' experiences. Now I know how mothers can lift cars or whatever.

Joyce, another cute little non-verbal autistic girl who lived with Qiaoqiao had this yellow stuffed monkey. She LOVED it. It went with her everywhere, and she chewed on it until it basically disintegrated. So we found another one at Walmart and got it. Then we secretly chucked her old one and gave the new one, hoping she wouldn't notice. But she did. She was so bummed, but over time she grew to like the new one.

After that holiday (for the Chinese, not for us), Mel was so nice she got me and Kandice a (separate) hotel room for the night at a super nice hotel. And man, that was much needed. Just silence and a bath and relaxing. Otherwise, we just kept busy doing everything that needed to be done.

By March I was sick, and slept 36 hours with a fever. Those contractors stiffed us, and did half the job building the three new apartments. So that was lame. The weather was cold and rainy. Cement buildings do *not* hold heat, and the hallways which had open windows all winter were colder than outside. Side note, I saw poo all the time on the sidewalks, and there's not a ton of pets in China... I saw a lady at Walmart wearing full body winter pyjamas and high heels. Some days people would park their scooter right at the elevator entrance. So close that we had to actually *move it* to get by. Smart eh. On top of that, half the time in China the elevators never work anyway.

We brought some kids to the dentist and they had a playground there, so that helped. Oh, here's one from Feb, when the people came from Mels church to help. Backing up a bit, I talked to my parents and said 'people are coming here from Texas. Can you ship my xbox to them so they can bring it?'. So it gets shipped to Texas and I tell Mel, 'tell them to put it in a carry-on, otherwise it could get broke in the luggage'. Well, it arrives loose, in a duffle bag, cracked. It still worked, but man, that was annoying. Anyway, this other time, me and Kandice just got the kids to bed at Mels and we're gonna sit for a bit and chill. So Kandice is making dessert for us, and I look, and it's literally just apple slices in the small oven. And I'm like "what are you making, hot apples?" We both died laughing. And yes, it was hot apples. Maybe she put sugar on them, I forget. But we laughed pretty much for five years about it.

One day driving, we saw a lady pushing her wide-as-a-car cart into oncoming traffic, taking up an entire lane. There was a line of about fifty cars trying to get by her. We went to buy paint, and they didn't have paint pan. I mean China didn't, not the store. Crazy talk. Twenty free urinals, the one guy who comes in goes right next to me. Classic China. Now, I have this other story, but I forget where or when I was flying. Here it is: I'm in line to get on the plane. We are the 'boarding time' in about one minute, so everyone is lined up waiting. I'm near the front, where they take the tickets, and I look to my right, and there's a kid, about 2.5 years old pissing on the glass railing/carpet. No one cared.

I also got to go back and visit Justin in Changsha. He and his family were finally moving back to Australia and sadly it was just him at the time. Anyway, he said "take as many movies and books as you want". Needless to say I filled an entire suitcase to the brim. Yay me! I did end up giving them to my other friend when I moved back to Canada like four years later. Oh, here's a fun culture thing.

**Chinese Culture: Black Cabs (not in Colour)**

So one thing I loved about China is black cabs. They were basically just ordinary people who would pick up strangers. Some guys did this as a job, so you'd always (and I mean always) hear people honking at you while they slowly drove by making eye contact. That meant "need a ride?" But it was so handy more often than not. You just open the door and tell them where you're going. If they could do it they'd give a price, to which you would always immediately cut in half. Then bargain it out. They were pretty fair usually. And most just wanted the opportunity to have a foreigner. So many guys said to me 'I've never had a foreigner in my car'. And of course it helped being able to speak Chinese.

Once Mel was at the Hospital and needed money, and I was downtown. So I needed to get home, grab a wad of cash and get to the Hospital as soon as I could. In China the doctors will literally not help you without cash in hand. So I waved down this one guy, and told him 'Xiaohe' (where we lived). He wasn't really stoked on that, and already had a dude with him. So I sad 100元. For him that was a lot, for me, 20$. So he agreed. Usually it's like 30 or 40元 to get home, but desperate time call for desperate measures eh.

~

The final story from April was, one day Mel sits me down and is like 'so... maybe you noticed, but me and Chen have been getting pretty close, and I think we're in love'. To which I did thee old '*huh*?' I hadn't noticed at *all*. Anyway, they basically dated and got married within a year I think. Since then they've adopted three kids, and had three of their own.

In May we got a few more kids. One, Luke, they said they found in a duffle bag. He had downs, and was 11/10 cute. I also forget most of the details on the three new apartments, but there was a rich Chinese business man who helped us out monetarily and within a few weeks of hard work they were ready! Finally we moved in! Mel took one, there was a new 'fun apartment' (where I had a room to live now) and the babies moved into the other. The brutal part was taking apart an entire caged trampoline, lifting every piece down 19 floors and up 12. The pieces barley fit and each turn of the stairwell we had to shift and turn and flip. It took hours. And now the trampoline was over Mel's, so no neighbours to annoy. At least not *under* us. Those ghetto half broken rusted springs were not quiet by any means and could even be heard outside. On top of the trampoline, the fun apartment included a ball pit and a 'autism room' which was dark, had mellow music playing, stuffed animals and coloured lights moving all over the walls.

So now we have 9 apartments, 29 kids. Around that time Kandice left China. Her time was up (I think she stayed 6-8 months or a bit more...). So that was super sad. 1 for the help, but 2 because she was a legit friend by now. Anyway, more random stories. I bought a Kinect for the xbox, and let the school aged girls play Fruit Ninja, some Dance game and others. They LOVED it so so much, but often, due to this 'fun' they would all hop in front of the TV, then the Kinect wouldn't be able to handle five bodies and it would mess up. But they still enjoyed it. We went to the park one day too, but there's crazy monkeys there who people feed all the time. They're so nutty that they'll just come up to you and grab food out of your hand, so we stayed away from them; just looked. Otherwise, I was still mad busy almost every single day.

One time, we and Mel we in line at this famous Baozi place; steamed bun with meat inside. So we finally got some, and Mel bites in, and the greasy juices squirt all over her new shirt. Well, we laughed. Anyway, time kept flying by. I don't know what I did that summer. Probably just crazy busy as usual.

By August we had two kids in the Hospital. No fun. Georges cries were louder than anything you've ever heard, so that got old fast. Had to nebulize him every hour or something. He hated it, and we'd have to hold the mask on his face so hard. Poor little guy. But he made it. By September I was burnt out, so I decided to get my own hotel. I booked one downtown and went; I think it was a Motel 8. Anyway, it was pretty rough, and of course the point of going was to get rest. But lo and behold, at 6AM I was awoken to a rooster. So loud, just outside my window. Yes, downtown Guiyang, with a rooster. So that ruined my day.

OK, here's some drama story: One night an Ayi came to Mel's at midnight. For three hours they talked. She told Mel of a ton of strange stuff. So Mel decided to fire her as we couldn't trust her. So that happened. Then she wanted ten thousand yuan (Chinese money), and we said no. She said she'd tell the cops and 'authorities' about what we do if we don't pay her. In theory she could get me and Mel sent home, 21-ish people lose their jobs and had 30-ish kids go back to the orphanage. After much negotiation she agreed to a month salary (3200). So the next day Mel found it in her heart to give 5000. But for some reason (don't ask me) she did a bank transfer. When Chen (the driver) was doing the transfer the computer messed up (he clicked twice I guess) and we sent 10k! Awesome. Needless to say, because she was beyond selfish and liked stealing from abandoned orphans she didn't give us any back. In fact she said 'it was God giving her the money she deserved because we were in the wrong'. Super rad.

Well, by October I was haggard as it gets and needed a vacation. So I flew to Texas to stay with some of Mels friends. That was super fun. Texas rules so hard, *and* I got to see Kandice which was nice. And then the two girls I worked with in Huangshi who live in/near Baton Rouge came to visit me as well. I also flew to California to visit my bother and his family as well during that time. So a few weeks in America ruled. I had a ton of fun and ate so so much good food.

When I was back it was as usual. As I mentioned previously, I lived in the 'fun apartment', and had a room. Well, since I lived there, one of my duties was to clean the ball pit once a week. You wouldn't believe how gross those balls get, or maybe you would. Anywho, it took me three hours one Friday night, which is ok. I listened to music and probably had a beer. Well, I wake up the next day to kids coming in the apartment. After some time they leave, and I creep out of my room. Then I notice it. Poop. Poop all over the balls and the walls of the ball pit. Hooray for me. So I was a little mad to say the least. Especially because I know some of the Ayis aren't the best, and often ignore the kids. So the next group that came in ten minutes later I had to tell to go away while I cleaned all the balls again. Gotta love poop eh.

Also around that time, Courtney came to help us for four months. She'd been in China a few years already doing work stuff. I forget. But she was super rad, and a *huge* help. When December came, the kids started rehearsing for the Christmas pageant performance thing. I forgot to mention, at this time, we turned one of the other apartments into a school, and had a few teachers. The kids would go to school every day and learn basic stuff, depending on their cognitive abilities. It was so great. So those teachers were prepping the kids for their big event. It was about that time that I started hanging out with Amy (a Chinese teacher Mel had hired). She was rad, and we started dating shortly after, in early December. But more on that later. Life was still happening, and Christmas was coming up. Mel had organized her 30-ish kids parts in the play (the Jesus story of course), and they all had costumes. Many babies were dressed as pigs and sheep. The older girls were Mary and Joseph etc... It was super amazing. And one cool thing was that many people from the Welfare Centre came. All in all we had about 120 people there. Everyone had a ton of fun and ate lots of food. Oh ya, it was held at a hotel just down the road a five minute walk away. And yes, there was a ton of dancing. Even the Ayis had their own little groups and did dancing.

# (Un?) Welcome, 2015!

Well, 2015 brought with it a bit of a mental Kevin. By now I'd been at Mels about fourteen months. It was a lot of stress, and I wasn't doing so hot. Looking back now, I was really having some serious mental issues. Me and Mel had a big long talk, and she basically said she couldn't trust me. That was hard for me, because I've always tried my best to have integrity, and be reliable. But it was true. I was snapping more, remembering less, and just gong a bit crazy. So that was 'behind the scenes'. Life, for the most, went on as usual. Me and Amy went on some dates and hung out lots. We even went to this super epic small village about three hours away. All the mountains there are entirely covered in houses. But it was almost colder than I've ever been in my life, and we left back home a few days early. One fun part of that little trip was, we were just walking around and knocked on some random door and asked if we could join the people inside to get warm. An old man welcomed us in, and he had his son there too. They, like all the village, were quite poor, but they gave us warm tea and we chatted for a good hour. I gotta say, most Chinese people are very very nice.

One little nugget of love we got was the cutest girl to ever exist named Emma, and the apple of my eye, but she would flip lids when Mel left, I suppose thinking Mel was abandoning her just like everyone else. She was about four years old at this time, and had a clef palette, so she couldn't really talk. But she was amazing, and chubby, and I think about her all the time, even to this day (as I do with all the kids). She was forced to leave us (back to the orphanage I think for some political reason I forget), and I will tell you, watching Mel give that girl up... it might as well have been her actual daughter. One of the saddest days of my (and I assume Mels) life. The only redemption in that was Emma got adopted to America, where she is today, somewhere, being cute I'm sure. I wish I could snuggle her again.

Around that time we had some kids birthdays too. So we took them out. All girls. To the mall. They got their nails done, hair washed and braided and then got Burger King. Funny to watch them eat their burgers one piece at a time. Top of the bun, then veg, then meat, then bottom of the bun. Anyway, time went on, and I started helping Mel a bit less because I was just having too hard of time dealing with life.

It was super hard living there. At Mels; but also in China. Like I said, we were busy every day, and there always seemed to be something about China that annoyed me. We couldn't go out without being stared at, like before, but now we had disabled kids. And, like I also said before, even seeing disabled kids is a rare thing in China, but seeing them with Whitey was even stranger. And Chinese love to stare. It just wore me thin. And the stupid traffic, and eating the same food every day, and having kids getting hurt, and fighting, and hitting, and biting, and eating garbage, and running away, and dealing with the Ayis, and organizing things, and taking kids for walks, and cleaning. It just never ended.

Here's a story that made me hate China even more, sorry. (I swear I don't actually hate China.) So I have Dylon, and I had to bring him to get a shot or something. Just me and him, and he was a super chill kid. About six years old with downs. Anyway, we were having a good time, we got the shot, it hurt, but I promised him I'd treat him to Burger King (BK) after. So we got in a taxi and headed to BK. As we get near to the mall (on a busy three lane road) the taxi pulls off to the side to let us out. So I pull the door handle, kick the door open and lean over to grab out Dylon. As soon as the door opens I hear a big crash. I look outside, and some absolute retard had tried to pass us on the right (a taxi keep in mind, who had just pulled over to the right side of the street) and tagged the door with his scooter. Well, since this is China, instantly thirty people were there watching.

### Chinese Culture: Observing

Now here's the thing. Curiosity is fine and well, but Chinese take it to an entirely new level. They are *obsessed* with watching things. They even have an idiom for it: 吃瓜群众 - to eat - melon - crowd - many. The meaning is 'peanut gallery' or 'onlookers who are interested in the spectacle but don't have anything knowledgable to say about it'. This happened all the time with *everything;* if there was a crash, dead body, fight, argument or whatever. And they would stand close, like sometimes even three feet away from a couple arguing just staring at them while they hit each other. There was absolutely no personal space in China. Sorry for the rant, but, that's how it was.

~

Anyway, back to the story. So I'm annoyed. I mean, honestly, who passes a taxi on the right just after it pulled over? This is one of those 'common sense doesn't exist in China' instances. So I get out with Dylon and check on the guy, seeing if he's ok. Meanwhile, while I'm talking with the scooter guy, some dude comes out of the crowd, holding a kid (a girl about the same age as Dylon) like me. And he just goes off, in English. He's like "you should say sorry!" and went on and on. And I just am loosing it. So I yell back at him to piss off, and try to tell him I was about to before he started raging on me. Anyway, we exchanged words, and I left, pushing through the crowd that was enamoured with the situation. That really ground my gears. After that we got BK, went to Walmart and had some fun, so that helped.

I hope all that doesn't come across too bad. You should understand that I dealt with these things all the time, and it wore me thin so so quick. I'm merely human; no more, no less. To be honest it was quite easy to let yourself get mad all the time and I constantly had to fight my hardest just to be calm when I was out and about. Another (fun?) challenge of China I suppose eh.

By Feb I was helping Mel even less. I just couldn't cope mentally or physically. If you know me you know I like naps (did I say that already?). That's because I've had insomnia for about fifteen years. I had, now that I think about it, compassion fatigue. Only back then I couldn't put a name to it. The name was basically 'asshole'. Because half the time I *was*. Couldn't be helped. But that's what it was. I was burnt out beyond words. Well, Chinese New Years came again, and we had volunteers for ten days. I don't remember any of it, so... there you go.

After that I went to Thailand for ten days to see a counsellor. There was a guy there who dealt with people from all over Asia who did volunteer work, and he was a good help. I also got a sweet themed hotel. I got the cowboy room, and slept in a caravan/trailer thing. It was so rad. He diagnosed me with A.D.D. which made so much sense. Bummer I found out at about age 33. Anyway, I went back to Guiyang and plugged along. Around this time I also joined a band for a while. Here's a funny tale.

So I join these dudes for jam sessions. One guy is basically a pro horn player, and the other played double bass in the local symphony. They were legit. And me? I am mediocre at drums at best. The band was guitar, drums, bass guitar, horn, and girl singer. This girl, to be honest, wasn't the best singer you've ever heard. But we jammed a few times and it seemed ok. Cover songs though, so please don't judge me. If you're wondering, one of them was that Taylor Swift song about 'haters gonna hate'. Anyway, the horn player was kinda of like our manager. He knew people, so he got us a gig, but it was soon, so we had limited time. I mean like, two jam sessions. Not enough if you're me. My memory is super bad, so it takes me a while to really let things sink in. We jam a few times, and it's not good, by any means, but it's not bad. Very ok. The day of the gig we go, and walk in, and there's about 1000-1500 chairs set up, tv camera booms and everything. A *huge* stage too. We're like 'dude, what's this?' The horn player didn't tell us that we would be on tv, along with about twenty other legitly professional performers. So I'm feeling rough. Like, I'm not prepared for something this monumental.

The event starts, and the room is full, and my girlfriend is there with Mel and Alex and a few other people we know. It's packed. And the show starts, and a few people go before us. The only one I actually really remember was a couple; a dude and a chick dancing, but I mean next level dancing. He was chucking her around like an uncooked pizza crust. They were flipping everywhere and had body paint and crazy techno music and lights and it was insane. Full-on.

Then *we* get up. Do a quick sound check and begin. Three songs. No biggie, except it's China, and the equipment setup is this: two large speakers facing forward. That's it. So I can't hear anything at all. I mean, maybe 15% at best. And I don't know these songs that good. So, here we go. Started playing, couldn't hear a thing, and hoped for the best. At one point there was a little break thing, where I had to build up the drum roll. Well, I came in at the wrong time. Unfortunately the girl signing wasn't musically inclined enough to be able to adapt. The other guys did, as they were professional. From what I heard it was an atrocity. And if you know me, you'll know I listen to heavy metal, so I may have added and few extra kick drum hits as well.

The review was so bad, the person who put on the gig didn't even want to pay us. We were of course mad with the shoddy setup (no monitors for the drummer), and moreover that no one told us the gig would be televised. I think we ended up getting paid, but the horn player didn't pay the singer girl. It was really brutal. Me and the bass player ended up putting our money together and dividing it three ways, so to be 'fair'. That whole event was really bad. And I quit the band after that, as did the bass player.

At the end of March, Amy (my girlfriend) said she got accepted to work in Thailand, and she'd be going to Beijing to prepare for a month, then leave shortly after. We'd been dating about three months by then. Looking back, in hindsight, we probably should of called it there and went our separate ways, but as they say "nothing worth while every came easy". So I thought we'd try to make it work and she went to Beijing. At that point I was thinking about the future, and what it would look like. What could I do for work? How could I stay in China? Well, the only option at that point was going back to Huangshi to work for a year teaching at the same middle school. That would keep me busy while Amy was gone. Then with the money I saved, I would attend the University in Guiyang (to be near Amy) and get a bachelor degree, then we'd get married and I'd teach English for the rest of my life. Easy. That was the plan.

While she was in Beijing, I had managed to get some free tickets for the symphony from the guy I was in the band with, the bass player. So when she returned, I picked her up from the train station and we immediately went to the symphony. The best part was not only was it free, but for some reason we got the VIP seats in the upper upper booth, and we were alone! So we just snuggled the whole time and watched epic music. One of the best days of my life for sure. But, Amy was prepping for Thailand by May, and then she left. Here's what I wrote in May of 2015:

Morning grabs me like a slow incline in gravity. I awake feeling like I haven't slept in days. The night before was once again wrought with insomnia. That feeling where you are trapped between two worlds. My brain never shuts down, even when I sleep. My thoughts merely turn into dreams and my sleep is comparable to just another life, yet stranger and less coherent.

My body aches, like I just finished exercising or running a marathon. Light hits my eyes and I feel as though someone is crushing my ocular chord with vice-grips, similar to a kick to the testicles. My brain receives a pound of pressure and I shy away. The worst part is, my curtain is closed. The next worst part is my curtain is what one normally would use in a shower to divide the 'washing room' with the bath tub.

As time goes by I wonder if my body can manage to bring itself to arise from bed. Motivation is, for the most, just a rumour I heard about. I feel like I could sleep my life away. My room is a disaster; generally, because I lack the energy to clean it. My brain tries to think about what I need to do, but the daily list floats behind a fog of incoherence. A man in the distance begins his daily routine of yelling. I guess it helps the vocal cords, but, like most Chinese customs, is based on tradition above anything else. Who needs logic and science when you have tradition?

It's a while before I get up. The oatmeal I eat is plain, with a little syrup as I'm out of sugar. I sit at my desk and read a little. Then I find that my computer is more interesting and open it. These days I'm researching a lot of different things at the same time. It makes for annoying mornings. I should read about Romans because I'm preaching this Sunday, but the way which Chinese people view their family has caught my attention for now. Having A.D.D. doesn't help the cause either.

I wonder a thousand things before an hour is past. Two hours later I find I can't focus. My body is shaking and my mind is shutting down. I need to sleep, but it's only 10:30am. I fall into bed like a meteor to the earth but I can't sleep. I also can't function. I am useless. Before long my brain thinks of something else that could be interesting to do: write about life, research actors, plan art, or whatever. I get up and attempt to make use of my day. Still unsure of why people do anything at all I contemplate moving back home and doing nothing with my life.

Life in China is daunting, beyond words. It takes all you are and pushes you until you become an involuntary agoraphobic. Leaving the house only means people will stare at you. How can a people group be so consistently rude?

Lunch time comes, and I trudge lethargically to Apt 19. I feel guilty, taking food I didn't pay for. Returning home I refry my food as rice and vegetables cooked in oil don't offer much in the way of flavour. Same food, every day. How can the Chinese people do this? I get asked often what my favourite Chinese food is. I say, 'what are the options?'. It's noodles or rice. They seem to think there are 'many Chinese foods'. There's not.

Time goes by. I'm convinced by now that time isn't what we think it is. We measure it to guide our life, but time isn't measurable. It began at creation and will end at the end. We comfort ourselves with it, like a blanket of consolation, but it's a guise.

Leaving the house I wait by the elevator. Only 1 of the 2 works. It's been that way for months. Why fix something when you can not fix it eh? Once inside the smell of lingering cigarette smoke burns through my nostrils. There's pee on the worn out plywood floor still left since construction over 3 years ago. The walls still hold their protective plastic cover, which is chipping away as years go by. Phone numbers for 'water delivery' or 'move home' litter not only the inside but outside of the elevator door and walls. The light fixture hangs precariously with wires falling out of the unfinished ceiling.

Outside is bland, as though God somehow desaturated China as a whole. Everything is covered in dust. In the distance I can hear drilling and construction. Each apartment is built as it is bought, not when the buildings are constructed. Multiply X amount of buildings by X amount of apartments, and you'll have a constant drilling noise almost every day you're alive.

At the bus stop cars will stop just to stare at me for a moment. When the bus comes, I will get on last because I was taught to line up. Chinese people are taught to put themselves first at the cost of everyone else. This entails pushing and shoving to get on first. Seats are treasured above all. It's summer. I'm in a t-shirt sweating. Everyone else is in a jacket or wool sweater. The windows are often closed, with rank BO seeping into the dank stuffy bus air.

Roads are of lesser grade quality. When they are fixed they quickly become ruined. Quality control in China is almost non-existent. Why fix something good when you can fix it bad? Why try when you can not try? This philosophy can sum up most things. A man answers his phone. His voice pierces my 'noise reducing headphones' and overtakes my music. Everything is loud in China. Eat loud, talk loud, drive loud, work loud. You can't escape it.

The bus stop I need is a 40 minute ride. On Saturdays over an hour. Exiting the bus I walk to the crosswalk only to be met by about 5 motorbike taxis sitting in the middle of the way. I have to step into oncoming traffic to avoid them. To cross the road I simply walk strategically through the cars driving by; they ignore me and no one has to stop.

On my way to eat noodles the sidewalk is covered in tables and chairs. Awnings hang so low I have to duck below them. The way through the self designated sidewalk-restaurant is small, and I must wait for people to first go through before I proceed. I arrive and order noodles. I can hear people talking about me.

After eating I set out to my usual routine of being downtown. It's always busy. People go to and fro. They are endless. I check if there are new dvds, and buy the good ones. Pirated moves for 2$ make me happy. I don't feel bad, either. If Hollywood stopped making them and gave all that 'movie money' to help starving kids I'd prefer it. But that's not the case, so I enjoy their products.

The way home is not much different from the way to town, except the odds of getting a seat home are quite minimal. As I watch the cars drive outside of the bus I find myself shaking my head more often than not. The single most often thing that goes through my head while I live here in China is 'what are they thinking?'. I have no words to express my bewilderment at the sheer stupidity of most drivers/ pedestrians here. Texting while driving a scooter, pulling a cart wider than a bus into oncoming traffic, parking in the middle of the sidewalk blocking 80% of it...

Back at home I feel like I traveled the world. My patience is depleted from getting stared at and hearing the clique 'hello' as people first see me then walk past me and say it, all the while laughing as though it's the most hilarious thing in the world. I feel alone, always. I want to do things but see no reason to. Everything is temporary. I cook a crappy meal and add the same spices I have been utilizing for the past 2 months. After dinner I feel like someone placed a nice bag of rocks on every inch of my body. I wish I had energy enough to get up and do something productive.

The nights, these days, are spent reading. Read this, read that. But nothing really sinks in. I'm trying to grow in wisdom and knowledge but it's near pointless to try. Few things remain in my memory bank. Sermons come after a brief movie session. I'm too A.D.D. to finish movies these days. I'm too A.D.D. to read a book for too long. Sermons help me fall asleep, but that doesn't last long. Once again I'm forced to do what I long for but can't.

One hour goes by, and I'm awake. It's the same thing every night. I pee. And I pee again. I'm up for an hour minimum or more, once again trapped in oblivion, between sleep and awake. Eventually my body exhausts itself and I sleep by about 3-4am. The sleep I get between then and 'the morning' is subpar at best, and never deep enough to make me feel better. Then morning comes, again, and I fall upward into the sad reality that I will be tired and alone this day, like the rest.

How can I change? People tell me to exercise. But it's the same thing as telling a child to do calculus. He can't do it if he doesn't understand it, and he can't understand it if he doesn't do it. When I applied for my credit card, they declined me on the basis I 'had no credit'. My logical reply was 'how can I get credit if you don't give me a credit card?'. So I'm trapped. I want to exercise but have no energy. But if I had energy, I could exercise. They call this a 'catch 22'.

People tell me to trust God. I do. The fact I'm still tired doesn't mean I have little faith, it means God isn't helping me. Maybe that's not true. Who am I to say? All I know is my eyes feel like their watching a television, through a set of goggles, through fog. My brain feels like a tangible physical ball of sludge sitting in my skull. My limbs seem as though they shouldn't exist, like an octopus man. They fumble through my life doing what they need to do, but for the most weigh my torso down. I'm always hungry. I can feel my gut churning in my belly like theres a rope around me getting tighter. I will eat the same thing; rice.

I can't seem to live in this world. My heart and soul can't relate to anything. People helping themselves, chasing money while others starve to death. Hollywood making movies for 100 million dollars while people starve to death. Billionaires buying cars while people starve to death. I mope around barley able to get out of bed while people starve to death.

I feel trapped between Christianity the Nihilism. I believe in God, and that we 'have a purpose', and yet find myself more often than not simply agreeing with Nietzsche. Why do anything? It's all circular. But it's not all that bad. The light at the end of the tunnel should come soon in the form of 'a job' and perhaps even Ritalin or some sort of replacement vitamin. It's sad when the only way I can function normal is with drugs not dissimilar to cocaine. Great world. Well, that's all. And don't worry, I'm not going to kill myself.

~

So May trudged by like like old cream of wheat. In June we got this little nuggety precious baby we named Grace. She had all sorts of problems, and was barely alive. She was born without an anus, and so she had a stoma. She was so tiny, and fragile. That was so hard to deal with, and I was almost hysterical helping Mel change her poo-bag. I was beside myself, just looking at this little life on the brink of death, pooing out her belly. Her life was 100% suffering. I think she finally get sent to ICU and then died, but I forget the details. We also had my favourite baby Jerry and his (maybe sister) Ruby taken from us. Again I don't remember all the details, but Mel told me there was some lies told, and some other bullshit politics involved, and we had to give those kids back. A lot had to do with another organization who will remain nameless. So that was more sadness to deal with. (On a side note, I emailed that organization the other day and they said Jerry got adopted to America, so that gave me some peace.)

Something good? We got little Mike and Chubby Bella. Mike had some disease, if you can call it that, where he was basically just like 50% smaller than everyone else. He was about two years old I think, and beyond cute. He was so so tiny! People thought he was three months old, and wouldn't believe us when we said he was two. Oh here's another funny story at the expense of Chinese people. Sorry.

Mike had a sexually transmitted disease from his mother. I think it was Hep C, or A, or something. Anyway, Mel told this to her Ayis, and they had never been so confused in their life. One even asked "how did he get a *sexual disease*?" They were bewildered. Haha. Anyway, Mel told them it was passed on from his mother. As for Bella, she was like a magic troll toy only with short hair. Her head was almost perfectly round, she smiled almost 100% of the time, was chubby, and about 2.5 years old. She was snuggled so hard by me every chance I had, and was the happiest girl to exist. Maddie, who has CP and was hilarious painted my nails. It turned out very not ideal, but she was happy, so I was happy. Honestly, there's too many stories to remember and tell. Every kid there at Mel's was a treasure beyond words.

In August (or September, I forget) we also went with Chen to the country side to celebrate winter solstice. In the country it's tradition to eat dog. So we did; with our shirts off. We drank Mijiu (rice wine) which means high alcohol level and bad taste. The girls/women of course kept their shirts on. It was a great time. And the dog meat soup tasted bitter and not really good.

On another day, as Mel's patience with her chef ladies was thinning she decided to let them go, aka fire them. Then later, we get this phone call at about 8PM from the people down below, saying their apartment is "being flooded from the ceiling". So, JP, our buddy helping us at the time goes to the cooking/fun apartment, opens the kitchen door and is hit with inches of water. The Ayis Mel had fired flooded the apartment. Nice one. Then I come up, and I'm raging. Absolutely just loosing it, so JP helps calm me down. He'd mopped it up with his wife for about an hour before I arrived. We checked our security camera, and we could see them close the kitchen door before they left. So it was definitely on purpose.

Anyway, the one lady comes back the next day, and it's awkward, and Mel tells her to go away. She says 'ok, but I forgot my purse, can I come in to get it?'. As Mel agrees she runs in, sits on a chair, refuses to move and says 'pay me money'. It was a big drama. So then me and JP come, and we finally get her to leave. But then her friend comes, the other chef lady, and we shut them out. Then they start pulling on the door to come back in, and it's a fight. Close the door vs open the door. And here we are, holding the handle to keep it closed as hard as we can, when the it breaks and just completely opens up JP's hand. Now there's blood everywhere, and I'm snapping and Mel's yelling at them to go away. My notes say 'we gave them some money', because as I said before, Chinese are sometimes unrelenting when it comes to revenge. Some (not all) will destroy your life without a second thought. The funny part was, the one chef lady lived in the same complex as us, and we sometimes saw her. Afterwards, it was like it never happened. We would even say hello.

The other fun thing that happened was in Mel's building, just outside her door. Well, you see, the neighbours had a cart. A cart they sold hot food from during the day. At night, they'd park said cart in the middle of the hallway, chained to the fire hose pipe. I guess one day, they didn't put out the coal (to heat the food), and the smoke set off the fire alarm/sprinklers. It flooded for two hours; just pouring *everywhere*, even down the elevator shafts. Both elevators were out for a week. Then, just one worked. Keep in mind that was a 24 story building. Good for us, we were on the 10, 11, and 12th floor. Not too bad, but not the best for sure.

We also got a lovely little girl, about seven years old named Mellissa. We were taking care of her short term, while she waited for her adoptive family to come get her. We call them the 'forever family'. So they came, and then they left. We heard from the middle man guy (who gives us the kids) that the parents refused to take her after meeting her. I think the reason was that they thought she had CP, but she didn't. She had a little wrong in her head, but barely noticeable, and cuter than anything. She was so sweet. Of course, me and Mel were 10/10 pissed off. Who flies around planet Earth to get a kid, then meets them and says 'no'? It's crazy and maddening beyond words. But to be honest, we were glad to have her. Time flew by and Mellissa adapted to her new environment. She was sassy, but just beyond cute and lovely. Eventually summer came and my time to depart was upon me. It was hard, but bitter sweet, much like leaving Changsha. Part of you wanted to get the hell out of there, and another simultaneously never wanted to leave. The eternal struggle of doing volunteer work.

Finally I left China. One last story for this chapter is, after arriving at the Vancouver airport I was "randomly" selected to have my bags checked. No biggie. So while they're searching my stuff there's a nice little Chinese elderly couple with zero English skills beside me. I can see the guy tell them they can't bring meat into the country, but they were thoroughly confused. I told the guy I could translate for him, and told them the same. Because Chinese have something called a Moon Cake (which they eat during holidays) and it contains meat they couldn't bring them in. On a side note, all the Moon Cakes I had were utterly disgusting. There were different flavours, but after a few gross ones, I gave them up for good.

Once I returned to my parents, summer officially had arrived and my next phase was beginning. I would return to Huangshi and teach. While I was gone, Mel and Chen got married! It was so amazing to hear (and see the pictures). The best news was that Mel's dad got to come and take part. The bummer was, her mom was too sick at the time to make the trip. But from what I heard it was amazing.

# Chapter 6: Huangshi, China - 1 year

Welp, summer was... I forget. Who even knows? Probably decent. I was off to Thailand to see Amy, then Huangshi to work. Arriving in Thailand I had to take out some money from the bank machine, so I did. The fee to take money was as much as the money I took. Then I realized I needed more, so I did it again. Whoops. The other whoops was, I was kinda in a rush to meet Amy at the other airport, so I left my Visa card in the machine and walked away. Smart eh. I did end up going back to the same airport days later as I had to fly to China, and I found my Visa at the Lost & Found, although I'd already cancelled it so it was basically useless.

I got a taxi and got the other airport and was supposed to meet Amy near the 'exit' (where you get off the planes) but we both didn't realize there were two areas. Something like that, so it took about an hour, but we finally found each other. We bummed around Bangkok for a few days, then flew to her town. Eight hour drive or 30 minute flight. It was fun and the food was amazing, of course. We mostly just adventured around her area and she showed me the sights. Oh, and we did end up renting a scooter and going to the nearby 'larger town', which still wasn't super big. Overall, it was awesome.

Then off to Huangshi. When I got in, again, the room was layered with dust. I mean, like insane amounts. So again, I spent a full day cleaning it. I had a new roommate this time too. Serge, from Kiev. And I gotta say, he was a bit of a weird dude. Very serious, even when joking. It's hard to explain, but we got along super good. He was a good guy, and we hung out a fair amount.

I started teaching again. Grade seven if I remember correctly. And it was awesome. I mean, after teaching two years, and having the experience at Mel's, I was now quite seasoned. Teaching came naturally, and I knew just what to do. The first week I basically just took all the kids pictures. All 600-ish. I made them hold a paper with their name on it, then would go home and study their names. It was as before, 12 classes, each class once a week. 8 hours of work total. But now, they had touch screen smart tvs, and I utilized the heck outta them. That really saved me. I definitely resorted to thee old 'games-to-teach' method often, but this year I spent about two hours each weekend doing my lesson plan, creating videos and PPTs (power points).

It was so nice having the confidence now. It really was. I had so much more fun with the kids, and they loved me more too. My lessons for this year went kinda like this (if I remember correctly). Quick warm-up, read the English book, work on pronunciation, play a game, then do the tv lessons. I had various English slang we commonly use like 'chill out' or 'bummer'. I did some literal translation from Chinese signs (ie. translate the translation) stolen from the internet. For example, the fire extinguisher would say 灭火瓶 = "to extinguish - fire - bottle", and underneath it would say 'hand grenade' in English. Only the kids didn't understand 'hand grenade', so then I'd put the translation of that underneath, and they'd all die laughing. I had about four of them a week, so that should tell you how many exist. Thanks internet.

I also would take an episode of Adventure Time and split it into parts. Each part, I would translate myself (add subtitles), then play one segment at a time. I'd pause, and ask things like 'what happened?' and 'what do you think will happen?' It got them talking. The last five minutes I'd give them free time to ask me questions; if they were a keener they could slack off, or get me to do/help them with homework. I had one time where the girls were asking me a question, and I gave the answer. They said I was wrong but I assured them I wasn't, and that the book was. But hey, it's China. Or sometimes they'd ask me some reason for this grammar, and I couldn't tell them. I know how to talk English, not grammar formulas. One class, near the beginning was a little rough around the edges, so I had this thing where I'd jump up onto a desk. It was just easier to command them that way, and get them to listen. I did that a few times. They thought I was mental.

Another amazing story is that I solved a three year mystery. I call it The Mystery of the Soft Fingernail. Back in the first years teaching, I thought I had some vitamin deficiency, because my fingernails were thin, and bent so easily. I even did research on it, but nothing came up that made sense. Finally, years later I discovered that it was because when I wrote with chalk, my fingers would rub on the blackboard. Doing that for a few hours every day for a year will definitely thin out your finger shells. What else? Here's a few randoms. One day I see this person handing out fliers, which is a job in China I guess. Anyway, they're lazy, and instead of giving them to people, they're putting them in car door handles, or in the windshield wipers etc. Then I look, and about fifty feet behind this person is an old granny, taking every flier off. Maybe to recycle? I'm really not sure, but it was funny to watch. There was also always garbage burning in the middle of the side walk, everywhere I went. No biggie eh. Often I'd encounter fruit carts, purposefully set up to block 90% of the side walk. I mean, there was literally human traffic jams on the sidewalk from the people. And they never (literally almost never) were off to the side of the sidewalk like you'd think. They blocked it. I guess to 'get more business'? I don't know.

Something else I found super funny, in the strange way, is that Chinese don't upkeep things. Like their car. They just drive it until it breaks. And they do the same thing with their teeth. There's no 'check ups' for your car or teeth. You just wait until they don't work anymore and go fix them. I thought that was curious. I also had a friend whose father was a contractor guy. He had a company that built apartment buildings. So she told me, in China, here's how they do business. They agree on a price, and build the structures. Then when pay time comes, they short the contractor guy a bunch of money, but they say 'you can have a free penthouse apartment'. It was super common in all sorts of businesses.

Anyway, enough about that. I was on a mission. Like I said, my goal was to work, save money, and prep for University. The requirements to be accepted were HSK 4 (remember that's the Chinese Language Level Test thing). I was at about level 3 by now, so every day I spent hours studying. I basically needed to double my language in three months. The test only happened like four times a year, and I had to pass it before I could apply to University, and you need to apply to University before summer arrives. So it was a bit of stress. But I knuckled down, listened to dubstep mixes and drank a beer while I studied. It ruled. It was nice to have a goal. Eventually I found a nice little coffee shop too, and would often go, find a seat in the back with my headphones and study. I mostly needed to able to read the characters. Till this point I didn't know a lot, as it never really mattered. You can do a lot with just verbal communication. So my work was cut out for me. I think I learned about over 1000 words and about 800-ish new characters. It was a ton, in a short time. But right before my test I knew 99% of the HSK 4 vocab and could read pretty good. The other nice thing was that test you could do on a computer. Let me explain writing Chinese on a computer.

Well, if you've seen Chinese (which you have), you'll know there's a stupid amount of characters, and there's almost no way to be able to write them all from memory unless you're a mad genius. I'm not. So luckily for me, we could use a computer for the test. Now, Chinese has a phonetic system called pinyin, as I wrote way back yonder, near the first pages of this book. Anyway, if I type something like 'chang' there will be a ton of options pop up. And then you use the numbers to choose which character. Do you want 'long' 长 or do you want 'sing' 唱? It's not super hard really. The nice part is, if you're writing a longer word, with a few characters you can just type the first letter of each character. So something like 'zhangjiajie', the place they filmed Avatar, you could type zjj, and this would come up.

Then you push number 1. Common words would almost always work, and come up at number 1 or 2. Computers are smart! Anyway, in December I went to the Wuhan University to do the test. Then, I had to wait a month for the results. If I failed, I think there may have been a chance I could try again, but who wants to do that? The news finally came in, I had passed almost flawlessly. There was three parts, reading, writing, and listening, and I got over 96% on one and 98% on the others I think. I was proud of myself. Oh, I forgot to mention, on top of all of that, I spent about six weeks making Amy's one year Anniversary present. It was a book comprised of various drawings and stuff pertaining to love. I'd add some pics, but I don't want to.

I went to Thailand for just four days to see Amy around Dec 30th. It was fun. The nice thing about Thailand is you can hold hands in public and no one cares. Chinese people, as I said, like to stare, and so we could never do that before. It was so refreshing to not have people judging you (mostly her to be honest) at every turn.

Jan was spent chilling out. Most of my hard work was done, and I was free-er. Of course, Chinese New Year was coming around early Feb (it changes every year depending on the moon cycles or something), and my plan was to go help Mel for a few days back in Guiyang. So I let all my classes slack off before the holiday. Don't forget, their stress is maximum, and my class was their only time to let loose all week. Just forty minutes a week for fun. I let them watch movies or whatever. On a side note, if you wanna watch an utterly insane Chinese Anime, go on youtube and look up '100,000 Bad Jokes: The Movie'. It has subtitles, and is...wacky.

I took the sixteen hour slow train to Mel's. Regrets of life, let me tell you. I was in a 'hard sleeper', as I said before, six thin bunks with no door. So five Chinese neighbours. That was normal, and usually that was ok, but my bed was located near the end of the train. And near the end of the train, between cars was the 'smoking area'. No windows of course, so all the smoke drifted to me! Yay! As you imagine, after twelve hours of second hand smoke I was done in. I went to the toilet and barfed. Acid mouth, tired, insane headache. No biggie eh. I'll just have some water. Oh yeah, it's China and the water on this train didn't work. Usually the water works, but not this time. I was dead. I crawled back into my bed and survived the rest of the the trip. Anyway, helped Mel for a few days while all her Ayis were gone. It was decent and nice to see the kids again.

Back in Huangshi, I also wanted to do the 'spoken Chinese test'. It wasn't mandatory, but I wanted to try. Amy came to visit around that time, in March. Her job had finished as in Thailand the summer is so hot there they take their holiday from around March to May. My spoken test was in at the Wuhan University again, only in a different location, so I decided to go on my own for a day and find out where to go. I didn't want to book the test, pay, then be late from being lost. Anyway, me and Amy went back a few weeks later and I did the test.

Now I gotta toot my own horn here, but by now my spoken Chinese was pretty good, at least for life. I spoke quickly in Chinese as English, with somewhat equal proficiency. So I go to the test, expecting to basically talk with a human for fifteen minutes. Nope. It was 25 people in a room, sitting at a computer with headphones. I was taken off guard, but prepared. Seemed easy enough. Listen and repeat, listen and answer. Ok. So the first thing is repeat the sentence. The voice reads out a sentence, and I begin to talk. I'd finished about 60% of the sentence before anyone in the entire room had started talking even! Then they all spoke, in unison, word by word like a slow robot. Now. Can. You. Imagine. How. Annoyed. I was. To. Talk. So. Slow? It was brutal. It threw me off so bad, I mean to the point I'd say half a sentence and then just stop because I couldn't concentrate with 24 other voices chanting like illiterate idiots. I finally gave up. Literally just stopped trying. When the 'answer the question' part came, for 'free talk', I just answered a few questions, got up and left. That whole ordeal really annoyed me.

If you care, I did receive the minimal passing grade, which I think was 60%. The University called and said I could come pick up my paper thing. But I never did. I didn't even care. Stupid robot test.

Oh I forgot. Just before Amy arrived from Thailand, I'd bought a tent and lights. I set it up in my room, with the lights inside. It was lovely. She slept there and I in my bed. As I only had a few months left, I tried to pick up side jobs. But I'll tell ya, most of them sucked hard. I mean, taking into account that 'spoiled brat syndrome' I talked about before, most of the kids were straight up assholes. But it worked out. I trudged through and saved some sweet cash. I applied to the University in Guiyang, and got accepted. So that was nice. The rest of my time in Huangshi was uneventful. But here's some final random stories.

Many Chinese people don't really cover their sneeze. I had a few people turn their head towards me and sneeze all over me on the bus. And once on the plane, this dude sneezed all over my arm on the armrest. Thanks eh! What are...germs?

I also got my iPhone SE, which I still use to this day. There's a reason I buy Apple. Oh, and one day I'm teaching, and I smell this gnarly odour. I recognize it from my days helping doing pest control for my Aunt. Chemicals. I look outside of the classroom, and there's some dude walking up the halls spraying the floors with copious amounts of some chemical. Don't ask. Another nice thing about China is there's no 'no loitering' signs or rules anywhere. Well, I guess it was also not ideal because KFC would always be full of people, but only about 30% of them eating. The rest were seniors, either talking or playing on their phone with free wifi. Last story: Chinese people clip their nails everywhere. I mean, *everywhere*. On the bus, in class, at restaurants etc... Makes my skin crawl every time. But that's just me, I digress.

# Chapter 7: University - 1.5 years

Well, Amy decided to do another year in Thailand teaching Chinese. So that was a bit sad for me. After summer though, I returned to see her in August for a visit. We got one hotel on Koh Samui, the wonderful island in the south. I think it was like 20$ CDN for a night, like forty feet from the beach. That was epic. We also did thee ol 'put your feet in the fish tank and let the small fish eat your dead skin' experience. I'm super ticklish, so it wasn't my favourite. I could barely do it. We also got another hotel, but they were renovating it, so that was the opposite of relaxing.

Besides all that we mostly toured around a bit more and 'saw more of the sights'. Man, Thailand is so legit. I love their culture. Did I say that already? Oh I just remembered this story. So I arrive at the airport in Thailand and have to go through customs. There's a million people, and the line to the booths was winding and long. Finally I get to choose a booth line to join. There's like ten booths open with customs officers. I never really care about a few people, so I just pick a random line without thinking. Then I watch.

The line directly beside me moves, and moves some more. Then I find that in about twenty minutes, around ten people passed through their line, but only *one* of mine. That's when I realize my mistake. I had lined up with "brown people". And since a few days before there'd been a 'terrorist bombing' in Thailand, they were getting scanned very thoroughly. I switched lines, and made in through the new line before two more guys had got through my *previous* line. Anyway, I was in. Now, back to my insane University life story. Where do I even begin?

Looking back now, my time at University was one of the best of life, despite all the bullshit I had to deal with, and there was a lot. So let's start at the beginning. I arrived and got my books - Ancient Chinese Literature. That meant this: Chinese has two types of characters. One set is 'traditional' and one is 'simplified'. As you guessed it, I'd been learning (just like all Chinese people) the simplified, as that was what they started using since 1949. Traditional characters were old, I mean thousands of years old, and hardly any Chinese person could read them. Not only that, almost every character had a different meaning from today's meaning. It was like giving Shakespeare to a toddler. Absolutely no difference. I went to every lesson for the next 1.5 years understanding 0% of everything. I mean, I got zero of it all, and my Chinese was decent. I will say, that 'requirement' to be accepted which was HSK 4 was wholly useless. I might as well have been in Korea. The classes were even hard for the Chinese students, which says a lot. (To make matters worse, Chinese has something they call 口音 'mouth sound' which means 'accent', and not all of our teachers were from Guiyang, which meant many had accents. So when I say it was hard for Chinese students, that's because it would be the equivalent for you listening to someone with a hard Irish or Scottish accent. Doable if you're fluent in English, hard if you're not.) So that was hard to deal with. Luckily for me, one of my two foreign classmates was the best dude I've ever met. And I'll tell you straight up, I couldn't have survived without him. (He wrote the forward (and Yin Yang part) for this book!)

Enter Antonio, a Colombian dude, about 24 years old. His native language was Spanish, but he knew a ton of Italian, French, and he'd basically taught himself English. He was totally a genius. He even began studying about two or three other languages while at University with me as well. Not only that, he was insanely musically gifted, and him being such a legit dude, we got along instantly and were best buddies. Now, as far as classes went, it got tricky. We were the only foreigners in history at this University to attempt this major. At any rate, due to our lack of proficiency in Chinese, we were unable to attend a few of the classes that required a higher Chinese skill level. Other foreigners were, to a degree, in the same situation. Most foreigners took majors like 'accounting' or whatever but some classes we just couldn't do.

So the school, being somewhat considerate in this matter made up some extra classes we could take for credits. Like tae kwon do, tai chi, calligraphy brush writing, culture and things like that. Basically free credits. And those classes were legitly fun. Especially the culture class. The teacher Mr. Soup was one of the best Chinese people I ever met during my entire time in China. He had studied in America, so was a little more sympathetic towards us, and his knowledge about the Chinese culture was unparalleled. Not only that, he was just an all around friendly guy. His class was the best one I ever had and was always the highlight of my week and I genuinely looked forward to it.

I forgot to mention, there was one other foreigner classmate we had. She was a meek, shy, quiet girl from Laos. So me and Antonio didn't really hang out with her. Moreover, she had all her own Laos friends there, so she was set up. As for me, I had a few American friends. They were a bit odd, but for the most it was nice to have some 'normal people' to talk with. I even found a church group which they held in their apartment. No Chinese allowed, or we could all get arrested. So that was made up of about three families, and about three of us students.

The dorms, they were about five stories high, maybe six. I had my own room, super small, with a bathroom. No kitchen. That was nice, because Amy told me her dorm room before had eight girls, and no bathroom. Four sets of bunks. That's crazy. I forget what we paid, but one month of rent for me was the entire year of rent for Amy. Once again I went to buy puzzle mat pieces for the floor. That tiled floor got COLD in winter. Remember, cement buildings... Anyway, the guy that moved in a week later across from me was from the Netherlands, and was super chill. We hung decent amounts, and I also helped him translate sometimes as his Chinese was about HSK 1 or 2 only. (People could also come to this University to study 'basic Chinese language'. He was one.) So that was nice. After he moved out, about six months later, I got this super nerd neighbour, but he was kinda a dick. One night when I was in bed trying to sleep at 11PM, he knocks on my door and asks if I have any booze. I didn't, of course. After days went by and I ignored him, I think he got the hint. Especially one night. Like I said, he was a nerd, and he was in China solely to slack off and play video games. So for *some* reason, he would leave his door open, and I could hear him furiously clicking and hitting the mouse on the desk. Like, not just a little. Mad amounts. Super nerd level.

Of course I snapped, as I do. Yelled at him and slammed his door for him. Well, it turned out that most of the foreigners hated him too, and he was one of those 'clingers'. He just invited himself along with people of his own volition. Felt a bit bad for the guy, but I wasn't mentally stable enough to have energy to care. I had a bunch of other crap to deal with. Classes were like lifting two fifty pound bags of rice up uneven stairs, blindfolded, forever. I strained to listen and follow along, but it was useless. Eventually we started this one class, with a legit teacher, but a teacher with integrity. He gave us so much strife, but at least we could empathize with him. He told us 'why should I pass you when you can't do the work?' The Chinese students (mostly 18 years old eh) had to bust their ass to learn this stuff. Why should we get a free ticket? Understandable, but also, not ideal for us. We never did end up being able to pass his class. The other major drama we encountered was this, and it pertained to the infamous 'Guanxi' (relationships).

Remember before (I'm sure you do by now, sorry), I said Guanxi was one of the most important things in China, but it could also be to your detriment. For example; I offend someone and break our Guanxi, I lose that connection to whatever. So in our case, we were the fodder for this broken relationship between the 'Foreigner Office' who took care of *us* and the 'Language Department' who was in charge of our *classes*. They'd had some falling out before we came onto the scene, but because they would't talk to each other, we got stiffed. So we had to basically try on our own accord to solve our 'unable to pass that class' problem. Most of it fell on deaf ears. One lady in the office yelled at me, calling me names for something totally asinine, so I laid into her. She was definitely taken aback. My point was correct and I was not about to take any of her crap. I forget what even happened with all that.

Besides that, we also had Gym class. That was fun, for the most part. That was the tae kwon do class, among other things. What else happened? I guess a few things. Christmas came, and the girls in the Foreign Office decided that me and Antonio should be hosts for the huge annual foreigner performance. We agreed. (I forgot to mention, I had previously bought a legit cheap suit in Thailand, so I wore it. Who knew I'd need a suit? I guess Amy did, as she convinced me to buy it. Smart girl.) Anyway, the event was mostly all the different countries doing something culturally related to themselves. I think there was about eight in all. There were also four other hosts. The bummer part was that the school provided some students to help us write our dialogue. So me and Antonio came up with a ton of great Chinese related jokes and puns and it was going to be great. Then, the 'boss-person' (whoever that was) reviewed what we'd written and cut most of it out. Bloody censorship eh. We still had some ok jokes though, mostly making fun of each country.

Also at some point I won the 'Top Ten Student' award (as did Antonio) and got a cool wooden plaque. It's on my mom's bookshelf as we speak. There was also a language competition after that event for us foreigners. I talked about my experience in Changsha and Sanmenxia, at the orphanage. Well, I didn't win that one due to me never being able to act professional and my Chinese sounding sloppy, but that was ok. Everyone said my speech was great none the less. By the time summer came the school said we had to move dorms. I did forget to mention, half our classes were about a two minute walk from the current dorm, and the other half were about a twenty minute walk away, at the "new campus" they were still constructing. Well, the new dorms were in this new building, which I found out later was classically made in China, and nothing worked. I think they didn't have showers (water) for about a month. And things were breaking etc... So I had this one buddy Jay. He was on of the best dudes too, at the university. We decided 'why not rent an apartment?' So we looked around. It was hard, but we found one right in the middle of the University. It was legit! And the same price as renting a dorm room. (A fun fact about China is, when their trucks back up, they don't make the 'beep' noise like in Canada. They actually talk. They say 'please pay attention, vehicle backing up' (请注意倒车) on repeat. It was SUPER annoying, and because our apartment was next to the mini school bus stop, we heard it like sixteen hours a day all day.)

The one nice thing was that there was a coffee shop below the apartment and I befriended the owners. A dude and his GF. And I know I've said it before about some other people, but they were and are seriously two of the greatest people I've ever met. We hung out a ton, and I was always there. So me and Antonio also decided to start a 'Chinese corner'. Remember how I said in Changsha we went to English corner? Well, that was for the Chinese people to improve their English. But we wanted to improve out Chinese, and to be honest it wasn't always easy to just have normal conversations with Chinese people. So we did it, and it was fun. A bunch of the foreigners from the Uni came out, and many Chinese students as well. It was a real good crew. And I still keep in touch with the owners to this day. They just had a baby!

Now, since me and Antonio were basically long lost brothers, we hung out a ton. It was great, as I said. The best part too was, since he actually learned Chinese from a good teacher for more than six months like I did, he was able to really *learn* the language, and he would frequently teach me interesting things I never knew. For me, I learned the basics and what was necessary to survive and converse, but the rest I learned from life. So one day, while we were walking to get pulled noodles he told me about the Yin Yang. When I was doing this book I asked him to write a little about it for me as I think you will appreciate it too. Also, before you read the next part, the pronunciation for Yin sounds like 'tin' and Yang sounds like 'young'; the 'a' in Chinese has a 'u' sound. Ok, proceed.

# The Yin-Yang

by Antonio Rodríguez Durán

According to Chinese mythology, before characters there were only two ways of putting thoughts into paper, a continuous line and an interrupted one. These two represented the forces that rule the natural world; the yin and the yang. This precedes all the other schools of thinking, religions and philosophies of China. The conception of yin and yang, although highly present in Daoism, is proper to a way of conceiving the world before there was any texts to explain it. These two lines had a third one added to them and thus the antagonistic, complementary and syncretic forces of Light/Darkness, Feminine/Masculine, Moon/Sun, Passive/Active were now expanded to represent those of Sky (Top line), Man (Middle line) and Earth (Lower line). These were called 'Trigrams' and are the base upon which the I-Ching, or the Classic of Mutations is written.

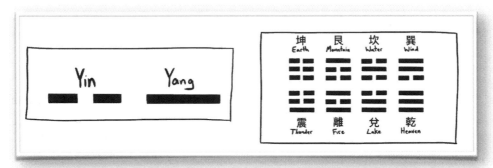

These lines were more than enough to speak of the world as we perceive it. "Fire" 离 does not affect the Sky, since its smoke blends with the clouds and it doesn't affect Earth either, since the ashes of what is burn goes back to the earth. It only affects man, thus "fire" is represented by a top uninterrupted line, a middle interrupted line, and a low uninterrupted line.

But once we were in need of weaving more complex ideas, characters arose. It is said that it was Cang Jie, a scribe for the Yellow Emperor, who by looking at the shadows of the leaves, the footprints of birds and the shape of the clouds, condensed the world into characters. These characters, nonetheless, did not lose the information its ancestors had in their trigrams. Yin and Yang were and still are a fundamental component of Chinese Characters.

China might be as ripe with historical facts as it is with stereotypes. One of the most hazardous misconceptions of China is that it is a mysterious country/

culture/tradition etc. China's hyper-exoticization (the conversion of something into a more exotic form) has lead to an apparently harmless image abroad, but it very much undermines its philosophies. Since what we consider mysterious is not only foreign but also dependent of the fact of remaining unclear, thus having no other choice than to approach only partially to all that China represents. Yin and Yang is the perfect example.

Perhaps the only two things Yin-Yang do not represent are "Good" and "Evil", and sadly through saying: "light and darkness" (which is exactly and most viscerally what yin-yang would stand for) we think of the good/evil divide. Nothing could be further from that.

And yet, we read these and tend to associate obscurity and passivity to negative aspects of life. Perhaps, we're more in need of perspective than in need of a dictionary. Plants need shadows to grow, as mushrooms do too. A face too light is pale, sign of sickness and even death. Chinese is ridden with yins and yangs.

The character 休 (combining a person 人 and a tree 木) means "to rest" and denotes a passive relationship with nature "you rest your back on the trunk of a tree" while 仙 (combining a person 人 and a mountain 山) which means "sage" denotes an active relationship, since "a sage is the person that climbs up a mountain in order to attain wisdom". We can see this balance between Yin and Yang all over Chinese words, not only individual characters. Such as:

左右 (zuǒ yòu): left + right = approximately
大小 (dà xiǎo): big + small = size
买卖 (mǎi mài): buy + sell = commerce
长短 (cháng duǎn): long + short = length

Chinese is an elusive language. Not in the sense that it is hard to learn, speak or use but rather because it's writing system is highly systematic, but not entirely so. You won't be able to deduce that a character is pronounced in a certain way or has a certain set of meanings. What you can do is take what the English language has expressed in the most beautiful way as an educated guess. Your conclusion will not then be entirely a logical one, since it is now tinged with imagination. I believe that if you are looking at the character 谢 for the first time, you wouldn't be able to know that it means "to thank" and that it is formed by the semantic radical 讠 (言) which means language,  and the phonetic element 射 which is pronounced shè, and therefore our original character 谢 is pronounced xiè, not at least through sheer logic, we need a little aid of our instinct, our imagination and sensibility. Much more difficult would it be to engage in a more in-depth analysis by just "thinking" in the most rational sense of the word. Since we could slice the character in three and remain with 讠, 身, and 寸 which would mean correlatively: "language, body, unit of measure" which may well be understood as "the reverence (bowing in the correct angle 寸) one does (with one's own body 身) when bidding farewell (with words 讠). That is: thanking our host when leaving, whence the meaning of 谢 is linked to the verb "to wither" (谢落), as well as the deep-rooted differences of politeness, particularly when saying "thank you" in China.

This elusiveness is hand-in-hand with coming to terms with the fact that the natural world follows its own rhythm, and we can just try to understand it in the most humble way possible. It tells us also that we should not come to hasty conclusions when met with a character as we might not know all that there is to it. And finally, it perhaps teaches us to make a responsible use of our imagination, and to educatedly guess.

~

Back to the story. I also bought a sweet flatland BMX off Taobao, the Chinese 'Amazon', only much better. I mean, Taobao sold frozen turkeys to your doorstep, or even live animals (for a pet). It had almost everything to exist that was legal. So that was rad. It was a Haro, and had a gyro and pegs. I even met these dudes who had trials bikes, so I befriended them and hung out a few times with them. They were pretty good. Sadly, after I left, I had to sell it, so Antonio bought it. Then he told me shortly after, it was locked up outside and someone stole it. Dang it! But I used that bike all the time to go to class. Why walk when you can ride? Oh ya, and back at the old dorm, the foreigners liked to party. I mean, fair enough. They were mostly all in their 20s, and most of them weren't there for a life altering degree and their entire future didn't depend on good sleep and study. Not me though. I was old, jaded, bitter and an insomniac.

One night, on a Sunday, they were in the hallways (which were exposed to the main hall) partying hard and loud. I snapped, came out in my undies and told them to "shut the eff up, it's Sunday and I have class tomorrow!" But they were cool. They eased up. At least there was no hard feelings, and we were all still buddies. Sometime I even did hang with them and have some beers. Good times. (Hopefully by this point you don't think all I do is get mad at people. I just have found these kinds of stories are seemingly more entertaining than the ones where life is perfect and everything goes smoothly. Ha.)

Another funny tale me and Antonio had was this. Well, first of all, I'll back up. Chinese people don't communicate really well, as I said. Anyway, so because me and Antonio had won the 'top ten student' thing, the school paper wanted to do an article about us. No biggie. We just had to meet up for some pictures and a quote or two. Well, Antonio didn't know about this and we waited about over an hour. Meanwhile I'm with some awkward Chinese people I don't want to talk with. We called and texted, but nothing came of it. Finally this one guy is like 'I'll go to his dorm and get him', so he leaves. A while later they saunter up, and Antonio is in full rage mode, only it's in his eyes, not his actions. He flashes me a warning like 'I'm going to cut someone', and I give him a nod in recognition. So we do the photo shoot and leave immediately for some lunch. Then he tells me what happened.

Well, I think I'll have to spare some details for his sake, but needless to say, the guy who went to his dorm was a jackass and super disrespectful. Food and conversation helped. Me and him bonded a lot on mere complaining during our time together. It was a good way to vent, a form of therapy for us. Ok, let me get into the 'bad communicating part' for a sec.

## Chinese Culture: Straight talk, and non-straight talk - Part 2
### -Abysmal Communication Skills-

There was a strange dichotomy in China. I found it went something like this. Someone would want to get a hold of you, and call over and over and over and over and over and over. (They did the same thing when knocking on doors. Knock, wait 0.3 seconds and knock again and again and again.) So they would put all this effort into it. Cells phones have caller ID now though, so there's not really a point in calling over and over. It was that, or the opposite. They'd plan to meet at

1:00PM, then call at 11:30AM and say "I'm free now let's meet". It was all over the place, and it happened more often than not.

One time my Chinese classmate (who was super rad) said he had a friend who had a few questions for me. I assumed he meant English language questions. Lesson 1 million, don't assume in China. You'll never be correct. So they call an hour early and say 'we're downstairs'. I'm not ready, of course, but I oblige. So we walk and talk. It was a dude and a chick; students. Anyway, I keep asking things like 'so what do you wanna know, my friend said you had questions', but them being Chinese ninja level in avoiding giving straight answers, they never told me. And we walked for about ten minutes in the direction of the market and restaurants. As we're walking they're like "oh, hey, let's just stop in this shop for a second", so I agree. Getting a little annoyed by now. Mostly because this always seemed to happen.

Upon entering the shop, which was for makeup or something female related, I have about twenty people turn and stare at me. Then I get swarmed. It was a ploy all along! To dupe me into coming. So I did the obligatory 'pictures'; selfies and the likes. I may be a dick, but I'm not 100% dick. I did what I could. Then they're like 'oh just come with us for dinner'. I was like 'fine, ok whatever'. (It makes for a good story though right?) So we go to dinner, and it's the usual large table with a huge lazy susan and a ton of food. So many people, so loud. I ate a bit, made some excuse and left. After I saw my classmate I told him they tricked me, and to never give my phone number to anyone else again. He felt a bit bad, but he was cool about it. I wasn't actually mad at him; he didn't know.

~

I also didn't mention, my absolute favourite noodle shop, the pulled noodles (soup or fried), was about a fifteen minute walk from my dorm. I went so so often. I mean, they were so good, and the other food was so mediocre; according to me at least. After six years of rice and misc fried-in-oil veggies and meat. Oh, and I never told you, there was a 'sour soup' shop. That noodle soup was one of the best things in life as well. Anyway, there was another area with restaurants, so I did an experiment. I walked all the four alleys looking for food that wasn't rice or noodles. That didn't exist. It was all rice and noodles. Kill me now. The good news was, about a quick 25-30 min walk there was a Starbucks, McDonalds, movie theatre and huge grocery store. So that helped.

This theatre was like Canada, as you'd expect. We went a few times. The American movies were in English, with subtitles. The funny thing was, the subtitles were often wrong, and my guess was that was on purpose as China isn't as perverted as America (sorry America). So lots of those kinds of jokes were translated quite differently. An example was, when we to see Guardian of the Galaxy 2. Near the beginning when Drax says something about his nipples, but the translation said 'chest'. I forget the actual quote by now.

Oh, here's another story I was thinking about last night. This one job I had teaching English was so stressful I even had panic attacks last night thinking about thinking about it. Here's how it went. Six hours, three classes of two hours. 200元 an hour, which is about $40 CDN. A good job, in theory. The main problem was two-fold. It was mad far, and the kids were, yes you guessed it, entitled little brats. Well, the one redeeming thing was they would send a driver for me to pick me up, but I still had to walk about twenty minutes to the main highway, then get driven about an hour. The first or second week I taught there, I literally walked out of class. I was losing it. The kids were just mental. So I'm raging, and I go sit in the office. Then some teacher comes in super confused. I told her "I'm not teaching these kids. They have no respect, don't listen, and are just running around the classroom throwing toys". Keep in mind, these classes were only about twelve kids, and I'd already taught classes of fifty kids for three years. I was no rookie.

The teacher went to the class, talked to the kids, then invited me back in. Anyway, who cares? Weeks went by, and they moved to a new building. I had a sort of obligation to this job by now. I was getting better, knowing the kids and figuring out how to manage them better. But for real, two hours per class, times three was exhausting. I mean, utterly insane. Because you gotta be top of your game for all six hours. The good part about that job was that the boss was super nice. Those days when I had to get picked up at like 1PM for that job, I would lay in bed shaking, in a fetal position. No breakfast, no nothing. Just anxiety to the max. The stress was beyond. But you do what you have to, and I would always just suck it up and give er. Getting $240 CDN at the end of the night helped the cause.

Well, here's a good job story to brighten your mood. Me and Antonio got this job for the day, $200 CDN for a day, which actually turned into about one hour of actual work, if you can call it that. Here's what happened. This super rich guy needed white people to pretend to be chefs. He said you just stand around behind a booth with some food. That's it. So he picked us up, along with four other people. Two of them were dating; a rad Mexican guy names Jesus, and his girlfriend from Italy. The other two were ladyboy students from Thailand who were super fun. (If you don't know what a ladyboy is, it's basically a dude who dresses and acts like a girl 100% of the time, but still has a penis.) The ladyboy's job was to dance on stage for like ten minutes. That was it. So he picked us up and we drove a few hours. This guy had a big event with food and music and a stage. I guess to bring people in to advertise his business. I'm not sure. Well, that evening, we didn't work because not many people came, so he bought us all dinner and a hotel. The next day, same thing, so we had lunch, then went to work. We stood around for a bit in a fake white shirt and chef hat, then that's it. We hung out more, and he drove us back.

Also during my time at University Amy brought me to see a traditional Chinese medicine doctor. He was super nice, and would feel my pulse, and check my tongue colour etc... I went because I could never sleep good. Well, I doubt you've ever had real traditional Chinese medicine before, so let me recount precisely as I can how it tasted. It was a drink, which I had to keep cold. I could only take one sip at a time or I'd dry heave. It was strong like plant extract, bitter and what you'd imagine vodka being without the alcohol. Just powerful as it gets. There's really no words for it. So I did that for a few months but I think ultimately it did nothing beneficial health-wise.

When summer came I returned home to Canada for a few months. It was then I started this book, well, the translation one. The entire next semester of classes, I would ignore the teacher and just work on my book, finding words and translating them. It was great. Side note, we had one chick teacher who said the same thing every few seconds. Compared to English, we would say something like "Eating properly and exercising is healthy, right? That "right?" has a Chinese equivalent. It's 是不是 or 对不对 - 'shi bu shi' or 'dui bu dui'. They basically mean 'yes not yes' (yes or no?) and 'correct not correct' (right or wrong?). But she would say it after almost *every* sentence. I finally started counting how many times she would say it per class. It was a *ton*. Me and Antonio loathed her with a burning passion. She was completely monotone and had no personality. Sorry to say. Eventually I just put headphones in and just listened to music. For real; it was a nightmare. I'm sure she was a nice human, and I didn't genuinely hate her as a person, just her teaching & talking style.

Well, I'd been trying to master HSK 5 for the past year by now, because they said 'for you to graduate you need to pass HSK 6'. Which was very, very intimidating. The main problem I had with the test was we were only allotted two hours to complete it, and this time it was by *hand*, not computer. We did a practice HSK 5 test, and I didn't even finish and failed it. Antonio passed though as he was a linguistic ninja/prodigy. At that time I knew about 50% of the 1300 new words. And HSK 6 had 2500 *more* words to learn. Oh my. I was pretty sure I'd never pass HSK 6.

Side stories: Early in the new year me and Amy went to this wedding for her cousin. The drive was two hours, only it was a holiday, and it took six. I was dying. But it was fun...sorta. More awkward than anything as there's this tradition in parts of China where the bride is locked in the house, and the groom has to break in to get her. The bride's family have to stop him, but he can pay them with fake (or real?) money. If you know me, I do not appreciate these "fun" events, and they make me uncomfortable, so I stood at a distance and watched. They seemed to be having good times, and I'm pretty sure the front door was destroyed and a few windows, but that's half the fun eh! Otherwise, I got some cool pictures in a new town.

Me and Amy also went to that place I mentioned before with all the small mountains that jutted up from the earth called Yangshuo. The best story there was this. We find a flier for a hot air balloon ride, and it looks *epic*. Like they bring you all over the area. Prime romance! For some reason which I forget now, we had to pay in advance, but it was worth it. Well, it was until we got there. What it was, was actually a hot air balloon tied to the ground. it would go up about 100 meters for about five minutes then come back down. That was it. So, I guess it makes for a funny story, but we were pretty bummed. I also bought an Xbox One in December, as I'd been tuning out life and playing that a decent amount. Yay for coping mechanisms that are fun!

That year me and Amy had made plans. Since I still had two and a half years left at school, and she wanted to do her masters, it made sense that she would be near me. So she applied to the same University, which was no small feat. It was a ton of work and stress. When she got the news she'd been accepted, that was great! Only, that was around Jan of 2018. And I was at my wits end. I mean, we were still dealing with the language department about that class, and there was a bunch of other things happening as well. I was really just tired of

China and the future was so daunting. The sad part is, I kinda knew all this by last summer, but part of me wanted to 'push on for the sake of love'. I really did try my best to succeed and create a viable future for me and Amy, but it just didn't happen that way, and that was super hard to deal with. Not just for me, but since I would go home (I finally decided) we would have to break up. She was only my second GF, and I was her first BF, so it was really emotionally exhausting and physically painful in my chest. Broken love due to 'life's circumstances' sucks. It's one thing to break for relationship reasons, but to break for other reasons sucks more.

Anyway, once I decided to go home, there was a huge weight lifted off me. I mean, as I wrote before, I'd been having mental problems since Mel's. It was beyond hard to go, but also beyond easy, if that makes sense. Bitter sweet I guess. And on top of that, I still hold a huge burden of disappointing Amy. I mean, she basically altered her entire life for me, applied to this (pretty crappy) school for me, and committed to three long years of abusive teachers and stupid classes. Her main teacher has been verbally abusing her, calling her stupid and useless for the entire time. She also would basically blackmail Amy, because as it is, she holds Amy's future in her hands. If she fails her, she loses three years and a masters degree. That happens a lot in China, sadly. So Amy had to do what she says out of fear.

That's about it I guess. My reflections on China? Well, it may seem from what I wrote it was mostly hell on Earth, and parts of it were, and elements of it were, but overall, I look back fondly on it all. I experienced a plethora of things most people who live in China never even get to experience. I was very blessed to meet a ton of super amazing people as well. If the world wasn't so crazy these days, I would highly recommend you visit China and see the sights and experience getting stared at for yourself. Just make sure you find pulled noodles made by Muslims and you're life will be complete.

# Out.

# The Alchemist and the Turtle

{A short story from 2010}

# The Alchemist: Part 1

As the summer sun shone high above, a small carriage traveled down a lonely road on it's way to a nearby city known as Brisdinville. Inside this particular carriage was an alchemist, but not just any alchemist; he was greatest in the land and his name was Galgeroth. Earlier on the same day, while at home, Galgeroth had received an urgent letter from the King of the nearby city asking him to brew a potion and that he would need it as soon as possible. So, much to the dismay of Galgeroth he prepared what he needed and set off.

The road they were currently on, although dirt, was soft and smooth, which was perfect for the alchemist who needed certain conditions to brew the potion the King desired. That is to say he needed a constant subtle vibration. And so the alchemist called Galgeroth brewed while they drove. Hours passed and then something unfortunate happened. Just as Galgeroth was about to finish his potion the carriage stopped moving. Everything he'd worked for was ruined.

"Why have we stopped?" thundered the alchemist shoving his head out of the window. "You know I said we must keep moving; I need the vibrations of the carriage constant to that my potion will brew properly. Now look!" he said throwing some liquid out of a flask into the fallen leaves nearby. "You've ruined it!"

His driver froze as he looked back at the alchemist. "A thousand hundred million apologies master" he screeched in a frightened voice, "There was a large rock and I didn't want to drive over it. But I have moved it now and we can travel without any more problems. I thought one *large* bump would be worse than no bumps at all..." he stammered awkwardly.

"It doesn't matter now!" shouted the angry alchemist, "I have to start over again." Then he popped his head back into his carriage and started all over mumbling to himself about how he was going to brew his driver a special potion that would make his body turn into wood, which made his spirits cheerful and he once more began to mix odd things together while the carriage proceeded on.

# The Turtle: Part 1

One day a turtle left it's pond in hopes of finding a new life in another part of the world. His friends had told him about larger ponds and great areas known as 'swamps' where there is marshland for miles. So the turtle, known to all simply as Ted, left his home. It was a sunny day and recently the leaves had just fallen. 'The weather is perfect' he thought 'for a good adventure. I've never left my pond, so I think I will leave to see the world and the great wonderers I hear so much about' and with that he said good-bye to his friends and headed off. The hours passed and Ted's excitement began to fade. How much longer would it take to find a new pond? Or new friends? But then he came to a road. 'This is where humans drive their carriages' he thought getting excited, 'maybe I will get to see one!' and he slowly began to cross the road.

As he crossed the shade the trees gave disappeared and soon Ted found himself very thirsty, and he noticed too that his shell was beginning to dry out. 'I ought to find some water soon or I shall die!' thought Ted while he put each leg in front of the other fast as he could, but since he was a turtle that wasn't very fast. Then he heard a strange rattling noise. 'A carriage!' he thought getting excited, 'maybe I can ask for some help from a human; I have heard such nice things about them' and he waited while the noise got louder.

Then as he was about to yell towards the driver of the carriage he noticed the man look at him. Panic struck, the human pulled the carriage to a full stop. 'This is it' thought the turtle, 'I didn't even have to *ask* for help, and the human is giving it to me.' Ted watched the human jump down and come towards him in a hurry. Then long human arms reached out and picked Ted up. Ted was just about to thank the man when he heard the man mumble something about 'stupid rock, who leaves a rock this big in the middle of the lane?' when he was tossed, tumbling and flipping way into the air. He could hear voices as he flew up and up. "Why have we stopped?" yelled one human, but right then Ted came down with a crash and his shell smashed upon the rocks that were near by. A sharp ringing noise hit him and pain flowed all over his body while he flopped out of his broken shell onto the ground.

He felt instantly cold and began to shiver. He struggled to look around and could see his split open shell laying beside him. 'What has happened?' though Ted while he lay dying. 'This is no adventure at all, but a murder. I have been murdered by a human! But I'm not dead yet' and he began to be filled with a strange feeling. He thought he would like to go back to the humans and tell them he was not a rock but in fact a turtle named Ted. So he rolled over, got up and looked at his new shell-less body. He still felt weak but began to climb over the rocks back to the area where the road was. He was ever so thirsty now.

# The Alchemist: Chapter 2

It was some time before the alchemist reached the city and entered through the large gates. He quickly reached the castle where the King lived and quickly entered. At once he was brought before the King and made to give the potion over. The alchemist was relieved too, for his potion had just only finished, and had the driver stopped any sooner it would not have been, and the alchemist knew that if the potion wasn't finished on time his head would be cut from his body. "You have my elixir?" asked the King as he sat lazily on his throne which was elegant like a petrified wind storm made of gold. The alchemist confirmed by giving it to a servant and then, bowing low, Galgeroth said "it is what you asked for my King, a concoction that will make a dying body well again."

The King gave some orders and the potion was brought into the next room. Then the door closed and silence fell upon the room. The alchemist knew that the King was waiting for news that the potion worked successfully, and hoped beyond hope that he had mixed it properly. It was a very hard potion to mix and he'd only made *one* before, although at that time it had worked. Then a shout of success came from the room and the King instantly turned into a whole different person. He rose with his hands in the air and yelled cheers of joy. Galgeroth simply stood, half bowed and wondered what to do next. The King it seemed had forgotten about him with the joyous occasion and left to the next room, but the alchemist knew were he not to wait for an order from the King to depart, his head would be cut from his body.

Then the King reappeared and walked up to the alchemist. "My son is well again thanks to you, potion maker. Now in return what can I do for you, name it and it shall be yours." Galgeroth was taken aback by such a statement. He'd not ever thought about being offered anything he wanted, but without thinking his mouth spoke words. "I want to be King."

The King laughed hardily and shook his gut, but then he realized the alchemist was serious. Galgeroth hadn't meant to say it, but now that he had, he knew it was true. There was part of him that wanted to rule the Kingdom. Then everything became awkward as the King wasn't about to go back on his word, because if he did he would lose the crown, and if he didn't he would lose face, and forsake the crown. The alchemist knew it, he had the King trapped. The servants had gone still as a morning pond and the room became dead silent and no one dared to do anything.

## The Turtle: Part 2

Ted climbed the final rock and felt as though he might die. He thirsted very badly by now and since his shell was gone his skin was not used of being out in the open. He looked and found some leaves on the ground with left over dew from the morning and perhaps rain from the pervious fall during the night. He began to take each leaf as though it held treasure and sipped each one dry. He sipped and sipped and then after drinking one leaf in particular his body began to feel strange. He looked and noticed that some of the water was a strange colour, and had he not been flying through the air would have known that the oddly coloured water he had just drunk was actually some ruined potion that Galgeroth the human had thrown from his window.

Ted began to feel very queer, and pain began to pulsate all over his body. He yelled and screamed and tore at his skin and he thought he might die just then, but he did not. Instead his body began to grow and his skin became thick and he sprouted large claws and his tail grew a large bunch of spikes. His legs became muscular and his mouth grew many sharp teeth. In a matter of minutes he had grown about the size of a human. The pain finally receded and Ted collapsed in exhaustion. 'What just happened?' He thought, 'what have I become?' He had no idea about the potion of course, but one thought went through his mind. 'Now that I have this body I can find the human faster, so that I may tell him I am not a rock.' Ted made a plan to follow the road. He thought it was yet another chance for a great adventure and so he began to walk, and soon realized he could stand, much like a human, and he would gain speed walking this way so he continued to do so.

After some hours Ted found himself approaching a large city. He had not seen a city in his whole life and thought it would be quite exciting to visit and converse with the humans that lived there, so he began to run towards it, all the while getting more and more excited.

The city was nothing spectacular, but it did have a decent sized wall surrounding it, and of course a gate with guards who didn't do a lot except stand around looking like guards. Once it was said one guard stopped someone bad, but that was told by someone who knew someone, so it may not be entirely true. And so on this particular day the guard had the honour of looking up to see an excited green beast running towards him with a spiked tail waving behind and a large grin showing razor teeth.

The guard fumbled his spear which flipped around and fell to the ground. He yelled to his partner who had his helmet tilted over his face while he slept in a leaning chair. The other guard lifted the helmet with much effort and peeked out. Then he flipped off his chair onto the ground with his mouth open about four inches. Ted of course didn't realize what he looked like to them, and only saw humans which he may talk to. He was quite intrigued by their action and wondered why they were holding out their spears toward him.

## The Alchemist: Part 3

The King had thought about what had happened and decided that since he had his son alive and well, that that was worth more than ruling the land, so he spoke loud so that all the room could hear. "I, King Gaventry hereby pass my crown the the alchemist known as Galgeroth so that he may rule over the land."

Everyone in the room gasped as the King removed the crown and put it upon Galgeroth's head. Then he bowed, and asked permission to go see his son. Galgeroth granted it, and then looked at the throne. He grinned large, and then made his way over to sit down. Then the sound to break the silence was a subtle cough from his driver. King Galgeroth looked up. "Ah yes, my trusted driver. I suppose now that I am King you would like a reward of some sort, for being so loyal and good to me, and stopping my carriage to move a rock from the road ruining my potion." The driver went white with fear. Then the new King laughed, "oh no, don't you see, it all worked out, and for that you are half the reason I am sitting here now. Yes, I will reward you, but I won't be so foolish as to say you may have anything you want." The driver took a sigh of relief and approached the new King. "Sir I wish for my family to have enough money to live without working for the rest of our lives." The King granted it, and the driver left a happy man and the King thought that being King wasn't so hard.

So Galgeroth sat at his throne for quite some time. He had told everyone except a few guards to leave the great hall so that he could just sit and think. For the alchemist liked to think, and think he did until there was a great clatter outside the main doors.

## The Turtle: Part 3

Ted stopped short of the guards who shook in their boots while they spoke like a shaky board. "You...stop right there...uh...what do you...or, what are you doing here?" Ted looked at them confused, "I'm looking for that carriage which passed here some hours ago, do you know it?" The one guard looked to his partner at a loss. "We've seen but one carriage all day; came into the city just one hour ago." Ted was very happy and his tail began to wag like a dog. The guards tightened their grip on the spears and looked at the green beast. "Thats so great!" said Ted, "I must find the humans on the carriage. You see, they thought I was a rock, but now I am here to tell them I am not a rock, but a turtle, and my name is Ted, and I am looking for great marshlands to find new adventures."

The guards didn't know what to do, but going on the base of self preservation they agreed to let Ted enter the city. One guard pulled the gate open, and Ted was about to enter when a boy came up them. Fortunately he'd not seen Ted and began to speak very fast. "Did you hear!? The alchemist has become King, he took the crown!" but just then he saw Ted and froze. "Hello" said Ted, "who is the alchemist?" What is an alchemist?" The boy stared for a minute, then shook himself. "Uh..." he said looking to the guards who were wide eyed and encouraged him to speak with a mere look of the face. "An alchemist is a man who makes potions. He just came to the city not one hour ago and saved the King's son's life, and then the King offered him anything he wanted and he wanted the crown, so now he is King."

Ted began to get excited. Now he knew where the human was who thought he was a rock, though he was mistaken; for it had actually been the driver. So Ted ran into the city while the guards looked after him in bewilderment and simply began to breath again dropping their spears and sitting down in disbelief at what had just happened.

Ted ran through the city and it seemed odd to him that almost every single human who looked at him stopped wherever they were and whatever they were doing to watch him run. He though 'I must be a great runner to be getting so much attention, perhaps the humans can't run, and that's why they carriage everywhere..." and Ted ran and ran until he found the castle. He ignored the guards at the gate and burst through the doors. He was finally about to find the human and tell him that he was not a rock, and then everything would be cleared up and maybe the human would know where the marshlands were and Ted would finally have his adventure.

## The Alchemist: Part 4

King Galgeroth sat on his throne curious. The noise outside his main doors got louder and louder and he heard shouting and crashing, and then screaming and then a great green monster burst through the doors. Galgeroth froze in his throne and gripped the arms of it until his knuckles were white. His posted guards stepped forward; perhaps the only men in the city who were skilled at fighting and had more confidence that a five year old child.

Ted yelled towards the King "Hello!" but the King did not reply. "Kill it" Galgeroth said simply, and the guards at once ran towards the giant turtle. Ted then thought a couple things at once. First, humans did indeed know how to run, which made him wonder why so many people were looking at him while he ran through the city, and two, the spears coming towards him might hurt him. 'These humans want to murder me!' he thought and he only had one thought right then. "Sir! King!" he yelled, and right before the spears stabbed at him he jumped towards the King. He thought he ought to get closer if he were to tell the human that he was not a rock, but he had not jumped since his change and he flew uncontrollably through the air towards the man in the throne.

Galgeroth sunk into his throne while the beast flew towards him and the more he sunk in the more he began to get scared. Then his crown tipped from his head and fell down his face just as Ted landed on him. The force of the large beast pushed the crown into Galgeroth face instantly ripping his jaw from his face and severing his spinal cord. Ted's claws also seemed to find their way into the Kings sides and blood began to profusely pour out.

The guards of course only had time to watch the beast fly through the air before they could react and while Ted lay on the King, with four large spears piercing through his back. The spiked crown that he'd so elegantly pushed through the face of the King had also entered his chest and Ted found he was bleeding all over. He looked down at the King and thought 'I've ruined everything, now the human will never know I wasn't a rock' and then Ted died while atop the King.

## The King: Part 1

Among all the commotion the King who had recently giving up his crown entered the room as did many other people. The women screamed and the men simply looked away in disgust. It was a mess, but the old King saw this as an opportunity. He walked over to the throne and pushed the bloody beast from the alchemist. Then he pulled the crown from the skull of Galgeroth and put it on his head. "I hereby reclaim the crown as King over the land!" he said in a booming voice over the silence. It seemed that no one found anything wrong with that and so the bodies were taken away and the room cleaned and once more the King sat at his throne lazily and ruled over the land, this time with his son by his side.

**The End**

Index

# House & Technology

Love seat - 双人沙发 (shuāng rén shā fā) = double - person - 'sha fa' *sofa transliterated*

Faucet - 水龙头 = (shuǐ lóng tóu) water - dragon - head

Fridge - 冰箱 (bīng xiāng) = ice - box

Flashlight - 手电筒 (shǒu diàn tǒng) = hand - electric - tube/cylinder/pipe

Toilet - 马桶 (mǎ tǒng) = horse - bucket

Toilet paper - 擦腚纸 (cā dìng zhǐ) = to wipe/clean - buttocks/butt - paper

**Toilet paper** - 卫生纸 (wēi shēng zhǐ) = health/hygiene/sanitation - paper (More commonly used, but the other was more funny.)

Oven - 烤箱 (kǎo xiāng) = bake/roast - box

Radio - 收音机 (shōu yīn jī) = receive - sound - machine

Desk - 书桌 (shū zhuō) = book - table

Cradle - 摇篮 (yáo lán) = to rock/to shake - basket

Toy - 玩具 (wán jù) = play/fun - device/tool/equipment

Peeler (Vegetable/Potato) - 刮皮刀 (guā pì dāo) = shave/scrape - skin - knife

Bunk bed - 上下床 (shàng xià chuáng) = up - down - bed

Spatula - 锅铲 (guō chǎn) = pot - shovel/spade

Urinal - 便器 (biàn qì) = 'to urinate or defecate' - device/tool

Generator - 发电器 (fā diàn qì) = 'to send out' - electricity - device/tool

Door Way - 门口 (mén kǒu) = door - mouth/entrance

Garage - 车库 (chē kù) = car/vehicle - wearhouse/storehouse

Weeds - 野草 (yě cǎo) = (of plants) wild/uncultivated - grass

Toaster - 烤面包机 (kǎo miàn baō jī) = roast/bake - bread - machine

Clothes dryer - 烘干机 (hōng gān jī) = to bake/heat by fire - dry - machine

Strainer - 漏锅 (lóu guō) = to leak - pot/pan

Blinds/Shutter - 百叶窗 (bǎi yè chuāng) = hundred - leaf/page - window/shutter

Office - 事务所 (shì wù suǒ) = matter of business/thing/affairs - place

Living room - 客厅 (kè tīng) = guest/visitor - hall/central room

Bathroom - 洗手间 (xǐ shǒu jiān) = to wash/bathe - hand - room

Whisk - 打蛋器 (dǎ dàn qì) = to beat/hit/strike/mix up - egg - device/tool/utensil

Thumbtack/pushpin - 图钉 (tú dīng) = picture/drawing - nail

**Thumbtack/pushpin** - 大头钉 (dà tóu dīng) = big - head - nail

Internet - 互联网 (hù lián wǎng) = mutual - to join/connect - net/network

Sprinkler - 喷水器 (pēn shuǐ qì) = to spray/to spurt/to spout - water/liquid - device/tool

Aquarium/fish tank - 养鱼缸 (yǎng yú gāng) = to raise - fish - jar/vat

Vacuum - 吸尘器 (xī chén qì) = to suck in/absorb - dust/dirt - device/tool

Elastic band - 松紧带 (sōng jǐn dài) = to loosen/relax - to tighten - band/belt/ribbon

Ceiling - 天花板 (tīan huā bǎn) = sky/Heaven - flower/pattern - board/plank

Duct tape - 宽胶带 (kūan jiāo dài) = wide - glue - belt

Mothball - 卫生丸 (wèi shēng wán) = health/hygiene/sanitation - ball/pellet

Body lotion - 润肤乳 (rùn fū rǔ) = to moisten/lubricate - skin - milk-like liquid/milk

Crayon - 蜡笔 (là bǐ) = wax/candle - pen/pencil/writing brush

Sleep in - 睡懒觉 (shuì lǎn jiào) = sleep - lazy - sleep

Chalk - 粉笔 (fěn bǐ) = powder/white - pen/pencil/writing brush

Whiteout - 乳白天空 (rǔ bái tiān kōng) = milk - to make clear/white/empty/blank - sky - to empty

Beaker - 烧杯 (shāo bēi) = burn - cup

Electrical outlet - 插座 (chā zuò) = to insert/stick in - base/stand

Magnifying glass - 放大镜 (fàng dà jìng) = to put - big/huge - lens/mirror

Highlighter - 荧光笔 (yíng guāng bǐ) = fluorescence/glimmering - light/bright - pen/pencil/writing brush

Crib - 娃娃床 (wá wá chuáng) = baby - baby - bed

Diaper - 尿布 (niào bù) = urine/to urinate - cloth

Mobile - 娃娃铃 (wá wá líng) = baby - baby - bell

**Mobile** - 床铃 (chuáng líng) = bed - bell

Timer - 计时器 (jì shí qì) = meter/gauge/to count - time/hour - device/tool

Cell Phone - 手机 (shǒu jī) = hand - machine

Flip Phone - 老人手机 (lǎo rén shǒu jī) = old - person - phone

Laser - 激光 (jī guāng) = sharp - light

Lighter - 打火机 (dǎ huǒ jī) = hit - fire - machine

Binoculars - 双目望远镜 (shuāng mù wàng yuǎn jìng) = double - eye - gaze at - far/distant - lens

Movie - 电影 (diàn yǐng) = electric - shadow/image

**Elevator** - 电梯 (diàn tī) = electric - stairs/ladder

Camera - 摄影机 (shè yǐng jī) = 'to take in' - shadow/image - machine

Audiobook - 有声书 (yǒu shēng shū) = 'to have' - sound - book

**Pencil Sharpener** - 卷笔刀 (juàn bǐ dāo) = roll - pencil - knife

Pencil Sharpener - 转笔刀 (zhuǎn bǐ dāo) = turn - pencil - knife

**Pencil Sharpener** - 刨笔刀 (páo bǐ dāo) = 'to deduce/subtract' - pencil - knife

Battery - 电池 (diàn chí) = electric - reservoir

RAM (Random Access Memory) - 内存 (nèi cún) = inner/internal - deposit/store

Hair dryer - 吹风机 (chuī fēng jī) = to blow - wind - machine

Walki-Talki - 步话机 (bù huà jī) = walk - speak - machine

Band-Aid - 胶布 (jiāo bù) = glue/adhesive/stick with glue/sticky - material/cloth

Chainsaw - 油锯 (yóu jù) = oil/grease/greasy - saw

Drone/Unmanned aerial vehicle - 无人飞行器 (wú rén fēi xíng qì) = not have - person - to fly - travel - device/tool

Boombox - 噪音盒 (zào yīn hé) = noise/disturbance - sound/noise - small box/case

Notebook - 笔记本 (bǐ jì běn) = pen - record/write down - 'classifier for books'

Compass - 指南针 (zhǐ nán zhēn) = 'to point towards' - south - needle

Hearing Aid - 助听器 (zhù tīng qì) = help/assist - hear - device/tool

**Hearing Aid** - 扩音机 (kuò yīn jī) = enlarge - sound - machine

Napkin - 餐巾 (cān jīn) = meal - cloth

Video game - 电玩 (diàn wán) = electricity/electric - fun/to play/toy

Computer - 电脑 (diàn nǎo) = electric - brain

T.V. - 电视 (diàn shì) = electric - 'to look at'

Speakers - 音箱 (yīn xiāng) = sound - box

Subwoofer - 低音炮 (dī yīn pào) = low - sound - cannon

Walker (for baby) - 学步车 (xué bù chē) = to study - walk/a step - vehicle/car

Malware - 流氓软件 (liú máng ruǎn jiàn) = hoodlum/gangster/immoral behaviour - software

Calculator - 计算机 (jì suàn jī) = to calculate/to compute/to count - machine

Thruster/propeller - 推进器 (tuī jìn qì) = to push - to go forward/to advance - device/tool

Thermometer - 温度计 (wēn dù jì) = temperature - to measure/degree - meter/gauge

Binary code - 二进制编码 (èr jìn zhì biān mǎ) = two - (math) base of a number system - system - code/to encode

Tripod - 三脚架 (sān jiǎo jià) = three - leg/foot - rack/frame/to support

Jackhammer = 风钻 (fēng zuàn) = wind - to drill/to bore/an auger

Pinball - 弹珠台 (dàn zhū tái) = marbles - desk/table

Humidifier - 加湿器 (jiā shī qì) = to add - moist/wet - device/took

Hose - 蛇管 (shé guǎn) = snake - tube

Dehumidifier - 除湿器 (chú shī qì) = to get rid of/remove/eliminate - moist/wet - device

Slot machine - 吃角子老虎 (chī jiǎo zi lǎo hǔ) = to eat/consume - one Jiao (Chinese coin) - tiger

CD Rom - 光盘 (guāng pán) = light/ray - hard drive (computing)

USB drive - 优盘 (yōu pán) = excellent/superior - hard drive (computing）

Monitor - 显示器 (xiǎn shì qì) = to show/display/make visible - device/tool

Moisturizing cream - 保湿霜 (bǎo shī shuāng) = to defend/protect/to ensure - wet/moist/damp/humid - cream

Rock Garden - 假山 (jiǎ shān) = fake/false/artificial - mountain

Hour Glass - 滴漏计时器 (dī lòu jì shí qì) = drip/drop - small hole/leak/trickle/funnel - meter/gauge/count/calculate - time/hour/period - device/tool/utensil

Water pump - 唧筒 (jī tǒng) = spurt/squirt - tube/cylinder/pipe

**Pneumatic** - 气动 (qì dòng) = air - move

**Hydraulic** - 水力 (shuǐ lì) = water - power/force

Tape measure - 卷尺 (juǎn chǐ) = roll (up)/spool/curl - ruler

Tape Measure - 软尺 (ruǎn chǐ) = soft - ruler

Light bulb - 灯泡 (dēng pào) = light/lamp/lantern - bubble

T-Square - 丁字尺 (dīng zì chǐ) = '丁' - character - ruler

**Micrometer** - 千分尺 (qiān fēn chǐ) = thousand/great amount/numerous - fraction/part/one tenth/ - ruler

Sleigh/Sled - 冰排子 (bīng pǎi zi) = ice - raft

Freezer/Deep Freeze - 冰柜 (bīng guì) = ice - cupboard/cabinet

Flint - 火石 (huǒ shí) = fire - stone/rock

Smoke Detector - 烟火探测器 (yān huǒ tàn cè qì) = smoke/mist - fire - detective/spy/scout - to measure - device/tool

Dental Floss - 牙线 (yá xiàn) = tooth/teeth - thread/string/wire

Goblet - 高脚杯 (gāo jiǎo bēi) = tall/high/height/above average/of a high level or degree - foot/base (of an object) - cup/glass

Tweeter (speaker) - 高音喇叭 (gāo yīn lǎ bā) = tall/high/height/above average/of a high level or degree - sound/musical sound/note/tone - loudspeaker/horn

Sound Proof Wall - 歌声强 (gē shēng qiáng) = separate/cut off/partition - sound/noise - wall

Abstract Art - 抽象艺术 (chōu xiàng yì shù) = take out (from in between)/take (a part from the whole)/obtain by drawing - appearance/shape/image - art

Screwdriver - 螺丝刀 (luó sī dāo) = spiral shell - threadlike thing - tool/something shaped like a knife

Phillips Screwdriver - 十字头螺刀 (shí zì tóu luó dāo) = '十' - character - head/top/end - screwdriver

Cling Wrap/Plastic Wrap - 保鲜膜 (bǎo xiān mó) = protect/defend/insure/care/safeguard - fresh/delicious/tasty - film/membrane

Canvas (for art) - 画布 (huà bù) = drawing/painting/picture - cloth

Blower Thingy (What's this even called?) - 喷粉器 (pēn fěn qì) = spurt/gush/to puff/to spray/blow out - powder - device/tool/utensil

Blowtorch - 喷灯 (pēn dēng) = spurt/gush/to puff//to spray/blow out - lamp/lantern/light/burner

Quill - 羽毛笔 (yǔ máo bǐ) = feather - pen/pencil/writing brush

Mug - 茶缸 (chá gāng) = tea - jar/vat/earthen jug

Joystick - 控制杆 (kòng zhì gān) = control/manipulate - pole

Detergent - 去垢剂 (qù gòu jì) = remove/get rid of/to reduce - dirt/filth/stains - dose (medicine)

Stapler - 订书机 (dìng shū jī) = staple together - book - machine

Beanbag (Chair) - 懒人沙发 (lǎn rén shā fā) = lazy/slothful/sluggish - person/people - sofa

Ottoman - 软垫凳 (ruǎn diàn dèng) = soft/mild/gentle - pad/cushion/mat - stool/bench

Kindling - 柴爿 (chái pán) = firewood - split wood

**Water Pick** - 冲牙器 (chōng yá qì) = (of water) to dash against/to rinse/to flush - tooth/teeth - device/tool/utensil

Post-it Note - 方便贴 (fāng biàn tiē) = convenient - sticker

Mop - 拖把 (tuō bǎ) = pull/drag/to tow/to mop (the floor) - handle

Scotch Tape - 透明胶 (tòu míng jiāo) = transparent - glue/rubber/gum

Caps Lock - 大写锁定 (dà xiě suǒ dìng) = big/large/huge/great/side - write/compose - to lock

Monkey-wrench - 活扳手 (huó bān shǒu) = alive/living/work/workmanship - to pull/to turn something around - hand

Mousetrap - 捕鼠器 (bǔ shǔ qì) = catch/seize/arrest/capture - mouse/rat - device/tool/utensil

Mousetrap - 鼠夹 (shǔ jiā) = mouse/rat - clamp/to press from either side/to sandwich/wedged between

Telescope - 望远镜 (wàng yuǎn jìng) = gaze into the distance/towards - far away/distant/remote - lens/mirror/looking glass

Toboggan - 平底雪橇 (píng dǐ xuě qiāo) = flat bottomed - sled/sledge/sleigh

Goggles - 护目镜 (hù mù jìng) = protect/guard/shield/defend - eye - lens/glasses/mirror

Hair Curler - 卷发夹 (juǎn fà jiā) = roll/roll up/curl - hair - clamp/to press from wither side

Tongs - 夹剪 (jiā jiǎn) = clamp/to press from wither side - scissors/shears/clippers

Clothes Pin - 晾衣架 (liàng yī jià) = dry in the air/air/dry in the sun/sun - clothing/clothes - clamp/to press from wither side

Lantern - 灯笼 (dēng lóng) = light/lamp/lantern - cage/basket/container

Level (Tool) = 水准仪 (shuǐ zhǔn yí) = water/liquid - accurate/exact - apparatus/instrument

Dowel - 木钉 (mù dīng) = tree/timber/wood - nail

Slide show - 幻灯 (huàn dēng) = unreal/imaginary/illusory/change magically - light/lamp

Allen Key (Tool) - 内六角扳手 (nèi liù jiǎo bān shǒu) = inside/interior - hexagon (six corner) - wrench/lever/spanner

Antivirus Software - 杀毒软件 (shā dú ruǎn jiàn) = kill/slaughter/butcher/murder - poison/toxin/virus - software

Thermos - 保温杯 (bǎo wēn bēi) = protect/defend/insure/care/safeguard - temperature - cup/glass

Combination Lock - 密码锁 (mì mǎ suǒ) = secret - code - lock

Spork - 叉勺 (chā sháo) = fork - spoon

Pitchfork - 干草叉 (gān cǎo chā) = dry - grass - fork

Electric Clock - 音叉钟 (yīn chā zhōng) = sound/note/noise - fork - clock

Microchip - 微晶片 (wéi jīng piàn) = minute/micro-/tiny/miniature - quarts (rock)/crystal/clear - thin piece/slice/flake

Defragmentation - 碎片整理 (suì piàn zhěng lǐ) = fragment/broken bit - put in order/straighten out/arrange/tidy up

**Pencil Lead** (Refill) - 笔芯 (bǐ xīn) = pencil/pen/writing brush - core/centre

Calendar - 日历 (rì lì) = sun/solar/day/time/season/date - record/experience/(also means calendar but I like record)

Bong/Hookah - 水烟袋 (shuǐ yān dài) = water/liquid - smoke/mist/vapour - pocket/bag/sack/pouch

Water Hose - 水龙带 (shuǐ lóng dài) = water - dragon/shaped like a dragon - belt/band/ribbon

Glitch - 程错 (chéng cuò) = programme/sequence - error/mistake/blunder

Hammock - 吊床 (diào chuáng) = hang/suspend - bed

Lottery Machine - 吹球机 (chuī qiú jī) = blow/puff/to end in failure/brag - game/match - machine

Nut (of 'nuts and bolts') - 螺丝帽 (luó sī mào) = screw - cap/hat

Washer (of 'nuts and bolts') - 螺丝垫 (luó sī diàn) = screw - mat/pad/cushion/to fill a gap

Blueprint - 图纸 (tú zhǐ) = picture/drawing/chart/diagram - paper

Car Jack - 千斤顶 (qiān jīn dǐng) = thousand/many/numerous - 500g - push from below/prop up

Doll/Stuffed Figure - 玩偶 (wán ǒu) = toy/to play/have fun with - image/idol

Chimney - 烟道 (yān dào) = smoke - road/way/path

Voltage - 电压 (diàn yā) = electricity/electric - pressure/press/oppress

Fax - 电传 (diàn chuán) = electricity/electric - to transmit/to spread/to pass on

Landline - 固网电信 (gù wǎng diàn xìn) = solid/firm/strong - network/net - telecommunications

Collect Call - 对方付款电话 (duì fāng fù kuǎn diàn huà) = receiving party - pay - phone call

Slide Show - 土电影 (tǔ diàn yǐng) = homemade/indigenous/unsophisticated - movie

Jumper Cable - 跨接电缆 (kuà jiē diàn lǎn) = crossing/crossover - electric/electricity - cable/thick rope

Spam (in e-mail) - 电子垃圾 (diàn zǐ lā jī) = electronic - garbage/rubbish/refuse/junk

**A Safe/Strongbox** - 保险柜 (bǎo xiǎn guì) = insure/safe/secure - cabinet/cupboard

A Safe/Strongbox - 金柜 (jīn guì) = gold/money/cash - cabinet/cupboard

**A Safe/Strongbox** - 铁柜 (tiě guì) = iron (metal)/hard/strong/unshakable - cabinet/cupboard

**Pantry** - 食物柜 (shí wù guì) = food/eatables - cabinet/cupboard

Electric Kettle - 快煮壶 (kuài zhǔ hú) = fast/quick/rapid/speedy - boil/cook - kettle/pot/jug/vase

Wok - 炒菜锅 (chǎo cài guō) = stir-fry/sauté - vegetables/greens - pot/pan/cauldron

Trowel - 小铲子 (xiǎo chǎn zi) = small/tiny/little - shovel/spade

Water Dispenser - 饮水机 (yǐn shuǐ jī) = drink/swallow - water/liquid/beverage - machine

Fountain Pen - 自来水笔 (zì lái shuǐ bǐ) = self/naturally - arrive/(to) come - liquid/water - pen/pencil

Nail Clippers - 指甲钳 (zhǐ jiǎ qián) = nail - tongs/pincers/pliers

Jackpot - 彩票头奖 (cǎi piào tóu jiǎng) = lottery ticket - first prize

**Textile/Fabric** - 织品 (zhī pǐn) = weave/knit - product/commodity/goods

Bar Code - 商品条码 (shāng pǐn tiáo mǎ) = commodity/goods/merchandise - strip/stripe - code

NFT - 非同质化代币 (fēi tóng zhí huà dài bì) = non-/un-/to not be - same as/alike/similar - quality/nature/material - change/transform/convert - acting substitute/replacement - money/currency ('To not be the same material transformed into replacement money' is my best translation.)

**Prototype** - 原型 (yuán xíng) = source/origin/start/beginning - mould/pattern/type/model

Router (computing) - 路由器 (lù yóu qì) = route/path/road/way - pass through/go by way of/via - device/tool

Hacksaw - 钢锯 (gāng jù) = steel - saw

Paperclip - 回形针 (huí xíng zhēn) = to curve/circle - shape/form - needle/something shaped like a needle (Paperclip also is 纸夹 (zhǐ jiā) which literally means 'paper - clip'.)

**Canopy Bed** - 八角床 (bā jiǎo chuáng) = eight - corner - bed

**Plunger** - 吸把 (x) = inhale/breath in/to suck - handle

**Dishwasher** - 洗碗机 (x) = to wash - bowl - machine

Mattress - 床垫 (chuáng diàn) = bed - pad/cushion/mat

**Cologne** - 香水 (xiāng shuǐ) = fragrant/sweet smelling/aromatic/perfume or spice - water/liquid

Mobile (Phone) Game - 手游 (shǒu yóu) = 'to hold'/hand - game

# People
(人 means people or person. I used my discretion.)

**People** - 人民 (rén mín) = people - nationality/citizen

Midget - 袖珍人 (xiù zhēn rén) = pocket size - person

Alien - 外星人 (wài xīng rén) = outside - star - person

Poet - 诗人 (shī rén) = poem - person

Assassin - 刺客 (cì kè) = stab (also means assassinate) - guest

Martian - 火星人 (huǒ xīng rén) = fire - planet - person

**Illegal immigrant** - 人蛇 (rén shé) = person - snake

Bidder - 出价人 (chū jià rén) = to rise/to go beyond - price/value - person

Santa Clause - 圣诞老人 (shèng dàn lǎo rén) = Christmas - old - person

**Ladyboy (She-male)** - 人妖 (rén yāo) = person - seductive/monster/demon/devil/strange/weird

Bumpkin - 土包子 (tǔ bāo zi)= earth - bun (包子 is a Chinese meat stuffed bun)

Ventriloquist - 口技表演者 (kǒu jì biǎo yǎn zhě) = mouth - skill - performance - 'the one who is' (Lit: the one who is skilled at mouth performances.)

**'Know-it-all'** - 万事通 (wàn shì tōng) = 10,000 - matters - 'to know well'

Elvis - 猫王 (māo wáng) = cat - king

Priest - 祭司 (jì sī) = 'offer sacrifice' - 'to take charge of'

Alchemist - 炼金术士 (liàn jīn shù shì) = refine/spelt - gold - method/technique - scholar

**Traitor** - 卖国 (mài guó) = 'to sell' - country

Buddhist Monk (mocking) - 秃驴 (tū lǘ) = bald - donkey

**Travel buddy** - 驴友 (lǘ yǒu) = donkey - friend

Sleepwalker - 梦游者 (mèng yóu zhě) = dream - travel - 'the one who' (Fig: the one who travels while dreaming.)

**Albino** - 天老儿 (tiān lao er) = sky/heaven - old man/father/husband

Albino - 白化病人 (bái huà bìng rén) = white - change (-ization)/to transform - illness/disease - person

Scarecrow - 稻草人 (dào cǎo rén) = rice - grass - person

White trash - 泥腿子 (ní tuǐ zi) = mud - leg

**Coward** - 胆小鬼 (dǎn xiǎo guǐ) = gall bladder - small - devil

**Coward** - 软脚虾 (ruǎn jiǎo xiā) = soft - foot - shrimp

'Smartphone addicts' - 低头组 (dī tóu zǔ) = 'to lower' - head - ethnicity/race

**"Mr. Perfect"** - 高富帅 (gāo fù shuài) = tall - rich - handsome

**"Mrs. Perfect"** - 白富美 (bái fù měi) = white - rich - beautiful

**Snob** - 狗眼看人低 (gǒu yǎn kàn rén dī) = dog - eye - 'to look at' - people - low/beneath

**Servant** - 用人 (yòng rén) = use - person

**Bitch** - 三八 (sān bā) = three - eight

**Fall Guy** - 黑锅 (hēi guō) = black - pot

Nazi - 纳粹 (nà cuì) = accept/receive - unmixed/pure

KKK - 三K党 (sān K dǎng) = three - K - party/club/association

**Useless/Good for nothing** - 饭桶 (fàn tǒng) = rice - bucket (Fig: all you're good for is eating.)

Robot - 机器人 (jī qì rén) = machine - person

Pirate - 海盗 (hǎi dào) = ocean/sea - thief/bandit

**Godfather** - 干爹 (gān diē) = to manage/capable - dad

**Scum** - 人渣 (rén zhā) = person - dregs (dregs of society)

Cart driver - 掌鞭的 (zhǎng biān de) = to hold in ones hand/to wield - whip/lash/flog - 'de'

**Loser** - 鲁蛇 (lǔ shé) = crass/stupid/rude - snake

Transvestite - 异装癖 (yì zhuāng pǐ) = different/unusual/strange - dress/clothing/pretend/to play a role - habit/hobby

**To meddle/nosey Parker** - 管闲事 (guǎn xián shì) = to care about - other people's business

Postman - 邮差 (yóu chāi) = post/mail - messenger/to send

Lawyer - 律师 (lǜ shī) = law - expert/master/teacher

Dentist - 牙医 (yá yī) = tooth - doctor

Farmer - 农民 (nóng mín) = peasant/to farm/agriculture - nationality/citizen

Cook/Chef - 厨师 (chú shī) = kitchen - expert/master/teacher

Bartender - 调酒师 (tiáo jiǔ shī) = to blend - liquor/wine/alcoholic beverage - expert/master/teacher

**Entrepreneur** - 企业家 (qǐ yè jiā) = to plan a project - line of business/occupation/employment/enterprise/to engage in - 'specialist'

Executioner - 刀斧手 (dāo fǔ shǒu) = knife - hatchet - 'tradesman'

Executioner - 刽子手 (guì zi shǒu) = to amputate - 'tradesman'

Old Person - 老头 (lǎo tóu) = old - head

**Metrosexual** - 型男 (xíng nán) = style/model - man/male (fashionable & good looking guy)

**Rookie** - 菜鸟 (cài niǎo) = weak (of ones skills) - bird/'to pay attention to'

**Rookie** - 新手 (xīn shǒu) = new - hand

Miser/scrooge - 守财奴 (shǒu cái nú) = to guard/defend/keep watch - money/wealth/riches - slave

**Cheapskate/stingy** - 铁公鸡 (tiě gōng jī) = iron - rooster (from which no feathers can be plucked)

Butcher - 卖肉者 (mài ròu zhě) = to sell - meat/flesh - 'the one who' (lit. the one who sells meat)

Ninja - 忍者 (rěn zhě) = to endure/bear/tolerate - 'the one who' (lit. the one who endures)

**Smug** - 臭美 (chòu měi) = repulsive/loathsome/terrible/stench/smelly - to be pleased with oneself/beauty/beautiful

**Worthless** - 不成器 (bù chéng qì) = not/no (negative prefix) - succeed/finish/complete - device/tool (fig. unable to make something of oneself)

**Masculine woman (Tom-boy)** - 女汉子 (nǚ hàn zi) = woman/female - man/fellow

Chiropractor - 脊椎指压治疗师 (jǐ chuí zhǐ yā zhì liáo shī) = backbone/vertebra - acupressure - medical treatment - master/expert

Mayor - 镇长 (zhèn zhǎng) = small town - chief/elder/head

**Cunning/sly** - 白鼻子 (bái bí zi) = white - nose

Nun/monk - 出家人 (chū jiā rén) = to go out - home/family - person

Pacifist - 和平主义者 (hé píng zhǔ yì zhě) = peaceful - ideology - 'the one who' (fig. the one who has a peaceful ideology)

**Popular comedian** - 笑星 (xiào xīng) = to laugh/smile - star/famous performer

**Private investigator** - 征信社 (zhēng xìn shè) = evidence - confidence/trust - group/agency

**Detective/Spy** - 侦探 (zhēn tàn) = to spy/to detect/to scout - to explore/search out/find

**Chain smoker** - 烟鬼 (yān guǐ) = smoke/cigarette - demon/derogatory term for one with bad habits

**Drunkard** - 酒鬼 (jiǔ guǐ) = alcoholic drink - demon/derogatory term for one with bad habits

**Mole/Rat/Traitor** - 内鬼 (nèi guǐ) = inside/interior - demon/derogatory term for one with bad habits

**Cross-dresser** - 中性人 (zhōng xìng rén) = middle/among/centre - disposition/character/sexuality/gender - person

**Ugly person** - 丑八怪 (chǒu bā guài) = ugly/hideous - eight - monster/demon

**Burglar** - 侵入家宅者 (qīn rù jiā zhái zhě) = to invade/encroach - to enter/go into - home/house - 'the one who' (fig. the one who enters and invades a residence)

Peeping Tom - 偷窥狂 (tōu kuī kuáng) = secretly/stealthily/steal - peep/watch/spy on - extremely/unrestrained/mad/crazy/insane

Stalker - 跟踪狂 (gēn zōng kuáng) = follow - track/footprint/trace - mad/crazy/insane/without being restrained

Detective/Spy - 侦察员 (zhēn chá yuán) = detect/scout/investigate - examine/look into/scrutinize - member (of an organization/employee/staff member/personal

Mutant/Freak of nature - 畸胎 (jī tāi) = irregular/abnormal - birth/fetus/embryo

Cat Burglar - 飞贼 (fēi zéi) = fly/go quickly/dart - thief/enemy

**Transgender** - 跨性别 (kuà xìng bié) = to step across/stride over - nature/character/sexuality/gender - leave/turn/change/to depart/separate/other/another

**Gold Digger** - 拜金女 (bài jīn nǚ) = worship - money/cash/gold - woman/female

Carpenter - 木匠 (mù jiàng) = tree/timber/wood - craftsman/master

Lumberjack - 伐木工人 (fá mù gōng rén) = fell/cut down - tree/timber/wood - worker

**Gay** - 同性恋 (tóng xìng liàn) = same/alike/similar/in common/together - sexuality/sex/gender/disposition/nature - (romantic) love/long for/feel attached to

Arsonist - 防火犯 (fáng huǒ fàn) = release/let go/light/kindle - fire - crime/criminal/violate

**Arsonist** - 纵火犯 (zòng huǒ fàn) = to release/set free - fire - crime/criminal/violate

Killer/Murderer - 杀手 (shā shǒu) = kill/murder/slaughter - person proficient or skilled at a certain activity

**Cinderella** - 灰姑娘 (huī gū niáng) = ash/dust - daughter/young woman/young lady

Busker - 街头艺人 (jiē tóu yì rén) = street corner - art - person

Bimbo - 胸大无脑 (xiōng dà wú nǎo) = chest/breast/bosom - big/large/great - be without/not have - brain

**Moron** - 脑残 (nǎo cán) = brain - deficient/incomplete

Peking Man (Homo Erectus) - 中国猿人 (zhōng guó yuán rén) = China - ape - man/person/people

**Peking Man** (Homo Erectus) - 北京猿人 (běi jīng yuán rén) = Beijing - ape - man/person/people

**Geisha** (Japanese Entertainer) - 艺妓 (yì jì) = skill/art/craft/talent/ability - prostitute

Veterinarian - 兽医 (shòu yī) = animal/beast - doctor

Lifeguard - 救生员 (jiù shēng yuán) = rescue/save/help/aid - life/living - employee/staff member/personnel

Magician - 魔术师 (mó shù shī) = magic/conjuring/slight of hand/tricks - teacher/master/expert/specialist

**Assassin** - 暗杀者 (an shā zhě) = hidden/secret/obscure/in the dark - kill/slaughter/butcher/murder - 'the one who'

Hermit - 岩穴之士 (yán xué zhī shì) = cave/cavern - 'of' - soldier/specialist/scholar (old term)/honorific

**Soloist** - (dú zòu zhě) = alone/single/independent - play (music)/preform (on a musical instrument) - 'the one who'

**Monk/Friar** - 修道士 (xiū dào shi) = repair/mend/overhaul/decorate/embellish/build/construct - way/method/path/doctrine/principle - specialist worker/person trained in a certain field/soldier/scholar

**Matchmaker** - 蹇修 (jiǎn xiū) = lame/cripple/unfortunate/unlucky - repair/mend/overhaul/decorate/embellish/build/construct

Bodyguard - 保镖 (bǎo biāo) = protect/defend/insure/care/safeguard - throwing weapon/dart/spear

**Sanitation Worker** - 保洁员 (bǎo jié yuán) = protect/defend//insure/care/safeguard - clean/purify - employee/member/person

Undertaker - 殡仪员 (bìn yí yuán) = funeral/embalm/to encoffin a corpse/to carry a burial - ceremony/rite - employee/personnel/staff

**Drag Queen** - 变装皇后 (biàn zhuāng huáng hòu) = transform/change/alter/become different - stage makeup and costume/dress up/plat the part of/pretend/feign/adornment/clothing/outfit - queen/empress

**Drag Queen** - 扮装皇后 (bàn zhuāng huáng hòu) = to put on make up - queen/empress

Paparazzi - 狗仔 (gǒu zǎi) = dog/cursed/damned - young man/child

**Refugee** - 难民 (nàn mín) = troublesome/bad/unpleasant/problem/not good/arduous - people/member of an ethnic group/citizen

**Spirit/Medium** - 乩童 (jī tóng) = divination - child/boy/servant boy

**Subcontractor** - 分包商 (fēn bāo shāng) = divide/separate/distribute/allot/to allocate - to contract (to or for) - trade/commerce/business/merchant

Mannequin - 人体模型 (rén tǐ mó xíng) = human body - model/mould/pattern

Hitch-hiker - 便车旅行者 (biàn chē lǚ xíng zhě) = convenient/ease/expedient - vehicle/car - travel/journey/trip - 'the one who' (the one who travels with a convenient vehicle)

**Shot-putter** - 铅球运动员 (qiān qiú yùn dòng yuán) = lead - ball/sphere/globe - athlete

Geek/Techie - 理工男 (lǐ gōng nán) = science and engineering - man/male

Skeleton - 骨人 (gǔ rén) = bone/skeleton - person/people

**Prehistoric Man** - 史前人 (shǐ qián rén) = history - ago/before/preceding/BC - person/people

Stenographer - 速记员 (sù jì yuán) = speedy/velocity/fast/rapid/quick - notes/record - employee/member/person/personnel/staff

Fraternal Twins - 异卵双胞胎 (yì luǎn shuāng bāo tāi) = different/to distinguish - ovum/egg/spawn - twins

Identical Twins - 同卵双胞胎 (tóng luǎn shuāng bāo tāi) = be the same as/similar/alike - ovum/egg/spawn - twins

**Mistress** (in an affair) - 小三 (xiǎo sān) = little/small/tine - three

Referee - 裁判员 (cái pàn yuán) = judge/decide - assess/dccide/judge/pass a verdict

Loan Shark - 大耳窿 (dà ěr lóng) = big/large/great/huge - ear - cavity/hole

**Horticulturalist** - 园艺师 (yuán yì shī) = garden - art - master/person skilled in a certain profession

**Nuns/Convent** - 修女团 (xiū nǚ tuán) = repair/mend/overhaul/decorate/embellish/build/construct - women/female - group/society/organization

**Potter** - 陶瓷工 (táo cí gōng) = pottery/make pottery/ceramics - porcelain/Chinaware - worker/craftsman/profession/trade

**Palaeontologist** - 古生物学家 (gǔ shēng wù xué jiā) = ancient/paleo-/old - living things - study/knowledge/branch of learning/-ology - specialist in a certain filed

Fool/Stupid - 傻瓜 (shǎ guā) = stupid/foolish/silly/imbecile - melon/gourd/squash

Cobbler - 修鞋匠 (xiū xié jiàng) = repair/mend/overhaul - shoes - craftsman/artisan/workman

Rich/Wealthy - 有钱人 (yǒu qián rén) = to have/possess/own - money/cash/currency

Stripper - 脱衣舞女郎 (tuō yī wǔ nǚ láng) = take or cast off/get out of - clothing/clothes - dance - young woman/girl

Plumber - 水管工 (shuǐ guǎn gōng) = water pipe - worker/craftsman/profession/trade

Electrician - 电工 (diàn gōng) = electricity - worker/craftsman/profession/trade

**Pedestrian** - 行人 (xíng rén) = travel/to walk - person/people

Cobbler - 制鞋工人 (zhì xié gōng rén) = make/manufacture - shoes - worker/workman

Milkman - 送奶人 (sòng nǎi rén) = deliver/give - milk - person/people/man

**Stay-at-home dad** - 家庭主夫 (jiā tíng zhǔ fū) = family/household - manage/in charge of - husband/man

**Whistle Blower** - 举报人 (jǔ bào rén) = act/deed - report/announce/declare - person

**Victim** - 受害人 (shòu hài rén) = receive/suffer/endure - evil/harm/calamity - person

Hermit/Recluse - 幽人 (yōu rén) = remote/hidden away/secluded - person

Inmate - 收容人 (shōu róng rén) = put away/take in/collect - contain/hold - person

**Trendsetter/Influencer** - 潮人 (cháo rén) = tide/social upsurge - person

Shepard - 牧羊人 (mù yáng rén) = tend (animals)/to herd - sheep/goat/ram - person

Barbarian - 野蛮人 (yě mán rén) = wilderness/open country/rude - rough/savage/fierce/(also is barbarian) - person

Conductor (in a symphony) - 指挥家 (zhǐ huī jiā) = finger/point (to)/to indicate or refer to - wave/wield/command/to conduct - specialist (in a certain field)

**Choreographer** - 舞蹈指导 (wǔ dǎo zhǐ dǎo) = preform a dance - to coach/guidance

**Pretentious Prick** - 装屄 (zhuāng bī) = adornment/to play the role - vagina aka 'the c' word'

**Grave Robber** - 盗墓者 (dào mù zhě) = steal/rob/plunder/thief/robber - grave/tomb - 'the one who' (the one who plunders tombs)

**Burglar** - 夜盗 (yè dào) = by night/nighttime/evening - steal/rob/plunder/thief/robber

**Burglar** - 穿窬之盗 (chuān yú zhī dào) = to bore or pass through/to penetrate - hole in a wall - of - steal/rob/plunder/thief/robber

**Archer** - 射箭手 (shè jiàn shǒu) = to shoot/to fire - arrow - person skilled in certain types of work

**Illiterate** (person) - 文盲 (wén máng) = writing/script/character - totally incompetent/blind/unable to distinguish things

**Alcoholic** - 嗜酒成癖 (shì jiǔ chéng pǐ) = addicted to/have a weakness for - alcohol/wine/liquor - become/turn into - addiction/craving

Yakuza (Japanese mafia) - 日本黑道 (rì běn hēi dào) = Japan - dark road/criminal ways/underworld

**Conman** - 男虫 (nán chóng) = man/male - insect/worm

# Animals

**Animal** - 动物 (dòng wù) = move - thing

Panda - 熊猫 (xióng māo) = bear - cat

Hippopotamus - 河马 (hé mǎ) = river - horse

Kangaroo - 袋鼠 (dài shǔ) = bag - rat/mouse

Giraffe - 长颈鹿 (cháng jǐng lù) = long - neck - deer

Alpaca - 羊驼 (yáng tuó) = sheep - camel

Cobra - 眼镜蛇 (yǎn jìng shé) = glasses - snake

Zebra - 斑马 (bān mǎ) = stripe - horse

Viper - 毒蛇 (dú shé) = poison - snake

Bald Eagle - 白头鹰 (bái tóu yīng) = white - head - eagle

Aardvark - 土猪 (tǔ zhū) = earth/soil - pig

Tarantula - 捕鸟蛛 (bǔ niǎo zhū) = seize - bird - spider

Platypus - 鸭嘴兽 (yā zuǐ shòu) = duck - mouth - beast

Condor - 神鹰 (shén yīng) = god - eagle

Centipede - 百脚 (bǎi jiǎo) = hundred - foot

Polar Bear - 北极熊 (běi jí xióng) = north - pole - bear

Squirrel - 松鼠 (sōng shǔ) = pine tree - rat/mouse

Raven - 大乌鸦 (dà wū yā) = big/large/huge - black - crow

Chipmunk - 栗鼠 (lì shǔ) = chestnut -rat/mouse

Skunk - 臭鼬 (chòu yòu) = smelly - weasel

Humming Bird - 蜂鸟 (fēng niǎo) = wasp/bee - bird

Narwhal - 独角鲸 (dú jiǎo jīng) = single - horn - whale

Porcupine - 箭猪 (jiàn zhū) = arrow - pig

Tusk - 长牙 (chǎng yá) = long - tooth

Owl - 猫头鹰 (māo tóu yīng) = cat - head - eagle

Hornbill (Bird) - 犀鸟 (xī niǎo) = rhinoceros - bird

Dinosaur - 恐龙 (kǒng lóng) = fearful - dragon

Mammoth - 毛象 (máo xiàng) = hair - elephant

Rattlesnake - 响尾蛇 (xiǎng wěi shé) = sound - tale - snake

Dolphin - 海豚 (hǎi tún) = ocean - pig

Seal - 海豹 (hǎi bào) = ocean/sea - leopard/panther

**Walrus** - 象海豹 (xiàng hǎi bào) = elephant - sea - leopard/panther

Walrus - 海象 (hǎi xiàng) – ocean/sca - elephant

Lobster - 龙虾 (lóng xiā) = dragon - shrimp

Octopus - 八爪鱼 (bā zhuǎ yú) = eight - claw - fish

Anteater - 食蚁兽 (shí yǐ shòu) = food/eat - ant - beast

Flamingo - 火烈鸟 (huǒ liè niǎo) = fire - upright - bird

Turkey - 火鸡 (huǒ jī) = fire - chicken

Penguin - 企鹅 (qì é) = 'to stand on tiptoes' - goose

Jellyfish - 海蜇 (hǎi zhē) = ocean - 'to sting'

Moose/Elk - 驼鹿 (tuó lù) = camel - deer

**Moose/Elk** - 大鹿 (dà lù) = big - deer

Swan - 天鹅 (tiān é) = sky - goose

Puma/Cougar - 美洲狮 (měi zhōu shī) = American - lion

Jaguar - 美洲虎 (měi zhōu hǔ) = American - tiger

Dalmatian - 斑点狗 (bān diǎn gǒu) = spotted - dog

Gerbil - 沙鼠 (shā shǔ) = sand - rat/mouse

Wombat - 袋熊 (dài xióng) = bag/pouch - bear

Koala - 树袋熊 (shù dài xióng) = tree - bag/pouch - bear

Chameleon - 变色龙 (biàn sè lóng) = change - colour - dragon

Caterpillar - 毛虫 (máo chóng) = hair - worm

Pony - 小马 (xiǎo mǎ) = small - horse

Toad - 癞蛤蟆 (lài há má) = scabies/skin disease - frog - toad

House lizard/Gecko - 壁虎 (bì hǔ) = wall - tiger

**House lizard/Gecko** - 守宫 (shǒu gōng) = defend - palace

Sloth - 树懒 (shù lǎn) = tree - lazy

Lemur - 狐猴 (hú hóu) = fox - monkey

Takin (Giant antelope) - 扭角羚 (niǔ jiǎo líng) = twist/turn - horn - antelope

Wildebeest/Gnu - 角马 (jiǎo mǎ) = horn - horse

Mammal - 哺乳动物 (bǔ rǔ dòng wù) = 'to feed' - breast/milk - animal (Fig: the animal which drinks milk.)

Reptile - 爬行动物 (pá xíng dòng wù) = crawl/climb - walk/go - animal (Fig: the animal which crawls.)

Amphibian - 两栖动物 (liǎng qī dòng wù) = two - 'to dwell/live' - animal (Fig: the animal which lives in two places; water and land.)

Reindeer - 驯鹿 (xùn lù) = to tame - deer

**Mare** - 母驴 (mǔ lǘ) = mother/female (of animals) - donkey

Coyote - 郊狼 (jiāo láng) = suburbs/outskirts - wolf

Sperm whale - 抹香鲸 (mǒ xiāng jīng) = to smear/wipe/erase - fragrant/sweet smelling - whale

Raccoon - 浣熊 (huàn xióng) = to wash/rinse - bear

Blue jay - 冠蓝鸦 (guān lán yā) = champion - blue - crow

Peacock - 孔雀 (kǒng què) = great - sparrow/small bird

**House centipede** - 蚰蜒 (yóu yán) = millipede - slug/millipede

Gecko - 蝎虎 (xiē hǔ) = scorpion - tiger

Lemming - 旅鼠 (lǚ shǔ) = to travel - mouse/rat

**Raptor (dinosaur)** - 盗龙 (dào lóng) = thief/robber - dragon

Beetle - 甲虫 (jiǎ chóng) = shell/amour - worm/insect

Ladybug - 瓢虫 (piáo chóng) = ladle/dipper - insect/worm

Caterpillar - 小毛虫 (xiǎo máo chóng) = small - hair/young/raw - insect/worm

Slug - 鼻涕虫 (bí tì chóng) = snot/nasal mucus - insect/worm

Stink Bug - 放屁虫 (fàng pì chóng) = fart - insect/worm

Trout - 尊鱼 (zūn yú) = respect/venerate/honour/senior - fish

Flounder - 左口鱼 (zuǒ kǒu yú) = left/wrong/opposite/differing - mouth - fish

Piranha - 水虎鱼 (shuǐ hǔ yú) = water/river/liquid - tiger - fish

Grizzly Bear - 灰熊 (huī xióng) = ash - bear

Poodle - 卷毛狗 (juǎn máo gǒu) = roll/roll up/curl - hair - dog

Greyhound - 灰猎犬 (huī liè quǎn) = ash - hunting/search for - dog

Pomeranian - 博美犬 (bó měi quǎn) = rich/abundant/plentiful - beautiful/beauty/pretty - dog

Gopher - 沙龟 (shā guī) = sand/powder/gravel - turtle/tortoise

Chimpanzee - 黑猩猩 (hēi xīng xīng) = black/dark/secret/wicked/sinister - ape/orangutang - ape/orangutang

Gorilla - 大猩猩 (dà xīng xīng) = big/large/great/eldest/huge - ape/orangutang - ape/orangutang

Falcon - 猎鹰 (liè yīng) = hunting/hunt - eagle/hawk

Iguana - 鬣蜥 (liè xī) = bristles/mane (of a horse)/fin/human whiskers - lizard

Rodent - 啮齿动物 (niè chǐ dòng wù) = (of rodents) gnaw/nibble/bite - teeth/tooth - animal

Carnivore - 肉食动物 (ròu shí dòng wù) = meat/flesh - meal/food/to eat - animal

Herbivore - 草食动物 (cǎo shí dòng wù) = grass/straw - meal/food/to eat - animal

Beaver - 河狸 (hé lí) = river/stream - fox-like animal/racoon dog

Porpoise - 鼠海豚 (shǔ hǎi tún) = mouse/rat - ocean/sea - pig

Triceratops - 三角恐龙 (sān jiǎo kǒng lóng) – three - horn - dinosaur

T-Rex - 霸王龙 (bà wáng lóng) = overlord/tyrant/bully/to rule by force - king/monarch/emperor/ruler - dinosaur

Brontosaurus - 迷惑龙 (mí huò lóng) = to confuse/confused/puzzled/to baffle - dinosaur

Stegosaurus - 剑龙 (jiàn lóng) = sword/sabre/rapier/dagger - dragon/dinosaur

Pterodactyl - 翼手龙 (yì shǒu lóng) = wing - hand/hold - dragon/dinosaur

Woodpecker - 啄木鸟 (zhuó mù niǎo) = peck - tree/timber/wood - bird

Dung Beetle - 屎壳郎 (shǐ ké làng) = excrement/feces/dung/shit - shell/housing/casing - official/gentleman

Ladybug - 花大姐 (huā dà jiě) = flower/blossom/bloom - large/big/huge/great/vast - elder sister/young lady

Blowfish - 河豚 (hé tún) = river - pig

Guinea Pig - 豚鼠 (tún shǔ) = pig - rat/mouse

Guinea Pig - 天竺鼠 (tiān zhú shǔ) = India - rat/mouse

Guinea Pig - 荷兰猪 (hé lán zhū) = Holland - pig

Meerkat - 狐獴 (hú měng) = fox - mongoose

Meerkat - 招狸 (zhāo lí) = pond/pool/lake - racoon dog/fox

Meerkat - 细尾獴 (xì wěi měng) = thin or slender/tiny/delicate - tail - mongoose

Canary - 金丝雀 (jīn sī què) = gold/golden - silk/a tiny bit/trace/a hint of - sparrow/small bird

Stray Dog - 流浪狗 (liú làng gǒu) = move from place to place/drift/wander - stroll - dog

Wolverine - 狼獾 (láng huān) = wolf - badger

Tasmanian Devil - 袋獾 (dài huān) = bag/sack/pouch/pocket - badger

Tiger Shark - 鼬鲨 (yòu shā) = weasel - shark

**Royal Eagle** - 狗鹫 (gǒu jiù) = dog - vulture/condor

Golden Retriever - 金毛狗 (jīn máo gǒu) = gold/golden - hair - dog

Kingfisher - 鱼狗 (yú gǒu) = fishing/to fish - dog

Archaeoraptor - 古盗鸟 (gǔ dào niǎo) = ancient/paleo-/old - thief/robber/bandit/to plunder - bird

Groundhog - 土拨鼠 (tǔ bō shǔ) = soil/earth/land/ground - move or adjust with the hand/dispel/distribute - mouse/rat

Marmot - 旱獭 (hàn tǎ) = dry/dry land/drought - otter

Sloth - 树獭 (shù tǎ) = tree - otter

Platypus - 鸭獭 (yā tǎ) = duck - otter

Gecko/House Lizard - 蝎虎 (xiē hǔ) = scorpion - tiger

Hadrosaurus - 巨龙 (jù lóng) = huge/tremendous/gigantic/chief - dragon

Hamster - 仓鼠 (cāng shǔ) = barn/storehouse/warehouse/cabin/hold (in a ship) - mouse/rat

**Squirrel** - 灰鼠 (huī shǔ) = ash/dust/grey - mouse/rat

Sponge - 海绵 (hǎi mián) = ocean/sea - spineless

**Moose** - 大鹿 (dà lù) = big/huge/large/great - deer

Husky (Dog) - 雪橇犬 (xuě qiāo quǎn) = snow - sled/sledge/sleigh - dog

Humpback Whale - 座头鲸 (zuò tóu jīng) = seat/base - head - whale

Killer Whale - 杀人鲸 (shā rén jīng) = kill/slaughter/butcher//murder - person/people - whale

Lay eggs - 甩子 (shuǎi zi) = leave behind/throw/fling - offspring/child

Chihuahua (dog) - 吉娃娃 (jí wá wá) = lucky/auspicious - baby (*transliterated*)

Sea Otter/Pipefish - 海龙 (hǎi lóng) = ocean/sea/lake - dragon/shaped like a dragon

Earthworm - 地龙 (de lóng) = earth/soil/ground - dragon/shaped like a dragon

Bottlenose Whale - 巨齿鲸 (jù chǐ jīng) = huge/tremendous/gigantic/chief - tooth - whale

Migrate (of animals) - 回游 (huí yóu) = return/go back/turn around - to travel/roam/drift/float/tour

Pilot Whale - 圆头鲸 (yuán tóu jīng) = circle/sphere/circular - head - whale

Giant Salamander - 娃娃鱼 (wá wá yú) = baby/child - fish

Jackal - 胡狼 (hú láng) = beard/whiskers/moustache - wolf

Pika - 鼠兔 (shǔ tù) = mouse/rat - rabbit/hare

Brachiosaurus - 腕龙 (wàn lóng) = wrist - dragon

Ostrich - 驼鸡 (tuó jī) = camel - chicken

Llama - 美洲驼 (měi zhōu tuó) = North America - camel

Toucan - 大嘴鸟 (dà zuǐ niǎo) = big/large/great/huge - mouth/beak - bird

Kiwi - 无翼鸟 (wú yì niǎo) = not have/without/to lack - wing - bird

Loon - 潜鸟 (qián niǎo) = to dive/to submerge - bird

Canary - 黄鸟 (huáng niǎo) = yellow - bird

Marlin - 枪鱼 (qiāng yú) = spear - fish

Water Flea - 金鱼虫 (jīn yú chóng) = goldfish - insect/worm

Pangolin - 穿山甲 (chuān shān jiǎ) = to penetrate/bore through - mountain - shell/amour

Partridge - 斑翅山鹑 (bān chì shān chún) = spotted/speck/striped - wing - mountain - quail

Sawfish - 尖齿锯鳐 (jiān chǐ jù yáo) = sharp/pointed - teeth - saw - ray (fish)

Addax - 旋角羚 (xuán jiǎo lǐng) = circle/revolve/spin - horn - antelope/gazelle

Longhorn beetle - 天牛 (tiān niú) = sky/heaven - cow

**Mackerel Sky** - 鱼鳞天 (yú lín tiān) = fish - fish scales - sky/heaven

Cuttlefish - 墨鱼 (mò yú) = ink/black/pitch-black - fish

Sloth - 懒熊 (lǎn xióng) = lazy - bear

**Dung Beetle** - 粪金龟 (fèn jīn guī) = dung/feces/excrement - gold/money - turtle/tortoise

'To mate animals' - 交尾 (jiāo wěi) = relationship/friend/acquaintance - tail/rear end (the relationship of the rear end?)

Koala - 无尾熊 (wú wěi xióng) = not/without - tail - bear

Velociraptor (dinosaur) - 伶盗龙 (líng dào lóng) = clever - steal/rob/plunder/thief/robber - dragon/dinosaur

Anglerfish - 琵琶鱼 (pí pá yú) = 'pipa' (instrument) - fish

Leech - 吸血者 (xī xiě zhě) = inhale/breath in/suck in/suck (liquids) - blood - 'the one who' (the one who sucks blood)

Larva - 幼虫 (yōu chóng) = children/the young/infant - insect/worm

Bumblebee - 大黄蜂 (dà huáng fēng) = big/large/huge/great - yellow - bee/wasp/hornet

Flea - 跳虱 (tiào shī) = jump/leap/bounce - louse/bug

Venom - 毒液 (dú yè) = poison - liquid/fluid/juice

**Guinea Foul** - 珍珠鸡 (zhēn zhū jī) = pearl - chicken

# Clothes

Headband - 头箍 (tóu gū) = head - hoop

Bra - 胸罩 (xiōng zhào) = breast - cover/shade

**Bra** - 乳罩 (rǔ zhào) = breast - cover

Wife Beater - 背心 (bèi xīn) = back - heart

Mask - 面具 (miàn jù) = face - equipment/tool/device

Glasses - 眼镜 (yǎn jìng) = eye - lens/mirror

Cape/cloak/poncho - 披风 (pī fēng) = 'wrap around the shoulders' - style

Sweater - 毛衣 (máo yī) = hair - clothes

**Sweater** - 卫衣 (wèi yī) = to defend/protect/guard - clothes

Contacts - 隐形眼镜 (yǐn xíng yǎn jìng) = invisible - eyeglasses

Slippers - 拖鞋 (tuō xié) = drag - shoes

Zipper - 拉链 (lā liàn) = pull - chain

Wallet - 钱包 (qián bāo) = money - bag/package

Sunglasses - 墨镜 (mò jìng) = ink - lens/mirror

Lip balm - 唇膏 (chún gāo) = lip - paste/ointment

**Chapstick/Lip Balm** - 润唇膏 (rùn chún gāo) = moisten/lubricate/smooth/glossy - lips - ointment/grease/fat/paste

Loafers - 懒汉鞋 (lǎn hàn xié) = lazy - man - shoes

Onesie - 连身衣 (lián shēn yī) = to connect/join - body - clothing

Suspenders - 吊袜带 (diào wà dài) = to suspend/hang - socks - belt

Scarf - 围巾 (wéi jīn) = to surround/to encircle/to wear (by wrapping around) - towel/kerchief/general purpose cloth

Bulletproof vest - 护甲 (hù jiǎ) = to protect - armour plating/shell

Lingerie - 亵服 (xiè fú) = obscene/disrespectful - clothes/garment

Pyjamas - 睡衣 (shuì yī) = to sleep - clothes

Bow tie - 蝶形领带 (dié xíng lǐng dài) = butterfly - form/shape - neck - belt/band/ribbon

Camouflage - 迷彩服 (mí cǎi fú) = confused/lost - colour (of clothes) - clothes

Split pants - 开裆裤 (kāi dāng kù) = to open - crotch - pants/trousers

(Chinese use pants with holes in them for their babies/toddlers because diapers are so expensive. This is why you see many babies/toddlers being held over the drainage vent in the street, spread eagle, to pee or poo. If you gotta go you gotta go right? I actually did this with one of our kids over a garbage can once. Although she was about 10, and had normal pants on. But what can you do eh?)

Mask - 假面 (jiǎ miàn) = fake/false/artificial- face

Panties - 三角裤 (sān jiǎo kù) = three - horn/horn-shaped/corner - underpants/pants/trousers

Clogs - 木鞋 (mù xié) = tree/timber/wood - shoes

**Mourning Apparel** - 殡服 (bìn fú) = funeral/embalm/to encoffin a corpse/to carry a burial - clothes

Pyjamas - 睡衣 (shuì yī) = sleep - clothes

Overalls/Coveralls - 工装裤 (gōng zhuāng kù) = worker/workman/labour/industry/trade/profession - attire/dress up/outfit/clothes/pants

Dress Shoes - 时装鞋 (shí zhuāng xié) = the latest fashion/fashionable clothes - shoes

Bib - 围兜 (wéi dōu) = to encircle/encompass/enclose/all around/to wear by wrapping around - pocket/bag

**Bib** - 围嘴 (wéi zuǐ) = to encircle/encompass/enclose/all around/to wear by wrapping around - mouth

Corset - 束衣 (shù yī) = bind/tie/restrain/bundle - clothes

Kitchen Apron - 油裙 (yóu qún) = oil/grease/fat - skirt (裙 also means apron, but I like 'oil skirt' more.)

Flared Skirt - 喇叭裙 (lǎ bā qún) = trumpet - skirt

Nightgown - 睡裙 (shuì qún) = sleep - skirt

Top Hat - 大礼帽 (dà lǐ mào) = big/huge/large/great - ceremony/rite/ritual/etiquette/manners/social custom - hat/cap

Hoodie Hood - 兜帽 (dōu mào) = to wrap up/pocket/bag - hap/cap

Biretta - 四角帽 (sì jiǎo mào) = four - something in the shape of a horn/corner - hap/cap

Flip-flops - 夹脚拖 (jiā jiǎo tuō) = place in between/wedged between - foot/leg - pull/drag

Sailor Hat - 水手帽 (shuǐ shǒu mào) = water/river/liquid - hand/person skilled in certain types of work - hat/cap

Earmuffs - 耳帽 (ěr mào) = ear/ear-like thing - hat/cap

Bonnet - 苏格兰帽 (sū gé lán mào) = Scotland - hat/cap

Beanie - 豆豆帽 (dòu dòu mào) = bean - bean - hat/cap

Miniskirt - 超短裙 (chāo duǎn qún) = ultra/super - short - skirt

**Wool/Fleece** - 羊毛 (yáng máo) = sheep/goat/ram - hair (also means 'wool' but I like hair more)

**Fire Proof Clothes** - 防火服 (fáng huǒ fú) = guard against/defence - fire - clothes

UGG Boots - 雪地靴 (xuě dì xuē) = snowfield - boots

Moccasins - 鹿皮靴 (lù pí xuē) = deer - skin/leather/hide/fur - boots

Coveralls/Overalls - 工装裤 (gōng zhuāng kù) = work/labour/profession - outfit/clothing/attire - pants

Flip-flops/Thongs - 人字拖鞋 (rén zì tuō xié) = '人' - character - drag shoes (slippers)

Mittens - 连指手套 (lián zhǐ shǒu tào) = link/join/connect - finger - gloves/(mittens)

Open-toed Shoe - 鱼嘴鞋 (yú zuǐ xié) = fish - mouth - shoes

Sweat Pants - 绒裤 (róng kù) = fine hair/down/woollen/cotton/silk - pants

**Underwear** - 内裤 (nèi kù) = inside/interior - underwear/pants/trousers

**Flat Shoes** - 平底鞋 (píng dǐ xié) = flat - bottom/base - shoes

**Shorts** - 短裤 (duǎn kù) = short - pants

Hoodie - 连帽卫衣 (lián mào wèi yī) = to link/join/connect - headgear/cap-like cover - sweater

**Life Jacket** - 救生衣 (jiù shēng yī) = rescue/save - life - clothes

**Ragged Clothes** - 鹑衣 (chún yī) = quail - clothes

**Ankle Socks** - 船袜 (chuán wà) = boat/ship - socks

# Body

Nipples - 奶头 (nǎi tóu) = milk - head

Weiner/dick (slang) - 鸡鸡 (jī jī) = chicken - chicken

Balls (slang) - 蛋蛋 (dàn dàn) = egg - egg

Testicles - 精巢 (jīng cháo) = sperm/semen - nest

Adams apple - 喉结 (hóu jié) = throat - knot

Boobies - 双峰 (shuāng fēng) = double - peak/summit

Goosebumps - 鸡皮疙瘩 (jī pí gē da) = chicken - skin - pimple

Thigh - 大腿 (dà tuǐ) = big - leg

Shin - 小腿 (xiǎo tuǐ) = small - leg

Pelvis - 骨盆 (gǔ pén) = bone - basin

Cleavage - 乳沟 (rǔ gōu) = breast - ditch

Wig - 假发 (jiǎ fà) = fake - hair

Acne - 青春痘 (qīng chūn dòu) = youthfulness - pimple

Sleepies - 眼屎 (yǎn shǐ) = eye - feces/excrement/shit

Earwax - 耳屎 (ěr shǐ) = ear - feces/excrement/shit

Snot - 鼻屎 (bí shǐ) = nose - feces/excrement/shit

Anus - 屁眼 (pì yǎn) = bum/buttocks - eye

**Anus** - 肛门 (gāng mén) = anus - door

Eyelid - 眼皮 (yǎn pí) = eye - skin

Iris - 虹膜 (hóng mó) = rainbow - membrane/film

Tonsil - 扁桃腺 (biǎn táo xiàn) = flat - peach - gland

Braces (on yer teeth) - 牙套 (yá tào) = tooth - harness/encase

Uterus - 子宫 (zǐ gōng) = child - temple/palace

**Cervix** - 宫颈 (gōng jǐng) = uterus/womb/palace/temple - neck/throat

Skull - 脑袋 (nǎo dai) = brain - bag

Pit of stomach - 胸口 (xiōng kǒu) = chest - mouth

Bald - 光头 (guāng tóu) = light/bright - head

Vein - 血管 (xiě guǎn) = blood - tube/pipe

Breast/Utter - 奶房 (nǎi fáng) = milk - room/house

Dark circles under the eyes - 熊猫眼 (xióng māo yǎn) = panda - eyes

Spit - 口水 (kǒu shuǐ) = mouth - water

Penis - 肉棒 (ròu bàng) = meat - stick/club

Pony tail - 马尾 (mǎ wěi) = horse - tail (Pony is 小马 = small - horse)

**Dreadlocks** - 脏辫 (zàng biàn) = dirty - braid

**Dreadlocks** - 未梳理的乱发串 (wèi shūlǐ de luàn fā chuàn) = not/did not - to comb/comb out - of - disorder/in a mess - hair - bunch/skewer/to string together & classifier for things that are strung together (lit. messy bunches of hair one didn't comb out)

Pregnant - 双身子 (shuāng shēn zi) = double - body/life (*身 can also mean pregnant) - child/seed/egg

Bladder (slang) - 尿袋 (niào dài) = urine - bag/pouch/sack

Belly button - 肚脐眼 (dù qí yǎn) = belly - navel - eye/small hole

Face cream - 香脂 (xiāng zhī) = fragrant/aromatic - fat/resin

Deodorant - 除臭剂 (chú chòu jì) = to get rid of/to remove/to eliminate - stench/to smell (bad) - dose (medicine)

Mascara - 睫毛膏 (jié máo gāo) = eyelashes - hair -paste/ointment/to grease/lubricate

Butt Crack - 股沟 (gǔ gōu) = thigh - ditch

Body odour - 体味 (tǐ wèi) = body - smell/taste

**Body odour** - 酸臭味儿 (suān chòu wèi er) = sour - smelly/stinky - smell/taste

Pigeon toed - 内八字脚 (nèi bāzì jiǎo) = inner/inside - 八 - character/word/symbol - foot

Dandruff - 头皮屑 (tóu pí xiè) = head - skin - crumbs/bits/filings

Bangs - 齐眉穗儿 (qí méi suì er) = 'level with' - eyebrow - fringe

**Vagina** - 阴道 (yīn dào) = genitalia - road/path

**Penis** - 阴茎 (yīn jīng) = genitalia - stalk/stem

Tattoo - 文身 (wén shēn) = writing/language - body

**Tattoo** - 纹身 (wén shēn) = line/trace/mark - body

Lipstick - 口红 (kǒu hóng) = mouth - red

Twins - 双胞胎 (shuāng bāo tāi) = set of two/pair/couple/double - womb/placenta - fetus/embryo/birth/unborn child/womb carrying a fetus

Testosterone - 睾丸激素 (gāo wán jī sù) = testicle - ball - arouse/stimulate/excite/surge - essence/nature

Fart - 放屁 (fàng pì) = let go/set free/release - wind/fart

**Sideburns** - 鬓脚 (bìn jiǎo) = hair on the temples - foot/base

**Sideburns** - 耳发 (ěr fà) = ear - hair

Sideburns - 腮胡 (sāi hú) = cheek - whiskers/beard

Sunburn - 日晒伤 (rì shài shāng) = sun/solar/daytime/day - (of the sun) shine upon/bask/dry in the sun - wound/injury/hurt

Bruise - 皮外伤 (pí wài shāng) = skin - outside/exterior/in addition/beyond/other place/external - wound/injury/hurt

Sphincter - 括约肌 (kuò yuē jī) = draw together (muscles etc.)/contract - restrict/restrain - muscle/flesh

Forehead - 脑门 (nǎo mén) = brain - door/gate/entrance/orifice in the human body

Cerebellum - 小脑 (xiǎo nǎo) = small - brain

Purse one's lips - 扁嘴 (biǎn zuǐ) = flat - mouth

Tonsils - 扁桃腺 (biǎn táo xiàn) = flat - peach shaped/walnut - gland

Cornea - 眼角膜 (yǎn jiǎo mó) = eye - corner - membrane/film

Slobber/Salivate - 口角流涎 (kǒu jiǎo liú xián) = mouth - corner - to flow/stream of water/current - saliva

**Slobber** - 淌口水 (tǎng kǒu shuǐ) = drip/trickle - mouth - water

Biceps - 二头肌 (er tóu jī) = two - head/top/chief/leading - muscle/flesh

Prosthetics - 修复术 (xiū fù shù) = repair/mend/overhaul/decorate/embellish/build/construct - duplicate/double - art/skill/technique/method

**Manicure** - 修手 (xiū shǒu) = repair/mend/overhaul/decorate/embellish/build/construct - hand

Manicure - 修指甲 (xiū zhǐ jiǎ) = repair/mend/overhaul/decorate/embellish/build/construct - finger - shell/nail

Pedicure - 修脚 (xiū jiǎo) = repair/mend/overhaul/decorate/embellish/build/construct - foot

Molar - 磨牙 (mó yá) = rub/grind/polish/wear down - tooth

Molar - 后牙 (hòu yá) = back/rear - tooth

Molar - 盘牙 (pán yá) = shallow/plate/dish/tray - tooth

Incisor - 门牙 (mén yá) = gate/door/opening - tooth

(Mouth) Gums - 压床 (yā chuáng) = tooth/teeth - bed

Front Tooth - 大牙 (dà yá) = big/large/huge/great/side - tooth

Fang/Canine Tooth - 尖牙 (jiān yá) = pointed/tip/tapering/sharp - tooth

Buck Teeth - 暴牙 (bào yá) = stick out/bulge/stand out - teeth/tooth

Dental Plaque - 牙垢 (yá gòu) = tooth/teeth - dirt/filth/stains

Enamel - 牙釉质 (yá yòu zhí) = teeth/tooth - glaze - quality/nature/character

Lactate - 泌乳 (mì rǔ) = secrete/excrete/to seep out - milk

Urinary Tract - 泌尿道 (mì niào dào) = secrete/excrete/to seep out - urine - path/road/channel

Part (in one's hair) - 分头路 (fēn tóu lù) = divide/separate/distribute/allot/to allocate - head/hair or hairstyle - road/path/street

**Part** (in one's hair) - 分缝 (fēn fèng) = divide/separate/distribute/allot/to allocate - seam/crack/narrow slit

Back of the head - 脑勺 (nǎo sháo) = brains/head - spoon/ladle/scoop

Brains - 脑汁 (nǎo zhī) = brains/head - juice/fluid/sauce

Brains - 脑浆 (nǎo jiāng) = brains/head - thick fluid/broth

Temple (of human head) - 太阳穴 (tài yáng xué) = sun - cave/den/hole/acupuncture point

Armpit - 肋窝 (lèi wō) = rib/chest - nest/lair/den/hollow of the human body

Spine - 背骨 (bèi gǔ) = back of the body/back side - bone/skeleton

Cartilage - 软骨 (ruǎn gǔ) = soft/flexible - bone/skeleton

Collarbone - 锁骨 (suǒ gǔ) = to lock/lock up - bone/skeleton

Fertile Egg - 受精卵 (shòu jīng luǎn) = receive/accept - sperm/semen/seed - ovum/egg/spawn

Dimple - 笑窝 (xiào wō) = smile/laugh - hollow on the human body/pit/nest

To Shave - 修面 (xiū miàn) = repair/mend/overhaul/decorate/embellish/build/construct - face

Concealer (Makeup) - 遮瑕膏 (zhē xiá gāo) = hide from view/cover/block/obstruct - blemish/defect - ointment/grease/fat/paste

**Manicure/Pedicure** - 美甲 (měi jiǎ) = beautiful/pretty - nail/shell

Hairspray - 喷发胶 (pēn fà jiāo) = spurt/gush/to puff//to spray/blow out - hair - gel/glue/rubber/resin

Orthodontic Braces - 牙齿矫正器 (yá chǐ jiǎo zhèng qì) = tooth/teeth - correct/rectify/to straighten - device/tool/utensil

Wart - 肉瘤 (ròu liú) = meat/flesh - tumor/lump/goitre

Achilles' Heel - 死穴 (sǐ xué) = die/death/dead - cave/den/hole/acupuncture point

Femur - 股骨 (gǔ gǔ) = thigh - bone

Pubic Hair - 阴毛 (yīn máo) = private parts/genitalia/secret - hair

Pubic Hair - 耻毛 (chǐ máo) = shame/humiliation/disgrace/ashamed - hair

Pacemaker - 心脏起搏器 (xīn zàng qǐ bó qì) = heart - raise/to initiate - (of heart) to beat - device/tool

Cochlea - 耳蜗 (ěr wō) = ear - snail

Ankle - 腿腕 (tuǐ wàn) = leg - wrist

Crow's Feet (Wrinkles near the eye) - 鱼尾纹 (yú wěi wén) = fish - tail - line/trace/mark/pattern/wrinkle

Ovary - 卵巢窝 (luǎn cháo wō) = ovum/egg/spawn - nest - nest/pit/lair/den

To Blush - 红晕 (hóng yùn) = red - swoon/faint/pass out

To Blush - 发红 (fà hóng) = send out/emit/give forth - red

# Fingers

Thumb - 大拇指 (dà mǔ zhǐ) = big - thumb - finger

**Index/forefinger** - 二拇指 (er mǔ zhǐ) = two - thumb - finger

Index/forefinger - 食指 (shí zhǐ) = food - finger

**Middle** - 三拇指 (sān mǔ zhǐ) = three - thumb - finger

Middle - 中指 (zhōng zhǐ) = middle - finger

**Ring** - 四拇指 (sì mǔ zhǐ) = four - thumb - finger

Ring - 无名指 (wú míng zhǐ) = nameless - finger

Pinkie - 小拇指 (xiǎo mǔ zhǐ) = small - thumb - finger

Fingernail - 指甲 (zhǐ jiǎ) = finger - shell (甲 also means 'finger nail', but I like finger shell more)

Knuckle - 指关节 (zhǐ guān jié) = finger - joint

Cuticle - 角皮 (jiǎo pí) = corner/angle - skin

# Musical Related Stuff

Oboe - 双簧管 (shuāng huáng guǎn) = double - reed - pipe/tube

Fiddle/Violin - 小提琴 (xiǎo tí qín) = small - lift - instrument

Tuba - 大号 (dà hào) = large/big - horn

Viola - 中提琴 (zhōng tí qín) = middle - lift - instrument

Cello - 大提琴 (dà tí qín) = big - lift - instrument

Double bass - 低音提琴 (dī yīn tí qín) = low - sound - lift - instrument

Harp - 竖琴 (shù qín) = vertical/upright - instrument

Piano - 钢琴 (gāng qín) = steel - instrument

Xylophone - 木琴 (mù qín) = wood - instrument

Harpsichord - 大键琴 (dà jiàn qín) = big - key (of an instrument) - instrument

Pipe Organ - 风琴 (fēng qín) = wind - instrument

**Falsetto** - 假嗓子 (jiǎ sǎng zi) = fake/false/to borrow/artificial - voice/throat

Bagpipes - 风笛 (fēng dí) = wind - flute

Accordion - 手风琴 (hǒu fēng qín) = hand - wind - instrument

Trombone - 拉管 (lā guǎn) = to pull - woodwind/pipe

**Trombone** - 长号 (cháng hào) = long - horn

Trumpet - 小号 (xiǎo hào) = small - horn

**Euphonium** - 低音大号 (dī yīn dà hào) = low - sound/tone - big - horn

French Horn - 圆号 (yuán hào) = round/circular/circle - horn

Cornet - 短号 (duǎn hào) = short - horn

Banjo - 班卓琴 (bān zhuō qín) = 'ban zhuo' - instrument *transliterated*

Clarinet - 单簧管 (dān huáng guǎn) = single/sole - metallic reed - woodwind/pipe

**Clarinet** - 黑管 (hēi guǎn) = black - tube/pipe/woodwind

Harmonica - 口琴 (kǒu qín) = mouth - instrument

**Guitar** - 吉他 = 'ji ta' *transliterated*

**Guitar** - 六弦琴 (liù xián qín) = six - string - instrument

Mandolin - 曼德琳 = 'man de lin' *transliterated*

**Mandolin** - 杨琵琶 (yáng pí pá) = foreign - pipa (Chinese lute)

Piccolo - 短笛 (duǎn dí) = short - flute

Saxophone - 萨克斯管 (sà kè sī guǎn) = 'sa ke si' - woodwind/pipe *transliterated*

Tambourine - 铃鼓 (líng gǔ) = (small) bell - drum

Chimes - 排钟 (pái zhōng) = to line up/a row/a line - bell

**Lip sync** - 假唱 (jiǎ chàng) = fake/false/artificial - to sing

**Mosh pit** - 舞台前的狂舞区 (wǔ tái qián de kuáng wǔ qū) = stage - front - crazy/mad/insane - area

National Anthem - 国歌 (guó gē) = country - song

Bassoon - 低音管 (dī yīn guǎn) = low - sound - woodwind

Guqin - 古琴 (gǔ qín) = ancient - instrument

Lyre - 七线竖琴 (qī xiàn shù qín) = seven - string - harp

Timpani - 定音鼓 (dìng yīn gǔ) = to set/fixed/determine - sound - drum

Chord (in music) - 和弦 (hé xián) = together with/union/harmony - bowstring/string of musical instrument

Soprano - 女高音 (nǚ gāo yīn) = woman/female - tall/high/height/above average/of a high level or degree - sound/musical sound/note/tone

Tenor - 男高音 (nán gāo yīn) = man/male - tall/high/height/above average/of a high level or degree - sound/musical sound/note/tone

Falsetto - 假声 (jiǎ shēng) = false/fake/phoney/artificial/deception - sound/voice/noise/tone

Pitch/Tone (music) - 音高 (yīn gāo) = sound/musical sound/note/tone - tall/high/height/above average/of a high level or degree

Ocarina (Instrument) - 陶笛 (táo dí) = pottery/earthenware - whistle/bamboo flute

Microphone - 传声器 (chuán shēng qì) = to pass on/to spread/to transmit - sound/noise/voice/tone - device/tool/instrument

Tuning Fork - 声叉 (shēng chā) = sound/noise/voice/tone - fork

Scat Singing - 拟声唱法 (nǐ shēng chàng fǎ) = onomatopoeia - singing style

Musical Box - 八音盒 (bā yīn hé) = eight -sound/note/syllable/tone - small box/case

Recorder (Instrument) - 木笛 (mù dí) = wood/tree/wooden - bamboo flute/flute

Recorder (Instrument) - 竖笛 (shù dí) = vertical/upright - bamboo flute/flute

**Cajón** - 木箱鼓 (mù xiāng gǔ) = tree/timber/wood - chest/box/case/trunk - drum/something resembling a drum

Beatboxing - 节奏口技 (jié zòu kǒu jì) = beat/rhythm/tempo - mouth - skill/ability/technique (Rhythm Ventriloquism)

**Arpeggio** (Music) - 分散和弦 (fēn sàn hé xián) = to disperse/to distribute - chord (music)

Turntable - 唱盘 (chàng pán) = sing/song - plate/tray/dish

Phonograph/Record Player - 唱机 (chàng jī) = sing/song - machine

Choir - 唱诗班 (chàng shī bān) = sing/song/chant - poetry/poem/verse - team/squad/group

A Capella - 无伴奏合唱 (wú bàn zòu hé chàng) = not have/without/none - accompany (with musical instruments) - chorus

Jukebox - 自动点唱机 (zì dòng diǎn chàng jī) = automatic - to choose - gramophone/record player

Onomatopoeia - 摹声词 (mó shēng cí) = copy/trace/duplicate/pattern - sound/noise/voice/tone - word/speech/statement/phrase/expression/lyrics

Tempo (in music) - 速度拍子 (sù dù pāi zi) = speed/velocity - degree of intensity/extent/degree/limit - beat/time

**Metronome** - 节拍计 (jié pāi jì) = section/segment/part - beat/time - device

# Drums

China - 中国钹 (zhōng guó bó) = China - cymbal

Ride - 叠音钹 (dié yīn bó) = to layer/pile up/repeat - cymbal

**Ride** - 节奏镲 (jié zòu chǎ) = rhythm/tempo/beat - small cymbal

Splash - 水钹 (shuǐ bó) = water - cymbal

Crash - 随音钹 (suí yīn bó) = smash/break/broken - sound - cymbal

Toms - 嗵嗵鼓 (tōng tōng gǔ) = thump/thud - thump/thud - drum

**Toms** - 筒鼓 (tǒng gǔ) = wide tube-shaped object - drug

Floor tom - 落地鼓 (luò dì gǔ) = to be set on the ground - drum

**Floor tom** - 低嗵鼓 (dī tōng gǔ) = low - thump/thud - drum

**Snare** - 小鼓 (xiǎo gǔ) = small - drum

Snare - 军鼓 (jūn gǔ) = army/military - drum

Kick drum - 低音大鼓 (dī yīn dà gǔ) = low - sound - big - drum

Hi-hats - 踩镲 (cǎi chǎ) = step on/stamp - small cymbal

Kick pedal - 踩锤 (cǎi chuí) – step on/stamp - hammer

Drum sicks - 鼓槌 (gǔ chuí) = drum - hammer/mallet

**Drum sicks** - 手锤 (shǒu chuí) = hand - hammer

## Vehicles & Stuff

('车' can mean 'vehicle' or 'car', so I used my own discretion.)

Airplane - 飞机 (fēi jī) = fly - machine/aircraft

Biplane - 双翼飞机 (shuāng yì fēi jī) = double/two/pair - wing - airplane

Cockpit - 座舱 (zuò cāng) = seat - cabin/module (of a spacecraft)

Tank - 战车 (zhàn chē) = war - vehicle

Train - 火车 (huǒ chē) = fire - vehicle

Taxi - 出租车 (chū zū chē) = 'to go out' - rent - vehicle

Scooter - 电动车 (diàn dòng chē) = electric - 'to move/set in movement' - vehicle

VW Bug - 金龟车 (jīn guī chē) = tortoise - vehicle

Truck - 卡车 (kǎ chē) = block - vehicle

Trolly Bus - 电车 (diàn chē) = electric - vehicle

Chariot/Carriage - 马车 (mǎ chē) = horse - vehicle

**Dining Car** - 餐车 (cān chē) = meal - vehicle

Hearse - 灵车 (líng chē) = spirit/departed soul/coffin - car

**Hearse** - 殡车 (bìn chē) = a funeral/to carry to a burial - car

Unlicensed Taxi (Black Cab) - 黑车 (hēi chē) = black - vehicle

The Ark - 方舟 (fāng zhōu) = square - boat

Roller Coaster - 过山车 (guò shān chē) = 'to cross' - mountain - vehicle

Forklift - 叉车 (chā chē) = fork - vehicle

Unicycle - 单轮车 (dān lún chē) = single - wheel - vehicle

Fire Truck - 消防车 (xiāo fáng chē) = eliminate - prevent/defend - vehicle

Ambulance - 救护车 (jiù hù chē) = save - protect - vehicle

Jet - 喷气式飞机 (pēn qì shì fēi jī) = spray/puff - gas/air - style/type - airplane

Blimp - 软式小型飞船 (ruǎn shì xiǎo xíng fēi chuán) = soft - small scale - fly - boat

Van - 货车 (huò chē) = goods/commodity - vehicle

Dump Truck - 倾斜汽车 (qīng xié qì chē) = 'to overturn/incline' - unload/get rid of - vehicle

**Dump Truck** - 自卸车 (zì xiè chē) = self - to unload/to get rid of - vehicle/car

Tractor - 拖拉机 (tuō lā jī) = to drag/tow - to pull - machine/engine

Snowmobile - 雪地车 (xuě dì chē) = snow - field/ground/land - vehicle

Yacht - 游艇 (yóu tǐng) = to tour/roam/travel - vessel/small ship

Limousine - 轿车 (jiào chē) = palanquin - car

Bumper car - 碰碰车 (pèng pèng chē) = to bump/to touch - to bump/to touch - car

**Crane/hoist** - 吊车 (diào chē) = to hang up/top suspend - vehicle

Crane/hoist - 起重机 (qǐ zhòng jī) = to raise/to rise - heavy - machine/engine

RV - 房车 (fáng chē) = house - vehicle/car

Submarine - 潜水艇 (qián shuǐ tǐng) = to submerge/dive/to hide/conceal - water - vessel/small ship

Mountain bike - 山地车 (shān dì chē) = mountain/hill - earth/ground - vehicle

Stroller - 娃娃车 (wá wá chē) = baby - vehicle/car

**Stern (of a ship)** - 船尾 (chuán wěi) = boat - tail

**To tailgate** - 追尾 (zhuī wěi) = to chase after - tail

Semi Truck - 货运卡车 (huò yùn kǎ chē) = goods/commodity - to move/transport - truck

Semi Truck - 拖挂车 (tuō guà chē) = to drag/tow/trail - trailer - vehicle

Semi trailer - 挂车 (guà chē) = to hang or suspend - vehicle

Oil rig - 钻井船 (zuǎn jǐng chuán) = to dig into/to drill/to bore - a well - boat/vessel

Aircraft Carrier - 航母 (háng mǔ) = ship/boat - mother

Rickshaw- 东洋车 (dōng yáng chē) = east/eastern - ocean/foreign/western - vehicle/car/carry in cart

Helicopter - 直升机 (zhí shēng jī) = vertical/straight/continuously - rise/go up/ascend - machine/aircraft

Hovercraft - 气垫船 (qì diàn chuán) = air/steam/vapour - pad/cushion/mat - boat/ship

Turbine - 涡轮机 (wō lún jī) = swirl/whirlpool - wheel/disc/revolve - machine/engine

SUV - 休旅车 (xiū lǚ chē) = to rest - travel/trip/journey/voyage - vehicle/car

Glider - 滑翔机 (huá xiáng jī) = slip/slide/smooth - soar/glide/hover - machine/aircraft/engine

Seaplane - 水上飞机 (shuǐ shàng fēi jī) = water - on top/upon/above/upper - airplane

Moped - 机动自行车 (jī dòng zì xíng chē) = power-driven/motorized - bicycle

Bulldozer - 推土机 (tuī tǔ jī) = push forward/shove - soil/earth/land/ground - machine

Scooter - 滑板车 (huá bǎn chē) = skateboard - vehicle/wheeled instrument

Tuk-tuk - 机动三轮车 (jī dòng sān lún chē) = power-driven/motorized - three - wheel - vehicle

Tuk-tuk - 三轮摩托车 (sān lún mó tuō chē) = three - wheel - motorcycle

Tuk-tuk - 突突车 (tú tú chē) = to dash/to move forward quickly/to rush out - to dash/to move forward quickly/to rush out - vehicle

**Cruise Ship** - 游轮 (yóu lún) = to tour/to roam/to travel - steamboat/steamer

Inflatable Dinghy - 充气筏 (chōng qì fá) = fill - air - raft

Kayak/Dugout Canoe - 独木舟 (dú mù zhōu) = alone/single/independent - wood - boat

Kayak - 皮艇 (pí tǐng) = leather/hide/skin - light boat/naval vessel

Snowcat - 雪地履带车 (xuě dì lǚ dài chē) = snowfield - track - vehicle

Drag Race - 短程加速赛车 (duǎn chéng jiā sù sài chē) = short distance - accelerate/speed up - auto race/race car

Pickup Truck - 小货车 (xiǎo huò chē) = small/tiny/few - goods/commodity/product - vehicle

Mining Car - 矿车 (kuàng chē) = ore/mine - vehicle/car (I like 'ore car' even though it also just means 'mine car'.)

Jet Ski - 水上电单车 (shuǐ shàng diàn dān chē) = on or above water - electric/electricity - bicycle

Jet Ski - 水上摩托车 (shuǐ shàng mó tuō chē) = on or above water - motorcycle

Carriage - 兽力车 (shòu lì chē) = beast/animal - power/strength - vehicle/car

Hybrid (Vehicle) - 混合动力车 (hùn hé dòng lì chē) = mix/blend - join/combine/together/unite - force - vehicle/car

4x4 (Vehicle) - 四驱车 (sì qū chē) = four - to drive - vehicle/car

Amphibious (Vehicle) - 水陆两用 (shuǐ lù liǎng yòng) = land and water - dual purpose

**Aircraft** (Slang) - 铁鸟 (tiě niǎo) = iron (metal) - bird

**Front-end Loader/Forklift** - 铲车 (chǎn chē) = shovel/spade - vehicle

**Pallet Jack** - 托盘车 (tuō pán chē) = prop/support - carry/transport - vehicle

# Car parts

Dipstick - 油尺 (yóu chǐ) = oil - ruler/measuring stick

**Dipstick** - 量油尺 (liàng yóu chǐ) = to measure - oil - ruler

Windshield wiper - 雨刷 (yǔ shuā) = rain - to brush

Carburetor - 化油器 (huà yóu qì) = to change into/transform - oil - device/tool

Alternator - 交流发电机 (jiāo liú fā diàn jī) = to exchange - to develop/to send out - electric/electricity/electrical - machine/engine

Clutch - 离合器 (lí hé qì) = to leave/to part from- to join/to fit - device/tool (lit. separation and reunion device)

Brake pedal - 制动踏板 (zhì dòng tà bǎn) = to regulate/control - to move/to set in movement - to press a pedal/to stamp/to step on - board/plank/plate

Gas pedal - 油门 (yóu mén) = petroleum/oil - door/opening/valve/switch

Ignition - 点火开关 (diǎn huǒ kāi guān) = to ignite/to light - fire - to turn on/switch on - to turn off/switch off

Muffler/exhaust - 减声器 (jiǎn shēng qì) = to reduce/decrease/diminish - sound/noise - device/tool

Piston - 活塞 (huó sāi) = living/alive - cork/stopper/to squeeze in

**Radiator** - 水箱 (shuǐ xiāng) = water/liquid - box

Radiator - 散热器 (sàn rè qì) = to disperse/dispel - heat - device/tool

**Radiator** - 暖气机 (nuǎn qì jī) = to warm - air/gas - machine/engine

Spark plug - 火花塞 (huǒ huā sāi) = fire - flower - cork/stopper (spark cork)

Hood - 引擎盖 (yǐn qíng gài) = to extend/lengthen - to raise (hand) - cover/canopy/top

Trunk - 行李箱 (xíng lǐ xiāng) = luggage - box/trunk/chest (also same characters as 'suitcase'.)

Bumper - 保险杠 (bǎo xiǎn gàng) = to defend/protect - danger/dangerous - bar/rod

Grille - 护删 (hù shān) = to protect - fence

Oil filter - 机油滤清器 (jī yóu lǜ qīng qì) = machine/engine - oil/petroleum - to strain/to filter - to clean or purge - device/tool

ABS - 防抱死系统 (fáng bào sǐ xì tǒng) = to protect/defend/prevent/guard against - to embrace - die/death - system

Sunroof - 天窗 (tiān chuāng) = sky/heaven - window

Spoiler - 导流板 (dǎo liú bǎn) = to direct/to conduct - to circulate or spread - board/plank

Brights/High beams - 远光灯 (yuǎn guāng dēng) = far/distant - light/bright - light/lamp/lantern

Windshield - 风挡 (fēng dǎng) = wind - to resist/obstruct/hinder/keep off/to block/cover

**Rearview mirror** - 反照镜 (fǎn zhào jìng) = in reverse - to reflect - mirror/lens

Rearview mirror - 后视镜 (hòu shì jìng) = behind/rear - to show/reveal - mirror/lens

Tachometer (RPM) - 转速表 (zhuǎn sù biǎo) = classifier for revolutions - velocity/rapid - meter

Defroster - 除霜器 (chú shuāng qì) = to remove/eliminate/get rid of - frost - device/tool

Emergency brake - 紧急闸 (jǐn jí zhá) = close at hand/urgent - hurried/urgent/quickly - brake

Antenna - 天线 (tiān xiàn) = sky/heaven - wire/line/thread

Stick Shift - 变速杆 (biàn sù gǎn) = change/alter - speed - pole/shaft/arm

Turn Signal - 泵等 (bèng děng) - pump - light/lamp

Fibreglass - 玻璃钢 (bō lí gāng) = glass - steel

Spoiler (on a car) - 扰流板 (rǎo liú bǎn) = disturb - flow/current - board

Spoiler (on a car) - 尾翼 (wěi yì) = tail/rear - wing

Rim (of a vehicle) = 车圈 (chē quān) = vehicle - circle/ring

# Food

Pumpkin - 南瓜 (nán guā) = south - melon

Watermelon - 西瓜 (xī guā) = west - melon

Bread - 面包 (miàn bāo) = wheat/flour - bundle

Eggnog - 蛋酒 (dàn jiǔ) = egg - alcohol

Sausage - 香肠 (xiāng cháng) = fragrant/savoury/appetizing - intestines

Lasagne - 千层面 (qiān céng miàn) = thousand - layer - noodles

Pasta/Spaghetti - 意大利面 (yì dà lì miàn) = Italy - noodles

Yogurt - 酸奶 (suān nǎi) = sour - milk

Passion fruit - 百香果 (bǎi xiāng guǒ) = hundred/all kinds of - fragrant/savoury/appetizing - fruit

**Pulp (in juice)** - 果肉 (guǒ ròu) = fruit - meat

Butter - 黄油 (huáng yóu) = yellow - oil/fat/grease

Butter - 牛油 (niú yóu) = cow - oil/fat/grease

Margarine - 植物牛油 (zhí wù niú yóu) = vegetation/plant - butter

Cream - 奶油 (nǎi yóu) = milk - oil/fat/grease

Kelp - 海带 (hǎi dài) = sea/ocean - belt/band/ribbon

Croissant - 羊角面包 (yáng jiǎo miàn bāo) = sheep - horn - bread

**Pig brain** (a somewhat common dish in China) - 脑花 (nǎo huā) = brain - flower

Shredded Meat - 肉丝 (ròu sī) = meat - silk

Nectarine - 油桃 (yóu táo) = oil/fat/grease - peach

Pancake - 热香饼 (rè xiāng bǐng) = hot/heat - fragrant/savoury or appetizing - round flat cake/cake

Sauerkraut - 德国酸菜 (dé guó suān cài) = Germany - sour - vegetable

Avocado - 牛油果 (niú yóu guǒ) = cow - oil/fat/grease - fruit

Oatmeal - 麦片 (mài piàn) = wheat - slice/piece

Smoothie - 冰沙 (bīng shā) = ice - sand

Broccoli - 西兰花 (xī lán huā) = west - orchid - flower

Skim Milk - 脱脂牛奶 (tuō zhī niú nǎi) = 'to shed' - fat - cow - milk

Macadamia Nut - 火山豆 (huǒ shān dòu) – volcano - bean

Walnut - 胡桃 (hú táo) = beard - peach

**Luffa** (Loofah?) - 丝瓜 (sī guā) = silk - melon

Buffet - 自助餐 (zì zhù cān) = self - 'to help/assist' - meal

**Pickled Cabbage** - 泡菜 (pào cài) = soaked - vegetable

Popsicle - 冰棒 (bīng bàng) = ice - stick/club

Pizza - 意大利肉饼 (yì dà lì ròu bǐng) = Italy - meat - pastry/round flat cake

Potato - 土豆 (tǔ dòu) = earth - bean

Peanut - 花生 (huā shēng) = flower/blossom - raw/uncooked/life

Soda/Pop - 汽水 (qì shuǐ) = air - water

**White gourd** - 冬瓜 (dōng guā) = winter - melon/gourd/squash

MSG - 味精 (wèi jīng) = taste - extract/essence

Hay - 马草 (mǎ cǎo) = horse - grass

Salami - 意大利香肠 (yì dà lì xiāng cháng) = 'yi da li' *Italy transliterated* - sausage

Bubble gum - 泡泡糖 (pào pào táng) = bubble - bubble - sweets/candy/sugar

**Parsley** - 洋香菜 (yáng xiāng cài) = foreign - cilantro

**Cilantro** - 香菜 (xiāng cài) = fragrant/savoury or appetizing - vegetable

Balut (fetus in egg) - 毛鸭蛋 (máo yā dàn) = hair/feather/young/raw - duck - egg

Balut (fetus in egg) - 屈头蛋 (qū tóu dàn) = bent/to bend- head - egg

Balut (fetus in egg) - 鸭仔蛋 (yā zǐ dàn) = duck - child/young animal - egg

Thousand-year old egg (Black egg/preserved egg) - 皮蛋 (pí dàn) = rubber - egg

Fondue - 奶酪火锅 (nǎi lào huǒ guō) = cheese - hot pot

**Soy Sauce** - 酱油 (jiàng yóu) = 'thick paste' - oil/fat/grease

**Nectarine** - 油桃 (yóu táo) = oil/fat/grease - peach

Corncob - 玉米芯 (yù mǐ xīn) = corn - core

Diet - 节食 (jié shí) = economize/save/conserve - meal/food/to eat

**Cranberry** - 小红莓 (xiǎo hóng méi) = small/tiny - red - berry

Cranberry - 酸莓 (suān méi) = sour/tart - berry

Raspberry - 山莓 (shān méi) = mountain/hill - berry

**Raspberry** - 木莓 (mù méi) = tree/wood - berry

Strawberry - 草莓 (cǎo méi) = grass/straw/countryside/wilderness

Frappuccino - 星冰乐 (xīng bīng lè) = small amount - ice - pleasure/enjoyment

Macadamia Nut - 火山豆 (huǒ shān dòu) = volcano - bean/pea/bean shaped thing

**Ham** (not common) - 火肉 (huǒ ròu) = fire - meat/flesh

Almond - 扁桃 (biǎn táo) = flat - walnut/peach

Nectarine - 油桃 (yóu táo) = oil/fat/grease/lard/greasy - walnut/peach

Protein - 蛋白 (dàn bái) = egg - white/pure

**Thaw Food** - 退冰 (tuì bīng) = remove/recede/cause to move back - ice

Lentil - 小扁豆 (xiǎo biǎn dòu) = small - flat - bean

Asparagus - 龙须菜 (lóng xū cài) = dragon/shaped like a dragon - tassel - vegetable/greens

Macaroni - 空心面 (kōng xīn miàn) = empty/hollow/void/vacant - centre/core - noodles

**Macaroni** - 水管面 (shuǐ guǎn miàn) = water - tube/pipe - noodles

**Macaroni** - 通心粉 (tōng xīn fěn) = to go through/open/pass through - centre/core - noodles

Brussels Sprouts - 球芽甘蓝 (qiú yá gān lán) = sphere/ball/anything shaped like a ball - bud/sprout - cabbage

Pasteurized Milk - 无菌牛奶 (wú jùn niú nǎi) = not have/without/none/to lack - germ/bacteria/mold/fungus - milk

**Rare** (Of Steak) - 一分熟 (yī fēn shú) = one - to allocate/part - cooked/done

**Medium Rare** (Of Steak) - 三分熟 (sān fēn shú) = three - to allocate/part - cooked/done

**Medium** (Of Steak) - 五分熟 (wǔ fēn shú) = five - to allocate/part - cooked/done

**Medium Well** (Of Steak) - 七分熟 (qī fēn shú) = seven - to allocate/part - cooked/done

**Fructose** - 左旋糖 (zuǒ xuán táng) = left/differing/improper/wrong - circle - sugar/sweets/candy

Beet - 甜菜 (tián cài) = sweet/sugary - vegetable/greens

Snow Pea - 荷兰豆 (hé lán dòu) = Holland - pea/bean

**Pecan/Hickory Nut** - 小核桃 (xiǎo hé táo) = small - walnut

Pecan/Hickory Nut - 山核桃 (shān hé táo) = mountain - walnut

Lime - 酸橙 (suān chéng) = sour/tart - orange

Pork Chop - 排骨 (pái gǔ) = row/line - bone/skeleton

Cabbage - 洋白菜 (yáng bái cài) = ocean/foreign/western - white/clear/plain - vegetable/greens/cuisine

Artichoke - 洋蓟 (yáng jì) = ocean/foreign/western - thistle

Egg Yolk - 卵黄 (luǎn huáng) = ovum/egg/spawn - yellow

Marmalade - 柑橘酱 (gān jú jiàng) = mandarin orange - tangerine - sauce/paste/jam

Mayonnaise - 蛋黄酱 (dàn huáng jiàng) = egg - yellow - sauce/paste/jam

String (Green/Snap) Bean - 豆角 (dòu jiǎo) = bean/bean-shaped - horn/horn-shaped/corner

Rutabaga - 芥菜疙瘩 (jiè cài gē da) = mustard/tiny - vegetable/greens/cuisine - pimple/swelling on the skin

Rutabaga/Kohlrabi - 大头菜 (dà tóu cài) = big/large/huge - head - vegetable

Cotton Candy - 棉花糖 (mián huā táng) = cotton/cotton-like material - flower/anything resembling a flower/cotton - sugar/sweets/candy

Instant Noodles - 方便面 (fāng biàn miàn) = convenient - noodles

Menu - 菜单 (cài dān) = dish/course/vegetable/cuisine - bill/list/sheet

Cottage Cheese - 乡村奶酪 (xiāng cūn nǎi lào) = village/countryside/rural area - cheese

Margarine - 人造奶油 (rén zào nǎi yóu) = man-made/artificial - cream/butter

Dairy Product - 乳品 (rǔ pǐn) = milk - product/commodity/goods

Kimchi - 韩式泡菜 (hán shì pào cài) = South Korea - style/type - pickled vegetables

Anchovy - 凤尾鱼 (fèng wěi yú) = phoenix - tail - fish

Sashimi - 生鱼片 (shēng yú piàn) = raw/uncooked - fish - slice/piece/flake

Wild Peach - 毛桃 (máo táo) = hair - peach

Dumpling - 团子 (tuán zi) = round/ball/lump - (noun suffix)

Cracker/Biscuit - 饼干 (bǐng gān) = round flat cake/biscuits/cookie/cake - dry

Taco/Burrito - 墨西哥卷饼 (mò xī gē juǎn bǐng) = Mexico - to roll up/curl - round flat cake

Cherry Tomato - 珍珠小番茄 (zhēn zhū xiǎo fān qié) = pearl - small/tiny - tomato

**Molasses** - 糖水 (táng shuǐ) = sugar/sweets/candy - water/liquid

**Molasses** - 糖汁 (táng zhī) = sugar/sweets/candy - juice

Molasses - 糖蜜 (táng mì) = sugar/sweets/candy - honey

Carrot - 胡萝卜 (hú luó bo) = beard/moustache/whiskers - radish/turnip - "meaningless bound form" (aka this character has no meaning here, really.)

Marshmallow - 果汁软糖 (guǒ zhī ruǎn táng) = fruit juice - soft/flexible - sugar/candy/sweets

Loaf Cake - 枕头蛋糕 (zhěn tou dàn gāo) = pillow - cake

Ginger Ale - 姜汁 (jiāng zhī) = ginger - juice/liquid/fluid

Root Beer - 根汁汽水 (gēn zhī qì shuǐ) = root (of a plant) - juice/liquid/fluid - soda/pop

Jalapeño - 墨西哥辣椒 (mò xī gē là jiāo) = Mexico - hot pepper

Horseradish - 辣根 (là gēn) = hot (spicy)/spicy/peppery - root (of a plant)

Popcorn - 玉米花 (yù mǐ huā) = corn - flower

Fortune Cookie - 签语饼 (qiān yǔ bǐng) = 'to make brief comments on a document'/label/inscribed bamboo stick (used in divination) - language/words/speak/say/speech - cookie/cake/biscuit

**Sweet Potato** - 红薯 (hóng shǔ) = red - potato/yam

Mead - 蜂蜜酒 (fēng mì jiǔ) = honey - alcohol/liquor

Zucchini - 意大利青瓜 (yì dà lì qīng guā) = Italy - cucumber

# Fantasy Stuff

Mermaid - 美人鱼 (měi rén yú) = beautiful - person - fish

Dryad - 树妖 (shù yāo) = tree - goblin/demon/evil spirit

Pegasus - 飞马 (fēi mǎ) = flying - horse

Werewolf - 狼人 (láng rén) = wolf - person

**Sphinx** - 人头狮身 (rén tóu shī shēn) = person - head - lion - body

Sphinx - 狮身人面 (shī shēn rén miàn) = lion - body - person - face

Cyclops - 独眼巨人 (dú yǎn jù rén) = single - eye - huge - person

Faun - 羊男 (yáng nán) = sheep - man

**Faun** - 牧神 (mù shén) = shepherd - god

**Faun** - 羊怪 (yáng guài) = sheep - monster

Basilisk - 蛇怪 (shé guài) = snake - monster

Valkyrie - 女武神 (nǚ wǔ shén) = female/woman - military - god/deity/supernatural being

Gargoyle - 石像鬼 (shí xiàng guǐ) = rock - image - devil/demon

Elf (Leprechaun) - 仙童 (xiān tóng) = immortal - child

Centaur - 半人马 (bàn rén mǎ) = half - person - horse

Griffin - 鹰头狮 (yīng tóu shī) = eagle - head - lion

Sasquatch - 大足野人 (dà zú yě rén) = big - foot - wild - person (barbarian/savage)

Gnome - 土神 (tǔ shén) = earth/soil - god/deity/supernatural being

Minotaur - 人身牛头怪物 (rén shēn niú tóu guài wù) = person - body - cow - head -monster

Vampire - 吸血鬼 (xī xuè guǐ) = to suck - blood - devil/demon

Orc - 半兽人 (bàn shòu rén) = half - beast - person

Satyr - 色魔 (sè mó) = sex - devil/demon (*Similar to faun, only the dark version. Don't look it up.* )

Goblin - 灵怪 (líng guài) = spirit/departed soul - monster/devil

Frankenstein - 科学怪人 (kē xué guài rén) = science - monster/devil - person

Golem - 魔像 (mó xiàng) = devil/demon - to resemble/appearance/to be like

Kraken - 北海巨妖 (běi hǎi jù yāo) = north - sea/ocean - huge/gigantic - monster/goblin/demon/spirit

Ogre - 食人魔 (shí rén mó) = to eat - person - devil/demon

Troll - 山精 (shān jīng) = mountain - mythical goblin spirit

Unicorn - 独角兽 (dú jiǎo shòu) = single - horn - beast/animal

Boogeyman - 夜半鬼开门 (yè bàn guǐ kāi mén) = midnight - ghost/demon - open - door

Grim Reaper (Shinigami) - 死神 (sǐ shén) = death - god/deity/supernatural being

**Asgard** - 仙宫 (xiān gōng) = immortal - palace/temple

Zombie - 僵尸 (jiāng shī) = rigid/stiff - corpse

Phoenix - 凤凰 (fèng huáng) = male phoenix/symbol of joy - female phoenix

**Throne** - 宝座 (bǎo zuò) = precious/treasure/gem/jewel - seat

Gargoyle - 滴水嘴兽 (dī shuǐ zuǐ shòu) = drip/bead - water - mouth - beast/animal

Succubus/Witch - 魔女 (mó nǚ) = demon/evil spirit/monster/devil/magic - woman/female

Cerberus - 地狱三头犬 (dì yù sān tóu quǎn) = hell/inferno/underworld - three - head - dog

Harpie - 鸟身女妖 (niǎo shēn nǚ yāo) = bird - body - women/female - goblin/demon/evil spirit/devil/witch

**Warlock/Sorcerer** - 妖术师 (yāo shù shī) = goblin/demon/evil spirit/devil/witch - art/skill/technique/method - master/teacher/expert/specialist

Siren (Seductress) - 妖精 (yāo jing) = goblin/demon/evil spirit/devil/witch - energy/spirit/mythical goblin spirit

Genie (Is also 'fairy or elf' as well) - 精灵 (jīng líng) = energy/spirit/mythical goblin spirit - fairy/elf/spirit

Spectre/Ghost - 魔影 (mó yǐng) = evil spirit/demon/devil/monster/magic/mystic - shadow/image/vague impression

Jackalope - 鹿角兔 (lù jiǎo tù) = deer - horn - rabbit/hare

Yeti - 雪人 (xuě rén) = snow - person/people (man or woman) *Also means snowman, of course...

**Hercules** - 大力神 (dà lì shén) = great strength - god/deity/immortal/divinity/supernatural being

(Irish) Banshee - 丧门神 (sàng mén shén) = mourning/mourn/funeral - door/gate - god/deity/immortal/divinity/supernatural being

**Banshee** (google said this meant 'slut') - 狺女 (yín nǚ) = 'the snarling of dogs'/barking/yapping dog - woman/female

Incubus - 梦魔 (mèng mó) = dream/fancy/illusion - evil spirit/demon/devil/monster

**Jack the Ripper** - 开膛手杰克 (kāi táng shǒu jié kè) = disembowel/gut/cut open the chest - person skilled in certain types of work - 'jie ke' (*transliterated)

# Sports & Game Related Stuff

Hockey - 冰球 (bīng qiú) = ice - ball

Rugby - 橄榄球 (gǎn lǎn qiú) = olive - olive - ball

Tennis - 网球 (wǎng qiú) = net - ball

Basketball - 篮球 (lán qiú) = basket - ball

Badminton - 羽毛球 (yǔ máo qiú) = feather - ball

Cricket - 板球 (bǎn qiú) = board/plank - ball

**Cricket** - 木球 (mù qiú) = wood - ball

Baseball - 棒球 (bàng qiú) = stick/club - ball

Soccer - 足球 (zú qiú) = foot - ball

Football - 美国足球 (měi guó zú qiú) = America(n) - foot - ball

Volleyball - 排球 (pái qiú) = a row/line - ball

Pool/billiards - 桌球 (zhuō qiú) = table - ball

Bowling - 滚球 (gǔn qiú) = to roll - ball

Squash - 壁球 (bì qiú) = wall - ball

Croquet - 门球 (mén qiú) = door/gate - ball

Polo - 马球 (mǎ qiú) = horse - ball

Curling - 冰壶 (bīng hú) = ice - pot/kettle

BMX - 小轮车 (xiǎo lún chē) = small - wheel - vehicle/car

**Ice skates** - 冰刀 (bīng dāo) = ice - knife/blade

Ice skates - 冰鞋 (bīng xié) = ice - shoe

Snorkeling - 浮潜 (fú qiǎn) = to float/floating - to dive/submerge

Snorkel - 呼吸管 (hū xī guǎn) = to breath out - to inhale - tube/pipe

Figure skating - 花样滑冰 (huā yàng huá bīng) = flower/fancy pattern - manner/appearance - to slip/slide - ice

Skiing - 滑雪 (huá xuě) = to slip/slide - snow

Water skiing - 滑水 (huá shuǐ) = to slip/slide - water

Skydiving - 特技跳伞 (tè jì tiào sǎn) = special/unique/distinguished - skill/ability - to jump - umbrella

Breaststroke (swimming) - 蛙泳 (wā yǒng) = frog - swimming/to swim

Balloon - 气球 (qì qiú) = air - ball

Ping pong - 乒乓球 (pīng pāng qiú) = 'ping pang' *transliterated* - ball

Race car - 赛车 (sài chē) = to compete/competition/match - vehicle/car

Drift (in a car) - 滑轮 (huá lún) = slip/slide - tire

Frisbee - 飞盘 (fēi pán) = flying - plate

Skateboard - 滑板 (huá bǎn) = slip/slide - board

Roller Skate - 轮滑 (lún huá) = wheel - slip/slide

Surfing - 冲浪运动 (chōng làng yùn dòng) = (of water) to dash against/to rise in the air - wave - sport

Surfboard - 冲浪板 (chōng làng bǎn) = (of water) to dash against/to rise in the air/to collide with - wave - board/plank

Scuba - 水肺 (shuǐ fèi) = water - lung

Heart (in cards) - 红桃 (hóng táo) = red - peach shaped

Spade (in cards) - 黑桃 (hēi táo) = black - peach shaped

Club (in cards) - 草花 (cǎo huā) = grass/straw - flower/blossom/florid

Diamond (in cards) - 方块 (fāng kuài) = square/upright/side - chunk/piece

Tic-tac-toe - 圈圈叉叉 (quān quān chā chā) = circle circle - cross cross

Skip stones - 打水漂 (dǎ shuǐ piào) = to play (a game) - water - to float/to drift

**Double dribble** - 两次运球 (liǎng cì yùn qiú) = two - times/next in sequence - to move/transport - ball

Cue ball (pool) - 主球 (zhǔ qiú) = main/master - ball

Monopoly - 地产大亨 (dì chǎn dà hēng) = real estate - bigwig

Javelin - 投枪 (tóu qiāng) = 'to cast/send' - spear

Tug of war - 拔河 (bá hé) = capture/seize - river

Parallel Bars (Gymnastics) - 双杠 (shuāng gàng) = double/two/pair/couple - bar/thick stick

Grand Prix - 大奖赛 (dà jiǎng sài) = big/large/huge - prize - race

**Cricket** - 木球 (mù qiú) = wood - ball

Putter (Golf) - 推杆 (tuī gǎn) = to push/shove/push forward - pole/shaft

Putter (Golf) - 轻击棒 (qīng jí bàng) = light/gentle/soft - hit/beat/strike - club/stick

Putting Green - 轻击区 (xīng jí qū) = light/gentle/soft - hit/beat/strike - area/region

The Rough (Golf) - 长草区 (cháng cǎo qū) = long - grass - area/region

Tee (Golf) - 球座 (qiú zuò) = ball - stand/seat/base

Caddie (Golf) - 球童 (qiú tóng) = ball - servant boy/child/boy

Caddie (Golf) - 杆第 (gān dì) = pole/staff - younger brother/junior male

Fore! (Golf) - 看球 (kàn qiú) = watch out/to see/to look at - ball

Driver (Golf) - 一号木杆 (yī hào mù gān) = one - number/size - wood - pole/staff

Driver (Golf) - 三号木杆 (sān hào mù gān) = three - number/size - wood - pole/staff

Chip Shot (Golf) - 切杆 (qiè gān) = slice/cut/carve - pole/staff

Bunker (Golf) - 沙坑 (shā kēng) = sand - pit/hole/trap

Roller Skates - 四轮鞋滑冰 (sì lún xié huá bīng) = four - wheel - shoes - skate

Roller Skates - 旱冰鞋 (hàn bīng xié) = dry land - ice - shoes (dry land ice skates)

Fins/Flippers (Swimming) - 蛙鞋 (wā xié) = frog - shoes

Flipper - 鳍状肢 (qí zhuàng zhī) = fin - shape - limb

Pole-Vaulting - 撑杆跳高 (chēng gān tiào gāo) = prop up/support/push (with a pole)/pole - pole/staff - jump/leap/bound/bounce - tall/high/height/above average/of a high level or degree

Seesaw - 跷跷板 (qiāo qiāo bǎn) = to lift/to raise/elevate/tilt/to rise on one end - to lift/to raise/elevate/tilt/to rise on one end - board/plank

Push-up (Exercise) - 俯卧撑 (fǔ wò chēng) = bend over/to look down/face down - to lie/to crouch - prop up/support/brace

Do the splits - 劈叉 (pī chā) = split/chop/cleave/to split open - fork/prong/cross/intersect/'x'/crotch

Slam Dunk - 扣篮 (kòu lán) = smash/spike/dunk - basket

Slam Dunk - 暴扣 (bào kòu) = cruel/fierce/savage/sudden/violent - smash/spike/dunk

Horse Spur - 踢马刺 (tī mǎ cì) = kick - horse - thorn/splinter/stab/prick/stimulate/to stab/prod

Quarterback (American Football) - 四分卫 (sì fēn wèi) = four - divide/separate/distribute/allot/to allocate - defend/guard/protect

Tap Dance - 踢跶舞 (tī dá wǔ) = kick - slip/stumble - dance

Tap Dance - 踢踏舞 (tī tà wǔ) = kick - stamp/step on/walk - dance

Breakdance - 霹雳舞 (pī lì wǔ) = thunderbolt/shocking/(slang) awesome - dance

'Twerk' - 电臀舞 (diàn tún wǔ) = electric/lightning - buttocks/butt - dance

Swimming Goggles - 泳镜 (yǒng jìng) = swim - lens/glasses/mirror

**Baseball Cap Visor** - 帽舌 (mào shé) = hat/cap - tongue

Pull-up - 引体向上 (yǐn tǐ xiàng shàng) = pull/stretch - body - towards/direction - up

Callisthenics - 柔软体操 (róu ruǎn tǐ cāo) = soft/flexible - gymnastics

Windsurfing - 帆板运动 (fān bǎn yùn dòng) = sail - board/plank - sport

Butterfly Stroke (Swimming) - 蝶泳 (dié yǒng) = butterfly - swim

Dog Paddle (Swimming) - 狗刨 (gǒu páo) = dog - dig/unearth

Yu-Gi-Oh! - 游戏王 (yóu xì wáng) = game/to play - king/chieftain/ruler/monarch

Marbles - 玻璃球 (bō lí qiú) = glass - ball/sphere/globe/round

Merry-go-round - 旋转木马 (xuán zhuǎn mù mǎ) = circle/to revolve/move in orbit - turn/revolve/rotate - tree/timber/wood - horse

Croquet - 槌球 (chuí qiú) = mallet - ball

Jigsaw Puzzle - 拼图玩具 (pīn tú wán jù) = to piece together/to join together/link - picture/drawing/chart/map - toy

Sudoku - 九宫格数独 (jiǔ gōng gé shù dú) = nine - imperial palace - square/frame/pattern - number/amount/figure/digit/count - alone/single/independent

Solitaire - 独立钻石 (dú lì zuàn shí) = to stand alone/independent - diamond/jewel

Peekaboo - 躲猫猫 (duǒ māo māo) = hide (oneself) - hide/conceal - hide/conceal

Board Game - 桌游 (zhuō yóu) = table - game

Rubik's Cube - 魔方 (mó fāng) = magic/mystic - square

**Rubik's Cube** - 魔术方块 (mó shù fāng kuài) = magic/slight of hand/tricks - cube

Merry-go-round - 旋转木马 (xuán zhuǎn mù mǎ) = revolve/rotate/to spin/to whirl - wooden horse

Yo-yo - 悠悠球 (yōu yōu qiú) = to swing - to swing - ball/sphere/globe

Parasail - 帆伞 (fān sǎn) = sail - umbrella

Balance Beam - 平衡木 (píng héng mù) = level/flat/even - weight/measure - tree/timber/wood

Marionette/Puppet - 牵线木偶 (qiān xiàn mù ǒu) = lead along/lead by hand - thread/string/wire - tree/timber/wood - image

Carnival - 狂欢节 (kuáng huān jié) = mad/insane/wild/violent - joyous/merry/jubilant/enjoy - festival/holiday

Bungee Jumping - 高空弹跳 (gāo kōng tán tiào) = tall/high/height/above average/of a high level or degree - empty/sky/air - to bounce/to jump/to leap

Hula Dance - 草裙舞 (cǎo qún wǔ) = grass/straw - skirt - dance

Dominos - 多米诺骨牌 (duō mǐ nuò gǔ pái) = 'duo mi nuo' (transliterated) - bone/skeleton - mahjong tile/game pieces

Home Run (Baseball) - 全垒打 (quán lěi dǎ) = whole/entire/complete - wall/base (baseball) - strike/hit/knock

Hang Glider - 滑翔翼 (huá xiáng yì) = slip/slide - soar/glide/hover/circle in the air - wing

Flush (Poker) - 同花 (tóng huā) = be the same as/alike/similar/same/alike - flower/pattern/design

Royal Flush (Poker) - 同花大顺 (tóng huā dà shùn) = be the same as/alike/similar/same/alike - flower/pattern/design - big/large/great - arrange/put in order/suit

Straight Flush (Poker) - 同花顺 (tóng huā shùn) = be the same as/alike/similar/same/alike - flower/pattern/design - arrange/put in order/suit

Arm Wrestling - 掰手腕 (bāi shǒu wàn) = break off with the fingers - hand/to hold - wrist

Arm Wrestling - 比腕力 (bǐ wàn lì) = compare/contrast - wrist - power/(physical) strength/force

**Wei Qi** (game; also called 'Go' in English) - 围棋 (wéi qí) = enclose/surround/encompass - chess/chess-like game

**Aerobic Dancing** - 健美舞 (jiàn měi wǔ) = healthy/strong/robust - good/beauty/pretty - dance

**Aerobic Dancing** - 健身舞 (jiàn shēn wǔ) = healthy/strong/robust - body - dance

**Moonwalk** (dance move) - 太空舞步 (tài kōng wǔ bù) = outer space - dance - step/go on foot/walk

**Lap Dance** - 膝上 (xī shàng wǔ) = knee - above/on top/upon/get onto - dance

**Erotic Dance** - 艳舞 (yàn wǔ) = envy/admire/romantic/sexy/voluptuous - dance

**Checkers** - 国际跳棋 (guó jì tiào qí) = international - jump/leap/bounce/hop - chess/chess-like game

**Burpee** - 立卧撑跳 (lì wò chēng tiào) = stand - lie/crouch - prop up/support/stay - jump/leap/bounce

**Hopscotch** - 跳间 (tiào jiān) = jump/leap/bounce - space/room

**Jungle Gym** - 攀登架 (pān dēng jià) = climb/clamber/hang on to - ascend/mount/scale - frame/rack/stand

Foosball - 桌上足球 (zhuō shàng zú qiú) = table/desk - top/on - soccer

Foosball - 足球游戏桌 (zú qiú yóu xì zhuō) = soccer - game - table/desk

Foosball - 手足球台 (shǒu zú qiú tái) = hand - soccer - desk/table

Juggle - 边抛边接 (biān pāo biān jiē) = side - throw/toss/fling - side - connect/join/put together

Wipeout (Gameshow) - 勇敢向前冲 (yǒng gǎn xiàng qián chōng) = brave/courageous - advance/forge ahead - charge/rush/dash/thoroughfare/important place

Waterpolo - 水球 (shuǐ qiú) = water - ball

Token - 代币 (dài bì) = take the place of/be in place of/substitute/replace - money

Arcade Game - 街机游戏 (jiē jī yóu xì) = street/road - machine - game

Pool - 撞球 (zhuàng qiú) = bump against/run into/strike/collide - ball

Blackjack - 二十一点 (èr shí yī diǎn) = twenty one - point/place/count

Rock-Paper-Scissors - 剪刀石头布 (jiǎn dāo shí tou bù) = scissors - rock - cloth

Rock-Paper-Scissors - 包剪锤 (bāo jiǎn chuí) = packet/bundle/container - scissors - hammer

Twister - 扭扭乐 (niǔ niǔ lè) = twist - twist - pleasure/enjoyment/happy/cheerful/joyful/glad

Fencing - 击剑 (jí jiàn) = beat/hit/attack/assault - sword

**Rollerblading** - 溜旱冰 (liū hàn bīng) = slide/glide/to skate - dry land - ice/something resembling ice

Risk (Board Game) - 大战役 (dà zhàn yì) = large-scale war/big clash/fierce competition/to wage war - battle/war/campaign/

Uppercut - 上钩拳 (shàng gōu quán) = up/send up - hook - fist/boxing

# Weapons

Weapons - 武器 (wǔ qì) = military - tool/device

Grenade - 榴弹 (liú dàn) = pomegranate - bullet/ball/shell

Grenade Launcher - 榴弹发射器 (liú dàn fā shè qì) = grenade - to send out - shoot - device/tool

RPG - 火箭推进榴弹 (huǒ jiàn tuī jìn liú dàn) = fire - arrow - to push - forward - grenade

Shotgun - 散弹枪 (sàn dàn qiāng) = to scatter/disperse - bullet/ball - gun

Air Gun - 鸟枪 (niǎo qiāng) = bird - gun

Gatling Gun - 加特林极抢 (jiā tè lín jí qiǎng) = 'jia te lin' * transliteration* - extreme - gun

Sniper Rifle - 狙击步枪 (jū jī bù qiāng) = 'to lie in ambush' - hit/strike - march/walk - gun

Bomb - 炸弹 (zhà dàn) = explode - bullet/ball/shell

Catapult - 弩炮 (nǔ pào) = crossbow - cannon

**Catapult** - 石弩 (shí nǔ) = rock - crossbow

Slingshot - 弹弓 (dàn gōng) = bullet/ball/shell - bow

Flare - 照明弹 (zhào míng dàn) = to shine/illuminate - bright - bullet/ball/shell

Tear Gas Grenade - 催泪弹 (cuī lèi dàn) = to urge/prompt/expedite - tears - bullet/ball/shell

Napalm - 凝固汽油弹 (níng gù qì yóu dàn) = to congeal - solid - gasoline - bullet/ball/shell

Sidewinder - 响尾蛇导弹 (xiǎng wěi shé dǎo dàn) = sound/noise - tail - snake - to guide - bullet/ball/shell

Dud - 未爆弹 (wèi bào dàn) = did not/not yet - explode - bullet/ball/shell

Flash Bomb - 照相弹 (zhào xiàng dàn) = to shine/illuminate - each other - bullet/ball/shell

Scud Missile - 飞毛腿导弹 (fēi máo tuǐ dǎo dàn) = fly - hair - leg - to guide - bullet/ball/shell

Stun Baton - 电击棒 (diàn jí bàng) = electric - hit/strike - stick/club

Switchblade - 弹簧刀 (tán huáng dāo) = to flick/to flip - spring of lock - knife/blade

Atom bomb - 原子弹 (yuán zǐ dàn) = primary/raw/original - bullet

Dynamite - 炸药 (zhà yào) = to explode - substance (used for a specific purpose)

Bayonet - 刺刀 (cì dāo) = stab - knife/blade

Broadsword - 大刀 (dà dāo) = big - knife/blade

Pocket Knife - 小刀 (xiǎo dāo) = small - knife/blade

Musket - 滑膛枪 (huá táng qiāng) = slippery/smooth - hollow - gun

Machete - 开山刀 (kāi shān dāo) = open - mountain - knife/blade

Sabre - 马刀 (mǎ dāo) = horse - knife

Mace - 钢鞭 (gāng biān) = steel - whip

Flamethrower - 喷火器 (pēn huǒ qì) = to spray/spurt - fire - device

Silencer - 消音器 (xiāo yīn qì) = to eliminate/to disappear - sound/noise - device/tool

**Fight organized crime** - 扫黑 (sǎo hēi) = to sweep - black

**Genocide** - 灭绝种族 (miè jué zhǒng zú) = to extinguish/to exterminate - to cut short/extinct/to disappear/vanish - ethnicity/race

**Human trafficking** - 贩卖人口 (fàn mài rén kǒu) = to deal in/buy & sell/to peddle - people

**Burglary** - 夜入私宅罪 (yè rù sī zhái zuì) = night - to enter/go into - personal/private - residence/home - crime/sin

**Smuggle** - 偷运 (tōu yùn) = to steal/pilfer/stealthily - to transport/to move

**Corporeal punishment (castration or amputation)** - 肉刑 (ròu xíng) = meat - penalty/punishment/sentence

Seppuku - 切腹自杀 (qiè fù zì shā) = cut - abdomen - suicide

**Assassinate** - 暗杀 (an shā) = hidden/in the dark/secret - kill

Torpedo - 鱼雷 (yú léi) = fish - mine (weapon)

(Gun) Scope - 望远瞄准镜 (wàng yuǎn miáo zhǔn jìng) = to gaze (into the distance)/look towards - far away/distant - take aim - accurate/exact - lens/glass

Rocket - 火箭 (huǒ jiàn) = firearms/ammunition/fire - arrow

Nunchucks - 双截棍 (shuāng jié gùn) = two/twin/double/pair/set of two - chunk/length - rod/stick/cudgel

Mauser Pistol - 盒子炮 (hé zǐ pào) = box/case - large gun/cannon

Uzi - 乌兹冲锋枪 (wū zī chōng fēng qiāng) = 'wu zi' (transliterated) - charge/assault - gun/firearm/rifle

Harpoon - 渔猎标枪 (yú liè biāo qiāng) = fish/to fish/seize/pursue - hunt - javelin

**Agent Orange** - 橙色战剂 (chéng sè zhàn jì) = orange - war/warfare/battle/fight - dose (medicine)

**Battering Ram** - 攻城木 (gōng chéng mù) = attack/city/wall/town - tree/timber/wood

Harpoon - 鱼叉 (yú chā) = fish - fork/prong

Weapons of Mass Destruction - 大量杀伤武器 (dà liàng shā shāng wǔ qì) = large in number or quantity/numerous - kill and wound/kill or injure/inflict casualties on - weapon/arms

**Holocaust/Massacre** - 大屠杀 (dà tú shā) = big/large/huge/vast - to massacre - kill/slaughter/butcher/murder

Stun Baton - 电警棍 (diàn jǐng gùn) = electricity/electric/lightening/get or give an electric shock - police/alert/to warn - rod/stick/cudgel

Short-hilted Broadsword - 单刀 (dān dāo) = single/only/thin - knife/blade/sword

Fuse (For Explosive) - 导火索 (dǎo huǒ suǒ) = lead/guide/to direct/to transmit - fire/flame/burn - rope/cable/cord/chain

# Diseases & Emotions

Pink Eye - 火眼 (huǒ yǎn) = fire - eye

Hay Fever - 花粉病 (huā fěn bìng) = flower - powder - illness/disease

Epilepsy - 癫痫 (diān xián) = mentally deranged/crazy - epilepsy/insanity/convulsions

Narcissism - 自恋 (zì liàn) = self - love

Diarrhea - 拉肚子 (lā dù zi) = 'to pull' - belly/abdomen

Carsick - 晕车 (yùn chē) = dizzy/faint - vehicle

Envy - 吃味 (chī wèi) = eat - flavour

Deep distress - 落汤鸡 (luò tāng jī) = to fall or drop - soup - chicken

Addiction - 痼癖 (gù pǐ) = obstinate disease/long-term - habit/craving

Euphoria - 喜孜孜 (xǐ zī zī) = to feel pleased/to feel happy - diligent/hard working

Infertility - 不孕症 (bù yùn zhèng) = cannot/not - pregnant - disease/illness

Hypothermia - 低体温症 (dī tǐ wēn zhèng) = low - body - temperature - disease

**Hypothermia** - 体温过低 (tǐ wēn guò dī) = body - temperature - excessively/too - low

Sad - 心伤 (xīn shāng) = heart - injury/wound

Dementia/Alzheimers - 老年痴呆症 (lǎo nián chī dāi zhèng) = old (of people) - year - imbecile/foolish/silly - stupid/foolish - disease

Chicken pox - 出水痘 (chū shuǐ dòu) = to come out/produce - water - pimple

**Bipolar/Manic** - 躁郁症 (zào yù zhèng) = impatient/hot-tempered - melancholy - disease

Tourettes - 抽动症 (chōu dòng zhèng) = to whip or thrash - to move/to stir (emotions) - disease

'Phobia' - 恐怖症 (kǒng bù zhèng) = afraid - frightened - disease

Sensitive - 敏感 (mǐn gǎn) = agile - feeling/emotion

Arthritis - 关节炎 (guān jié yán) = to close/shut - joint - flame/inflammation

To be distressed - 肉痛 (ròu tòng) = meat - pain/ache/sorrow

Stutter - 口吃 (kǒu chī) = mouth - eat

Cross-Eyed - 斗鸡眼 (dòu jī yǎn) = 'coming together'/struggle - chicken - eye

One Track Mind - 死脑筋 (sǐ nǎo jīn) = dead - brain - muscle/tendon

Shameless - 厚脸皮 (hòu liǎn pí) = thick - face - skin

Jealous - 吃醋 (chī cù) = eat - vinegar

Apathetic - 壁上观 (bì shàng guān) = wall - to go up - to observe/watch (lit. to watch the wall go up)

Halitosis - 口臭 (kǒu chòu) = mouth - stench/to smell (bad)

Catch a cold - 伤风 (shāng fēng) = injury - wind

Disillusionment - 幻灭 (huàn miè) = fantasy - to extinguish or put out

Feeling giddy = 发昏 (fā hūn) = to show (ones feelings)/to send out - muddle headed/to faint

Schizophrenia - 精神分裂症 (jīng shén fēn liè zhèng) = psychological/mental - to split up/to divide/to break up - disease/illness

Déjà vu - 即视感 (jí shì gǎn) = already - to show/to look at - feeling/emotion

**OCD** - 强迫症 (qiǎng pò zhèng) = strong/powerful - to force/compel/urgent - illness/disease

OCD - 洁癖 (jié pǐ) = clean - habit/hobby/weakness for

Flashing - 露阴癖 (lù yīn pǐ) = to reveal/to expose - genitalia - habit/hobby/weakness for

Emaciated/thin - 骨立 (gǔ lì) = bone - to stand (fig. standing bones)

Snivel - 假哭 (jiǎ kū) = fake/false/artificial - to cry

Manic Depression - 躁狂抑郁症 (zào kuáng yì yù zhèng) = restless/impetuous - extremely/to the utmost/crazy/insane - depressed/gloomy - disease/illness

PTSD (Post traumatic stress syndrome) - 创伤后压力紊乱 (chuāng shāng hòu yā lì wěn luàn) = wound/trauma/injury - later/future/afterwards - pressure/overwhelming force/burden/strain - disorderly/chaotic/confused

Cerebral Palsy - 脑瘫 (nǎo tān) = brain - be physically paralyzed

Bloodthirsty - 嗜杀成性 (shì shā chéng xìng) = be fond of/addicted to - kill/slaughter/butcher/murder - become second nature to somebody/by nature

**Autism** - 孤独症 (gū dú zhèng) = solitary/isolated/alone/lonely/orphan - alone/single/independent - disease/illness

**Night Blindness** - 雀盲眼 (qiǎo mang yǎn) = sparrow/small bird - blind/unable to distinguish things/blindly/shortsighted - eye/look/glance

Allergies - 花粉病 (huā fěn bìng) = flower/blossom - powder - disease/illness/sickness

Dyslexia - 诵读困难症 (sòng dú kùn nán zhèng) = read aloud - difficulty/challenging - disease/illness/ailment

Dyslexia - 失读症 (shī dú zhèng) = slip/mistake/defect/mishap/to fail - read aloud/pronounce - disease/illness/ailment

**Split Personality** - 人格分裂 (rén gé fēn liè) = personality/character/moral quality - to split up/divide/break up

Half-hearted - 三心二意 (sān xīn èr yì) = three - heart/mind/feeling/intention - two - wish/desire/opinion

Fever - 发烧 (fā shāo) = emit/give forth/to develop - burn/cook/heat/bake/roast (烧 also means fever, but I like 'emit heat' more.)

'Butthurt' - 玻璃心 (bō lí xīn) = glass - heart

**Euphoria** - 欣快症 (xīn kuài zhèng) = glad/joyful - disease/illness

Scoliosis - 脊柱侧弯 (jǐ zhù cè wān) = vertebra - incline to one side/to lean/slant - turn/curve/bend

**Polio** - 脊髓灰质炎 (jǐ suǐ huī zhí yán) = spinal cord - grey matter - inflammation/-itis

Battle Cry - 喊杀声 (hǎn 'shā' shēng) = to shout/to yell/howl/cry/call out - 'kill/slaughter/butcher/murder' - sound/noise/voice/tone

**Plague** - 鼠疫 (shǔ yì) = mouse/rat - epidemic/disease/pestilence/plague

Lockjaw - 牙关紧闭正 (yá guān jǐn bì zhèng) = tooth/teeth - to close - tight - shut/close - disease/illness

**Gender Dysphoria** - 性别认同障碍 (xìng bié rèn tóng zhàng ài) = gender/sex - identify - impediment/barrier/hinder/obstruct

Tapeworm - 绦虫 (tāo chóng) = cord/silk ribbon/ribbon - insect/worm

Careless/Negligent - 马虎 (mǎ hǔ) = horse - tiger

Kiss-ass/Boot-licking - 马屁 (mǎ pì) = horse - fart/buttocks

Mumps - 流行性腮腺炎 (liú xíng xìng sāi xiàn yán) = epidemic - cheek - gland - inflammation

Diabetes - 糖尿病 (táng niào bìng) = sugar - urine - illness/disease

Shingles - 带状疱疹 (dài zhuàng pào zhěn) = area - appearance/state/condition - blister/acne/boil - rash/measles

Chlamydia - skin/clothing - raw - fungus/germ/mushroom

Bronchitis - 支气管炎 (zhī qì guǎn yán) = protrude/raise - air/breath - tube/pipe - inflammation

Careless - 马虎 (mǎ hǔ) = horse - tiger

**Overjoyed** - 欢欣雀跃 (huān xīn què yuè) = joyous/happy/pleased/glad/merry - delighted/happy/joyous - sparrow/small bird - leap/jump

Bored - 无聊 (wú liáo) = without/have not - to chat

**Pretentious** - 神气 (shén qì) = expression/look - gas/air/vapour/steam

**Pretentious** - 浮华 (fú huá) = excessive/surplus - flashy/extravagant/splendid

# Religion & Holiday Stuff

Religion - 宗教 (zōng jiào) = school/sect - teaching/religion

Christmas - 圣诞节 (shèng dàn jié) = holy - birth - holiday

**Easter** - 复活节 (fù huó jié) = 'to return to' - life - holiday

The Cross - 十字架 (shí zì jià) = 十 - character - rack

Baptize - 施洗 (shī xǐ) = to act/bestow/carry out - wash/bathe

Witchcraft - 巫术 (wū shù) = witch/wizard - method/technique

**Witchcraft** - 魔法 (mó fǎ) = devil/magic - method/way

Heretic/heathen/pagan - 异教徒 (yì jiào tú) = strange/unusual - disciple/follower of a religion

**Carnival (Christian)** - 谢肉节 (xiè ròu jié) = to thank (be thankful for) - meat/flesh - holiday/festival

The Gospel - 福音 (fú yīn) = good fortune/happiness - news

Apocrypha - 伪经 (wěi jīng) = false/fake/forged -scripture

Pentagram - 五角星 (wǔ jiǎo xīng) = five - angle/corner - star

Spell - 咒语 (zhòu yǔ) = incantation/magic spell/curse - speech/language

Alchemy - 炼金术 (liàn jīn shù) = to refine/to smelt - gold - method/technique

Divination - 命理学 (mìng lǐ xué) = life/fate - inner essence/logic/truth - to study

Dogma - 教条 (jiào tiáo) = religion/teaching - law/order

**Dogma** - 死理 (sǐ lǐ) = rigid/inflexible - logic/truth/reason

Numerology - 数字命理学 (shù zì mìng lǐ xué) = number - life/fate - science (fig. the science of fate)

Bahá'í - 巴哈伊 = 'bā hā yī' *transliterated*

Christian - 基督徒 (jī dū tú) = 'ji du' (Christ) - disciple/apprentice/believer

Christianity - 基督教 (jī dū jiào) = 'ji du' (Christ) - religion/teaching

Orthodox Christianity - 正教 (zhèng jiào) = main/proper/upright - religion/teaching

Catholicism - 天主教 (tiān zhǔ jiào) = heaven - God/Lord/host/master - religion/teaching

**Catholicism** - 旧教 (jiù jiào) = old - religion/teaching

**Muslim** - 穆斯林 = 'mù sī lín' *transliteration*

Buddhism - 佛教 (fó jiào) = Buddha - religion/teaching

Hinduism - 印度教 (yìn dù jiào) = India - religion/teaching

Judaism - 犹太教 (yóu tài jiào) = just as/as if - highest/greatest - religion/teaching

("Critic" - 论者 (lùn zhě) = Fig. the one with an opinion/theory/doctrine. I put this here because the next few translation contain this, but it translates to critic, so I used that. Also is 批评家 (pī píng jiā) = to criticize - specialist in a certain field (lit. specialist at criticism)

Atheism/Atheist - 无神论者 (wú shén lùn zhě) = no/none/not/to lack - God/deity - critic

Agnostic - 不可知论者 (bù kě zhī lùn zhě) = not/no - can/able to - to know - critic

Shinto - 神道教 (shén dào jiào) = God/deity - principal/truth/road - religion/teaching

Zoroastrianism - 拜火教 (bài huǒ jiào) = to worship - the sun/fire - religion/teaching

Zoroastrianism - 祆教 (xiān jiào) = Ormazda the Sun God - religion/teaching

**Confucianism** - 儒教 (rú jiào) = Confucian/scholar - religion/teaching

Confucianism - 孔教 (kǒng jiào) = Confucius - religion/teaching

Daoism (Taoism) - 道教 (dào jiào) = the road/path/'The Way' - religion/teaching

*(During my time at University in China, a mere one and a half years, much of my time was spent studying Daoism, and I highly recommend you check it out for yourself. Although I am Christian, there was a lot of interesting thoughts and things to learn. Look for the book: Dao De Jing - 道德经)*

Satanism - 撒旦崇拜 (sā dàn chóng bài) = 'sa dan' *transliterated* - to worship

Hermeneutics - 诠释学 (quán shì xué) = to explain/to comment - interpret/explain - to study

Reincarnation - 转世 (zhuǎn shì) = to transfer/classifier for revolutions & repeated actions - life/age (lit. to transfer life)

Monotheism - 一神教 (yī shén jiào) = one - God/deity - religion/teaching

Pantheism - 泛神论 (fàn shén lùn) = non-specific/pan- (prefix) - God/deity - doctrine/theory/opinion/view

Polytheism - 多神教 (duō shén jiào) = many/much/multi - God/deity - religion/teaching

Purgatory - 炼狱 (liàn yù) = to refine/to smelt - prison

Nihilism - 虚无主义 (xū wú zhǔ yì) = emptiness/void - not have/none/to lack - ideology

Voodoo - 巫毒教 (wū dú jiào) = 'wu' witch/wizard - 'du' to poison/malicious/cruel - religion/teaching

Bible - 圣经 (shèng jīng) = holy/sacred - scripture/sacred book

Church - 教堂 (jiào táng) = religion/teaching - (main) hall/large room for a specific purpose

Hell - 地狱 (dì yù) = earth/ground - prison

Heaven - 天堂 (tiān táng) = sky/heaven - room

Hymn - 圣歌 (shèng gē) = holy/sacred - song/to sing

Karma - 因果 (yīn guǒ) = cause - result

Missionary - 传教士 (chuán jiào shì) = to pass on/spread - religion/teaching - specialist worker/soldier

Omnipotent & omniscience - 全知全能 (quán zhī quán néng) = all/whole/entire - to know/be aware - all/whole/entire - can/to be able to/ability (fig. to know all and be able to do all)

Preach - 说教 (shuō jiào) = to speak/say/explain - religion/teaching

Sermon - 传道 (chuán dào) = to pass on/spread/transmit - truth/road/path

Prophet - 预言家 (yù yán jiā) = beforehand/in advance - to say/speech - specialist

Psalm - 圣诗 (shèng shī) = holy/sacred - poem/verse

Repent - 悔改 (huǐ gǎi) = to regret - to change/alter/transform/correct

Enlightenment - 启蒙主义 (qǐ méng zhǔ yì) = to enlighten or awaken/to inform - ignorant/blind/dim-sighted - ideology/-ism

Testimony - 证词 (zhèng cí) = to prove/demonstrate/confirm - speech/statement/word

Communion - 圣餐 (shèng cān) = holy - meal

**Jack-o-lantern** - 南瓜灯 (nán guā dēng) = pumpkin - lantern/lamp

**Valentines day** - 情人节 (qíng rén jié) = lover/sweetheart - festival/holiday

**Thanksgiving** - 感恩节 (gǎn ēn jié) = emotion/to feel/sense of - grace/favour/kindness - festival/holiday

**April fools** - 愚人节 (yú rén jié) = to cheat or deceive/to be stupid - person - festival/holiday

Astrology (fortune telling) - 占星术 (zhān xīng shù) = to observe/to divine - star/heavenly body - method/skill/art/technique

**Astrology (fortune telling)** - 谈星 (tán xīng) = to discuss/talk (about)/speak - star

**Celibacy** - 独身主义 (dú shēn zhǔ yì) = alone/single/independent - body/life - ideology/doctrine

Convent - 女修道 (nǚ xiū dào) = women/female - repair/mend/overhaul/decorate/embellish/build/construct - way/method/path/doctrine/principle

Monastery - 修道院 (xiū dào yuàn) = repair/mend/overhaul/decorate/embellish/build/construct - way/method/path/doctrine/principle - academy/school/yard/court/compound

An Effigy - 假人像 (jiǎ rén xiàng) = fake/false/phoney/sham/artificial - person/people - likeness (of somebody)/statue/to resemble/to look as if/figure

Effigy - 模拟人像 (mó nǐ rén xiàng) = imitate/simulation - person/people - likeness (of somebody)/statue/to resemble/to look as if/figure

Exorcism - 驱邪 (qū xié) = expel/disperse/drive away - demonic/nefarious/evil/abnormal

Orthodox School - 正宗 (zhèng zōng) = set right/make right/correct one's thinking/honest/upright - sect/faction/school

Sleep Paralysis - 鬼压身 (guǐ yā shēn) = ghost/spirit/demon/devil - press/push down/hold down/weigh down/control - body

**God** (Capital 'G') - 上帝 (shàng dì) = above/upper/superior/highest - god/supreme being

Hanukkah - 光明节 (guāng míng jié) = light/radiance/openhearted - festival/holiday

Passover - 逾越节 (yú yuè jié) = to cross over/to jump over/to exceed/go beyond - pass/go through - festival/holiday

Netherworld - 泉壤 (quán rǎng) = mythical abode of the dead - earth/area/soil

Heretical Ideas/Heresy - 邪说 (xié shuō) = demonic/iniquitous/nefarious/evil - talk/speak/to say

To Indoctrinate - 教化 (jiào huà) = teach/instruct/religion - convert/influence/reform

Coffin - 寿木 (shòu mù) = funerary/life/age/long life/birthday - coffin

Memorial Speech/Eulogy - 悼词 (dào cí) = mourn/grieve - words/speech

Ark of the Covenant - 约柜 (yuē guì) = pact/agreement/treaty/covenant - cabinet/cupboard

Podium - 讲桌 (jiǎng zhuō) = lecture/speech/speak/discuss - table/desk/stand

**Tongues** (spiritual gift) - 灵语 (líng yǔ) = spirit/soul - language/words/speak/say/speech

**Hedonism** - 快乐主义 (kuài lè zhǔ yì) = happy/joyful/cheerful - ideology/-ism

# Study Related

Math - 数学 (shù xué) = number - study

Algebra - 代数学 (dài shù xué) = to replace/to substitute - number - study

Geometry - 几何学 (jǐ hé xué) = how much/how many - how/why/which - study

Trigonometry - 三角学 (sān jiǎo xué) = three - corner/angle - study

Calculus - 分析学 (fēn xī xué) = fraction/part or subdivision/to allocate - to analyze/to separate/to divide - study

Statistics - 统计学 (tǒng jì xué) = to unify/to unite/gather - to calculate/compute/count - study

Chemistry - 化学 (huà xué) = to change into/transform - study

Physics - 物理学 (wù lǐ xué) = thing/object/matter - science/truth/logic/reason - study

**Metaphysics** - 形而上学 (xíng ér shàng xué) = form/shape/body/entity - and - up/ascend/higher/upper/superior - study

Logic - 逻辑 = 'luo ji' *transliterated*

Philosophy - 哲学 (zhé xué) = wise man/sage - study

Biology - 生物学 (shēng wù xué) = organism - study

Botany - 植物学 (zhí wù xué) = plant - study

Zoology - 动物学 (dòng wù xué) = animal - study

Sociology - 社会学 (shè huì xué) = society - study

Theology - 神学 (shén xué) = God/deity - study

Mythology - 神话学 (shén huà xué) = legend/fairytale/myth - study

Linguistics - 语言学 (yǔ yán xué) = language - study

**Communism** - 共产主义 (gòng chǎn zhǔ yì) = common/together/to share - product/resource/estate - ideology/-ism (lit. the ideology of sharing produce)

Neurology - 神经学 (shén jīng xué) = mental state - study

Anaesthesiology - 麻醉学 (má zuì xué) = to feel numb/pins & needles - intoxicated - study

Radiology - 放射学 (fàng shè xué) = to release/to let out - radio (chemistry) - study

Psychiatry - 精神病学 (jīng shén bìng xué) = mental disorder - study

Geology - 地质学 (dì zhí xué) = earth/ground - quality/nature - study

Astronomy - 天文学 (tiān wén xué) = heaven - culture - study

Architecture - 建筑学 (jiàn zhú xué) = to construct/building - study

Pharmacology - 药物学 (yào wù xué) = medicine/pharmaceuticals - study

Toxicology - 毒理学 (dú lǐ xué) = poison/narcotics - to manage/science/to handle - study

Business - 商业 (shāng yè) = commerce/merchant/dealer - industry/occupation/enterprise/to engage in

Literature - 文学 (wén xué) = culture/language/writing/literary - study

Anatomy- 解剖学 (jiě pōu xué) = to divide/to break up/to split/to explain/to understand/to know/a dissection - to cut open/to analyze - study

**Physiology** - 生理学 (shēng lǐ xué) = life - intrinsic order/science - study

Anthropology - 人类学 (rén lèi xué) = people/person - kind/type/class - study

Engineering - 工程学 (gōng chéng xué) = trade/profession/work - rule/order/regulations - study

Forestry - 森林学 (sēn lín xué) = forrest - study

Aesthetics - 美学 (měi xué) = beautiful/to beautify/pretty - study

Optics - 光学 (guāng xué) = light/ray/bright - study

Demography - 人口学 (rén kǒu xué) = people - mouth - study (lit. the study of population)

Science - 科学 (kē xué) = law/rule/branch of study/field/division - study

Mechanics - 力学 (lì xué) = power/force/strength/ability - study

Archaeology - 考古学 (kǎo gǔ xué) = to hit/test/inspect - ancient/old - study

Criminology - 犯罪学 (fàn zuì xué) = to violate/to assault/criminal/crime - guilt/crime/fault/sin/blame - study

**Fallacy/misconception** - 谬论 (miù lùn) = to cheat/confuse/deceive - opinion/view/theory/doctrine

**Antiestablishmentarianism** - 反正统主义 (fǎn zhèng tǒng zhǔ yì) = to oppose/against/-anti - main/principle - to unify/to gather - ideology/-ism

**Contradiction** - 矛盾 (máo dùn) = spear - shield

**Contradiction** - 相悖 (xiāng bèi) = mutually - to go against/to be contrary to

**Fundamentally/at the deepest level** - 骨子里 (gǔ zi lǐ) = ribs/frame - lining/interior/inside/internal

**Cognitive dissonance** - 认知失调 (rèn zhī shī tiáo) = cognition/understanding/awareness - imbalance

Glaciology - 冰川学 (bīng chuān xué) = glacier - study

**Somatology** - 口腔学 (kǒu qiāng xué) = oral cavity - to study/learning/knowledge/branch of learning/-ology

Traumatology - 外伤学 (wài shāng xué) = outside/exterior/in addition/beyond/other place/external - wound/injury/hurt/be distressed/hinder - study

Horticulture - 园艺学 (yuán yì xué) = gardening - study

Cryptography - 密码学 (mì mǎ xué) = secret - code - study

Paleoanthropology - 古人类学 (gǔ rén lèi xué) = ancient/paleo-/old - person/people/human being - kind/type/group - study

Palaeontology - 古生物学 (gǔ shēng wù xué) = ancient/paleo-/old - living things - study

**Archaeology** - 考古学 (kǎo gǔ xué) = examine/test/study/investigate - ancient/paleo-/old - study

**Chiropractic** - 脊骨神经医学 (jǐ gǔ shén jīng yī xué) = backbone - nerve - medicine/medical science/study of medicine

Toxicology - 毒理学 (dú lǐ xué) = poison/toxin/narcotics - natural science/science - study

Virology - 病毒学 (bìng dú xué) = virus - study

Ornithology - 鸟类学 (niǎo lèi xué) = bird - type/kind/class/group - study

Robotics - 机器人学 (jī qì rén xué) = robot - study

# Video Games

Diablo - 暗黑破坏神 (àn hēi pò huài shén) = dark - to destroy/wreck - God/deity

Far Cry - 孤岛惊魂 (gū dǎo jīng hún) = isolated island - 'the state of being frightened'

GTA - 侠盗猎车手 (xiá dào liè chē shǒu) = heroic/brave and chivalrous - steal/rob - hunt - vehicle - skill/a person proficient or engaged in a certain activity

Minecraft - 我的世界 (wǒ de shì jiè) = my - world

Grim Fandango - 冥界狂想曲 (míng jiè kuáng xiǎng qǔ) = ghost world/under world - rhapsody (music)

The Sims - 模拟人生 (mó nǐ rén shēng) = simulate - life

Doom - 毁灭战士 (huǐ miè zhàn shì) = destroy/exterminate - soldier/warrior

Wolfeinstien - 德军司令部 (dé jūn sī lìng bù) = Germany - army - headquarters

Quake - 雷神之锤 (léi shén zhī chuí) = thunder - god - 'of' - hammer (Hammer of the Thunder God)

Starcraft - 星际争霸 (xīng jì zhēng bà) = star - edge - 'contend for power'

Portal - 传送门 (chuán sòng mén) = deliver/convey - door

Need For Speed - 极品飞车 (jí pǐn fēi chē) = highest grade - go quickly/flying - car

Myst - 神秘岛 (shén mì dǎo) = mysterious - island

Tetris - 俄罗斯方块 (è luó sī fāng kuài) = Russia - square - piece

World of Warcraft - 魔兽世界 (mó shòu shì jiè) = magic/monster - beast - world

Street Fighter - 街头霸王 (jiē tóu bà wáng) = street - leading overload

Mortal Kombat - 格斗之王 (gé dǒu zhī wáng) = fist fight/grapple/wrestle - king (fig. King of Fist Fighting)

Left 4 Dead - 求生之路 (qiú shēng zhī lù) = seek - life - 'of' - road (The Road to Survival)

Trials - 特技摩托 (tè jì mó tuō) = stunt - motorbike

Temple Run - 神庙逃亡 (shén miào táo wáng) = religious shrine/god's temple - runaway

Tomb Raider - 古墓丽影 (gǔ mù lì yǐng) = ancient/old - tomb/grave - beautiful - picture/image/photograph/movie

Quest for Glory - 荣耀任务 (róng yào rèn wù) = honourable - task/mission

Carmageddon - 死亡赛车 (sǐ wáng sài chē) = death - race car

Castlevania - 恶魔城 (è mó chéng) = evil - devil - city

Pac-man - 吃豆人 (chī dòu rén) = to eat - bean - person

Twisted Metal - 烈火战车 (liè huǒ zhàn chē) = raging inferno - tank

**Devil May Cry** - 鬼泣 (guǐ qì) = devil/demon - tears/to sob

Metroid - 银河战士 (yín hé zhàn shì) = milky way - soldier/warrior

**Crash Bandicoot** - 古惑狼 (gǔ huò láng) = ancient - confused/be puzzled - wolf

PUBG - 吃鸡 (chī jī) = to eat/eradicate/destroy - chicken

Tekken - 铁拳 (tiě quán) = iron/hard/strong/violent - boxing/fist

# Movies

Totoro - 龙猫 (lóng māo) = dragon - cat

Sisterhood of the Traveling Pants - 牛仔裤的夏天 (niú zǎi kù de xià tiān) = jeans' - summer

Up - 飞屋环游记 (fēi wū huán yóu jì) = flying - house - bad - travel - memory

Homeward Bound - 看狗在说话 (kàn gǒu zài shuō huà) = look - dog - at - speaking (Fig: look at the speaking dog.)

**Star Trek** - 星际迷航 (xīng jì mí háng) = interstellar - lost - ship

Star Trek - 星际旅行 (xīng jì lǚ xíng) = interstellar - journey

The Goonies - 七宝奇谋 (qī bǎo qí móu) = seven - treasure - ingenious - plan

Pokémon - 口袋妖怪 (kǒu dài yāo guài) = pocket - monster

Finding Nemo - 海底总动员 (hǎi dǐ zǒng dòng yuán) = seabed - general mobilization

Frozen - 冰雪奇缘 (bīng xuě qí yuán) = ice - snow - witch

Minions - 小黄人 (xiǎo huáng rén) = small - yellow - people/person

Zootopia - 疯狂动物城 (fēng kuáng dòng wù chéng) = crazy - animal - city

Despicable Me - 神偷奶爸 (shén tōu nǎi bà) = lively - steal/thief - milk dad (stay at home dad)

Willy Wonka and the Chocolate Factory - 欢乐糖果屋 (huān lè táng guǒ wū) = happy - candy - house

Tangled - 长发公主 (chǎng fā gōng zhǔ) = long - hair - princess

Toy Story - 玩具总动员 (wán jù zǒng dòng yuán) = toy - general mobilization

Big Hero 6 - 超能陆战队 (chāo néng lù zhàn duì) = super - land battle - team

Ponyo - 悬崖上的金鱼公主 (xuán yá shàng de jīn yú gōng zhǔ) = overhanging steep cliff - on top - goldfish - princess

Wreck-it Ralph - 无敌破坏王 (wú dí pò huài wáng) = unmatched - destruction - king

Cloudy With a Chance of Meatballs - 天降美食 (tiān jiàng měi shí) = sky/heaven - drop - delicious food

Ghostbusters - 捉鬼敢死队 (zhuō guǐ gǎn sǐ duì) = catch - ghost - suicide team

Shrek- 怪物史瑞克 (guài wù shǐ ruì kè) = monster - 'shi rui ke'

Bambi - 小鹿斑比 (xiǎo lù bān bǐ) = small - deer - 'ban bi'

Pinocchio - 木偶奇遇记 (mù ǒu qí yù jì) = 'wood image' (puppet) - strange meeting - record

The Muppet Show - 大青蛙布偶秀 (dà qīng wā bù ǒu xiù) = big - frog - 'cloth image' (muppet) - show

**Walking Dead** - 行尸走肉 (xíng shī zǒu ròu) = walking - corpse - to walk/go - meat

World of Warcraft - 魔兽世界 (mó shòu shì jiè) = magic/monster/demon - beast - world

**Tarzan** - 丛林之王 (2013) (cóng lín zhī wáng) = jungle - 'of' - king (King of the Jungle)

Tarzan - 泰山归来:险战丛林 (2016) (tài shān guī lái: xiǎn zhàn cóng lín) = Mount Tai - return: dangerous - war - jungle

Ghost in the Shell - 攻壳机动队 (gōng ké jī dòng duì) = attack - shell/housing/casing - power driven - team

Resident Evil - 生化危机 (shēng huà wéi jī) = biochemistry - crisis

Guardians of the Galaxy - 银河护卫队 (yín hé hù wèi duì) = Milky Way - guard/protect - team

Jungle Book - 奇幻森林 (qí huàn sēn lín) = strange - forest

Smurfs - 蓝色小精灵 (lán sè xiǎo jīng líng) = blue - small - spirit/demon

Zoolander - 超级名模 (chāo jí míng mó) = super - top model

Men in Black - 黑衣人 (hēi yī rén) = black - clothes - people

Benjamin Button - 返老还童 (fǎn lǎo huán tóng) = return - old - 'go back' - child (This one is also transliterated as '本杰明·巴顿' 奇事 - 'ben jie ming · ba du' -  strange - affair/matter.)

Die Hard - 虎胆龙威 (hǔ dǎn lóng wēi) = brave - gallbladder/guts - dragon - strength/might

Sex and the City - 欲望都市 (yù wàng dū shì) = lust - metropolis

Where the Wild Things Are - 野兽家园 (yě shòu jiā yuán) = wild - beast - homeland

Ghost Rider - 灵魂战车 (líng hún zhàn chē) = soul - war chariot

A-Team - 天龙特攻队 (tiān lóng tè gōng duì) = sky - dragon - attack - team

**A-Team** - A字特攻队 (A zì tè gōng duì) = A - character - attack - team

Evan/Bruce Almighty - 冒牌天神 (mào pái tiān shén) = impostor - deity

Knocked Up - 一夜大肚 (yī yè dà dù) = one - night - big - belly

Kick-Ass - 海扁王 (hǎi biǎn wáng) = 'to beat somebody up' - king

High School Musical - 歌舞青春 (gē wǔ qīng chūn) = sing - dance - youthfulness

**Music & Lyrics** - K歌情人 (K gē qíng rén) = KTV - lovers

Music & Lyrics - 共谱恋曲 (gòng pǔ liàn qū) = mutual - compose - love song

The Big Lebowski - 谋杀绿脚趾 (móu shā lǜ jiǎo zhǐ) = murder - green - toe

Final Destination - 死神来了 (sǐ shén lái le) = death - god - comes

**Paul Blart: Mall Cop** - 百货战警 (bǎi huò zhàn jǐng) = general merchandise - war - police

Balls of Fury - 愤怒乒乓球 (fèn nù pīng pāng qiú) = anger/rage - ping pong

Eight Below - 南极大冒险 (nán jí dà mào xiǎn) = south pole - big - adventure

50 First Dates - 初恋五十次 (chū liàn wǔ shí cì) = first love - fifty - times

Click - 人生遥控器 (rén shēng yáo kòng qì) = life - remote control

The Matrix - 黑客帝国 (hēi kè dì guó) = hacker - kingdom/empire

Spy Kids - 非常小特务 (fēi cháng xiǎo tè wù) = extremely - small - spy/special agent

Meet the Fockers - 拜见岳父大人 (bài jiàn yuè fù dà rén) = pay a visit to - wife's father - adult

Anchorman - 王牌播音员 (wáng pái bò yīn yuán) = trump card - announcer

Tron - 电子世界争霸战 (diàn zǐ shì jiè zhēng bà zhàn) = electron - world - 'to contend for power' - war/battle

Spongebob Squarepants - 海绵宝宝 (hǎi mián bǎo bǎo) = sponge - baby

**Oblivion** - 遗落战境 (yí luò zhàn jìng) = leave behind - war - boarder

Ferris Bueller's Day Off - 春天不是读书天 (chūn tiān bù shì dú shū tiān) = springtime - 'is not' - study - day

Donnie Darko - 死亡幻觉 (sǐ wáng huàn jué) = death - hallucination

Karate Kid - 功夫梦 (gōng fū mèng) = kung fu - dream

**Indiana Jones** - 夺宝奇兵 (duó bǎo qí bīng) = take by force/seize - treasure/jewel/gem - surprising - an army/soldiers (army suddenly appearing from nowhere)

Wall-E - 机器人总动员 (jī qì rén zǒng dòng yuán) = robot - general mobilization

Mallrats - 耍酷一族 (shuǎ kù yī zú) = to act - cool - social group/subculture

Pulp Fiction - 低俗小说 (dī sú xiǎo shuō) = vulgar/poor taste - novel/fiction

The Nightmare Before Christmas - 圣诞夜惊魂 (shèng dàn yè jīng hún) = Christmas - night terror - soul/spirit

Good Will Hunting - 心灵捕手 (xīn líng bǔ shǒu) = bright/smart/clever/quick-witted - catcher

Shutter Island - 禁闭岛 (jìn bì dǎo) = confinement (as a punishment) - island

Lord of the Rings - 指环王 (zhǐ huán wáng) = (finger) ring - king/emperor

Pleasantville - 欢乐谷 (huān lè gǔ) = pleasure/happy/glee/gladness - valley/gorge

Scream - 惊声尖叫 (jīng shēng jiān jiào) = startled/frightened/shock/alarm/to be scared - sound/noise/voice/tone - scream/shriek/yell

Joe Dirt - 摇滚电台 (yáo gǔn diàn tái) = rock and roll - radio station

Punch-Drunk Love - 私恋失调 (sī liàn shī tiáo) = private - love - imbalance

6 Underground - 鬼影特攻：以暴制暴 (guǐ yǐng tè gōng: yǐ bào zhì bào) = ghost/spirit/apparition/clever/crafty - shadow/trace - special/unique/distinguished - attack - 'to use violence to curb violence' (google translate: Ghost Strike: Fighting Violence with Violence)

IT - 小丑回魂 (xiǎo chǒu huí hún) = clown - return/go back - soul/spirit

Childs Play - 鬼娃回魂 (guǐ wá huí hún) = ghost/spirit/apparition/clever/sly/terrible/ghastly - child/baby/doll - return/go back - soul/spirit

Gremlins - 小魔怪 (xiǎo mó guài) = small/tiny/children/young - fiends/demons and ghosts

Psycho (1960) - 惊魂记 (jīng hún jì) = fearful/in a panicked state/frightened - notes/record/to remember

Evil Dead - 鬼玩人 ( guǐ wán rén) = ghost/spirit/apparition/clever/sly/terrible/ghastly - play (with)/have fun/amuse oneself/engage in/toy with/trifle with - person/people

Shaun of the Dead - 僵尸肖恩 (jiāng shī xiào ēn) = zombie/rigid corpse - 'xiao en' (Shawn transliterated)

Texas Chainsaw Massacre - 德州电锯杀人狂 (dé zhōu diàn jù shārén kuáng) = Texas - electric saw - homicidal maniac/spree killer

Dr. Jeckel & Mr. Hyde - 化身博士 (huà shēn bó shì) = incarnation/personification - doctor

Coco - 寻梦环游记 (xún mèng huán yóu jì) = to search/to look for/seek - dream/illusion - tour around (a place) - notes/record/remember

Baby Driver - 极盗车神 (jí dào chē shén) = extreme/utmost - steal/rob/to plunder/thief/bandit/robber - vehicle/car - god/deity/divinity/immortal/supernatural being

Blade Runner - 仿生人会梦见电子羊 (fǎng shēng rén huì mèng jiàn diàn zǐ yáng) = imitate living things - person/people - can/to be able to/to be possible - to dream about (something or somebody) - electronic - sheep/goat (do robots dream of electric sheep?)

No Country for Old Men - 老无所依 (lǎo wú suǒ yī) = old (of people)/experienced/aged - to lack/without/not/no/none - place/location - depend on/rely on

Dumbo - 小飞象 (xiǎo fēi xiàng) = small/tiny/little/young - to fly/flying/hover or flutter in the air - elephant

Ratatouille - 美食总动员 (měi shí zǒng dòng yuán) = gourmet food/culinary delicacy - general mobilization (for war etc...)

About Time - 时空恋旅人 (shí kōng liàn lǚ rén) = time and space/(physics) space-time - (romantic) love/to love/to long for - traveller/passenger

Truman Show - 楚门的世界 (chǔ mén de shì jiè) = 'chu men' - 's - world

The Mask - 变相怪杰 (biàn xiàng guài jié) = in disguise form/convert - strange/odd/devil/monster - hero/outstanding person

The Grinch - 圣诞怪杰 (shèng dàn guài jié) = Christmas - strange/odd/devil/monster - hero/outstanding person

Jumanji - 勇敢者的游戏 (yǒng gǎn zhě de yóu xì) = brave/courageous - 'the one who' - 's - game/recreation

Pitch Black - 星际传奇 (xīng jì chuán qí) = interstellar/interplanetary - legend/fantasy sega

John Carter - 异星战场 (yì xīng zhàn chǎng) = different/other/unusual/strange - star/heavenly body/planet - battlefield

John Wick - 疾速追杀 (jí sù zhuī shā) = great speed/very fast - chase/pursue/seek/go after - kill/slaughter/murder/butcher

The Devil Wears Prada - 穿普拉达的女王 (chuān pǔ lā dá de nǚ wáng) = to wear/be dressed in - 'prada (brand)' - 's' - queen (The Queen Wears Prada)

Judge Dread - 特警判官 (tè jǐng pàn guān) = special police - judge/sentence/pass a verdict - government official/public servant

Snow Piercer - 雪国列车 (xuě guó liè chē) = snow - country/nation - train

RoboCop - 机械战警 (jī xiè zhàn jǐng) = machine/machinery - war/warfare/battle/fight - police/guard

There's Something About Mary - 我为玛丽狂 (wǒ wèi mǎ lì kuáng) = I/me - to act as/for/to be/to behave as - 'ma li' (Mary transliterated) - crazy/mad/insane

Teletubbies - 天线宝宝 (tiān xiàn bǎo bǎo) = antenna - baby/darling

A Night at the Roxbury - 舞翻天 (wǔ fān tiān) = dance - behave wildly

354

Home Alone - 小鬼当家 (xiǎo guǐ dāng jiā) = little devil/mischievous child - manage the household/to be in charge

Ace Ventura - 神探飞机头 (shén tàn fēi jī tóu) = smart/clever - detective/spy/scout - airplane - hair style

Clueless - 独领风骚 (dú lǐng fēng sāo) = independent/only/sole - lead/guide - flirtatious behaviour

The Naked Gun - 白头神探 (bái tóu shén tàn) = white - head/hair - smart/clever - detective/spy/scout

The Flintstones - 摩登原始人 (mó dēng yuán shǐ rén) = modern *transliterated* - primitive/first - people/person

Half Baked - 半仙半死 (bàn xiān bàn sǐ) = half - immortal - half - dead

Point Break - 极盗者 (jí dào zhě) = extreme/utmost - thief/robber - 'the one who' (The (one who is an) extreme thief.)

Virtuosity - 时空悍将 (shí kōng hàn jiāng) = time and space - heroic/valiant/violent/fierce - general/commander in chief

Space Jam - 空中大灌篮 (kōng zhōng dà guàn lán) = 'in the sky or air' - big/large - slam dunk

Big Trouble in Little China - 妖魔大闹唐人街 (yāo mó dà nào táng rén jiē) = evil spirit/demon - 'to cause havoc'/'to run amok' - Chinatown

Snakes on a Plane - 航班蛇患 (háng bān shé huàn) = scheduled flight/plane - snake - trouble/misfortune

Momento - 记忆碎片 (jì yì suì piàn) = memory - fragment

Event Horizon - 黑洞表面 (hēi dòng biǎo miàn) = black hole - surface/appearance

Ron's Gone Wrong - 天赐灵机 (tiān cì líng jī) = bestowed by heaven - clever/intelligence/mind - machine

Blind Side - 弱点 (ruò diǎn) = weak point

Trainspotting - 猜火车 (cāi huǒ chē) = 'to guess' - train

Billy Madison - 超龄插班生 (chāo líng chā bān shēng) = overage - 'a student who joins class midstream'

Happy Gilmore - 高尔夫球也疯狂 (gāo ěr fū qiú yě fēng kuáng) = golf - crazy/insane/frantic

Wedding Crashers - 婚礼傲客 (hūn lǐ ào kè) = wedding - overbearing/haughty/arrogant - guest

Taken - 飓风营救 (jù fēng yíng jiù) = hurricane - rescue

Stranger Than Fiction - 奇幻人生 (qí huàn rén shēng) = fantasy/fantastic - life

Rad - 单车小子 (dān chē xiǎo zi) = bicycle - boy

**Stand By Me** - 伴我同行 (bàn wǒ tóng xíng) = accompany/partner/companion/comrade - me - travel together

Game of Thrones - 权力的游戏 (quán lì de yóu xì) = power/authority - game

The Never Ending Story - 大魔域 (dà mó yù) = large/big/huge - monster/demon/devil/evil/magic - land within certain boundaries/territory/region

The Burbs - 邻居 (lín jū) = neighbour

Heathers - 希德姐妹帮 (xī dé jiě mèi bāng) = rare/uncommon/sparse - virtue/morals/moral character/ethics - sisters - group/gang/clique/party/secret society

Willow - 风云际会 (fēng yún jì huì) = wind and cloud/stormy or unstable situation - come across/opportunity/chance

Fast Times at Ridgemont High - 开放的美国学府 (kāi fàng dì měi guó xué fǔ) = unconstrained in one's sexuality/unrestrained by convention - America - educational establishment/institution of higher learning

The Running Man - 过关斩将 (guò guān zhǎn jiàng) = go through a strategic pass by killing the garrison commander in battle/beat one's opponents one by one/overcome one difficulty after another/to surmount all difficulties (on the way to success)

Short Circuit - 霹雳五号 (pī lì wǔ hào) = thunderbolt - number five (actually is 'five number')

Pee-Wee's Big Adventure - 荒唐小混蛋奇遇记 (huāng táng xiǎo hún dàn qí yù jì) = absurd/fantastic/preposterous/beyond belief - small/young - bastard/hoodlum/scoundrel - happy encounter/fortuitous meeting/adventure - to record/remember/remember (Google says "Absurd Little Bastard Adventures)

Strange Brew - 神奇酒酿 (shén qí jiǔ niàng) = magical/mystical/miraculous/effective and startling - fermented glutinous rice wine

Dazed and Confused - 年少轻狂 (nián shào qīng kuáng) = young/youngster/junior - extremely frivolous

Death Becomes Her - 飞越长生 (fēi yuè cháng shēng) = unexpected/accidental/unfounded/groundless - to exceed/surpass/pass - long - life (or 'to live forever')

**Weird Science** - 摩登保姆 (mó dēng bǎo mǔ) = modern/fashionable - housemaid/nanny/(children's nurse)

# Earth, Nature, and Infrastructure

Fossil - 化石 (huà shí) = to change into/to transform - rock

Petroleum - 石油 (shí yóu) = rock/stone - oil (also means petroleum)

Sunflower - 向阳花 (xiàng yáng huā) = towards/to face - sun - flower

Volcano - 火山 (huǒ shān) = fire - mountain

Icicle - 冰柱 (bīng zhù) = ice - pillar

Snowflake - 雪花 (xuě huā) = snow - flower

Pyramid - 金字塔 (jīn zì tǎ) = '金' - character/symbol - tower

Dead end road - 死路 (sǐ lù) = impassible/uncrossable/to die/dead - road/street

Sunset - 日落 (rì luò) = sun/day - to fall or drop/to lower (also 'of the sun to set', so it's the same as English yay!)

Sunrise - 日出 (rì chū) = sun/day - to come out/to rise/to produce

Stalagmite - 石笋 (shí sǔn) = rock/stone - bamboo shoot

Tsunami - 海啸 (hǎi xiào) = ocean/sea - to roar/to howl

Storm - 风暴 (fēng bào) = wind - sudden/violent/cruel

Grand Canyon - 大峡谷 (dà xiá gǔ) = big/large/wide/deep - canyon/ravine - valley

Cliff - 峭壁 (qiào bì) = high and steep/precipitous - wall

Iceberg - 冰山 (bīng shān) = ice - mountain

Mirage - 幻景 (huàn jǐng) = fantasy - scenery

Pollution - 污染 (wū rǎn) = dirty/filthy/to defile - to contaminate

**Beehive** - 蜂箱 (fēng xiāng) = bee - box/trunk/chest

Beehive - 蜜蜂房 (mì fēng fáng) = honey - bee/wasp - house/room

Pinecone - 松球 (sōng qiú) = pine - ball

Chimes - 风铃 (fēng líng) = wind - (small) bells

Opal (stone) - 蛋白石 (dàn bái shí) = egg - white - stone

Fig - 无花果 (wú huā guǒ) = flowerless - fruit

**Cactus** - 仙人掌 (xiān rén zhǎng) = immortal - person - 'palm of the hand'/sole of the foot (more common)

Cactus - 霸王树 (bà wáng shù) = to rule by force/tyrant - king/grand/great - tree

Tornado - 龙卷风 (lóng juǎn fēng) = dragon - roll - wind

**Tornado** - 旋风 (xuàn fēng) = loop/whirl - wind

Switchback (Road) - 之字路 (zhī zì lù) = 之 - character/symbol - road/route

Sewer - 下水道 (xià shuǐ dào) = down - water - road

Subway - 地下铁道 (dì xià tiě dào) = underground/subterranean - iron (metal) - road/path

Sewage - 脏水 (zàng shuǐ) = dirty - water

Population - 人口 (rén kǒu) = people - mouth

Ghetto/Slums - 贫民区 (pín mín qū) = poor - citizen/'the people' - district/area

Traffic Light - 红绿灯 (hóng lǜ dēng) = red - green - light

Cement - 水泥 (shuǐ ní) = water - mud

Windmill - 风车 (fēng chē) = wind - machine/vehicle/car

Emergency exit - 太平门 (tài píng mén) = peace and security - door

Tunnel - 地道 (dì dào) = earth/ground/land - road/path

University - 大学 (dà xué) = big - study

Elementary School - 小学 (xiǎo xué) = small - study

Middle School - 中学 (zhōng xué) = middle - study

Dorm - 宿舍 (sù shè) = 'lodge for the night' - residence

Workshop - 车间 (chē jiān) = vehicle/car/machine - room

Address - 地址 (dì zhǐ) = place - location/site

Bank - 银行 (yín háng) = silver - profession

Crop circle - 麦田怪圈 (mài tián guài quān) = oats/wheat - field/farm - bewildering/odd/strange - circle/ring/loop

Puddle - 水坑 (shuǐ kēng) = water - pit/hole

Hurricane - 狂飙 (kuáng biāo) = crazy/insane/mad/furious/violent - whirlwind

Lighthouse - 灯塔 (dēng tǎ) = light/lamp/lantern - tower

Orchard - 果木园 (guǒ mù yuán) = fruit - tree/timber/wood - garden/land for growing plants/area for special purposes

**Glacier** - 冰川 (bīng chuān) = ice - river

Glacier - 冰河 (bīng hé) = ice - river

Pebble - 河卵石 (hé luǎn shí) = river/stream - sperm/semen/seed/spawn - rock/stone

Aloe Vera - 芦荟胶 (lú huì jiāo) = reed/rush - thriving/flourishing - gel/resin/glue

Log - 圆形木材 (yuán xíng mù cái) = round/circular - shape/form/appear - tree/timber/wood - material/timber

Iceland - 冰岛 (bīng dǎo) = ice - island

Horticulture - 园艺 (yuán yì) = garden - art

Concrete - 石屎 (shí shǐ) = rock/stone - excrement/poo/stool/dung/droppings/shit

Peninsula - 半岛 (bàn dǎo) = half/in the middle - island

Lava/Magma - 岩浆 (yán jiāng) = rock/mountain - thick liquid/broth

Lava/Magma - 熔浆 (róng jiāng) = melt/fuse/smelt - thick liquid/broth

Magma - 岩石 (yán shí) = rock/mountain - rock

Marble (Stone) - 大理岩 (dà lǐ yán) = big/large/huge - texture/inner essence/science - rock/mountain

Obsidian - 黑曜岩 (hēi yào yán) = black/dark - sunlight/bright/glorious - rock/mountain

Clay - 粘土 (nián tǔ) = sticky/glutinous/adhesive - dirt/soil/earth/land/ground/clay

Geyser - 间歇喷泉 (jiàn xiē pēn quán) = occur intermittently - fountain

Pollination - 传粉 (chuán fěn) = pass on/hand down/spread/transmit - powder

Pollen - 花粉 (huā fěn) = flower/blossom - powder

Diamond - 金刚 (jīn gāng) = metals/money/gold/golden/precious - hard/tough/rigid/strong

Amethyst - 紫水晶 (zǐ shuǐ jīng) = purple/violet - water/liquid - quartz (rock)/crystal

Topaz - 茶晶 (chá jīng) = dark brown - quartz (rock)/crystal

**The Equinox** - 昼夜平分点 (zhòu yè píng fēn diǎn) = day and night - divide equally/share alike - aspect/feature/to light

Mahogany - 桃花心木 (táo huā xīn mù) = peach blossom - heart/centre/core - tree/timber/wood

Ebony - 乌木 (wū mù) = dark/black - tree/timber/wood

Maple - 醉红 (zuì hóng) = drunk/intoxicated - red

Teak - 柚木 (yòu mù) = grapefruit/pomelo - tree/timber/wood

Deciduous - 落叶树 (luò yè shù) = to fall or drop - leaf/foliage - tree

God-Forsaken/Remote and Desolate - 鸟不拉屎鸡不生蛋 (niǎo bù lā shǐ jī bù shēng dàn) = bird - not/no - shit - chicken - not/no - lay eggs

Monsoon - 季候风 (jì hòu fēng) = season - wind/air

A Landslide - 山泥倾泻 (shān ní qīng xiè) = mountain/hill - mud/clay/earth - collapse/overflow - flow swiftly/rush down/pour down

Lagoon - 泻湖 (xiè hú) = flow swiftly/rush down/pour down - lake

Fire Hose - 消防水龙 (xiāo fáng shuǐ lóng) = disperse/vanish/eliminate/dispel/remove - defend/protect/to prevent - water - dragon

Sleet - 雨夹雪 (yǔ jiā xuě) = rain - place in between/wedged between - snow

High School - 高中 (gāo zhōng) = tall/high/height/above average/of a high level or degree - centre/middle/intermediary

Graft (Horticulture) - 接木 (jiē mù) = connect/join/put together - tree/timber/wood

Bird's Eye View - 俯瞰图 (fǔ kàn tú) = bend over/to look down/face down - look down from a height/overlook/watch - picture/drawing/chart/map/diagram

Manhole - 检查口 (jiǎn chá kǒu) = inspect/examine - opening/mouth/entrance/hole

Yurt - 圆顶帐篷 (yuán dǐng zhàng péng) = dome - tent

Burr/Barb - 毛刺 (máo cì) = hair/plant - thorn/splinter/stab/prick/stimulate/to stab/prod

Sweatshop - 血汗工厂 (xiě hàn gōng chǎng) = blood and sweat - factory/plant/mill

Escalator - 电扶梯 (diàn fú tī) = electric/electricity - staircase/ladder (also means escalator, but I like 'electric staircase' better.)

Canal - 人工河 (rén gōng hé) = artificial/man-made - river

Tropical - 热带 (rè dài) = hot/heat/warm - area/region/zone/belt

**Drizzle** - 毛毛雨滴 (máo máo yǔ dī) = hair - hair - rain - drop

**Castle** - 城堡 (chéng bǎo) = city wall/wall/city/town - fortress/fort/castle

# Idioms

Unexpected misfortune - 山高水低 (shān gāo shuǐ dī) = mountain - high - water - low

Shotgun wedding - 因孕而婚 (yīn yùn ér hūn) = because - pregnant - and so/and - marry/wedding

Extravagant - 大手大脚 (dà shǒu dà jiǎo) = big - hand - big - foot

To toot your own horn - 自炒 (zì chǎo) = oneself/self - fry/sauté

A brief period of enthusiasm - 三分钟热度 (sān fēn zhōng rè dù) = three - minutes - heat/hot - temperature

To talk big - 满嘴跑火车 (mǎn zuǐ pǎo huǒ chē) = full/to fill - mouth - to run away/to escape - train

To make life difficult for someone - 穿小鞋 (chuān xiǎo xié) = to wear - small - shoes

**To make a hasty last minute effort** - 抱佛脚 (bào fó jiǎo) = to hug/embrace - Buddha - foot/feet (lit. to clasp at Buddha's feet (without ever having burned incense/fig. to profess devotion only when in trouble)

To cheat/Trickery - 挂羊头, 卖狗肉 (guà yáng tóu, mài gǒu ròu) = hang - sheep - head - sell - dog - meat

To have a brainstorm - 心血来潮 (xīn xuè lái cháo) = heart - blood - to arrive/come - tide

Be the object of flattery - 戴高帽子 (dài gāo mào zi) = to wear - tall - hat

**Beside the point** - 驴唇不对马嘴 (lǘ chún bù duì mǎ zuǐ) = donkey - lip - not/no - for/suit/match together - horse - mouth (lit. a donkey's lips do not match a horses mouth)

Freeload/Sponge off others - 吃白饭 (chī bái fàn) = to eat - white - rice

Fame has its price - 人怕出名猪怕肥 (rén pà chū míng zhū pà féi) = people - to fear - 'fame' - pig - to fear - fat (lit. people fear getting famous like pigs fear fattening up (for the slaughter)

To endure all sorts of hardships - 一把屎一把尿 (yī bǎ shǐ yī bǎ niào) = handful of - feces/poo - handful of - urine/pee (fig. to raise ones children while they poo and pee)

To hoodwink people - 偷天换日 (tōu tiān huàn rì) = to steal/pilfer - sky/day - to exchange/to switch/change - sun (fig. to steal the sky and put up a sham sun/perpetrate a gigantic fraud)

**Have a strong start but a weak finish** - 龙头蛇尾 (lóng tóu shé wěi) = dragon - head - snake - tail

**'Blows ones brains out'** - 脑袋开花 (nǎo dai kāi huā) = brain - bag/sack - explode/break up

Very complicated - 千头万绪 (qiān tóu wàn xù) = thousand - head/aspect - ten thousand - string

Complete confusion (earth shaking) - 翻天覆地 (fān tiān fù dì) = turn over/turn upside down - sky/heaven - tip over/capsize/to cover - the earth/'indicating a state of mind'

Outdoing one another - 争先恐后 (zhēng xiān kǒng hòu) = contend/strive - first - fear/dread - last

**Satisfied with what one has** - 知足常乐 (zhī zú cháng lè) = know/realize/be aware of - to be sufficient/enough/attain - common/often/usually - pleasure/enjoy/happy/cheerful

**Empty headed** - 丢三落四 (diū sān là sì) = to lose/mislay - three - to lag or fall behind/to fall or drop - four

**To give up halfway** - 半途而废 (bàn tú ér fèi) = half/in the middle - way/road/route - and - give up/abandon

**When in Rome, do as the Romans do** - 入乡随俗 (rù xiāng suí sú) = to enter/go into - village/countryside - to follow/comply with/adapt to - social customs/convention

Looking for a needle in a haystack - 大海捞针 (dà hǎi lāo zhēn) = big/large -ocean/sea - fish for/scoop out of water - needle

**An eye for an eye, a tooth for a tooth** - 以眼还眼以牙还牙 (yǐ yǎn hái yǎn yǐ yá hái yá) = because of - eye - in addition - eye - because of - tooth - in addition - tooth

**Easier said than done** - 知易行难 (zhī yì xíng nán) = to know - easy - behaviour/conduct - difficult/hard

**Stab somebody in the back** - 暗箭伤人 (àn jiàn shāng rén) = hidden/secret - arrow - injure/hurt - person

Light-fingered/Prone to stealing - 手脚不干净 (shǒu jiǎo bù gān jìng) = hand - foot - not - clean

**Love at first sight** - 一见钟情 (yī jiàn zhōng qíng) = first/as soon as - view/see/meet - concentrate - feeling/affection/emotion/passion

**To act without taking time to think/react instantly** - 不加思索 (bù jiā sī suǒ) = not/no/negative prefix - increase/add - to think/consider

**Running as fast as flying** - 健步如飞 (jiàn bù rú fēi) = healthy/strong - step/walk - like/as if - fly

**Where there's a will there's a way** - 有志者事竟成 (yǒu zhì zhě shì jìng chéng) = to have - will/aspiration - 'the one who' - matter/affair - finish/complete/in the end - accomplish/succeed

**By every possible means** - 千方百计 (qiān fāng bǎi jì) = thousand - way/method - hundred - plan/idea

Eyes brimming with tears of excitement - 热烈盈眶 (rè liè yíng kuàng) = hot - tears - to be full of/be filled with - eye socket

To wolf down ones food/to devour ravenously - 狼吞虎咽 (láng tūn hǔ yàn) = wolf - swallow/gulp down - tiger - swallow

To receive worldwide attention - 举世瞩目 (jǔ shì zhǔ mù) = whole/entire - world - gaze/look steadily - regard/look/eye

To suddenly see the light - 恍然大悟 (huǎng rán dà wù) = all of a sudden - right/correct - large/big/great - realize/awaken/become aware

**Survival of the fittest** - 优胜劣汰 (yōu shèng liè tài) = superior/excellent - defeat/victory - weak/inferior - discard/eliminate

**Plain sailing/To go smoothly** - 一帆风顺 (yī fān fēng shùn) = one - sail - wind - favourable

One disaster on top of another - 雪上加霜 (xuě shàng jiā shuāng) = snow - go up/up - add/increase - frost

**A bargain** - 物美价廉 (wù měi jià lián) = thing/object - beautiful - price - inexpensive/cheap

Every cloud has a silver lining - 雨过天晴 (yǔ guò tiān qíng) = rain - to cross/pass/to go over - sky/heaven/day/season/weather - fine (weather)/clear

To let the cat out of the bag - 漏泄天机 (lòu xiè tiān jī) = to leak/divulge/drip/fall out/let out - let out/discharge/leak out/vent/flow - sky/heaven/day/season/weather - important affairs/secret/idea/intention

To punish an individual as an example to others - 杀鸡儆猴 (shā jī jìng hóu) = kill/slaughter/murder/butcher - chicken - warn/warning - monkey/ape

**Dead Set/Hell Bent** - 死心踏地 (sǐ xīn tā dì) = die/be dead/inflexible/rigid - heart/mind/feeling/intention - step on/ground/earth/land/soil

Burning the candle at both ends - 劳累过度 (láo lèi guò dù) = work/labour/strain/toil - (be) tired/weary/fatigued/to work hard - pass/cross/excessively - degree of intensity/limit/extent

Stereotype - 刻板印象 (kè bǎn yìn xiàng) = stiff/inflexible/stubborn - impression

Erratic/Fickle/Unstable - 反复无常 (fǎn fù wú cháng) = repeatedly/over and over/reversal/relapse - variable/changeable

You get out what you put in - 一分耕耘一分收获 (yī fēn gēng yún yī fēn shōu huò) = one - part - cultivate - one - part - results/gains

To pledge undying love - 海誓山盟 (hǎi shì shān méng) = ocean/sea/big lake - oath/vow/to swear/to pledge - mountain - swear/oath/union/covenant

To do one's utmost - 尽心竭力 (jìn xīn jié lì) = to the greatest extent - heart/mind/feeling/intention - exhaust - power/strength

**To overdo it** - 画蛇添足 (huà shé tiān zú) = to draw//to paint/picture - snake - add/increase - foot/leg

**There's more than one way to skin a cat** - 不要在一棵树上吊死 (bù yào zài yī kē shù shàng diào sǐ) = don't - at - a tree - hang oneself - die (don't hang yourself on a tree to die)

**What's gone can never come back** - 肉包子打狗 (ròu bāo zi dǎ gǒu) = meat - stuffed bun - attack/strike/hit/break - dog (to throw a meat bun at a dog)

# Relationships, Behaviour & Life/Work Stuff

Picky (about food) - 挑食 (tiāo shí) = to pick/nitpick/to choose - food/to eat

Eavesdrop - 偷听 (tōu tīng) = to steal/pilfer/stealthily - to listen/hear

Hunt for a job - 找饭碗 (zhǎo fàn wǎn) = to look for/find/seek - rice - bowl

Fire somebody - 炒鱿鱼 (chǎo yóu yú) = to fry/sauté - squid

To silence somebody - 灭口 (miè kǒu) = to extinguish/to exterminate - mouth

Affair - 偷情 (tōu qíng) = steal/stealthily - passion/situation

Long distance relationship - 异地恋 (yì dì liàn) = different/other - place - to love/to long for

Break up - 分手 (fēn shǒu) = separate - hands

Chase women - 猎艳 (liè yàn) = hunt - romance

Stand someone up - 放鸽子 (fàng gē zi) = to release/let go/to free - dove

One-way love - 单相思 (dān xiàng sī) = single/sole/only - to yearn/to pine after

To live off a woman (esp. a mistress) - 吃软饭 (chī ruǎn fàn) = to eat/consume - soft - rice/devotee

To propose - 求婚 (qiú hūn) = to request/to look for/to seek - marriage/wedding/to take a wife

To joke/jest - 玩笑 (wán xiào) = to play/to have fun/to trifle with - laugh/smile

Blurt out - 脱口 (tuō kǒu) = to get away from/escape - mouth

Slip of the tongue - 矢口 (shǐ kǒu) = to lose/miss/fail - mouth

To 'hog' something - 独吞 (dú tūn) = alone/single/independent - to take/to swallow

Gossip - 嚼舌头 (jiáo shé tou) = to chew - tongue

Harbour a grudge - 挟怨 (xié yuàn) = to clasp under the arm - to complain/blame

Crack a joke - 打牙 (dǎ yá) = to hit/strike - tooth

Talk big/Brag - 吹牛 (chuī niú) = the blow (also brag/boast) - cow

Suppose/assume - 假定 (jiǎ dìng) = fake/false/suppose - to decide/to determine

Get a beating - 吃生活 (chī shēng huó) = to eat - life

To get fired - 回家吃自己 (huí jiā chī zì jǐ) = return - home - eat - oneself

To go bankrupt - 破产 (pò chǎn) = to break, split or cleave/to get rid of/to destroy - product/resource/estate/property

Train of Thought - 心路 (xīn lù) = heart - road

Lose ones job - 丢饭碗 (diū fàn wǎn) = the lose - rice - bowl

Suicide - 自杀 (zì shā) = self - kill

Swearing - 脏话 (zāng huà) = dirty/filthy - words/speech/language

Third Wheel - 大灯泡 (dà dēng pào) = big - light bulb

One night stand - 约炮 (yuē pào) = to make an appointment/to invite - firecracker

To Bargain - 砍价 (kǎn jià) = to cut/reduce - price

Nap/Doze Off - 假寐 (jiǎ mèi) = fake/false/artificial - sleep

Retire - 退休 (tuì xiū) = retreat/decline/withdraw/quit - rest/retire/stop/cease

Characterization - 人物塑造 (rén wù sù zào) = personage/character - model/portray

Rumour/Gossip/Slander - 诽闻 (fěi wén) = slander/vilify/condemn - news/story/make known

Blind Date - 相亲 (xiāng qīn) = see for oneself - marriage/bride/intimate/in person/first-hand

Gifted/Talented - 天分高 (tiān fèn gāo) = sky/heaven/overhead/nature/inborn/innate - distribute/assign/allot - tall/high/height/above average/of a high level or degree

Strangle - 扼杀 (è shā) = clutch/grip/choke - kill/slaughter/butcher/murder

Divorce - 离婚 (lí hūn) = leave/depart/to part from - marriage/wedding

**Fidelity** (Faithful/Loyal) - 保真度 (bǎo zhēn dù) = protect/defend/insure/care/safeguard - true/real/genuine/actual - degree of intensity/extent/degree/limit

Adventure - 冒险 (mào xiǎn) = to face/to brave/reckless - dangerous/perilous/narrow pass/danger/dangerous

To fall flat on one's face - 狗吃屎 (gǒu chī shǐ) = dog - to eat - excrement/shit/dung/feces

(Other people's) Dumb Luck - 狗屎运 (gǒu shǐ yùn) = dog - excrement/shit/dung/feces - luck/fate/fortune

Imagination - 想象 (xiǎng xiàng) = to think/ponder/consider/to believe/to wish - image/shape/form

Nightmare - 恶梦 (è mèng) = shocking/upsetting/bad/startling - dream

Couch Surfing - 沙发客 (shā fā kè) = sofa - visitor/guest/patron/traveller/passenger

To Share - 分享 (fēn xiǎng) = divide/separate/distribute/assign/allot - enjoy/to benefit/to have the use of

To follow someone closely - 跟屁股 (gēn pì gu) = follow closely/to go with - buttocks/butt/ass

Unexpected mistake or mishap - 乌龙 (wū lóng ) = crow/black/dark - dragon

To mechanically memorize - 死记硬背 (sǐ jì yìng bèi) = to the death/extremely - remember/bear in mind/memorize - good (quality) - to learn by heart/to recite from memory

To Bluff - 虚张声势 (xū zhāng shēng shì) = false - display/look - voice/sound/tone - outward appearance/gesture

To be the object of flattery - 戴高帽子 (dài gāo mào zi) = to wear - tall/high/elevated - hat/cap

To blow a kiss - 飞吻 (fēi wěn) = fly/hover or flutter in the air - lips/kiss

Ill-gotten Gains - 邪财 (xié cái) = demonic/iniquitous/nefarious/evil - wealth/money/fortune

Having a hangover - 宿酒未醒 (sù jiǔ wèi xǐng) = lodge for the night/rest/stay overnight - alcoholic beverage/liquor - have not/did not - sober up/regain consciousness/wake up/be in clear mind

To Eavesdrop - 听墙根 (tīng qiáng gēn) = listen/hear - wall - origin/source (to listen to the wall source)

Attempted Murder - 杀人未遂 (shā rén wèi suì) = kill a person/murder/homicide - have not/did not/not - succeed/to satisfy

'Jack of all trades' - 杂家 (zá jiā) = miscellaneous/mixed/various - specialist in a certain field

**Jack-of-all-trades** - 万事通 (wàn shì tōng) = ten thousand - matter/thing/item/work/job - to know/understand/authority/expert

Drug Trafficking - 毒品交易 (dú pǐn jiāo yì) = narcotics/drugs - transaction/engage in/business deal

J-Walk - 乱穿马路 (luàn chuān mǎ lù) = random/indiscriminate/arbitrary - cross - road/street/avenue

# Science, Medicine & Drugs

Radioactive - 放射 (fàng shè) = to send out/release - radio (chemistry)

Hieroglyph - 象形文字 (xiàng xíng wén zì) = shape/form - to appear/to look - character/script/writing/written language

Sterilize/disinfect - 消毒 (xiāo dú) = to eliminate - poison

**Sterilize/disinfect** - 杀毒 (shā dú) = to kill/attack - poison

Latex glove - 胶乳手套 (jiāo rǔ shǒu tào) = glue/gum/rubber - milk - hand - sheath

Cremate - 火化 (huǒ huà) = fire - to make into/-ization/transform

Surgery - 手术 (shǒu shù) = hand - art

Viagra - 伟哥 (wěi gē) = big/large - elder brother (slang for penis)

**Viagra** - 威而钢 (wēi ér gāng) = power/might - and - steel

Drugs - 毒品 (dú pǐn) = poison - product

LSD - 迷幻药 (mí huàn yào) = confused - fantasy - medicine/drug

Methamphetamine - 冰 (bīng) = ice (slang)

Magic mushroom - 迷幻蘑菇 (mí huàn mó gū) = to bewilder/confused - fantasy - mushroom

MDMA/Ecstasy - 摇头丸 (yáo tóu wán) = to shake/to rock - head - pill/ball/pellet

Ketamine - K粉 (K fěn) = K - powder

Nicotine - 烟碱 (yān jiǎn) = tobacco plant - base/alkali

Overdose - 超剂量 (chāo jì liàng) = to exceed/surpass - dose (medicine) - amount/capacity/quantity

Scalpel - 解剖刀 (jiě pǒu dāo) = a dissection/to open/separate/split - to cut open/to analyze - knife/blade

**Scalpel** - 手术刀 (shǒu shù dāo) = surgery - knife/blade

Cesarean section - 剖宫产 (pōu gōng chǎn) = to cut open - palace/temple - to give birth/reproduce

Digest (food) - 消化 (xiāo huà) = to eliminate/to disappear - to transform/-ization/to change into

Rhythm of the Heartbeat - 心律 (xīn lǜ) = heart - law

Amputate - 截肢 (jié zhī) = to cut off - limb

Adrenaline - 肾上腺素 (shèn shàng xiàn sù) = kidney - above/upper - gland - essence/element

Catheter - 导尿管 (dǎo niào guǎn) = guide - urine - tube

Virus - 病毒 (bìng dú) = illness/disease - poison

**Symptom** - 症状 (zhèng zhuàng) = disease/illness - condition/state

Facelift - 拉皮 (lā pí) = to pull - skin

Stoma - 气孔 (qì kǒng) = air/gas/smell - hole/opening

Stethoscope - 听诊器 (tīng zhěn qì) = to listen/hear - examine (a patient)/diagnose - device/tool

Deep distress - 落汤鸡 (luò tāng jī) = to fall or drop - soup - chicken

Ayahuasca - 死藤水 (sǐ téng shuǐ) = death/to die - cane/vine - water/liquid/beverage

CT Scan - 电脑断层扫描 (diàn nǎo duàn céng sǎo miáo) = computer - judge/decide - layer/stratum - scan

Plastic surgery (Face Lift) - 整容 (zhěng róng) = repair/mend/renovate - facial expression/appearance/looks

Herbicide - 杀草剂 (shā cǎo jì) = kill/slaughter/butcher/murder - grass/straw - dose (medicine)

Cremate - 火葬 (huǒ zàng) = fire - bury (the dead)/bury in a specific way according to local customs

Gravity - 重力 (zhòng lì) = weight - power/force

Insecticide - 杀虫剂 (shā chóng jì) = kill/slaughter/butcher/to murder - insect/worm - dose (medicine)

Anesthesia - 麻醉 (má zuì) = to feel numb - intoxicated/drunk/tipsy

Urn - 骨坛 (gǔ tán) = bone/skeleton - earthen jar/vat/jug

Defibrillator - 除颤器 (chú chàn qì) = to eliminate/to remove/to wipe out - quiver/tremble - device/tool/utensil

Sling (For injured limb) - 悬带 (xuán dài) = hang/suspend/lift/raise - belt/girdle/ribbon/band/to carry

Sling (For a wounded arm) - 三角巾 (sān jiǎo jīn) = three - horn/horn-shaped/corner - general purpose cloth/towel/kerchief

Coca (Source of cocaine) - 古柯 (gǔ kē) = ancient/paleo-/old - stalk/branch

Antibacterial/Antibiotic - 抗菌素 (kàng jùn sù) = resist/combat/anti-/to fight - germ/bacteria/mold/fungus - essence/element

Pasteurizer - 杀菌器 (shā jùn qì) = kill/slaughter/butcher/fight/to attack - germ/bacteria/mold/fungus - device/tool/utensil

EMG (Electromyogram) - 肌电图 (jī diàn tú) = muscle/flesh - electric/electricity - picture/drawing/chart/diagram

Incubator (For Newborns) - 保育箱 (bǎo yù xiāng) = protect/defend/insure/care/safeguard - raise/bring up/rear/produce - chest/box/case/trunk

Artificial - 人工 (rén gōng) = person/people - work (ie. something made by people)

Artificial Insemination - 人工受孕 (rén gōng shòu yùn) = artificial - receive/to accept - pregnancy/be pregnant

Artificial Insemination - 人工授精 (rén gōng shòu jīng) = artificial - receive/to accept - sperm

**Artificial Insemination** - 人工授精受孕 (rén gōng shòu jīng shòu yùn) = artificial - receive/to accept - sperm - receive/to accept - pregnancy/be pregnant

**Encrypt** - 加密 (jiā mì) = add/increase - secret/confidential

Reference Book - 工具书 (gōng jù shū) = tool/instrument - book

Antidote - 解毒药 (jiě dú yào) = to dissolve/to solve/to separate/to remove - poison/toxin - medicine/drug

Tonic - 补品 (bǔ pǐn) = mend/patch/repair/nourish - product/commodity/goods

**Trachoma** - 沙眼 (shā yǎn) = sand - eye

**Bile** - 胆汁 (dǎn zhī) = gallbladder - juice/liquid/fluid

# Time Related

Months

January - 一月 (yī yuè) = one - month

February - 二月 (èr yuè) = two - month

March - 三月 (sān yuè) = three - month

April - 四月 (sì yuè) = four - month

May - 五月 (wǔ yuè) = five - month

June - 六月 (liù yuè) = six - month

Jul有- 七月 (qī yuè) = seven - month

August - 八月 (bā yuè) = eight - month

September - 九月 (jiǔ yuè) = nine - month

October - 十月 (shí yuè) = ten - month

November - 十一月 (shí yī yuè) = ten - one - month

December - 十二月 (shí èr yuè) = ten - two - month

Days

Monday - 周一/星期一 (zhōu yī/xīng qí yī) = week - one//star - phase/stage - one

Tuesday - 周二/星期二 (zhōu èr/xīng qí èr) = week - two//star - phase/stage - two

Wednesday - 周三/星期三 (zhōu sān/xīng qí sān) = week - three//star - phase/stage - three

Thursday - 周四/星期四 (zhōu sì/xīng qí sì) = week - four//star - phase/stage - four

Friday - 周五/星期五 (zhōu wǔ/xīng qí wǔ) = week - five//star - phase/stage - five

Saturday - 周六/星期六 (zhōu liù/xīng qí liù) = week - six/s/tar - phase/stage - six

Sunday -星期天 (xīng qí tiān) = star - phase//stage - day

365

Times

| | | |
|---|---|---|
| Early morning | 5am-8am | 早上 (zǎo shàng) |
| Morning | 9am-11am | 上午 (shàng wǔ) |
| Noon | 12pm | 中午 (zhōng wǔ) |
| Afternoon | 1pm-6pm | 下午 (xià wǔ) |
| Evening | 7pm-12am | 晚上 (wǎn shàng) |
| Night | 1am-4am | 凌晨 (líng chén) |

# Randoms
### (Nouns, verbs, sayings and miscellaneous crap)

Priority - 先河 (xiān hé) = first - river (Ancient tradition of worshipping the river first, then the sea)

Massage - 按摩 (àn mó) = to press/push - to rub

Poach - 盗猎 (dào liè) = to steal/to rob/thief/bandit - hunting

Exploitative - 吃人 (chī rén) = to eat/to suffer/to destroy - person

Challenge - 挑战 (tiǎo zhàn) = to incite/stir up - to fight/battle/war

Size - 大小 (dà xiǎo) = big - small

Cartoon - 漫画 (màn huà) = free/unrestrained - to draw/picture/painting

Sharp tongue - 刀子嘴 (dāo zi zuǐ) = knife - mouth

Stuff - 东西 (dōng xī) = east - west

Uneven/Bumpy - 凹凸 (āo tú) = concave - convex

Tip/Gratuity - 赏钱 (shǎng qián) = to bestow/to give/to hand down - money/coin

Banner - 徽帜 (huī zhì) = badge/emblem/insignia/logo - flag

Free - 免费 (miǎn fèi) = to avoid/to escape - fee/cost/expenses

Hint - 暗示 (àn shì) = hidden/secret/obscure - to show/to reveal

Be careful - 小心 (xiǎo xīn) = small/tiny - heart/intention/mind

Walk a tightrope - 走钢丝 (zǒu gāng sī) = to walk/to go - steel - thread/silk

Cube - 立方 (lì fāng) = to stand - square (lit. standing square)

**Perception/awareness** - 感知 (gǎn zhī) = to feel/to touch/feeling/emotion/sense of - to know/to be aware

Tampon - 卫生棉条 (wèi shēng mián tiáo) = to guard/protect/health/hygiene - cotton/padded or quilted with cotton strip/item/article - long narrow piece/strip

Oh dear! - 糟糕 (zāo gāo) = rotten - cake

Go crazy - 抓狂 (zhuā kuáng) = grab - crazy

Slang - 俚语 (lǐ yǔ) = rustic/vulgar/unrefined - language/speech

Enjoy your meal! - 慢慢吃 (màn man chī) = slow - slow - eat

Very popular - 吃香 (chī xiāng) = to eat - fragrance/sweet smelling

Chinese (Mandarin) - 普通话 (pǔ tōng huà) = common/ordinary/general - language/dialect

**Drop dead!/Go to hell!** - 扑街 (pū jiē) = to fall forward/to fall prostrate - street (Lit. to fall prostrate in the street)

Damn it! - 该死 (gāi sǐ) = should/to deserve - to die/damned

To hell with it! - 见鬼 (jiàn guǐ) = to see/to meet - ghost/demon

Mosaic - 镶嵌画 (xiāng qiàn huà) = rim/edge - inlay/set - picture/painting

Rigged ball game - 假球 (jiǎ qiú) = fake/false/sham - ball

**Literary hack** - 帮闲文人 (bāng xián wén rén) = clique/gang - irrelevant words - person

Pronunciation - 读音 (dú yīn) = to read (aloud) - sound/syllable

Narcolepsy - 发作性嗜睡病 (fā zuò xìng shì shuì bìng) = become/come to be/show effect - disposition - addicted to - sleep - disease/illness

Horseplay - 打打闹闹 (dǎ dǎ nào nào) = fight - fight - noisy - noisy

Adopt (a child) - 收养 (shōu yǎng) = receive/take in - raise/provide for/support/help (also means foster/adoptive)

News - 信息 (xìn xī) = information/to trust or believe - news

Ballet shoe - 足尖鞋 (zú jiān xié) = foot - sharp/pointed/tip - shoe

Air conditioner - 空调 (kòng tiáo) = air - transfer/shift/move

Wardrobe - 衣柜 (yī guì) = clothing/clothes - cupboard/cabinet

House pet - 宠物 (chǒng wù) = pamper/spoil/love - creature/thing

Blender - 搅拌机 (jiǎo bàn jī) = to stir - to mix - machine

LP (record) - 唱片 (chàng piàn) = sing/song - slice/flake/thin piece

Jewelry - 首饰 (shǒu shì) = head - decorations/ornaments/adorn

Yodel - 岳得尔歌 (yuè dé ěr gē) = high mountain/mountain peak - [structural particle] - like - song

Wheelbarrow - 独轮车 (dú lún chē) = single - wheel - vehicle

Nocturnal - 夜行 (yè xíng) = night/in the dark/by night - behaviour/conduct/travel

UFO - 不明飞行物 (bù míng fēi xíng wù) = no/not/negative prefix - to show/reveal/sight - to fly/hover/move swiftly - behaviour/conduct/travel - thing/object

**Aquarium (for the public)** - 水族馆 (shuǐ zú guǎn) = collective term for aquatic animals - public building/place for cultural activities

**Hepatitis** - 肝炎 (gān yán) = liver - inflammation/-itis

Syringe - 注射器 (zhù shè qì) = to inject/pour into - discharge in a jet/spout/shoot/launch/emit - device/tool

Scales (for body weight) - 体重器 (tǐ zhòng qì) = body - weight - device/tool

CPR - 心肺复苏术 (xīn fèi fù sū shù) = heart - lung - to resume/to recover/to return to original state - to revive/resurrect - skill/technique/method

Funny - 搞笑 (gǎo xiào) = to make/produce/cause to become - laugh/smile

X-Rated movie - 儿童不宜片 (er tóng bù yí piàn) = children - unsuitable/inadvisable - film

Birth defect - 畸态 (jī tài) = abnormal/irregular/lopsided - appearance/shape/form

Vulgar/Indecent - 不雅 (bù yǎ) = not/no - elegant

Kitten - 猫儿 (māo er) = cat - child

Flea market - 小市 (xiǎo shì) = small - market

Rigor mortis - 尸僵 (shī jiāng) = corpse/dead body - stiff and motionless/numb/rigid

Pop rocks (candy) - 跳跳糖 (tiào tiào táng) = jump/bounce/leap - jump/bounce/leap - candy/sweets/sugar

Transliterate - 音译 (yīn yì) = sound/syllable - translate/interpret

Snicker (laugh up ones sleeve) - 暗笑 (àn xiào) = secret/hidden - laugh/smile/ridicule

Stonehenge - 巨石柱群 (jù shí zhù qún) = huge/gigantic - stone/rock - pillar/column - group/crowd

Firecracker - 爆竹 (bào zhú) = explode/burst/pop - bamboo

**To pirate/illegally copy and sell** - 盗版 (dào bǎn) = steal/rob - edition/version/page/block of printing

**Arrogant** - 自命不凡 (zì mìng bù fán) = self - life/fate/luck - not/no - ordinary/commonplace

**Illegitimate child** - 私生子女 (sī shēng zǐ nǚ) = illegal/secret/private - give birth to/bear - boy - girl (sons and daughters/offspring)

Diamond - 金刚石 (jīn gāng shí) = gold/precious - hard/firm/tough/unyielding - stone/rock

Terracotta warriors - 兵马俑 (bīng mǎ yǒng) = army/warfare/troops - horse - tomb figure/figurine

Veal - 小牛肉 (xiǎo niú ròu) = small/little ones/children/young - cow - meat

**Fractal** - 分形 (fēn xíng) = to divide/distribute/part or subdivision/fraction - form/shape/appearance

Approximately - 左右 (zuǒ yòu) = left - right

Happy - 高兴 (gāo xìng) = high level/above average - excitement/mood or desire to do something

Liposuction - 抽脂 (chōu zhī) = to draw out/pull out - fat/lard/grease

Oedema - 浮肿 (fú zhǒng) = inflated/excessive/surplus - swelling/swollen

Urinal - 便器 (biàn qì) = 'to urinate or defecate' - device/tool

Cat litter - 猫沙 (māo shā) = cat - sand/powder

Breakfast - 早饭 (zǎo fàn) = early - meal/rice

Lunch - 午饭 (wǔ fàn) = noon/midday - meal/rice

Dinner - 晚饭 (wǎn fàn) = evening/night/late - meal/rice

**Cork** - 软木塞 (ruǎn mù sāi) = soft - wood - to stop up/stopper/cork

Female gossip - 长舌妇 (cháng shé fù) = long/always/constantly/forever - tongue - woman

Burn the Midnight Oil - 吃夜草 (chī yè cǎo) = eat - night - grass

**Charitable auction** - 义卖 (yì mài) = justice/righteousness - to sell

Moral (of a story) - 寓意 (yù yì) = to contain/reside - meaning/idea/thought

Irony - 反话 (fǎn huà) = reverse - talk

Ghostwriter - 捉刀人 (zhuō dāo rén) = grab/clutch - knife - person

Novel - 小说 (xiǎo shuō) = small - speak/to say

Plot - 情节 (qíng jié) = feeling/emotion/passion/situation - part/segment/section

Phrase - 短语 (duǎn yǔ) = short/brief - language/speech

**Blog** - 博客 (bó kè) = obtain/to get/plentiful - customer/visitor/guest

Blog - 网志 (wǎng zhì) = net/network - to record/to write a footnote

Spoiler/Plot leak - 剧透 (jù tòu) = theatrical work - to show/appear/pass through

Tongue twister - 绕口令 (rào kǒu lìng) = confuse/wind/coil - mouth - to cause/make something happen/order/command (Lit: to cause the mouth to be confused)

Fireworks - 烟花 (yān huā) = smoke - flower

Parade/march - 游行 (yóu xíng) = to walk/roam - to walk/go/travel

Circus - 马戏团 (mǎ xì tuán) = horse - play/show/drama - group/society

Hide-and-Seek/Peek-a-boo - 藏猫猫 (cáng māo māo) = to hide away/conceal - cat - cat

Waltz - 慢三步 (màn sān bù) = slow - three - step/pace/walk/march

Emoji - 表情符号 (biǎo qíng fú hào) = facial expression - symbol/mark/sign

Copy - 复印 (fù yìn) = to duplicate - to print/to mark/image

Poker face - 板脸 (bǎn liǎn) = board/plank/hard/stiff - face

Streaking - 裸奔 (luǒ bēn) = naked - to hurry/rush/run quickly

Foreshadow - 预兆 (yù zhào) = beforehand/in advance - omen/to foretell

Hide-and-Seek - 藏猫猫 (cáng māo māo) = hide/conceal - hide/conceal - hide/conceal

Plasticine - 蜡泥 (là ní) = wax - mud

Styrofoam - 保丽龙 (bǎo lì lóng) = protect/defend/insure/care/safeguard - beautiful/pretty/elegant - dragon

Password - 密码 (mì mǎ) = secret - code

**Pun** - 双关语 (shuāng guān yǔ) = double/two/pair/couple - connection/relation - language/saying/expression

Harness - 挽具 (wǎn jù) = to pull/draw - tool/utensil

Index (in a book) - 检字表 (jiǎn zì biǎo) = collect/gather - word - table/form/list/chart

Meter (unit of length) - 公尺 (gōng chǐ) = metric - ruler/Chinese measurement approx 'foot'

Booth (In a restaurant) - 火车坐 (huǒ chē zuò) = train - seat/place

Glitter - 金葱粉 (jīn cōng fěn) = gold/metal/money - scallion/green onion/leeks - powder

Guidebook - 指南 (zhǐ nán) = finger/toe/point to/indicate/refer to - south/southward

Pink - 桃红色 (táo hóng sè) = peach - red - colour

**Dictatorship** - 独裁 (dú cái) = alone/single/independent - judge/decide/decision

B Movie - 二级影片 (er jí yǐng piàn) = two (second) - rank/grade/class/level - film/movie

Sketch - 写生画 (xiě shēng huà) = write/paint/draw - life/unrefined - drawing/painting/picture

Stop-motion Animation - 逐帧动画 (zhú zhèn dòng huà) = one by one - frame/picture - cartoon

Talk Nonsense/Bullshit - 满嘴喷粪 (mǎn zuǐ pēn fèn) = full/filled/packed - mouth - spurt/gush/to puff//to spray/blow out - excrement/feces/dung/shit/manure

Magnum Opus - 巨著 (jù zhù) = huge/tremendous/gigantic/enormous - book/work/manifest

Schedule - 预定 (yù dìng) = in advance/beforehand/prior/preparatory - decide/fix/set/to determine

Dictation - 听写 (tīng xiě) = listen/hear/obey - write/compose/describe/draw

Silhouette - 侧影 (cè yǐng) = side/lateral - shadow/image/reflection/photograph/picture

Siphon - 虹吸管 (hóng xī guǎn) = rainbow - inhale/breath in/draw/suck (liquids)/suck up - tube/pipe

Movie Trailer - 预告片 (yù gào piàn) = prior/in advance/beforehand - tell/inform/notify/announce - film/tv/incomplete/fragmentary

Cog - 轮牙 (lún yá) = wheel/disc/to rotate - tooth

Partition/Divide - 瓜分 (guā fēn) = melon/gourd/squash - divide/separate/distribute/allot/to allocate

369

Semicolon - 分号 (fēn hào) = divide/separate/distribute/allot/to allocate - mark/sign/signal/number

**Micrometer** - 千分尺 (qiān fēn chǐ) = thousand - divide/separate/distribute/allot/to allocate - ruler/tape-measure

Graffiti - 涂鸦 (tú yā) = spread on/apply/smear/scribble/scrawl/street - crow

Graffiti - 涂鸭 (tú yā) = spread on/apply/smear/scribble/scrawl/street - duck

Vowel - 元音 (yuán yīn) = (key) element/essential factor/fundamental - sound/note/noise/syllable

An Epic/Poetic Saga - 史诗 (shǐ shī) = history/annals - poetry/poem/verse/ode

Onomatopoeia - 拟声 (nǐ shēng) = imitate/mimic/simulate - sound/noise/tone/voice

@ Symbol - 小老鼠 (xiǎo lǎo shǔ) = small/tiny - mouse/rat

@ Symbol - A圈儿 (A quān er) = A - circle/ring

Why - 为什么 (wèi shén me) = for the purpose of/because of - what

Telepathy - 心电感应 (xīn diàn gǎn yìng) = heart/mind/feeling/soul - get (or give) an electric shock - response/reaction

Jack-o-lantern - 鬼火 (guǐ huǒ) = ghost/demon/devil - fire/flame/burning

Fragile - 易碎 (yì suì) = easy - smash/break to pieces/break

Contraband - 禁运品 (jìn yùn pǐn) = taboo/prohibit/forbid/ban - movement/to transport - product/commodity/goods

Caricature - 讽刺画 (fèng cì huà) = satirize/mock - criticize - drawing/painting/picture

Censorship - 审查制度 (shěn chá zhì dù) = examine/investigate/judge - to research/check/investigate/examine - system/institution

Facebook - 非死不可 = 'fei si bu ke' *transliterated* (also means 'you must die' - to not be/not - to die - can't (pun. can't not die))

Cleansing lotion - 洁面乳 (jié miàn rǔ) = clean - face - milk

Cleansing lotion - 洗面奶 (xǐ miàn nǎi) = to wash - face - milk-like liquid

Eye of the needle - 针鼻 (zhēn bí) = needle/pin - nose

Crayon - 炭棒 (tàn bàng) = coal-like substance/charcoal - stick/club

Compass - 指北针 (zhǐ běi zhēn) = 'to point towards' - north - needle

Sleigh/Sled - 冰床 (bīng chuáng) = ice - bed/something shaped like a bed

Shampoo - 洗头膏 (xǐ tóu gāo) = to wash/bathe/rinse/clean/purify - head/hair - ointment/grease/fat/paste

Reclining Chair (Lay-Z-Boy) - 睡椅 (shuì yǐ) = sleep - chair

Sofa-bed - 两用沙发 (liǎng yòng shā fā) = two - use - sofa

(Upholstered) Armchair - 单人沙发 (dān rén shā fā) = single/sole/only - person/people - sofa

Humble Abode - 蜗庐 (wō lú) = snail - hut/cottage

**Chest of Drawers** - 五屉橱 (wǔ tì chú) = five - drawer/tray - cabinet/wardrobe/closet/cupboard

Weeds - 杂草 (zá cǎo) = mixed/miscellaneous/various - grass/straw

Weeds/Wild Grasslands - 荒草 (huāng cǎo) = wasteland/uncultivated land/wilderness/desolate - grass/straw

Laxative - 泻药 (xiè yào) = flow swiftly/rush down/pour down - medicine/medication/drug

Laxative - 轻泻剂 (qīng xiè jì) = relaxing/gentle/soft/unstressed - flow swiftly/rush down/pour down - dose (medicine)

Monochrome (picture/painting) - 单色话 (dān sè huà) = single/only/individual - colour - drawing/painting/picture

Straw - 吸管 (xī guǎn) = inhale/breath in/draw/suck (liquids)/suck up - tube/pipe

Outhouse - 茅厕 (máo cè) = reeds/rushes/grass - lavatory/toilet/restroom/washroom

**Visor/Face Guard** - 面罩 (miàn zhào) = face - cover/shade/hood/casing

D Size Battery - 一号电池 (yī hào diàn chí) = one - size/number - battery

C Size Battery - 二号电池 (èr hào diàn chí) = two - size/number - battery

AA Size Battery - 三号电池 (sān hào diàn chí) = three - size/number - battery

AAA Size Battery - 四号电池 (sì hào diàn chí) = four - size/number - battery

AA Size Battery - 五号电池 (wǔ hào diàn chí) = five - size/number - battery

AAA Size Battery - 七号电池 (qī hào diàn chí) = seven - size/number - battery

Hand Sanitizer - 消毒洗手液 (xiāo dú xǐ shǒu yè) = to disinfect/to sterilize - liquid soap

Dunce's Cap - 高帽 (gāo mào) = tall/high/elevated - hat/cap

Velcro - 魔术贴 (mó shù tiē) = magic - stick/glue/paste

**Labyrinth** - 迷宫 (mí gōng) = to bewilder/confused/lost - temple/palace

(Sports) Jersey - 球衣 (qiú yī) = ball/(sports) match - clothes/garment

(Sports) Jersey - 毛织运动衫 (máo zhī yùn dòng shān) = woollen - sports/to exercise - shirt/robe/garment

Crowbar - 撬杠 (qiào gàng) = to pry open - bar/rod/thick pole

Barbed Wire - 刺钢丝 (cì gāng sī) = thorn/splinter/stab/prick/stimulate/to stab/prod - steel - threadlike thing/wire/string

Barbed Wire - 刺铁丝 (cì tiě sī) = thorn/splinter/stab/prick/stimulate/to stab/prod - iron/weapon - threadlike thing/wire/string

**Overpass** - 高架路 (gāo jià lù) = tall/high/height/above average/of a high level or degree - to support/frame/rack/prop/put up (a bridge) - road/path/way/means/street

The Nutcracker (ballet) - 胡桃夹子 (hú táo jiá zi) = walnut - clamp/tongs

Vegetarian - 素食者 (sù shí zhě) = vegetable/basic element - food/meal/eat - 'the one who' (the one who eats vegetables)

Sleep in - 睡懒觉 (shuì lǎn jiào) = sleep - lazy - sleep

Auction - 拍卖 (pāi mài) = to slap/swat = to sell

Horseshoe - 马蹄铁 (tǎ tí tiě) = horse - hoof - iron

Black Friday - 黑五 (hēi wǔ) = black - five (five being the fifth day of the week aka Friday)

Braille - 点字 (diǎn zì) = dot - word/character

Suffix - 字尾 (zì wěi) = word/character - tail/end

**Wake (of a boat)** - 尾漏 (wěi lòu) = tail/rear end - funnel

Dub (voiceover in a film) - 配音 (pèi yīn) = to match/find something to fit or replace something else - sound

**Pixelated or censored (of video)** - 有码 (yǒu mǎ) = to have/contain - code

**Defame/Smear someones name** - 抹黑 (mǒhēi) = to smcar/wipe - black

**Ozone** - 臭氧 (chòu yǎng) = stinky/stench/smelly/foul - oxygen

Decapitate - 斩首 (zhǎn shǒu) = to cut - head

**Suffocate** - 窒息 (zhì xí) = to obstruct/stop up - breath

Infinite - 无限 (wú xiàn) = without/have not - limit/boundary

Goodnight - 晚安 (wǎn ān) = evening/nighttime - safe/peaceful

An extra in a movie - 临时演员 (lín shí yǎn yuán) = temporary/provisional - actor

Paradox (logic) - 悖论 (bèi lùn) = contrary/go against - theory/doctrine

Microscope - 显微镜 (xiǎn wéi jìng) = to reveal/display/show - tiny/minute/miniature/micro - lens/looking glass

Cryptocurrency - 电子钱 (diàn zǐ qián) = electronic - money/currency

**Paperback Book** - 简装书 (jiǎn zhuāng shū) = simple/basic - assemble - book

Lawnmower - 剪草机 (jiǎn cǎo jī) = to cut with scissors/trim/clip - grass - machine

**To Trot** - 快步跑 (kuài bù pǎo) = fast/quick/rapid/swift - step/walk/go on foot/stroll - run/flee

Inhaler - 吸入器 (xī rù qì) = inhale/breath in/suck in - go into/enter - device/tool

Velcro - 黏扣带 (nián kòu dài) = sticky/adhesive/to glue - buckle/clasp/to fasten - belt/band/ribbon/strap

Drowsy - 想睡 (xiǎng shuì) = think/ponder/consider/to wish/to want - sleep

Morse Code - 摩尔斯电码 (mó ěr sī diàn mǎ) = 'mo er si' - telegram/cable/telephone/call - code/number

**Jungle** - 丛林 (cóng lín) = cluster/thicket - forrest/woods

**Jungle** - 密林 (mì lín) = close/thick/dense - forrest

**Bad Luck** - 霉头 (méi tóu) = mildew/mold - head

Guano - 海鸟粪 (hǎi niǎo fèn) = seabird - excrement/feces/dung/droppings

Cosmetics - 脂粉 (zhī fěn) = rouge - powder/face powder

Cosmetics - 化妆品 (huà zhuāng pǐn) = makeup - product

**Elasticity** - 弹力 (tán lì) = spring/leap/bounce - power/strength/ability/force

To Smoke - 吸烟 (xī yān) = inhale/breath in/suck in - smoke/cigarette

Whisper - 私语 (sī yǔ) = secret/private - language/words/speak/say/speech

Chinglish - 中式英语 (zhōng shì yīng yǔ) = Chinese style - english

Synonym - 同义语 (tóng yì yǔ) = be the same as/same/alike/similar - meaning/significance - language/words/speak/say/speech

Sign Language - 手语 (shǒu yǔ) = hand - language/words/speak/say/speech

**Thumbnail** (computing) - 缩略图 (suō lüè tú) = contract/shrink/to reduce - summery/outline - picture

**Ventriloquism** - 腹语 (fù yǔ) = belly (of the body)/abdomen/stomach - language/words/speak/say/speech

Thesaurus - 类语词典 (lèi yǔ cí diǎn) = resemble/be similar to/like - language/words/speak/say/speech - dictionary

The Great Wall - 长城 (cháng chéng) = long/chief/head - wall

**Smirk** - 假笑 (jiǎ xiào) = false/fake/sham/phoney/artificial - smile/laugh

To Punch - 动手 (dòng shǒu) = use/move/happen/action - hand

Breast Pump - 吸奶器 (xī nǎi qì) = inhale/breath in/suck in - milk - device/tool

Passport - 护照 (hù zhào) = protect/guard/defend - photo/licence/permit

**Tiger Balm** - 万金油 (wàn jīn yóu) = ten thousand/a great number - gold/money - oil/fat/grease/lard

**P.S.** - 附言 (fù yán) = to add/attach - words/speech

**Union Jack** - 米字旗 (mǐ zì qí) = '米' - character - flag

**Headphones** - 耳机 (ěr jī) = ear - machine

**Wild game (as in 'hunt for animals' for food or sport)** - 野味 (yě wèi) = open country/illicit/unlicensed - taste/smell/odor/delicacy

# Space

Space - 外太空 (wài tài kōng) = outside/exterior - greatest - void/sky/air

Planet - 行星 (xíng xīng) = travel - planet/star

Mercury - 水星 (shuǐ xīng) = water - planet/star

Venus - 金星 (jīn xīng) = gold - planet/star

Mars - 火星 (huǒ xīng) = fire - planet/star

Jupiter - 木星 (mù xīng) = wood - planet/star

Saturn - 土星 (tǔ xīng) = earth/soil - planet/star

Uranus - 天王星 (tiān wáng xīng) = sky/heavenly - king - planet/star

Neptune - 海王星 (hǎi wáng xīng) = ocean - king - planet/star

Pluto - 冥王星 (míng wáng xīng) = dark/obscure - king - planet/star

Earth - 地球 (dì qiú) = earth/dirt/land - sphere/ball/globe

Asteroid - 小行星 (xiǎo xíng xīng) = small - to travel - planet/star

Meteor - 流星 (liú xīng) = to drift or move - planet/star

Sun - 太阳 (tài yáng) = greatest - light/sun

Solar System - 太阳系 (tài yáng xì) = sun - system

Milky Way - 银河 (jín hé) = silver - river

Milky Way - 天河 (tiān hé) = sky/heaven - river

Satellite - 卫星 (wèi xīng) = guard/protect/defend - planet/star

Spaceship - 宇宙飞船 (yǔ zhòu fēi chuán) = universe - fly - boat

Big bang - 大爆炸 (dà bào zhà) = big/large - explosion

Nebula - 星云 (xīng yún) = star/planet/heavenly body - cloud

**Cluster of galaxies** - 星系团 (xīng xì tuán) = star/planet/heavenly body - system - group/to gather/mass

Atmosphere - 大气层 (dà qì céng) = big/large/huge - gas/air/weather - layer

**The Moon** (slang) - 冰轮 (bīng lún) = ice - wheel/disc/ring

# Books
(I was too lazy to draw any of these...)

The Great Gatsby - 了不起的盖茨比 (liǎo bù qǐ de gài cí bǐ) = amazing/terrific/extraordinary - 's - 'gai ci bi'

Moby Dick - 白鲸 (bái jīng) = white - whale

The Devine Comedy - 神曲 (shén qū) = god/deity/divinity/immortal/mysterious/amazing - bend/curved/wrong/unjustifiable/false

The Catcher and the Rye - 麦田里的守望者 (mài tián lǐ de shǒu wàng zhě) = wheat field - neighbourhood/native place - 's - to keep watch/on guard - 'the one who' (the one who watches the neighbourhood fields of wheat)

Gone with the Wind - 乱世佳人 (luàn shì jiā rén) = disorder/in confusion/riot/to mix up/revolt/turmoil - life/lifetime/generation/age/era/world - beautiful/fine/good/delightful

Robinson Crusoe - (lǔ bīn xùn piāo liú jì) = 'lu bin' (name) - modest/humble - to float on the current/to drift along/rafting - notes/record/to remember

The Hitchhiker's Guide to the Galaxy - 银河系漫游指南 (xín hé xì màn yóu zhǐ nán) = Milky Way Galaxy - to travel around/to roam - guidebook

Winnie the Pooh - 小熊维尼阿噗 (xiǎo xióng wéi ní ā pū) - small/tiny - bear - 'wei ni a pu'

Dune - 沙丘 (shā qiū) = sand - mound/hillock/grave

Brave New World - 美丽新世界 (měi lì xīn shì jiè) = beautiful - new - world

The Wizard of Oz - 绿野仙踪 (lǜ yě xiān zōng) = green - field/plain/open country/wilderness - celestial being/immortal - footprint/tracks/trace

# Questionable words

Condom - 安全套 (ān quán tào) = safety/security - sheath/case/cover/that which covers/cover with/slip over/encase in

Condom - 保险套 (bǎo xiǎn tào) = safe/insurance/secure - sheath/case/cover/that which covers/cover with/slip over/encase in

Slut - 贱人 (jiàn rén) = low-priced/cheap/inexpensive - person

Son of a Bitch - 王八蛋 (wáng bā dàn) = king - eight - egg

Bastard - 龟儿子 (guī ér zi) = turtle - son

Loser - 屌丝 (diǎo sī) = penis - silk (aka silk penis)

Hickey - 吻痕 (wěn hén) = kiss - scar/mark

Hickey - 唇印 (chún yìn) = lip - mark/trace

Bastard - 兔崽子 (tù zǎi zi) = rabbit - child

Red light district - 烟花巷 (yān huā xiàng) = tobacco/smoke - lustful/'to spend money or time' - lane/alley

Shoddy Stuff/Whore - 烂货 (làn huò) = rotten/fester/decay/worn-out/crappy - goods/product

Pervert (One who gropes women in public) - 咸猪手 (xián zhū shǒu) = widespread - pig - hand

Thong (Underwear) - 丁字裤 (dīng zì kù) = '丁' - character - underpants/pants/trousers

### From 'Dumb & Dumber'

(*This one was hard to translate. The 阿 doesn't directly translate into any specific word in English. The main gist of the meaning is 'to form terms of endearment or before pet names', or also 'kinship terms etc to indicate familiarity'. So with that being said, I didn't include it in the translation due to the fact it holds a subtle connotation unexplainable with a few words. Also, 'melon' also can mean 'stupid'.)

Chinese Poetry

Here's some famous poems in China. This is one reason I really love the Chinese language. Because English is so specific, which can be good, but when it comes to poetry, the non-specificity of Chinese is far superior in this case. It leaves so much room for interpretation, as in, the characters give the general idea, and your mind gets to fill in the rest. See the example below. I think it's super interesting and wonderful. When I was first learning Chinese I stumbled upon this and thought "what a stupid poem". Later I realized it was lovely.

# 《Thoughts in the Silent Night》
## 静夜思
(jìng yè sī)

### 床前明月光, 疑是地上霜. 举头望明月, 低头思故乡.

**The 'general' translation is:**
Before my bed there's a pool of light
I wonder if it's frost on the ground
Looking up, I find the moon bright
Then bowing my head, I drown in homesickness

**But, the literal translation is this:**
bed - front - bright - moon
light/ray - doubt - is - on the ground - frost
raise - head - look at - bright - moon
lower - head - ponder - former - native place/home village

# 《Spring Morning》
## 春晓
(chūn xiǎo)

春眠不觉晓, 处处闻啼鸟. 夜来风雨声, 花落知多少.

**The 'general' translation is:**
This spring morning in bed I'm lying
Not to awake till the birds are crying
After one night of wind and showers
How many are the fallen flowers?

**But, the literal translation is this:**
spring - sleep - not - awake - dawn
everywhere - hear - twitter/cry - bird
in the night - wind and rain
flower - 'to fall or drop' - 'to know' - how many?

# Note

I had to scrap all the video game and movie art I did due to copyright infringement, which makes me sad. So I've put it on my website. Feel free to look. Oh, and if you're wondering my favourite translations, I'd go with these few: Sauerkraut, Tetris, diapers, dandruff, acne, kangaroo, flashing, Pac-Man, Frisbee, ghetto, and kitten.

# Fun Stuff

Here's some final stuff. Did you make it this far? Well, here's a thought I had. If you want, go into your computer keyboard settings and add the 'simplified Chinese keyboard'. The next step is go into google translate, hit a bunch of random keys (something like bjasufhsdk jfhsdfjbapan) then press number '1'. Then see what the translation says. I just tried and got "What about his ordinary mom u Me and Minnesota send i three meals, onlookers watching documents and water". It's fun! You can play with your friends, and see whoever can get the funniest one.

Also available is the 'Coffee Table Edition'. It exists for those people who just want the drawings/translations. It doesn't include My China Adventure Story, or the other stuff. Just the drawings; meant for a quick read.

You can get it from my website.
www.kevinsbook.ca

# References

[ Ref 1: https://zhuanlan.zhihu.com/p/49579380 ]
[ Ref 2: https://www.wukong.com/question/6792950299502838029/ ]
[ Ref 3: https://baijiahao.baidu.com/s?id=1619840848064503719&wfr=spider&for=pc ]
[ Ref 4: https://baike.baidu.com/item/王八蛋/68796?fr=aladdin ]

Manufactured by Amazon.ca
Bolton, ON

29300030R00208